THE LIBERATOR

ALSO BY THE AUTHOR

The Envoy

Escape from the Deep

The Few

The Longest Winter

The Bedford Boys

Blood and Champagne

Jack London

After five hundred days of combat, Lieutenant Colonel Felix Sparks fires his pistol into the air to stop his men slaughtering captured SS soldiers during the liberation of Dachau on April 29, 1945. [Courtesy David Israel]

ONE WORLD WAR II SOLDIER'S

500-DAY ODYSSEY FROM THE BEACHES OF SICILY

TO THE GATES OF DACHAU

THE LIBERATOR

ALEX KERSHAW

B\D\W\Y

BROADWAY BOOKS

NEW YORK

Published in the United States by Broadway Books, an imprint of the Crown Publishing Group, a division of Random House LLC, a Penguin Random House Company, New York.
www.crownpublishing.com

BROADWAY BOOKS and its logo, B \ D \ W \ Y, are trademarks of Random House LLC.

Originally published in hardcover in the United States by Crown Publishers, an imprint of the Crown Publishing Group, a division of Random House LLC, New York, in 2012.

Library of Congress Cataloging-in-Publication Data
Kershaw, Alex.
The Liberator: One World War II Soldier's 500-Day Odyssey from the Beaches of Sicily to the Gates of Dachau / Alex Kershaw.—First Edition.
Includes bibliographical references and index.
1. Sparks, Felix Laurence, 1917–2007. 2. United States. Army. Infantry Regiment, 157th. Battalion, 3rd. 3. United States. Army—Officers—Biography. 4. World War, 1939–1945—Campaigns—Western Front. 5. World War, 1939–1945—Campaigns—Italy. I. Title. II. Title: Five hundred days. III. Title: One soldier's odyssey from the beaches of Sicily to the gates of Dachau.
D769.31157th.K47 2012
940.54'1273092—dc23 2012017064

ISBN 978-0-307-88800-6
eISBN 978-0-307-88801-3

PRINTED IN THE UNITED STATES OF AMERICA

Maps by David Lindroth, Inc.
Cover design by Eric White
Cover photography by Robert Capa/International Center of Photography/ Magnum Photos

10 9 8 7 6 5 4 3

First Paperback Edition

In memory of Jack Hallowell

CONTENTS

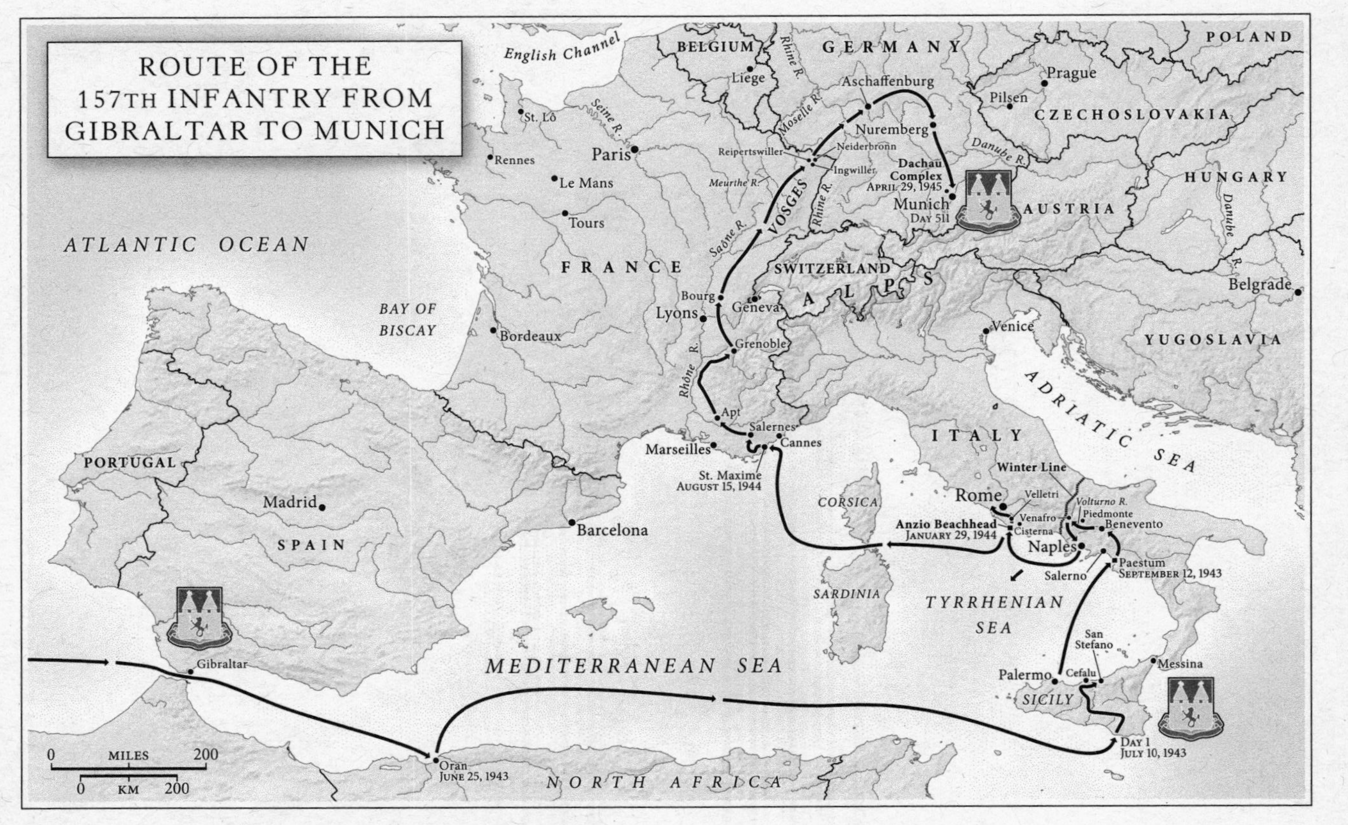

ROUTE OF THE
157TH INFANTRY FROM
GIBRALTAR TO MUNICH
English Channel
BELGIUM
Liege
Rhine R.
GERMANY
Aschaffenburg
POLAND
Prague
Pilsen
CZECHOSLOVAKIA
St. Lô
Seine R.
Moselle R.
Nuremberg
Rennes
Paris
Reipertswiller
Neiderbronn
Ingwiller
Danube R.
Le Mans
Meurthe R.
Dachau Complex
April 29, 1945
Munich
Day 511
HUNGARY
Danube R.
Tours
VOSGES
Rhine R.
AUSTRIA
Saône R.
ATLANTIC OCEAN
FRANCE
SWITZERLAND
ALPS
Belgrade
Bourg
Lyons
Geneva
BAY OF BISCAY
Bordeaux
Venice
YUGOSLAVIA
Grenoble
Rhône R.
ADRIATIC SEA
Apt
Salernes
ITALY
Marseilles
Cannes
PORTUGAL
St. Maxime
August 15, 1944
Winter Line
CORSICA
Rome
Velletri
Volturno R.
Madrid
Piedmonte
Venafro
Anzio Beachhead
January 29, 1944
Cisterna
Benevento
Barcelona
Naples
SPAIN
Paestum
September 12, 1943
Salerno
SARDINIA
TYRRHENIAN SEA
San Stefano
Gibraltar
MEDITERRANEAN SEA
Messina
Palermo
Cefalu
SICILY
Day 1
July 10, 1943
0 MILES 200
0 KM 200
Oran
June 25, 1943
NORTH AFRICA

American casualty in Europe, 1944. [National Archives]

PROLOGUE

THE GRAVES

EUROPE, OCTOBER 1989

THEY LAY BENEATH PERFECT rows of white graves that lined lush green lawns. He knew where they were buried. He had their names. Finding all of them meant walking back and forth, all across the graveyard, through avenues of thousands of white crosses. But he could manage the strain. His heart had given him problems for years, yet he still had the strength, the will, to search for his men. They had died near here, at Anzio, the bloodiest piece of ground occupied by American and British forces during World War II. Seventy-two thousand men lost in all—killed, wounded, sent insane, blown to shreds, missing, or captured, now a mere statistic in a history book.

The men he had commanded had achieved something of lasting greatness, something of permanence. They had defeated barbarism. He had seen it. He had been there, poisoned and heartbroken but somehow blessed, or rather damned, with the strength to fight on, to beat Hitler's most violent men.

Often he had questioned what kept his men going. The American Army was on the attack all the time in Europe. He had kept thinking:

Why do they go? It was hard to explain why his men had not hesitated. Many times he had said: "Let's go!" Every time, they had gone. Now that he was back in Europe, he marveled once more at the American spirit, as he called it, that had kept them advancing toward death or at best debilitating injury. It was this spirit that had mattered so much when the odds had been even.

The American soldiers under his command had performed magnificently. He wanted to pay his respects to some of those who had fallen. That was why he was back. There had been no time during combat to stand over them and grieve, no time to say how he felt, to show his love other than by trying his best to keep them alive. At that, he had failed, over and over, and over again.

Never give up. That was what had counted most. He had never given up, not once in his entire life. He had fought since he could remember—to eat, to stay alive, to overcome everything a vengeful God could throw at him. He had survived, somehow, perhaps through grit and rage, perhaps because God took the good first and left the rotten until last.

He had never been afraid of God or any man. Fear had never thrown him off balance, but he had felt great anxiety, mostly about what was going to happen to his men. Thankfully, he had always been able to think and act fast. In fact, he had functioned extraordinarily well in combat, remaining for the most part calm and focused. He had some of the fighting Irish in him plus a lot of anger. It was in his blood. His great grandfather had fought at the Alamo.

The graves of his men stretched across Europe, over two thousand miles. They had died in Sicily, in France, at the dark heart of Nazi Germany. There had been several hundred killed under his command, half of them buried in Europe. Near a crossing over the fast-flowing Moselle, he looked for Sergeant Vanderpool and Lieutenant Railsback's final resting places. Railsback had looked like a high school valedictorian with his confident, easy smile and neatly cropped hair. He had been a hell of an officer, like Sparks at his age. As for Vanderpool—he should never have died. He should have ignored the fact that he wanted to stay with his brother and pulled him off the line, but he had left it too late.

On the German border, near a small village, he traipsed along the ridge where he had been beaten just that one time, where in snow and ice the SS had humiliated him. His men's foxholes were still there as well as their spent cartridges. He had never gotten over their loss. How could anyone recover from losing so many men? Thirty platoon leaders and six hundred warriors who had never hesitated to carry out his every command.

Then it was on into the dark forests where you could get lost after a hundred yards without a compass, a place of primeval fears, to the border of Germany and the Siegfried Line with its famous dragon's teeth, now decomposing concrete and rusted iron; across the swirling Rhine to a city on the banks of the Main River where a grateful mayor and townspeople honored him and left him beaming with pride; south toward the Alps and a pretty town where he pointedly reminded the good burghers that the German government had authorized the building of a center for the study of the Holocaust. Why hadn't it been built? Much as they might want to forget, future generations should not.

He had never been able to forget that day. He could still picture the girl lying on top of all the bodies. It was as if she and others were looking at him with reproach, asking: "What took you so long?"

Why hadn't he been able to save them in time?

He had lost control here, in the outskirts of this town in Bavaria, in this place of evil, for perhaps as much as half an hour. It had been impossible to stop his men from going crazy. The horrors had robbed their minds of reason. He had never liked to see people killed unnecessarily, no matter their color or nationality or whatever terrible things they had done. He had never allowed his men to kill without good reason. He had tried to take prisoners and treat them honorably. But at the end, with his back turned, near piles of dead, his men had killed unnecessarily.

Events that day, one of more than five hundred at war, nagged at him like an old wound. The rumors festered still, the published falsehoods. Just once, just that time, among thousands of emaciated, stinking corpses, he had failed to control his men when they had gone on the rampage. But he had then done the right thing. He had stopped the madness. It was painful to think people thought otherwise.

Time had not healed. It had not erased the memories. That fall of 1989, seventy-two-year-old General Felix Sparks wandered through towns he had set free, across battlefields, and through several graveyards. The white crosses were silent. The men who had died for him could not be resurrected. They could not be brought back. He knew one thing for certain. It didn't matter how well he had waged war. The cost had been too great.

PART ONE

THE DUST BOWL

CHAPTER ONE

THE WEST

Corporal Felix Sparks, U.S. Army Coast Guard Artillery, Camp Kamehameha, 1936. [Courtesy the Sparks Family]

MIAMI, ARIZONA, 1931

FELIX SPARKS WOKE EARLY. It was getting light outside. He pulled on his jacket, grabbed his shotgun, and headed out into the dusty canyon, past miners' shacks and mountains of tailings from the nearby mine, and into the red-rocked canyons, eyes darting here and there as he checked his traplines. The Tonto forest and mountains surrounding his home were full of bounty and menace: snapping lizards, tarantulas the size of his fist, and several deadly types of scorpion. It was important to tread carefully, avoiding porcupines beneath the Ponderosa pines and always being alert for the raised hackles of the diamondback rattler and the quick slither of the sidewinder snake, with its cream and light brown blotches.

Each morning, he checked his traplines and hunted game, hoping to bag with just one shot a quail or a cottontailed rabbit or a Sonora dove. He couldn't afford to waste a single cartridge. As the sun started to warm the cold, still air in the base of canyons, he returned to the small frame house he shared with his younger brother, Earl, and three sisters, Ladelle, Frances, and Margaret. His mother, Martha, of English descent and raised in Mississippi, and his father, Felix, of Irish and German blood, counted themselves lucky to have running water. They had moved to Arizona a decade before to find work. But now there was none. Every animal their eldest son brought home was needed to feed the family.

The economic panic and failure that followed the October 1929 Wall Street crash had swept like a tsunami across America; more than nine thousand banks had failed, and unemployment had shot up tenfold, from around 1.5 million to 13 million, a quarter of the workforce. There was no stimulus spending, nothing done to stop the catastrophe enveloping the nation like one of the dust storms that buried entire towns in Oklahoma.

By 1931, the copper mines in Miami had closed down and a terrible silence had descended on the town that stood three thousand feet in the lee of Mount Webster. The rumble of machines far below, the distant growl made by their grinding and lifting, was gone. Over Christmas, at age fourteen, Sparks hiked far into the mountains with his father and Earl, laid traps and hunted for two full weeks, then skinned and dried pelts. They also fished for perch. But none of it was enough.

When he was just sixteen, Sparks's mother and father sent him to live with his uncle Laurence in Glendale, Arizona. There were too many mouths to feed. It hurt to see the anguish and guilt in his father's eyes as they said good-bye. In Glendale, he had to pay his way by doing chores, milking cows and working in his uncle's store on Saturdays.

When he returned to Miami a year later, in 1934, a government program had been set up, part of President Roosevelt's New Deal, to provide people with basic food requirements. Families in Miami were able to at least eat, even if there was no work. Once a week, he went down to the train depot in town and drew free groceries, staples such as flour, beans, and lard, salt pork, so many pounds per person, per family. Nothing was wasted. His mother was a resourceful woman, cooking salt pork gravy and biscuits for breakfast, feeding her five children as best she could, making them clothes on an old sewing machine, and cutting their hair.

When he wasn't hunting or studying, he became a regular visitor to the public library in Miami. His passion was military history: the Indian Wars, tales of the mighty Cherokee and Custer's Last Stand, and the heroics at the Alamo, where his great-grandfather, Stephen Franklin Sparks, had fought. He hoped someday to go to college and become a lawyer. But he was also drawn toward the military and applied to the Citizens' Military Training Program. To his delight, he was one of just fifty young men from around the state accepted into the program. Those who completed it became second lieutenants in the U.S. infantry. Training took place every summer in Fort Huachuca, Arizona, a hundred and fifty miles from Miami, at an old cavalry post. He hitchhiked to the camp, saving his travel allowance until he had enough to order a new pair of corduroy trousers from the J. C. Penney catalog.

The long marches and drills in more than one-hundred-degree heat tested the hardiest, and many youths did not return after the first summer, but Sparks enjoyed playing war with real weapons in the desert and nearby canyons. Aged eighteen, he was fully grown, around 140 pounds, slim, and tall, as wiry as a mesquite tree, with a toothy smile, thick black hair, and a broad and handsome face.

In his last semester at high school, he won a nationwide essay competition and received a $100 pocket watch. In June 1935, he graduated, the most gifted student in his senior year. He knew he had it in him to go far. Of one thing he was certain: He would never be a miner like his father. He would earn his living with his mind, not his hands. But he did not even have enough money to buy a suit for the graduation prom. Nor did he have a way to escape the poverty that had engulfed so much of America. There was not a spare dime for him to go to college, no loans to be had, and no jobs in Miami. He would have to leave home to find work of any kind.

Late that summer, his father borrowed $18 from a friend and gave it all to his oldest child. It was a grubstake for a new life somewhere else. His mother, Martha, sewed a secret pocket in his trousers for the borrowed money, which would have to last him until he found a job. He had no clear plan other than to head east and maybe get a berth on a ship out of Corpus Christi, on the Gulf Coast. At least he might get to see some of the world he had read about.

One morning, he put a change of clothes and a toothbrush in a pack, slipped a small metal club he'd bought for a dollar into a pocket, said a wrenching good-bye to his family, and then got a ride from a friend to Tucson, where he was dropped off near some rail tracks. Other men were hanging around, waiting to "catch out." One of them pointed out a train due to go east, south of the Gila Mountains, through the Chiricahua Desert, toward El Paso, Texas. The hobo warned Sparks to make sure he got off the train before it arrived in the rail yards in El Paso; otherwise he might be beaten or shot by railroad security men—"bulls"—armed with clubs and Winchester shotguns.

Sparks pulled himself up into a chest-high boxcar. There was the acrid odor of hot oil mixed with steam. He was suddenly aware of dark shapes in the recesses, movements in the shadows, other men. It was safer, he knew, to travel alone. He had bought the club just in case he had to defend himself. Instead of backing away, he moved to an empty corner and lay down.

"THE JUNGLES," THE DUST BOWL, 1936

THE TRAIN JERKED to life, shuddering as it began to move. The shaking slowly became an almost comforting, rhythmic *click-clack* of iron wheels on rails. Then came the adrenaline rush. For the first time, Sparks felt the exhilaration and intense sense of freedom that came with all the dangers of riding the "rods." It was like being on an iron horse, snaking back and forth through canyons, through the desert, headed east, toward the sea.

When the train built up speed, acting like a runaway colt, it was wise to stand up and brace oneself. When the boxcars slowed, it was possible to actually relax, to lie on one's back with a pack as a pillow and gaze out of the open doors, watching the desert pass leisurely by: the brittle mesquite trees, the greasewood bushes, and the cactus that dotted the horizon.

He wanted to stay awake, in case he was jumped by the other hobos, but the sweet syncopation of the wheels on the tracks and the train's rocking motion eventually sent him into a deep slumber.

"Kid! It's time to get off."

The train was approaching San Antonio, Texas, the city where he had been born on August 2, 1917. Its rail yards, patrolled by ruthless bulls, were up ahead.

"We got to get off here, buddy," the hobo added. "If they catch you, they put you on a chain gang or make you join the army."

When the train slowed, Sparks jumped down. He hiked into San Antonio, where he spent the night in a flophouse. In the morning, he walked to the other side of the city and hopped another train, bound for Corpus Christi. For several days, he watched what other bums did and copied them, learning how vital it was to carry a water jug and to hop freights with covered boxcars to protect him from sun, sandstorms, and rain. He adapted fast to the ways of the "jungles"—the rail-side camps—as did a quarter million other teenage boys during the height of the Depression, thousands of whom were killed in accidents or violent encounters with bulls or predatory older men.

Once in Corpus Christi, he searched without luck for a job. Hundreds of men with families waited in lines for just a few openings. The prospects were dire, so when he heard things were better out west he hopped another freight train and rode the high desert to Los Angeles, first glimpsing the Pacific from a rattling boxcar. But there again scores of men queued for every opportunity. Not knowing where else to go, he hung around for a few weeks, sleeping rough in parks, learning the feral habits of the urban homeless, getting by on just 25 cents a day: hotcakes for a dime in the morning, a candy bar for lunch, and a hamburger for dinner.

He decided to try his luck farther north, caught out again, and was soon watching the Sierra Nevada Mountains slip slowly by to the east. In San Francisco, he went to yet another hiring hall, this time on a dockside. There were jobs, but he would have to pay $15 to join a union to get one. He was down to his last couple of dollars. Again he slept rough. Then he ran out of cash.

One morning, as he was walking along Market Street, hungry and penniless, he passed a man in uniform.

"Hey, buddy," said the man. "Do you want to join the army?"

Sparks walked on.

What the hell else have I got to do?

He turned around.

"Yeah, I do."

"Are you kidding me, buddy?"

"No, I'm not kidding you—I want to join the army."

The recruiter gave him a token and pointed at a streetcar.

"Get on that streetcar. At two o'clock there will be a small boat coming in from Angel Island."

He was soon heading across the bay to Angel Island. From his boat, on a clear day, he would have been able to see the infamous Alcatraz prison, built on a craggy rock that rose from the riptides like an obsolete battleship, and where Depression-era killers like Al Capone and "Machine Gun" Kelly were kept under maximum security. At the army post on Angel Island, he was sworn in and given a choice of wherever he wanted to serve. So it was that one fall day in 1936 he found himself on a troopship, passing beneath the cables and iron girders of the half-constructed Golden Gate Bridge. He went below to his assigned bunk amid hundreds of others stacked three high in the fetid hold. He couldn't stand the crowding, so he grabbed his mattress and took it up on deck. The journey to Honolulu lasted a week. He slept every night under the stars and ate three square meals a day as he headed toward the land of lanais, perpetual sunshine, and coconut shell cocktails.

CAMP KAMEHAMEHA, HAWAII, 1936

THE BARRACKS WERE airy and spacious, with fans lazily circling on the high wooden ceilings. The palms shading the base, located at the mouth of a channel leading to Pearl Harbor, were taller than those back in Arizona, the air humid and the breezes warm. Sparks's days began at 6 A.M. with the sharp call of a bugle, followed by training in how to operate huge sixteen-inch guns.

Army life suited him. He didn't mind the routine and discipline, the hurry-up-and-wait bureaucracy and boring details, the endless hours mowing the grass and practicing drills on the parade ground surrounded by sugarcane fields. He was warm and well fed. There were no bums waiting to jump him in a boxcar or a rail-side jungle. His barracks had a library, a pool table, and a piano. His weekends were free and his days ended at 4:30 P.M., leaving him plenty of time to explore Honolulu, eight miles away.

One day, he bought a camera from a soldier for $2 and photographed the base as well as other soldiers. Then he discovered that the only place he could develop his images of fellow artillerymen and nearby beaches was at an expensive camera shop in Honolulu. Some men saved money and time by developing their negatives in the barracks latrine, but the prints were crude and faded. He quickly saw an opportunity. In Honolulu, he bought a book about photography and then asked his company commander if he could get him an appointment with the Post Exchange Council, which operated a large store on the base. He told the council he was an experienced photographer and suggested they set up a shop where soldiers could drop off film to be developed. To his delight, the council agreed to loan him money and equipment to set up the print shop. A week later, he was in business, developing roll after roll by hand, bent over developing trays in a red-lit darkroom. Soon, he had to hire a fellow soldier to help him. Within a month, he was "rolling in money," he later recalled, earning more than the battery commander. He put it all in a postal savings account that paid 2 percent interest.

He also taught himself how to take high-quality portraits and began snapping officers, their families, and the various tourist attractions. He scanned newspapers for details about arrivals of Hollywood stars at the pink-hued Royal Hawaiian hotel in Honolulu, so he could capture them lounging under sunshades. The musical star Alice Faye, a twenty-two-year-old natural blonde, was one of several actresses who agreed to be photographed, despite the protests of a boyfriend. He promptly sold the pictures as pinups back at base. By the time his enlistment was up, he had saved $3,000, more than enough to finance a college education.

He returned the same way he had arrived, by boat, passing beneath the now completed Golden Gate Bridge, which stretched 4,200 feet across the Pacific, making it the longest suspension bridge in the world. In San Francisco, he treated himself to his first suit, tailor-made for $15. He then visited nearby Palo Alto, where he toured the campus of Stanford University. The facilities impressed him, but the cost of tuition was too much, even with three thousand in savings. So he took a bus home, back to Arizona, where he was joyfully reunited with his family. Soon after, he enrolled at the state university in Tucson. The fees for a semester were just $25.

He studied hard and was popular with the other freshman students, almost all of them two years younger. Two students in his class were from his hometown of Miami: Mary and John Blair, brother and sister. Eighteen-year-old Mary was easygoing and studious, majoring in Business Administration. She had a slim, attractive figure and strawberry blond hair, and loved to dance to swing music. Mary had first set eyes on Sparks four years earlier outside Miami High School and had not been overly impressed. He'd been in a fistfight the principal had to break up. Now he was taller, his thick black hair swept back, and clearly ambitious, worldly compared to the callow freshmen her own age. He was going somewhere, just like her. They began to date and soon fell in love. In a photograph Mary would always treasure, they pretended to be characters in a great romance, she looking like Juliette, perched atop a boulder, he professing his love like Romeo, the Arizona desert as their backdrop.

At the end of his freshman year, Sparks returned to the summer training camp for prospective officers he'd attended during high school. After his time in Hawaii, he was quickly rated an outstanding cadet and received a much-coveted Pershing Award, which entitled him to an all-expenses-paid vacation to Washington, DC. In early 1940, he and eight others visited Congress and met George C. Marshall, army chief of staff, who pinned an award to the bespoke jacket Sparks had bought in San Francisco.

Over the next months, he followed events across the Atlantic with growing concern as Hitler's superbly equipped and highly mobile forces stormed through one democracy after another. By July 1940, most of Europe lay under brutal Nazi repression: France, Belgium, Holland, Poland, Norway, and Denmark. The British were holding out, but only just, thanks to the English Channel and the brave fighter pilots of the Royal Air Force. America began to re-arm in earnest and build up its military forces. That September, when he returned to college, he received a letter from the U.S. Army that began with the word "Greetings" and went on to inform him that he was being called back to service. He could finish his fall semester but would have to report for active duty for a full year before he could return to his studies. Instead of walking off a stage with a bachelor's degree, his dream of becoming a lawyer within reach, he found himself where he had started before college, back in a uniform.

He reported in January 1941 to Fort Sill in Oklahoma, where he would serve as a second lieutenant in the 157th Infantry Regiment of the 45th Infantry Division, a National Guard outfit that had been mobilized. The regiment's motto, he learned, was "Eager for Duty." He was willing to play his part but hardly eager.

Fort Sill was notable for being where the last great leader of the Apache, Geronimo, had died in 1909. It was easy to understand why the last of the great braves had been banished to this godforsaken corner of the Dust Bowl. Through the flaps of his tented barracks, Sparks could see nothing but yellowed grass, dusty brush, and ugly scrub for mile after mile. Local bars posted NO MEXICANS AND INDIANS signs, much to the fury of the many hundreds of such men in the 45th "Thunderbird" Division, so named because of the shoulder patch each soldier wore showing the image of the mythical Thunderbird. It was a far cry from his last base in Hawaii.

The 157th Infantry Regiment was no instant infantry, cobbled from draftees. It was drawn from Colorado and had a storied past, having fought with distinction in the Indian Wars and in the Spanish American War of 1898, when it had stormed the beaches near Manila and then raised the first American flag above the walled city. It had then clashed with Pancho Villa's raiders in 1916 on the Arizona-Mexico border and served in the trenches in World War I. In September 1940, the regiment had become part of the 45th Division and had then been mustered into service at Fort Sill.

Sparks loathed Fort Sill but quickly came to admire his regiment's commander, a straight-backed and extremely strict Washington, DC, native called Colonel Charles Ankcorn, who had seen combat in World War I. Everyone on the base seemed to be afraid of Ankcorn, who rarely spoke to him other than to issue crisp, short orders. One day, Sparks learned that he was to be in charge of training 60mm mortar crews.

In silence, Ankcorn watched as he put trainees through drills. Sparks wondered if he had done a good job; Ankcorn gave no indication. But several weeks later Ankcorn announced suddenly that Sparks was now his adjutant, responsible for the organization, administration, and discipline of the regiment. He simply showed him a desk and told him to get on with it, having also promoted him to captain. It was clear that Ankcorn's silence over the months had been a way of testing and teaching him to think for himself and act decisively. In the heat of battle, there would be precious little time for consultation. On the killing fields of Flanders in 1918, Ankcorn himself had learned that lesson fast.

CHAPTER TWO

OFF TO WAR

Felix Sparks and his future wife, Mary, in the desert near Tucson, Arizona, 1939. [Courtesy of Mary Sparks]

CAMP KAMEHAMEHA, HAWAII, DECEMBER 7, 1941

THE NAVY ZEROS ZOOMED low, spitting bullets, dropping bombs, ending peace, the red suns on their fuselages, soon to be known as "meatballs," flashing by in the early Sunday morning light above Pearl Harbor. The massive sixteen-inch artillery guns that Sparks had operated for two years were utterly useless as the Japanese bombed and strafed, sinking four battleships and two destroyers and killing more than two thousand men. The surprise attack on Hawaii had come not from the sea but the air.

Just four days later, on December 11, in an eighty-eight-minute-speech before the Reichstag, Adolf Hitler dramatically announced that the Third Reich was also going to wage war on the United States. Sparks was only a few days from completing his year's call-up to active duty. There was no way now he would be able to go back to school. Like others serving, he would have to stay in the army until the war was lost or won. He soon received yet more bad news, this time from a college friend: Mary Blair was socializing with other men. He called her immediately. She was at a party. It was a bad line. All he could hear was young men's voices, swing music, and laughter. She was clearly having a good time. He couldn't bear to lose her.

"Let's get married."

What was he saying? Mary couldn't hear him properly. Annoyed she had not immediately agreed, he asked again.

They tied the knot at the end of her junior year, on June 17, 1942, in front of their families and some of their college professors in Tucson, and then shared a car with another couple, driving west to the Pacific, and honeymooned in San Diego for a few days. They had made a deal. He knew how much finishing college meant to her, and how hard she had worked, so he insisted she complete her degree, then join him at whatever base he was on.

In September 1942, having finished college, Mary arrived in Massachusetts in time to experience a spectacular New England fall. Gold and orange leaves piled up in front of white clapboard houses and churches while Sparks and his regiment practiced landing on the pristine beaches of Cape Cod. Like many other young wives who had joined their husbands that autumn, Mary became pregnant. But then, in November, the relative idyll ended and the division moved to Pine Camp in upstate New York, where it encountered its first blast of a true New England winter: four feet of snow and a temperature of minus fifty-four degrees.

The men had not been issued winter gear, and frostbite became a problem. Thunderbirds took out their frustration in fistfights in local bars, and two disaffected soldiers even held up a bank with tommy guns, earning five-year jail sentences.

Much to the relief of local bar owners and banks, in January 1943 the division moved to the balmier climes of Virginia to train in the Blue Ridge Mountains. Morale was soon restored with the help of a powerful local moonshine. Rumor had it the division would ship out soon for Europe or the Pacific. The odds of surviving combat began to weigh heavily on the minds of soldiers and their families. Sparks and his fellow Thunderbirds knew with certainty that many of them would never return.

Early that May of 1943, Sparks held Mary in his arms. The baby was showing. She had been told she could not travel after seven months and had to return to her family in Tucson, where she would have the baby. They clung to each other and kissed good-bye, knowing they might not see each other again. Would he get to see his child? What would happen to Mary and the baby if he didn't make it back? In a May 19 letter, he asked his parents to take care of the baby if anything should happen to Mary in birth. "If ever there was a time in my life that I wanted to be home, it's now," he added. "It can't be done."

He would be back one day, he vowed, when the war was over in Europe.

HAMPTON ROADS, VIRGINIA, JUNE 3, 1943

THE DOCKSIDE WAS filled with a long, snaking line of men in green uniforms. Towering above Sparks was the USS *Charles Carroll*, a five-hundred-foot-long attack transport bristling with twenty-two anti-aircraft guns. There was much debate as men filed up the gangways. Where were they headed? Some thought they were going straight to France to open a second front. Others insisted, though they were on the Atlantic coast, that they were bound for the Pacific via the Panama Canal. To some of Sparks's exhausted fellow officers, it didn't matter where they were going, so long as the fifty-mile marches, day and night, and the endless packing and repacking and checking on equipment were finally over.

For brothers Otis, nineteen, and Ervin Vanderpool, twenty-nine, as with most of the men, it was the first time they were departing the United States. When the brothers had left the cornfields of Olathe in Colorado to join the regiment at Fort Sill, where Sparks became their platoon commander, it had been the first time they had even ventured beyond state lines. Ervin thought it best if he went to war with his younger brother, hoping he might be able to protect him in some way. Like dozens of other brothers serving side by side in the 45th Infantry Division, they dared not imagine returning alone.

It was 0800 on June 8, 1943, when whistles sounded, anchor chains clanked, and the convoy transporting the 157th Infantry Regiment moved slowly out of Hampton Roads. Men crowded railings to watch America recede into the distance. Some felt strangely empty as they headed out into the Atlantic. The convoy zigzagged southeast, with several destroyers providing escort, to avoid U-boats before heading north toward Gibraltar.

Sparks remembered listening to Axis Sally radio broadcasts from Berlin as he drew closer to North Africa. "You boys in the 45th Division know you are on the high seas and I'm going to play a song for you," announced Sally one day. "It's 'The Last Roundup' and it's going to be the last roundup for many of you." After two weeks at sea, he had learned to block out Axis Sally but not the popular music she played.

On June 21, 1943, the convoy passed through the Straits of Gibraltar. The Mediterranean was a bright blue and so clear that the men could see deep into it when they leaned over the rails and looked down. Dolphins played in the ships' wakes. The convoy then approached the crowded harbor at Oran in French Algeria. To their great frustration, the Thunderbirds were kept cooped up on their crowded, foul-smelling troopships for four more days. The reason became clear on June 25, when the whole division moved ashore in a practice landing on nearby beaches, with the 36th Infantry Division playing the role of defenders. It proved a fiasco, largely due to the absence of many experienced coxswains and ensigns who had been reassigned due to chronic shortages of landing craft crews in Europe and the Pacific, just minutes before the 45th Division had left the States.

What would happen, corps commanders and senior Allied planners wondered, when the green Thunderbirds actually landed on a foreign shore under enemy fire? On June 27, the anxious Seventh Army commander, George S. Patton, assembled all of the division's officers for what was clearly a much-needed pep talk. Sparks was among a crowd of several hundred who listened to Patton from a hillside, looking down on a stage set up in a dry riverbed.

"Gentlemen," said Patton, "in a few days we're going to hit the mainland of Europe for the first time. Most of you have never been in combat before and you may be afraid. But don't be afraid! You can stick a red feather up your ass and run around in front of them and they can't hit you."

Patton added that if the Italians and Germans wanted to surrender, then let them surrender. But if they didn't, Sparks and his fellow Thunderbirds were to "kill the bastards."

Inspired and also somewhat bemused by Patton's ripe language, Sparks and the other officers returned to their command posts and resumed training in the North African desert. At the end of June, he learned that the division was to begin boarding invasion craft in less than a week's time. Men soon crowded religious services. There were no fireworks that July 4. For Sparks and his fellow fifteen thousand Thunderbirds, about to enter combat for the first time, there seemed precious little to celebrate.

The following day, at 4:30 P.M., Sparks's regiment left the harbor at Oran aboard five boats. Only now was the Thunderbirds' ultimate destination revealed as men were handed government-issued books titled

The Soldier's Guide Book to Sicily. Thirty other ships transported the rest of the division. The force gathered strength as it steamed east, skirting the North African coast, collecting hundreds more vessels that carried the British Eighth Army, commanded by General Bernard Montgomery, as well the remainder of Patton's U.S. Seventh Army. When the entire armada finally assembled, it comprised some two thousand ships, the greatest invasion fleet in the history of war.

The plan to invade Sicily, code-named Operation Husky, entailed landing along a hundred miles of coast with an initial seven divisions split into two task forces, one led by Patton, the other by the equally controversial and colorful Montgomery, a national hero in Britain thanks to his impressive defeat of Rommel at El Alamein in November 1942.

It was after dark on July 9 when orders were given on the boats carrying the 45th Division for men to sew on shoulder patches.* Men pulled out needle and cotton, took off their combat jackets, and then attached soft felt patches, colored red and gold, showing the image of the mythical thunderbird. Ironically, before the war, the division's patch had been a swastika but it had been dropped in 1938 because of the Nazis' appropriation of the symbol. There had been many suggestions for a new patch, including a smoking Colt .45, the gun that had won the West. But to reflect the division's roots in Indian country, the symbol of a thunderbird had been chosen instead.

Among the fifteen hundred Apache, Seminole, Cherokee, Sioux, and Choctaw Indians who had earned the division headlines in the East Coast newspapers during training by performing a war dance on Boston Common, the thunderbird was a potent symbol indeed. In their eyes, it was an avenging spirit, dealing death and destruction to evildoers. But it was also a source of hope, a harbinger of victory, for those who were noble and deserving.

*The patch showed a bird against a background of scarlet. The patch was a diamond shape, the four sides representing the four states from which the troops were drawn: New Mexico, Arizona, Colorado, and Oklahoma.

PART TWO

ITALY

Everyone was talking about Rome by Christmas.

—PAUL CUNDIFF, 45TH DIVISION HEADQUARTERS STAFF

CHAPTER THREE

SICILY

(LEFT) Captured Italian troops under guard, Sicily, July 1943. [National Archives]
(RIGHT) Seventh Army commander George Patton (pointing) in Gela, Sicily, July 11, 1943. [National Archives]

THE MEDITERRANEAN, JULY 9, 1943

NEAR HIS HEADQUARTERS IN MALTA, fifty-three-year-old General Dwight Eisenhower, the supreme commander of Allied forces in the Mediterranean, stood rubbing several lucky coins together and chain-smoking as he counted planes carrying paratroopers bound for Sicily. He had never led a more vital mission. He knew only too well that the next few hours would decide his fate and place in history. Nothing so vast, entailing so many troops, had been attempted before. Italy had in fact never been invaded successfully from the south. As Napoleon had quipped, given that the country was shaped like a boot, the best way to occupy it was not to enter by its toe.

Operation Husky was an ambitious plan indeed. In Eisenhower's war room at his Lascaris HQ in Malta later that evening, Air Marshal Sir Arthur Tedder commented: "Hannibal had the sense to come in with his elephants over the Alps." And even if the landings succeeded, colossal challenges remained. Could the Allies prevail in Italy and then push on to the very heart of the Third Reich? Could the young citizen soldiers, drawn from "the ways of peace," as President Roosevelt put it, defeat the superbly armed and fanatical forces of fascism?

At ten that night, Eisenhower found time to write a few lines to his wife back in the States: "Men do anything to keep from going slightly mad. Walk, talk, try to work, smoke (all the time)—anything to push the minutes along. . . . Everything we could think of to do has been done; the troops are fit; everybody is doing his best. The answer is in the lap of the gods."

In Rome, Eisenhower's opposite number, fifty-eight-year-old Albert Kesselring, overall German commander in the Mediterranean, also spent that evening in his headquarters. He had not fallen for an ingenious counterintelligence operation, code-named Mincemeat, aimed at convincing the Germans that the Allies were going to land elsewhere. He had not chosen to place his faith in any divine intervention. Instead, he was now putting final touches to carefully laid plans to destroy Eisenhower's armies once they were ashore.

Unlike Eisenhower, Kesselring was an undisputed master of war and had already achieved near-perfect coordination between the nationalities and forces under his command. Highly popular with his men, who had nicknamed him Uncle Albert (the Allies called him Smiling Albert because he always seemed to be grinning with confidence in photos), he had served on the Eastern and Western fronts in World War I before setting up the Luftwaffe, serving as its chief of staff until 1938. He had then led the Luftwaffe with great success during the invasions of Poland, France, and Russia.

Kesselring had for some time expected the Allies to invade Sicily, figuring they would chose to do so because they could enjoy fighter cover from air bases in Tunisia and Malta. So he had strengthened the four mobile and the six coast-based Italian divisions on the island with two German ones, the Fifteenth *Panzergrenadier* and the Hermann Göring Panzer Division. He knew these forces could not stop a large-scale landing, but by careful deployment of his formidable Panzer tanks he intended to roll over the Allies as soon as they tried to break out of their beachhead.

ABOARD THE USS *Monrovia*, fifty-seven-year-old General George Patton, commander of the U.S. Seventh Army, watched the swelling waters, unable to quell his anxiety. A full gale was blowing. The invasion appeared cursed by the Boreas, the north wind so prevalent in Greek myth, and now so very real as it whistled south from the Alps, turning the Mediterranean into a menace every bit as unforgiving as Hitler's best troops.

"George, this shows every sign of becoming more intense," said fifty-seven-year-old Admiral Hewitt, commander of the invasion fleet. "I think I'll signal [Eisenhower] to delay the landings."

"Wait a minute, Henry," said Patton. "Have you spoken to Steere?"

Steere was a meteorologist who had proved comfortingly accurate in his predictions in the past.

"Yes."

"Did he say how long this goddamn storm will last?"

"He thinks it will calm down by D-day."

Steere was soon standing in front of Patton, who had nicknamed him "Houdini."

"Well, what do you say?"

"This is a mistral, sir, violent but abrupt. I would say it will moderate by twenty-two hundred, and the weather will be fine by H-hour, General."

"It had better."

"I'm positive, sir."

ABOARD A blacked-out ship a few miles across the storm-whipped waters, Felix Sparks also waited for H-hour to arrive. The winds were still high. Thunderbirds struggled to stand upright as the ship rocked up and down in the bucking waves. An inch of vomit covered some decks. The convoy nearing Sicily comprised hundreds of boats, yet so strict was the blackout that he could not see a single speck of light in any direction.

Sparks watched as the 157th Infantry Regiment vessels broke away from the armada and began to steam toward their assigned positions off the southern shore of Sicily. It was 9:45 P.M. There were flashes of light on the horizon. The Allies were bombing targets on the Camerina plain, which stretched several miles inland from the Seventh Army's landing beaches that lay north and south of the fishing village of Scoglitti. Yellow flames stabbed upward and faded in the night sky. At times, war could look unforgettably beautiful.

At 10:30 p.m., HMS *Seraph*, a British submarine acting as a beacon, began to signal the flotilla carrying Sparks's regiment. It was time to take up a position seven miles from the coast. *Seraph* had played a crucial role in Operation Mincemeat, dropping off the Spanish coast that spring a corpse clothed in a Royal Marine uniform and bearing false intelligence. Now her captain stood on the bridge, looking in awe through his night glasses at the Allied armada. "The English language needs a new descriptive noun to replace the hackneyed word 'armada,'" he would later reflect. "After all, the original Invincible Spanish Armada could boast only 129 sizable ships and a scattering of small fry." The armada then gathering off the southern shores of Sicily had twenty times as many ships and was carrying almost two hundred thousand men.

NO BRITON UNDERSTOOD the enormity of events that evening better than Prime Minister Winston Churchill, who had written lyrically about the Spanish Armada and every other critical juncture in his nation's history. It was Churchill who had pushed longest and hardest for the imminent invasion as the best way to tie up German forces until the Second Front, impatiently demanded by Stalin, could be opened up in France.

At his country retreat, Chequers, in England the sixty-nine-year-old warlord could not sleep, so great was the strain. His immensely supportive wife, Clementine, was too tired to stay up through the night, so she had asked her daughter-in-law, Pamela, to keep the restless British wartime leader company. Pamela and Churchill passed the time playing bezique, one of Churchill's favorite card games. But no matter how many times he cut and shuffled the pack, no matter how often he came up with the trump card, he could not keep his mind off the imminent landings.

"So many brave young men going to their death tonight," said Churchill. "It is a grave responsibility."

All through the night, Churchill received updates on the Allies' progress. More than any Allied leader he had cause to be worried. His previous adventures in the Mediterranean—the "soft underbelly" of Nazi Europe, as he had recently labeled it—had been disastrous. In 1915, as first lord of the admiralty, he had urged a landing at Gallipoli, in Turkey, that had turned into a disaster, incurring fifty-five thousand casualties. It had not been forgotten or forgiven by many of the Australians, who had suffered disproportionately. Yet, despite his failures there, the region still held a spell over Churchill, just as the Russian steppes had with Hitler.

Churchill kept cutting and dealing, coming up trumps, asking for the latest news from the Mediterranean. "I'm sure," recalled Pamela, "he was wondering if another fiasco could happen." A supernaturally gifted politician and orator, her father-in-law was at best a mediocre military strategist, too prone to aggressive adventurism. He knew only too well that his grand scheme to defeat Hitler via the Mediterranean, which the Americans had only grudgingly supported, could very well end up as yet another bloody shambles. Indeed, would it prove just as ill-fated as Gallipoli?

AT HIS HEADQUARTERS in Poland, the "Wolf's Lair," fifty-four-year-old Adolf Hitler also awaited the Anglo-American onslaught. Unlike Kesselring, he had fallen for Operation Mincemeat and had assumed the invasion would come in Greece and Sardinia, not Sicily. Nevertheless, Hitler was confident of victory wherever the Allies chose to land. The Luftwaffe would soon cut the Allied supply lines across the Mediterranean, and any force that did manage to secure a foothold in Europe would then be starved into submission. The question that troubled Hitler was whether or not the Italians could be counted on in Greece, Sardinia, or indeed anywhere they might be asked to fight.

"The Italians never lose a war," he had once complained. "No matter what happens, they always end up on the winning side."

USS *MONROVIA*, JULY 10, 1943

CLOCKS STRUCK ONE minute after midnight. D-day had arrived. Thankfully, Patton's favorite meteorologist, "Houdini," had been right: The gale was fast abating as Patton and his staff gathered on the blacked-out bridge deck.

"Gentlemen," said Patton. "I have the honor and the privilege to activate the Seventh United States Army. This is the first army in history to be activated after midnight and baptized in blood before daylight."

Admiral Hewitt stood nearby. He watched as an honor guard marched onto the deck and presented a gift for Patton—a flag for his new army. The anti-Semitic, "A-rab"-hating, British-loathing southern aristocrat General George Smith Patton Jr., commander of the new Seventh Army, was deeply moved. According to one bystander, there were tears and a "fire of pride in his eyes."

SPARKS STOOD ON a deck of the 157th's command ship, seven miles from the coast of Sicily, beside his tall regimental commander, Colonel Charles M. Ankcorn. He looked up as the sky filled with droning bombers, headed to batter defensive installations on the Sicilian coast. A few minutes later, huge explosions lit up the horizon, casting ships into stark silhouette. Italian shore batteries responded and shells thundered across the swelling waters, several exploding close to Sparks's ship.

Before long, he noticed that the boat was moving back out to sea. Colonel Ankcorn was furious. Sparks followed him up a ladder to the bridge deck, where Ankcorn approached the flotilla's commodore.

"Commodore, why are we heading back out to sea?" asked Ankcorn.

"We are coming under fire from the shore," replied the commodore, "and I am taking the convoy out to a safer distance of eleven miles."

Sparks saw Ankcorn pull out his pistol. Unbelievably, he then placed it to the commodore's head.

"Commodore, our scheduled station is seven miles offshore. Now, you turn this convoy around and get back on proper station."

The commodore didn't say a word to Ankcorn but did give the order to turn around.

IT WAS 2:30 A.M. when the call came for the men to go to their boat stations. Among the nervous Thunderbirds was twenty-four-year-old Montanan Jack Hallowell, a witty former journalist whose father had fought with the British in the Boer War. He belonged to a mortar unit in the regiment's E Company. "They had trained often with live ammunition," he would write of his fellow Thunderbirds, "but this was the first time they could expect their fire to be answered by fire. It made a difference. It made one hell of a difference."

The worst of the storm had passed, but the decks were still heaving, knocking frightened men into one another in the darkness. Whistles and loud-hailers sounded as some wished one another good luck. Tensions ran high. One private in the regiment's I Company, a jumpy young machine gunner called Jackson "Cowboy" Wisecarver, bumped into another nervous Thunderbird by accident.

"Son of a . . ."

Wisecarver promptly hit the other infantryman so hard he almost knocked him out.

Men clambered down chain ladders to landing craft bobbing and pitching below. There were anguished cries as some lost their grip and fell from the ladders. Several were injured and one man drowned. The absence of experienced coxswains had cost the regiment its first life.

3:45 A.M. A loudspeaker sounded.

"Go! Good luck!"

Landing craft pulled away from the mother ships, formed a long V, and made for the dark shore. Although the wind had dropped, the waves were more than nine feet as the craft bucked and bounced toward their assigned landing area, "Bailey's Beach," five miles south of the fishing village of Scoglitti. In bad weather, it was among the most treacherous places on the Sicilian coastline. The Sicilians believed it was in fact impregnable because of its rocky shoreline and many sandbanks, and they had not bothered to set up extensive beach defenses. All the same, stretches of rusted barbed wire and several gun emplacements would welcome the Thunderbirds to Sicily. A hundred yards from the waterline were sand dunes that stretched two hundred yards farther inland toward olive orchards.

The regiment was to land in several waves preceded by an intense naval bombardment. Once it had secured Bailey's Beach, it was to push inland two miles due east to a small, dusty village called San Croce Camerina, the regiment's first objective on D-day.

Two hundred and thirty thousand Italian troops were garrisoned Sicily. Would they resist the Allied invaders or would they capitulate as so many had in North Africa when the prospect of dying for their increasingly comical Il Duce—Benito Mussolini—suddenly became very real indeed? By contrast, there was no doubting the willpower or the potential for immense violence of the 60,000 Germans ready to counterattack if the Italians buckled when the first bullets and shells started to fly. These storm troopers were exceptionally well armed and led by one of the most brilliant and courageous of Hitler's battlefield commanders, General of Panzer Troops Hans Valentin Hube, who in turn answered to Kesselring, the finest practitioner of defensive warfare in World War II.

It was 4 A.M.

"We're going in!" a Thunderbird cried.

Men grabbed the handles of ammunition boxes. Others picked up bangalore torpedoes. Riflemen snapped clips into their M1 rifles.

It was 4:20 A.M. when the first craft approached Bailey's Beach and began to bounce up and down ominously in the nine-foot-high surf. In the hands of inexperienced coxswains, many of the craft veered off course in the high seas. Others were swept toward jagged rocks by rip-tides. Some finally ground onto the sands.

H-hour had arrived. The liberation of Europe had begun.

CHAPTER FOUR

THE RACE FOR MESSINA

Thunderbirds march into Cefalu, Sicily, July 1943. [National Archives]

SAN CROCE CAMERINA, SICILY, JULY 10, 1943

THERE WAS NO BUZZING of MG-42 machine gun bullets or the ear-splitting thunder from German guns. Ramps dropped and the Thunderbirds began staggering ashore. More men were lost in the regiment that morning in accidents, as landing craft were blown off course, than were killed by enemy fire. Over half the landing craft were damaged or sunk in the heavy surf. Two boats collided and were driven into a cove and broken apart on sharp rocks, with one boat overturning. Twenty-seven men from F Company were drowned.

The regiment was soon over the dunes on Bailey's Beach and crossing through the olive orchards farther inland. A dead young 82nd Airborne paratrooper, who had made his first and only combat jump just a few hours earlier, dangled from a parachute caught up in one of the trees. Cowboys in the regiment, from ranches across Colorado and Oklahoma, cut swathes from the young American's billowing silk chute and used them as neckerchiefs.

With the crucial support of the 158th Artillery, the regiment seized ground above San Croce Camerina by early afternoon. "Hits on buildings near the village public square were very effective," recalled Colonel Ankcorn, "and had a marked effect on the garrison commander's attitude."

When Sparks arrived in the village, he was greeted by dozens of white flags fluttering from windows. Five hundred Italian soldiers had given up without the loss of a single American life. "Those goddamn Italians came right out with their hands up," Sparks recalled, "with their bags packed, ready to go to the States." He pressed on that afternoon under a fierce sun, following a trail of unnecessary equipment and clothing men had discarded.

Spirits were high. "We had gone over the side of ships that morning as boys," recalled one man. "Now we were men." There had been no bloodbath when they broke out from the beach, as had been predicted. Elsewhere along the southern coast of Sicily the Allies had met only limited resistance and now advanced rapidly on key cities and towns. The regiment's next objective was Comiso Airport, around ten miles inland. By late on the afternoon of July 11, it had been seized along with over 450 prisoners, 200,000 gallons of aviation fuel, and a nickel-plated bicycle, which the regiment's chaplain, Leland L. Loy, quickly put to use. Men would soon call out "Hi yo Chappie" whenever they saw him pedaling their way. The fight for the airport was the last time the regiment encountered an Italian foe in Sicily. From now on, the men firing back at them would be German, few of whom would be eager to give up without a fight.

THE FOLLOWING MORNING, Chaplain Loy visited the regimental command post that Sparks had set up at the airport. He looked upset. "Colonel," he told Ankcorn, "we have bodies lying all over the beach down there, and nobody's burying them or picking them up or anything."

Ankcorn frowned, thought for a few moments, and then turned to his adjutant.

"Sparks," said Ankcorn. "I don't care how you do it, but I rely on you to see that they are buried with honor."

It was his first challenge of the war. But how was he to do it? The only men at hand were members of the regimental band near his command post. He gathered them together on a truck, then headed back to Bailey's Beach. Dozens of landing craft wallowed in the surf, their engines having burned out as they tried to cross sandbanks. Everywhere there was debris, the flotsam and jetsam of a chaotic invasion crowding the high-water line: smashed boxes of K rations, abandoned bazookas and bangalore torpedoes, packs, and washed-up life belts. More disturbing were the bloated and disfigured corpses, most of them men from F Company who had drowned when their craft broke up on the rocks.

For several hours, Sparks went from one dead American to another, looking for their dog tags. It was gruesome work. The drowned men had been washed back and forth by the tide. Some had been stripped bare, parts of their bodies blue and purple, as if covered in bruises, the whites of their bulging eyes gone gray. He also found the remains of an Air Corps lieutenant named Goldberg, from Utica, New York, in the cockpit of a crashed plane on the beach. He could not find dog tags on five of the corpses, so he took the men's fingerprints with a kit the army

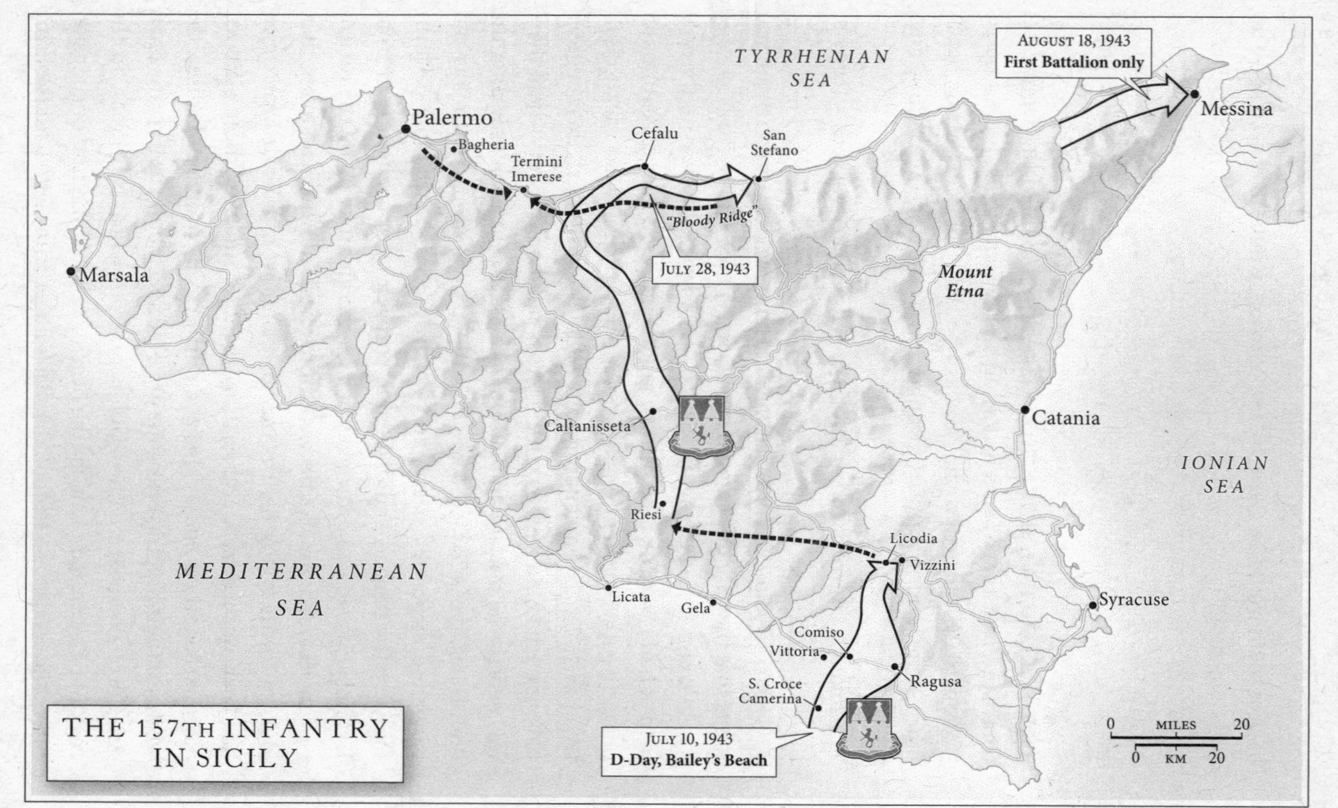

THE 157TH INFANTRY IN SICILY
TYRRHENIAN SEA
IONIAN SEA
MEDITERRANEAN SEA
AUGUST 18, 1943
First Battalion only
Messina
Palermo
Bagheria
Termini Imerese
Cefalu
San Stefano
"Bloody Ridge"
JULY 28, 1943
Marsala
Mount Etna
Catania
Caltanisseta
Riesi
Licodia
Vizzini
Licata
Gela
Syracuse
Comiso
Vittoria
S. Croce Camerina
Ragusa
JULY 10, 1943
D-Day, Bailey's Beach
0 MILES 20
0 KM 20

supplied to every regimental adjutant. Wondering how to shroud the fast-decomposing corpses, he searched the beach and discovered abandoned survival kits that contained blankets. Knowing how important it was to Ankcorn that the men receive a decent burial, he found a field where he and his burial party of musicians then dug three-foot-deep graves in the rocky soil. Finally, they gathered wood from a nearby village and made each man a cross, from which Sparks hung a dog tag.

LICODIA, SICILY, JULY 14, 1943

CAKED IN A dust that seemed to coat every soldier, building, and vehicle a ghoulish gray, Sparks arrived in a small mountain town called Licodia, thirty miles to the east of Bailey's Beach. Thankfully, the locals welcomed him and his fellow Thunderbirds as liberators, even though Italy was still at war with the United States. After enduring millennia of invasion, Sicilians clearly knew when to resist and when to shower well-fed and well-supplied young Americans with flowers. "When we take a town," Sparks soon wrote his parents, "the whole town turns out with flags, flowers, and much shouting. The natives are very friendly and amazed by our generosity. They have been in pretty bad shape and hate the Germans."

The regiment pushed farther into the sunbaked heart of Sicily. German snipers hid in olive trees and even fired at medics. Furious Thunderbirds replied with chemical mortars, showering the marksmen's lairs with white phosphorous, which burned through their uniforms and flesh to the bone. Abandoned vehicles littered the roadsides looking like bizarre skeletons after the locals had scavenged their metal to forge into tools and plows. The Thunderbirds marched on, past buildings with red stucco walls that belonged to the Cantonieri, the Italian Fascists, who had scrawled messages on walls all across Sicily: "*Credere, Obediere, Combattere*"—"Believe, Obey, Fight"—instructions few locals carried out.

As he sped north in a jeep, planning where next to set up the regimental command post, Sparks encountered his most senior commander in Sicily, General George Patton himself. Patton was being driven in a jeep. Just days before, the silver-haired Seventh Army commander had admitted to a fellow general that the two things he loved most in life were "fucking and fighting."

Patton got out of the jeep and approached Sparks, who quickly saluted.

"Where's your commander?" asked Patton, three stars clearly visible on his helmet.

"He's up ahead," said Sparks. "We've got a hard fight up there."

The following day, July 15, the regiment reached the vital Vizzini-Caltagirone Road, which led to Mount Etna. But then the regiment was suddenly ordered to halt. Eighth Army's General Montgomery wanted to use the crucial road, so the entire 45th Division, much to Patton's fury, was forced to give way and march back the way it had come, toward the landing beaches. "My God," US II Corps commander Omar Bradley exclaimed to Patton, "you can't allow him to do that." As far as Bradley was concerned, Montgomery's theft of the road was "the most arrogant, egotistical, selfish and dangerous move in the whole of combined operations in World War II."

Patton allowed Montgomery to take the road, not wanting to provoke Eisenhower, who had recently criticized him unfairly for poor planning. But in private he exploded. "Tell Montgomery to stay out of my way or I'll drive those Krauts right up his ass," he raged at his deputy, Major General Geoffrey Keyes, who diplomatically neglected to do so. It was a humiliating reversal but quickly forgotten by the hot and sweaty infantrymen, if not their peeved officers, as the Thunderbirds pulled back and then swung northwest toward Palermo, trailing a seemingly endless dust cloud behind them.

Montgomery had stolen Patton's road cutting through the central mountains toward Messina, the closest port to mainland Italy. But he now failed to exploit it and was soon stalled west of Mount Etna, held up by determined Panzer units. The ancient home of the Cyclops and the Mafia, the Roman Empire's first province was no longer a "soft underbelly" as Churchill had promised. Kesselring had decided during a flying visit to Sicily three days before, on July 12, to abandon the island. But he was determined to slow the Allied advance and buy time for a full evacuation. It was crucial to defend key routes east toward Messina, from where thousands of men and hundreds of vehicles were being ferried to mainland Italy each day.

Montgomery's woe would be Patton's gain. Determined to upstage the British, Patton decided to strike along Sicily's northeastern shore and get to Messina first, ahead of his British archrival—"that little fart," as he called Montgomery in his diary. "This is a horse race in which the prestige of the US Army is at stake," Patton stressed in a note to the 45th's Troy Middleton. "We must take Messina before the British. Please use your best efforts to facilitate the success of our race."

The Thunderbirds now became the front runners in the race for American glory in Sicily. On July 27, the regiment attacked along the coastal highway toward Messina. Facing the 45th was the Ulrich Combat Group, made up of two well-armed and tenacious regiments of the 29th Panzergrenadier Division: men who would "say Heil Hitler with their dying breath," as one Thunderbird officer put it. They had been ordered to stop the American advance, come what may, in order to shield tens of thousands of other Axis troops who were being evacuated.

The Germans had left mines along the coastal highway to slow the advance and had then retreated into the mountains, where they now began to zero in on the Americans with alarming accuracy. Mortar shells seemed to drop like hail as the Thunderbirds pushed toward San Stefano along the coast through booby-trapped groves of ripening olives and lemons, below a barren mountain that jutted to the ocean's edge. The mountain had to be crossed if Patton was to seize Messina first. The natives called it San Rosso. It would be forever remembered by Thunderbirds as "Bloody Ridge."

That first day of battle for the ridge, July 27, the regiment suffered

108 casualties, by far its highest one-day total so far. Exhausted and stunned by the ferocity of German counterattacks with tanks, that evening the regiment formed a circle defense with men positioned no more than three yards from one another, just as many of their forefathers had done in the Indian Wars. Mules carried up ammunition and food. So steep was the climb that some of the poor animals died from exhaustion. Men cussed as they picked up the supplies and carried them on their own backs.

The "Battle of Bloody Ridge" resumed the next day. Again the Germans countered the regiment's every attempt to push forward. A machine-gun squad in Company A fought with great courage to hold off one such strike, the fiercest the regiment had yet encountered. The gunners were later awarded the Distinguished Service Cross. None would be alive to receive it. Twenty-year-old Private First Class Bernie Kaczorowski, another machine gunner in A Company, saw friends sliced in half by German shells. Under heavy fire, he jumped in a foxhole, only to find himself beside a young man from Philadelphia with his head blown off. Kaczorowski quickly understood how frail the human body was and how easily it could be shredded and reduced to hamburger. Fighting on Bloody Ridge, he remembered, was just like being in a meat grinder. At the epicenter of the carnage, he found American flesh splattered everywhere: on the sturdy stock of his M1 rifle, in shallow foxholes, seemingly wherever he cowered for cover from the flying hot metal and machine-gun bullets that buzzed over his head.

The deeply religious, who had chaplains praying for their survival, appeared to be more forsaken than the sinners, who swore, whored, and drank themselves unconscious whenever they could scrounge cheap, sour-tasting wine from the locals. "They [used to] say God only takes the good," a still-traumatized Kaczorowski would say more than sixty years later. "Maybe that's why I'm still here—because I'm rotten."

On July 31, the regiment finally arrived in San Stefano, a port midway along the northern coast. German corpses lay rotting, black with flies, in the streets. Here the Thunderbirds were relieved by the 3rd Division and trucked to a rest area near another port, called Termini Immerse, where men sat in the shade, stunned and utterly exhausted by their first real battle. When nearby watermelon patches had been cleared of mines, some men lay in the sun, juice running in bright lines down their throats, while others waded in cold streams where they washed off the infernal sand and dust.

At the regimental command post, Sparks received mail from his wife, Mary. He was now the proud father of a baby boy. Mary had sent a photo of his new son, Kirk, who had been born on May 20, just days before Sparks left America. He was delighted and relieved that Mary had fast recovered from a long and difficult birth. "I have been getting lots of letters from Mary in the past ten days," he told his parents in a V-mail addressed simply from "Sicily." "The baby seems to be doing fine," he added, "which is good news to me. It's reassuring to know that everyone is interested in him." That August 2 was Sparks's 26th birthday. "I wasn't able to do any celebrating on my birthday," he wrote his parents, "although there were plenty of fireworks. It's plenty hot over here and very dusty."

Two days later, the first blood transfusion began: The regiment received its first batch of nervous replacements, 123 enlisted men and nine officers. They were pitiful neophytes in the ways of war, one officer noted, "not mentally, physically, and technically ready for combat." The same officer recommended that in the future "every man must be drilled to withstand mental shock."

The replacements had barely learned their fellow platoon members' names when they were told to get ready to board landing craft. The aim was to perform an "end run" by leapfrogging points of German resistance on the northern coast of Sicily. Yet again, lives were lost as the Thunderbirds moved from ship to shore. A davit failure caused one assault boat to fall into the sea, killing most of the men aboard. But these were the only casualties during the operation: To their great relief, the

Thunderbirds discovered that the 3rd Division had already managed to secure their assigned landing beaches with ease.

The Allied race to Messina ended on August 18, around 4 A.M. Men from Sparks's regiment, a party from the First Battalion, marched into the city's heavily bombed suburbs, beating the 3rd Division, the Rangers, and, notably, the entire British Eighth Army to the first great prize in the campaign to liberate Europe.

"Where you tourists been?" asked GIs when the British arrived just two hours later.

"Hello, you bloody bastards!" replied British tankers.

It was not much of a prize. Messina had endured earthquake, plague, and Carthaginian slaughter but nothing as calamitous as American Flying Fortresses.

Patton entered the shattered city later that day, a phalanx of press and photographers in his wake. A senior British officer greeted him with a snappy salute.

"It was a jolly good race," said the gracious limey. "I congratulate you."

Patton was elated. He was the American general of the hour. PATTON, not MONTY, would appear in the front-page headlines around the world.

The Battle for Sicily had lasted thirty-eight days and cost 25,000 Allied casualties. By contrast, the Germans had suffered fewer than 20,000. Almost 150,000 Italians had surrendered. Crucially, Axis forces were no longer able to control the Mediterranean.

Sparks would later consider Sicily to be something of a bitter victory, given that so many of the enemy had escaped unscathed. Kesselring's divisions had performed superbly, stalling the Allies just long enough to pull out more than a hundred thousand troops and ten thousand vehicles to fight another day. "We should have murdered them," one of Sparks's fellow captains complained. "It would have saved us a hell of a lot of trouble later on."

TRABIA, SICILY, LATE AUGUST 1943

IF HE WANTED, he could wander through the ripening lemon groves nearby or pick grapes lining the roads on the verdant north shore of Sicily, where red geraniums formed hedges in the lee of the rugged mountains just inland. The sunsets were spectacular, vast swathes of yellow and red splashed across the Mediterranean, and at night the moon's pale light seemed to make the olive leaves glow like polished silver.

Day after day, the Thunderbirds practiced war, advancing under live fire to test men's nerves and their commanders' competency. Sparks sat typing, organizing, reading reports, and readying maps while the booming of guns reminded him, like a nagging aunt, that he was a pen pusher, not a true soldier. He knew the division was going to move out soon. Long lines of vehicles blocked the coastal road to the nearby port of Termini Imerese, where they were to be waterproofed in preparation for another amphibious operation. Rumor had it Sardinia or the Balkans would be next.

Sparks wanted to lead men in combat, not follow behind and sit out battles in the safety of a command post, however essential his duties were as adjutant. He'd spent the whole summer in Sicily typing reports and arranging maps while men had been fighting and dying. So when he learned that a vacancy had opened up in the regiment for a company commander, he immediately approached Colonel Ankcorn.

"We've got a vacancy and I'd like to fill it."

"No, you're doing all right where you are."

A few days later, Ankcorn stomped into the tented command post in an olive grove where Sparks was working. Ankcorn had watched with growing rage as E Company, from the regiment's Second Battalion, had failed a live-fire test.

"All right, Sparks, you asked for it! You take over E Company. We're going to run through those tests again tomorrow and they'd better pass."

Sparks packed his personal belongings, quickly relieved E Company's temporary commander, and then called the unit's sergeants to an urgent meeting.

"What's your problem?" asked Sparks.

"We don't like our commanding officer," said one man. "We don't think he's competent."

"You have a new one now and I assure you I'm competent. We're going to go through this test again and we're going to pass or some of you are going to be privates."

The sergeants knew Sparks was not one to make idle threats. Before leaving the States, he had been placed in charge of a special J Company (*J* for "Jailbird") comprising men who had gone AWOL. Through his "gentle persuasion" and with the help of several tough sergeants, including a former prizefighter, he had quickly prepared them for combat, earning a fearsome reputation in the regiment in the process. "If anyone gave me a problem," he recalled, "I had a sergeant beat up on them. I don't think that was legal, but that's the way we did it."

A reinvigorated E Company passed the test with high marks, and Sparks found himself officially assigned as the commander of E Company. He had not wanted war, but neither had he wanted to sit on the sidelines. Since his days as a teenager at Fort Huachuca in Arizona, he had worked hard to become an infantry officer. Combat was what he had been trained for. There was no doubt he would now experience it.

From the day he took control of E Company, Sparks was in his element. He loved being a rifle company commander. He had a keen memory and quickly learned the name of every soldier in his company, all 192. He did not make windy speeches or give lectures like some officers. Instead, he got to know his men by asking them direct questions and quizzing them about their families and where they were from. There was Jack Turner, a popular medic from Lamar, Colorado, one of the original members of E Company when it had been a National Guard unit based in his hometown. Other stalwarts included the twenty-four-year-old Montana-born journalist Jack Hallowell, who belonged to one of Sparks's three mortar squads. With these men and the rest of his company, Sparks quickly enjoyed what he would later describe as a wonderful relationship.

He now had three rifle platoons of forty men each under his command, most of them battle-tested, plus a heavy-weapons platoon that contained two machine-gun squads and three 60mm mortar squads that could fire shells three times the weight of hand grenades more than a mile. He knew that in combat he would have to deploy the machine guns in pairs so their fields of fire covered as much of his front as possible. Two rifle platoons would be engaged at any one time, while the third rotated in reserve, hence the term "two up and one back" used to describe a company's basic triangle organization and that of battalions, regiments, divisions, and corps.

With his new responsibilities came new worries. The life expectancy of company commanders in the infantry was almost as short as that of the fresh-faced lieutenants who led his three rifle platoons—ninety days, if he was lucky.

BAGHERIA, SICILY, AUGUST 25, 1943

THE SUN BLAZED with the kind of intensity Sparks had experienced during summers spent wandering the Arizona desert, shotgun under his arm, alert for rattlesnakes and prey. In an olive grove, he stood with hundreds of other young officers in the shade of gnarled trees. The men around him smiled, laughed, and clapped wildly as they listened to General George Patton.

Before the invasion, Patton had worried about the green National Guard Thunderbirds. Were they up for the fight? Would they cut and run when the first Panzers started to clank their way? Now he could not have been more pleased with the men, drawn mostly from Oklahoma, New Mexico, Arizona, and Colorado, and their incisive, hard-charging division commander, Troy Middleton. They had confounded all his fears. They had fought like wily veterans from day one.

"The Forty-fifth Infantry Division is one of the best," said Patton, "if not *the* best division that the American Army has ever produced."

Patton stressed that the Thunderbirds still confronted a skilled and determined enemy.

"But you, as Americans," added Patton, "are his superior. When you meet him, as you will some day on the plains of Europe, you may expect him to throw large masses of armor at you. He will seek to drive through your center with a point of armor but, by God, this point will not get through!"

Patton turned sentimental.

"I love every bone in your heads," he declared, "but be very careful. Do not go to sleep, or someone's liable to slip up behind you and hit you over the head with a sock full of shit, and that's a hell of an embarrassing way in which to die!"

A few days later, Sparks was surprised to learn that Patton, who had given such a rousing performance in the olive grove, would no longer lead the Thunderbirds in combat. In fact, the entire Seventh Army was being broken up, the Thunderbirds were being transferred to the Fifth Army, and Patton himself was being demoted to the role of military governor of Sicily.

Patton had won the island. Now he could keep it, indefinitely, confined to a grand old villa, the Palermo Palace, where he would carry out administrative duties, like some disgraced Roman senator, for the foreseeable future. He had only himself to blame for his fall from grace. In two different hospitals that July, he had slapped and verbally abused shell-shocked casualties, to the outrage of medical staff. When Omar Bradley had read a report on the incidents, though "sickened and soured" by it, he had chosen not to forward the career-ending dossier to higher-ups. Others had not been so diplomatic, passing on information to several reporters who threatened to go public if Patton was not sacked.

"This would be a nasty story to get out," reporter Quentin Reynolds from *Collier's* warned Eisenhower. "Goebbels could do a lot with it. Every mother in America would think that her son was being subjected to this sort of treatment."

"I know," replied a weary Eisenhower. "I know."

Patton was forced to make groveling apologies to both of his victims and his superiors. A deeply dismayed Eisenhower confided to an aide: "George is one of the best generals I have, but he's like a time bomb. You can never be sure when he's going to go off. All you can be sure of is that it will probably be at the wrong place at the wrong time." To his credit, Eisenhower refused to fire the man who was, arguably, his finest general. There was still a long way to go before the Allies reached Berlin. One day he might need him.

A humiliated Patton sank quickly into depression and despair, appearing to one fellow general "very old and desiccated." He was also increasingly paranoid, believing the envious British cousins had somehow been out to get him. "Sometimes I think there is a deliberate campaign to hurt me," he wrote in his diary. A few days later, he added: "One British general said, 'George is such a pushing fellow that if we don't stop him he will have Monty surrounded.' I know I can outfight the little fart anytime."

Eisenhower had saved him from the shame of returning to the United States in disgrace. But would he ever give him the opportunity to outfight Montgomery with an army again?

TERMINI IMERESE, SICILY, SEPTEMBER 7, 1943

NEPTUNE WAS ANGRY. For several days a violent storm had buffeted the scores of ships in the harbor, hampering loading and causing much concern among senior officers gathered around map tables in the

45th Division's headquarters. The high seas had abated somewhat but gale force winds persisted as Sparks waited to board a boat in Termini Imerese. A long column of waterproofed vehicles wound back and forth through the mountains, like a dusty snake, toward the port and its rows of landing craft. He and his men were bound for the port of Salerno, south of Naples. For the first time, he was heading into combat, not as an adjutant armed with a typewriter, but as a young leader of two hundred men.

CHAPTER FIVE

MOUNTAIN COUNTRY

Three Thunderbirds using a cave for protection from enemy shelling, December 27, 1943, near Venafro, Italy. [National Archives]

USS *ANCON*, OFF THE COAST OF ITALY, SEPTEMBER 8, 1943

GENERAL MARK CLARK SAT down behind a desk in the spacious stateroom. H-hour for planned landings in mainland Italy, Operation Avalanche, was just a few hours away. Forty-seven-year-old Clark could not hide his nerves. Indeed, he looked anxious, his handsome face gaunt. Before him were gathered several wily and skeptical correspondents whom he had just briefed on Avalanche. To his most generous critics, Clark was a tenacious and even capable commander. But to others, such as the legendary "Wild Bill" Donovan, head of the OSS, he was vain, superficial, and worst of all, ineffectual. Churchill affectionately called him his "American Eagle" because of the prominence of his aquiline nose, which Clark always insisted should be photographed from the most flattering angle. Among the press corps, because of such gross egotism, he was widely derided and in many cases truly loathed.

Known as Wayne to his friends, Clark had graduated almost bottom of his class at West Point and languished as a captain for sixteen years before his friendship with Eisenhower—they had shared a house in England—saw him become the youngest lieutenant general in U.S. Army history. Now Clark faced the greatest challenge of his career—securing a foothold on mainland Italy. Unlike in Sicily, the Germans would do everything in their power to throw the Allies back into the sea, and they stood every chance of doing so. Only three Allied divisions from Clark's Fifth Army were scheduled to land at Salerno on D-day, due to shortages in landing craft.

"So what do you think of my plan, gentlemen?" Clark asked.

"Daring," replied forty-one-year-old Quentin Reynolds of *Collier's*.

"My God, it is, isn't it!" exclaimed Clark. "I guess it's the most daring plan of the war. We're spitting into the lion's mouth and we know it."

Another correspondent asked: "Is it perhaps too daring, sir?"

"You've got to remember we've been working on invasion plans for months," replied Clark. "I can assure you the Fifth Army is ready."

"So you hope to achieve surprise, sir, by the sheer daring of the plan?"

"With a few breaks we'll pull it off."

"Have you any serious reservations, sir?"

"None."

The same could not be said of other senior generals, namely Bernard Montgomery, who decried the lack of a carefully crafted master plan for the invasion of mainland Italy and believed the gamble of landing just three divisions at Salerno was ill-advised. As far as he was concerned, little had been learned from Sicily, where infighting among the Allies (much of which he had caused) and the failure to cut off the Germans in retreat had left some senior strategists wondering if the battle for the island had cost more than it gained.

Montgomery also believed Clark's invasion plans depended too much on the naïve belief that a secretly negotiated surrender by the Italians would act in the Allies' favor. The Germans had long suspected that the Italians would throw in the towel, he maintained, and had made elaborate plans to quickly seize control of the country. He was right. The news of the Italian capitulation on September 8, the day of Clark's press conference, did nothing to impair the Germans' ability to defend Italy. For several weeks, Erwin Rommel had gathered eight German divisions and quickly disarmed Italian troops. Meanwhile, the commander of German troops in southern Italy, Kesselring, seized key defenses along the western coast and promptly instructed six experienced divisions, including Panzer forces, to prepare for an invasion in the Salerno area.

Mark Clark had also told correspondents that the invasion beaches would be lightly defended. He had decided not to precede the landings with bombardment, in order to maintain the element of surprise. But when the first wave of troops from the green 36th Infantry Division, a Texas National Guard unit, approached Salerno early on September 9, the day after Clark's press conference, they were stunned to find heavily armed Germans waiting in force.

In propaganda leaflets dropped on the Allies before the invasion, the Germans had warned that Salerno would be a death trap, and so it proved that morning. The air was soon thick with machine-gun bullets stitching their way across soft sands toward hastily beached boats. Men vainly tried to dig foxholes in the shallows, others froze in the face of the intense fire, none had a safe place to run back to, just the bullet-spattered sea. More than two hundred men from the 36th Division were killed as they came ashore, many mown down before they got off their landing craft. Two British divisions, the 46th and the 56th, also met fierce resistance on their assigned beaches farther north. The Germans were lying in wait, so well-informed by intelligence sources that they had marked the Fifth Army's Green, Red, and Yellow landing beaches on their maps. Forced to concentrate their forces, the British were unable to link up with the traumatized Texans to the south. Kesselring sent a message to his commanders: "The invading enemy . . . must be completely annihilated and, in addition, thrown into the sea. . . . British and Americans must realize that they are hopelessly lost against the concentrated German might."

By sundown on D-day, more than fifty thousand Allies were ashore and had pushed inland as much as eight miles, but a ten-mile gap lay open between the British and the Americans, who were both badly in need of reinforcement. Only continuous supporting fire from naval batteries and great courage saved the 36th Division from being wiped out on its first day in battle. In the Temple of Neptune near Paestum, built by the Greeks in 470 B.C., beneath thirty-six ornate Doric columns that had survived the Allied shelling, medics rushed from litter to litter, desperately trying to keep at least some of their fellow Texans alive.

The Allies were ashore but only just. On September 13, Mark Clark found himself trying desperately to claw his way out of the jaws of defeat. Relief was a long way off: Montgomery's Eighth Army had landed a hundred miles farther south, at the toe of Italy, and would take several more days to link up. The Germans commanded all the high ground and were massing tanks and striking at weak points all along the Allied lines. Clark's gamble had been daring indeed, but it had failed. There had been no element of surprise. "The Germans actually needed only a pair of average magnitude binoculars," recalled one disgusted soldier, "to spot the approaching Allied convoys far out to sea."

What Churchill feared most—another Galliopli—looked more and more probable. The man who had called loudest and longest for the invasion of Italy, much to American strategists' dismay, spent that "Black Monday" of September 13 with President Roosevelt at his Hyde Park estate. Both Churchill and Roosevelt were understandably perturbed by early reports of the invasion. It was all chillingly similar to the Sulva

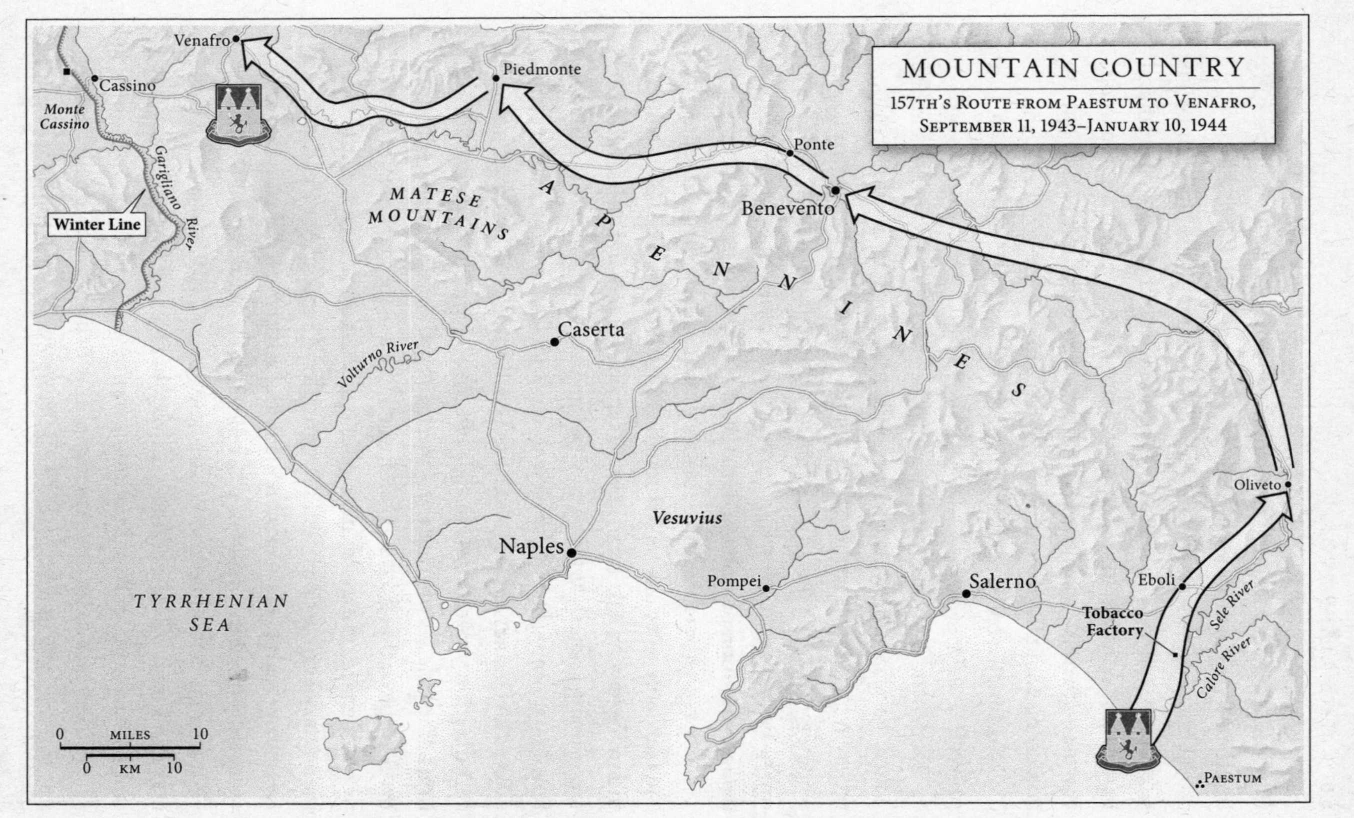
MOUNTAIN COUNTRY
157TH'S ROUTE FROM PAESTUM TO VENAFRO, SEPTEMBER 11, 1943–JANUARY 10, 1944
Venafro
Piedmonte
Cassino
Monte Cassino
Garigliano River
Winter Line
MATESE MOUNTAINS
APENNINES
Ponte
Benevento
Caserta
Volturno River
Vesuvius
Naples
Pompei
Salerno
Oliveto
Eboli
Tobacco Factory
Sele River
Calore River
PAESTUM
TYRRHENIAN SEA
0 MILES 10
0 KM 10

Bay landing in the Gallipoli campaign, when troops landed successfully but then failed to advance inland.

At his headquarters, Mark Clark conferred with his corps and division commanders. The reports were dire: Everywhere, the push inland had ground to a halt. In some sectors, announced VI Corps commander General Ernest Dawley, the Germans had broken through. "What are you doing about it?" asked Clark. "What can you do?"

"Nothing," replied Dawley. "I have no reserves. All I've got is a prayer."

Kesselring had the upper hand. If he threw all his reserves at the Allies, he would prevail. Clark hastily tried to plug his lines, calling on every Allied soldier he could muster. When two-star general Troy Middleton, leading the Thunderbird Division, learned that withdrawal might be an option, he sent a curt message to his superiors: "Put food and ammunition behind the 45th. We are going to stay here."

Across the beachhead, the Allies prepared defenses and waited for the Germans to attack. All through September 14, Kesselring's forces did so. Crucially, Allied artillery was massed in critical areas, with gun crews firing as many as ten rounds per minute from hundreds of 105mm howitzers, timing the fire so that shells landed every couple of seconds where the Germans tried hardest to break through. This "fire on time" coordination proved devastatingly effective, so much so that Kesselring himself wondered whether the Americans had devised a repeat-loading artillery piece that fired shell after shell like a giant machine gun.

In the face of massive naval and land-based artillery fire, the German attacks broke down and by nightfall on September 14 had stalled. Kesselring had failed to exploit his initial advantage, not realizing how weak the Fifth Army had been. A relieved Clark contacted Eisenhower. "We are in good shape now. We are here to stay. . . . We have made mistakes and we have learned the hard way, but we will improve every day and I am sure we will not disappoint you."

On September 16, the American and British forces finally linked up. The critical gap was closed. Kesselring ordered his divisions to pull back to higher ground to fight another day. Everything Eighth Army commander Montgomery had predicted would go wrong had indeed done so. That same day, forward patrols of the Eighth Army made contact with the battered Fifth. A smug Montgomery told *Collier's* reporter Quentin Reynolds: "We have landed on the enemy mainland. Now we are really at grips with him. It has just begun."

PAESTUM, ITALY, SEPTEMBER 18, 1943

THEY LOOKED AT him for the first time as their leader, about to enter combat. Their destination was a beach four miles north of the seaside town of Paestum, some forty miles south of Naples. The regiment's Second Battalion, including Sparks's E Company, had been held back in floating reserve during the height of the fighting at Salerno. Now, on September 18, it was ordered to land and then press north toward Naples, the Allies' next major objective.

"You know the drill," said Sparks. "Now it's up to us. See you on the beach."

Once again, Sparks had missed the action. He had yet to lead men in battle and was understandably nervous as he headed toward the front for the first time as a company commander. But one of the many things he had learned from Colonel Ankcorn in Sicily was that he should always appear calm and collected. Indeed, good leaders were often good actors, able to convince their men if not themselves that they would somehow prevail. "The truth of the matter was I was scared shitless but my men didn't know it," Sparks later confessed. "Sometimes you just have to take care of business. Just do it, get through it. That's all."

Sparks and his men climbed down netting and into the landing craft that would take them to the shore. It was around 8 A.M. when E Company's boats left the mother ship and made for the beach. The air was soft, the skies a bright blue except where scarred by ugly black puffs from anti-aircraft fire. Before them lay the Gulf of Salerno with its long beaches of white sands. In the distance, to the north of the bay, Sparks could see 3,556-foot Monte Soprano and adjacent Monte Sottane, which had provided the perfect vantage points for German artillery observers.

Ramps came down. The landing craft disgorged a foul soup of puke and seawater. Men pushed forward onto the churned sands and began weaving through piles of Allied supplies. Sparks led his men inland, passing the ancient ruins of Paestum, famous for its three great temples, whose towering columns still stood, seemingly in defiance. Evidence of fierce and desperate fighting lay all around as he moved farther inland: abandoned German anti-tank guns, packs dropped by men in a hurry, vehicles blackened and still smoldering. Not far from one temple stood the charred hulk of a German tank that had received a direct hit and then "brewed up" as the British put it, exploding into flames. The Germans had been trapped inside, and a puddle of their fat, coated in brightly colored flies, spread slowly beneath the tracks.

As Sparks moved off the plain of Salerno and onto higher ground, one of his men couldn't help show his feelings.

"Captain, I'm scared," said a young private.

"Well, soldier, we're all scared," Sparks reassured him. "Don't let that bother you."

E Company was soon soaking wet. The famous Italian autumn rains began, turning road junctions into muddy bottlenecks and slowing the Allied advance. The mud caused as much delay as Kesslering's divisions, which had destroyed bridges and blocked roads with felled trees covered in booby traps. Early on September 24, Sparks learned that Colonel Ankcorn had been injured on a reconnaissance patrol when his jeep hit one of the countless mines the Germans had also left in their wake. The Thunderbirds' commanding general, Troy Middleton, was as worried as Sparks at the possible loss of the man he regarded as the finest regimental commander he had ever encountered.

At first, it was reported that Ankcorn had a bad fracture near his ankle. He might return to duty soon, the injury being relatively minor. Middleton waited, like Sparks and others throughout the division, for more news. When it arrived, it was not good. Ankcorn's leg was so badly mangled, it would have to be amputated. His war was over, and Sparks had lost his mentor, the man who had taught him more than any other about leadership. Colonel John Church, the 45th Division's chief of staff, took over command of the regiment, but as far as a bereft Sparks was concerned, Ankcorn could "never adequately be replaced."

The Allied advance continued. On October 1, the Fifth Army seized Naples. As if the gods had ordained it, nearby Mount Vesuvius erupted for the first time in thirty-eight years and began to spew ominous clouds of soot and ash. The city was in a woeful state, with no water or electricity and a starving population, having been sacked by the departing Germans.

Naples was a harbinger of greater disappointment still. In front of the Allied advance, Kesselring had constructed three defensive lines across Italy from east to west. The strongest of these was the Gustav Line, which spanned the narrowest part of the country, some eighty miles south of Rome and seventy north of Naples. Its strongpoint was the ancient town of Monte Cassino, notable for a wondrous Benedictine monastery established on a mountain almost fifteen hundred years before. To reach Rome, the Gustav Line had to be breached and Monte Cassino taken.

In early October, Sparks received orders to advance toward the Upper Volturno Valley, a key objective if the Allies were to reach the Gustav Line before winter set in. Heavy rain fell and rivers burst their banks, washing away the few bridges that the Germans had not destroyed. As Caesar's legions had before them, Sparks and his men passed through the town of Benevento's famous archway in jeeps and trucks. Most of the men couldn't have cared less that they were now the ones making history as they headed toward the small town of Ponte, where division commander Middleton hoped to trap German forces retreating toward the Gustav Line. Dead Germans lay by the roadside like carrion, hawks and crows circling above limbless corpses that looked like large hams wrapped in gray uniform.

PONTE, ITALY, OCTOBER 6, 1943

DAWN WAS NIGH. A cold mist clung to the ground near the village of Ponte, providing cover as Sparks led his men across a hillside. E Company was acting as the point of the regiment's advance.

"I want your squad to secure our flank," Sparks told Sergeant Vinnie Stigliani, a fluent Italian speaker who had joined E Company at Salerno. Also a gifted musician, Stigliani had quickly learned to dig his hands into the earth whenever he came under fire, terrified he might never play an instrument again. Since arriving at Salerno, Sparks had come to rely on this short and wiry eighteen-year-old rifle squad leader from Boston to converse with the often surly locals in order to obtain chickens and other fresh food.

Stigliani and his squad set out, each man fifteen yards from the other. They had not gone far when the mist lifted, leaving E Company terribly exposed. German machine gunners opened up. Volleys of bullets swept the open ground, sounding like rough fabric being ripped apart. Stigliani hit the dirt and flattened himself. "I was lower than a rat on the ground," he recalled. "Machine gun bullets passed over my head, buzzing like bees, and I could hear guys moaning all around me." Something hit his back. Then he felt warm blood trickle down his leg.

Sparks meanwhile shouted for his other rifle squads to pull back to a bare hillside to his left. They could take cover from the German machine guns there. He and his men had just reached the hill when he spotted enemy tanks four hundred yards farther to his left. The tanks opened fire. There wasn't time to think. All he could do was react. He tried to make himself heard above the firing, which sounded like hammer blows close to the ear, and the explosions that peppered the bare hillside with lethal shards of hot metal. A few men no doubt urinated and defecated as their shocked bodies automatically rid themselves of excess ballast and locked into survival mode.

Sparks stayed focused and shouted as loud as he could. There was a ridge, around half a mile to the rear. His men were to head for it.

They should bring their weapons. It was to be an orderly retreat. But few could hear him as the sky seemed to collapse on them and explosions ripped the earth apart.

Mortarman Jack Hallowell watched as some men panicked and ran for trees. He didn't follow them, knowing that one shell burst in the treetops would shower fragments of wood and metal, killing anyone cowering below. It was safer to stay in the open. And then it happened. A shell screeched through the air and exploded amid the trees. Three or four men were hit. Hallowell would never forget their last screams. He was tempted to drop the mortar barrel he was carrying over his shoulder and run for his life, back to the ridgeline, but he knew Sparks would be furious if he left any part of the weapon behind. He ran as fast he could, but the barrel was so heavy he had to stop and catch his breath. A shell whistled over his head. He had been spotted. Another shell landed closer. He knew the next would kill him, so he jumped up and ran, setting what surely must have been a new world record for the hundred-yard dash, before finally reaching the ridgeline to his rear.

Several wounded men lay in agony. Medics were busy tending to them, slapping on dressings and punching morphine spikes into their torn bodies. Sparks stood nearby, still shouting orders to his platoon leaders.

As machine-gun bullets raked the ridgeline, Hallowell and others took cover in a farm building where a small and frightened boy sat crying.

"You're going to be okay," Hallowell said to soothe him. "You're going to be okay."

Back on the exposed hillside, where the mist had lifted, Vinnie Stigliani heard the guttural sound of German soldiers. He dared to glance up and saw them examining American corpses.

"Oh, Jesus."

Stigliani decided to pretend to be dead. It didn't work. One of the soldiers grabbed his head and pulled him up by his helmet. The German was all of sixteen years old. He was wearing an Afrika Korps hat with a bull's-eye marked on it. Soon, another German was helping drag Stigliani toward captivity.

On the ridgeline, Sparks examined some of his injured men. Among them was a young private called Campbell. He had been hit in the chest and was a blood-drenched mess with a serious wound to one of his lungs. The medics had done their best to stem the blood flow, but Sparks gave him little chance, knowing such "sucking wounds" were almost always fatal.

The German tanks finally moved away, no doubt low on ammunition and gas, much to the traumatized riflemen's relief. Like the men under his command, Sparks would now have experienced the backlash from the stress of combat. A profound exhaustion probably hit him as his adrenaline ebbed.

Sparks had seen young men ripped apart, felt the ground shudder beneath him and groan as 88mm shells exploded all around. He had lost more than a dozen men, the highest count so far in combat for his company. But it could have been far worse. Thankfully he had been able to pull most of his men out of danger before even more could be captured or killed.

He had not panicked. He had been able to think and act quickly once the shooting began, and he had felt little fear. Important lessons had been learned. Only a few of his men could be counted on to advance under heavy fire. Good lieutenants and experienced sergeants were essential. Before long, he would place a particularly formidable sergeant, an ex–football player, just to the rear of his most vulnerable men to stop them turning tail.

He was delighted with most of his company, however, and particularly pleased with several Mexican-Americans under his command. He had wondered how they would behave in combat, knowing they had been discriminated against throughout their lives and might therefore lack the will to fight for a country that had treated them so shabbily. In Miami, Arizona, more than half his classmates had been Hispanic, and he could fully understand why some would not want to give their all for

Uncle Sam. But like all the other poor boys in his company, they had turned out to be excellent soldiers.

Later that day, in a farmhouse behind German lines, a badly wounded Vinnie Stigliani sat opposite a German intelligence officer. The lieutenant had already examined Stigliani's dog tags and discovered that he came from Charlestown, Massachusetts.

"Did you belong to the Boys' Club?" the officer asked in perfect English.

"Yeah. Everybody belonged to it."

"Do you know who I am?"

"No."

"I was a swimming instructor at the club before the war."

The German had worked at the club while attending MIT in Boston as a German army officer.

"Did you find any ponds destroyed?" asked the German.

"I don't know what you mean."

"Oh, you know what I mean," the German said, and then placed a Luger pistol to Stigliani's head.

Stigliani started to cry. The German asked him again. He said he didn't understand the question. Then the German pushed Stigliani into an adjoining room. But he did not shoot him. Only later, as a POW, would Stigliani realize that the German's English had not been perfect after all. The German must have forgotten the English word *bridges* and used the Italian instead. *Pontes* had sounded just like "ponds" to a terrified eighteen-year-old bleeding from shrapnel wounds. The German had wanted to know if E Company had found destroyed bridges, not poisoned ponds, during its advance.

PONTE-CASALDUNI, ITALY, OCTOBER 12, 1943

THE MOUNTAINS OF Matese towered to the north, skirted by forests of beech and black pine. The leaves were turning, especially at higher altitudes, where they resembled the yellowing aspen back in the mountains of Arizona. The disappearing cover was beautiful to behold, but it also exposed men to German artillery observers hiding on ridgelines, as cunning as the Apennine foxes that roamed the area.

Sparks set up his command post a mile and a half east of the town of Ponte, where the Volturno and Calore rivers met, and awaited his next orders. He had been on the line almost three weeks. He had reached the period of maximum efficiency for young officers in World War II, no longer a battle virgin, too soon to become overconfident and then exhausted as his mind and body shut down because of accumulated stress and deprivation.

It was around 10:30 A.M. on October 12 when he heard the regiment's 40mm Bofors anti-aircraft guns open up, filling the area with their frantic barking. Enemy planes came in low, wings spitting fire, strafing E Company's positions. There was no time to take cover. Caught in the open, near his command post, Sparks fell to the ground. Blood poured from a serious wound in his abdomen. Medic Jack Turner may have been the first to get to him and stem the bleeding, possibly with a compress, and then inject morphine to kill what must have been excruciating pain. Mortarman Jack Hallowell was there to help carry him to an ambulance. So great was the blood loss that he quickly lost consciousness. He had been felled by friendly fire: a splinter from a 40mm American anti-aircraft shell had in fact penetrated all the way to his liver. For Captain Felix Sparks, the war appeared to be over.

THE APENNINES, NOVEMBER 1943

THE ALLIES' BLOODY slog up the mountainous spine of Italy continued, the cost in lives growing higher and the gain in ground less every day. "I do not think we can conduct a winter campaign in this country," wrote General Montgomery on October 31. "If I remember, Caesar used to go to winter quarters—a very sound thing to do!" Nevertheless, Eisenhower insisted on pushing ahead: "It is essential for us to retain the initiative." Tying down German forces was crucial to his preparations for Overlord, the planned 1944 invasion of northwestern Europe via Normandy.

As the weather worsened late that fall, the Allied advance slowed to an average of less than two miles each week, each German life costing an astronomical $25,000 in shells. "To infantrymen the war in Italy was one fortified German line after another," recalled the British journalist Alan Whicker. "Break through one and there was always the next, just ahead. Ford a river—and there's its twin, behind an identical mountain."

The Thunderbirds succeeded in crossing the raging Volturno River, most of whose bridges had been swept away in floods, and then pressed on to the mountain town of Venafro, some seventy miles north of Naples, where they finally confronted the fabled Gustav Line, defenses so strong that, in Kesselring's words, the Allies would "break their teeth on it." Winter had arrived in the central Apennines, marked simply as a "mountainous hinterland" on the Americans' maps. The bare, vertiginous slopes, which even bears and wolves seemed to have abandoned, crisscrossed with almost vertical mule trails, were assigned coordinates and numbers but no names. "The country was shockingly beautiful," recalled Ernie Pyle, who covered the Allied advance, "and just as shockingly hard to capture from the enemy."

On November 7, a bitterly cold day, the 157th Infantry regiment moved north of Venafro and set up positions some fifteen miles due east of Monte Cassino in the Matese Mountains. Still in their summer field jackets, men shivered, their teeth chattering so hard their jaws ached as they slapped their arms against their bodies. When they looked back over their shoulders, they saw a long valley stretching to the south, dotted with orchards, vineyards, and hundreds of anti-aircraft guns and howitzers.

It was destined to be a long stay. The Germans had been ordered by Hitler to cease all withdrawals, and the Thunderbirds came under devastating fire whenever they tried to advance. Medic Warren Wall spent day after day crawling over sharp rocks to reach fellow Thunderbirds wounded by shrapnel, which would account for almost 80 percent of fatalities among American infantrymen in Europe. To stop his cold metal dog tags from rattling against his chest as he sprinted to the wounded, he had wrapped German insulation rubber around them. They would be his sole possession by war's end.

That November in mountain country, Wall got lucky. In heavy rain, around 10 A.M. one morning, he came under intense machine-gun fire. The bullets were so close they ricocheted off nearby rocks. A fellow medic beside Wall cracked under the strain and ran away. Wall tried to find better cover as mortars exploded nearby, but he was flipped into the air by one explosion and hit in the neck by shrapnel. Blood poured down his neck and soaked his chest. He knew he would bleed to death if he did not get treatment quickly. Adrenaline coursing through him, he ran to the bottom of a ridge and caught up with the medic who had broken down in tears and fled.

"Stop!" he begged his fellow medic. "See how bad I'm hit."

The medic kept running. Wall followed. At the next ridge, he caught up with him.

"How bad am I hit?"

The medic looked at Wall's wound and began to shake.

"You're hit bad."

Then the shell-shocked medic took off running again.

Two miles behind the lines, Wall finally got to a doctor who stopped the bleeding. A few days later, at the 45th Division General Hospital, he learned that a nerve in the back of his neck had been severed and he would be reclassified as fit for noncombat duties only. He had received the "million-dollar wound" so many of his fellow Thunderbirds, shivering above the Volturno Valley, now hoped for.

The freezing temperatures and soaking rains began to cause as many casualties as the German guns. Dozens of men in the regiment came down with trench foot, no matter how many times they changed into dry socks and rubbed Barbasol shaving cream on their blackened toes. Mule trains carried supplies to the shivering Thunderbirds, who had still not received full winter kit, and brought back dozens of crippled men. Sometimes mules slipped and fell to their deaths, screaming and kicking as they tumbled onto rocks hundreds of feet below. Rotations with men spending eight days up on the line and four days in a rest camp did little to improve morale or reduce the incidence of trench foot. "Dry feet? Sure we had dry feet," recalled E Company's Jack Hallowell. "We had dry feet like we had electric toasters and blondes to sing us to sleep. Dry feet were something we dreamed about when we weren't too damn cold to dream."

NAPLES, ITALY, NOVEMBER 11, 1943

MARK CLARK WALKED past fresh graves in a new graveyard full of American dead south of Naples. On Veterans Day, the Fifth Army commander stood to attention and then addressed a group of officers. It was the twenty-fifth anniversary of the signing of the armistice that had ended the First World War, the war to end all wars, as generals and politicians had claimed.

"Here we are, a quarter of a century later," declared Clark, "with the same Allies as before, fighting the same mad dogs that were let loose in 1918."

Clark stood beside a flagpole. Reporters and photographers watched as he straightened his back to deliver a passionate exhortation: "We must not think about going home. None of us is going home until it's over. We've caught the torch that these men have flung us, and we'll carry it to Berlin."

ALGIERS, NOVEMBER 1943

IT WAS GOOD to see a familiar face, especially Colonel Ankcorn's. A few weeks after his arrival at a hospital in Algiers, while receiving an injection as he lay in bed recovering, tubes running in and out of his body, Sparks was delighted to see Colonel Ankcorn enter his ward on crutches and hobble toward him. Ankcorn had heard that Sparks was in the hospital and wanted to see him before being shipped back to America. His mood improved further when he also received a visit from Private Campbell, the young man with the sucking chest wound whom he had given up for dead.

Meanwhile, back in Arizona, Sparks's wife, Mary, waited for news from her husband. She was working part-time in a Social Security office and also kept herself busy organizing a club for other women whose husbands were overseas. She always found time each night to write to Felix, and she received V-mail replies whenever he had the time to respond. One day that fall of 1943, she received a telegram from the War Department, informing her that he had been wounded. The message did not state the nature of his wound. She had to wait for news from Sparks himself to learn that he had not lost a leg like Ankcorn or been otherwise maimed.

In Algiers, Sparks made a quick recovery thanks to superb medical provision. Astonishingly, less than 4 percent of men admitted to field hospitals during the war died. But Sparks was far from happy. He had commanded men in combat for less than a month. The sacrifice, the years lost to the army—it all now seemed as if it had been for nothing. He knew from news reports that the Allied advance had stalled in Italy. Rome was still in Nazi hands. As he grew stronger in a recuperation hospital, he yearned to be back with his men. So long as the war continued, that was where he belonged, not in North Africa.

One day, doctors examined him and told him he was going to be given a "B rating."

"What's that?"

"You can't go back to combat."

"There's nothing wrong with me," he protested. "I can get around as well as anybody. I want to go back to my unit."

He was again told he could not return to the front lines. Instead, he would help run the recuperation hospital. The prospect of spending the rest of the war in Algiers scared him far more than facing the Germans again, so the very next day, determined to get the hell out of North Africa, he visited a nearby replacement depot.

"I want to go back to Italy to rejoin my unit," Sparks told a major.

"We're short on transportation," said the major. "I'll let you know when something comes up."

Sparks returned to his jeep.

"Let's go to the airfield," he ordered his driver.

When he arrived at the nearby airfield, he saw men repairing massive B-17 Flying Fortress bombers that had been shot up over Europe. So many planes had been lost in disastrous daylight raids, seventy-seven on October 14, 1943, alone, that the USAAF had suspended missions deep into Germany.

He found the officer in charge.

"Have you got anything going to Italy tomorrow?"

"Yeah, we got a B-17 and we just got a flight crew that's flying it back."

"Can I get on it?"

"Sure."

Early the next morning, back at the hospital, he began to pack his things.

"Captain," asked a nurse, "what do you think you're doing?"

"What the hell does it look like I'm doing?"

"You don't even have discharge orders. You can't leave without the doctor's authority."

"I'm discharging myself under my own authority. I've a war to fight and my men are out there."

Later that morning, Sparks boarded a repaired B-17 bomber bound for Italy. The crew was comprised of a radio operator and two pilots. He was the only passenger. After landing near Naples, he walked to a road leading to the front. An endless stream of olive-drab vehicles passed by. It was easy to hitch rides. To his amazement, one driver was a Mexican-American from his hometown called "Shorty" Suarez. He said he would take Sparks wherever he wanted to go. Sparks told him to head for the 45th Infantry Division's headquarters, where he learned that his regiment was still positioned on a mountain above Venafro, facing Kesselring's Tenth Army on the "Winter Line," as the Gustav Line was now known.

The next day, he drove in a jeep to regimental headquarters near Venafro. As he climbed out of the vehicle, he heard a familiar voice greet him. It belonged to Jack Hallowell, the lanky journalist from Montana, who had helped him to an ambulance back in October. Hallowell had been transferred to the regimental headquarters staff during Sparks's six-week absence.

"You're still here!" Sparks said.

He then met with Colonel John Church, who had replaced Ankcorn as regimental commander.

"I want my company back," said Sparks.

To his delight, Church agreed to let him resume his command. E Company was up on the line, dug in on the top of some nameless mountain. He climbed up to rejoin his men the next morning. Sparks recognized medic Jack Turner, who had been with the company since before the war. There were precious few other familiar faces. Only a hundred men were left in the company, about half its full strength. All but a dozen of the men he had commanded in Sicily had become casualties. He didn't know a single officer. Every one of his lieutenants was gone.

THE WINTER LINE, DECEMBER 7, 1943

IT WAS THE second anniversary of the bombing of Pearl Harbor. Orders had come from division headquarters for Sparks to attack north at 6:30 A.M. and to seize a mountain labeled simply as "640" on his map. It would be his first action since returning to his company. He knew he could expect stiff resistance. Later that morning, after a fierce firefight, he seized the assigned mountain. The Germans pushed back but had only fifty men compared to Sparks's hundred and fifty and were soon beaten off by withering machine-gun fire. Later that day, they attacked once more and Sparks's machine gunners again mowed them down. One of the Germans, a captain, fell around seventy-five feet from where Sparks was taking cover. He was badly wounded and began to cry out in pain.

Medic Jack Turner volunteered to help the wounded German officer.

"I want to go get him."

"No, Jack, you can't go out there," ordered Sparks.

The firing died down. Sparks was exhausted and tried to get some sleep. He had almost nodded off when he heard one of his men cry out.

"Captain! Turner's out there!"

Sparks looked up and saw Turner running toward the injured German captain. He had taken off his Red Cross armband and was waving it in the air. Then a German machine gun opened up. Sparks watched as Turner was killed instantly, almost cut in half. It was so unnecessary, so cruel. If only Turner had not been so compassionate.

Under cover of darkness, Sparks went out and tied a piece of communication wire to Turner's leg and to the German captain's, then dragged them both back to E Company's lines. For the first time, he felt real anger toward the enemy. But a few days later he realized that the Germans could be every bit as humane as his own men. E Company seized another hillside, where two sergeants from G Company had been killed. The Germans had taken their bodies and dug two graves for them in ground that seemed as hard as granite. They had even placed two wooden crosses on their graves and hung the Americans' dog tags from them.

Not long after losing Turner, Sparks received an urgent message. He was to go see Colonel Church at the regimental command post.

"They want you back in Africa," announced Church. "They're going to court-martial you there for being AWOL."

"I'm not going back," insisted Sparks.

Church knew how much Sparks was respected by his men in E Company and fellow officers. He had been greatly missed.

"Don't worry," Church promised. "I'll take care of it."

Instead of returning to face charges in Africa, Sparks celebrated his first Christmas at war in a freezing foxhole above Venafro. The few men in his company who had landed with him in Sicily and were still alive had enjoyed just six days' rest in the last ninety-four. Indeed, there was precious little cheer as the New Year approached on the Winter Line. What was left of E Company's esprit de corps was fast evaporating, unlike the chilling mists and soupy fogs that settled for days on end in the sullen valleys and ravines below. His men could only endure so much. Unlike Sparks, those lucky enough to be alive had spent almost four months on the line, fighting to stay sane amid the freezing mud and the howling wind and rain.

Two weeks later, on January 10, 1944, the long nightmare in the mountains came to an end. The 45th Division was relieved of its positions along the Winter Line by French troops called Goums who had been recruited from the Atlas Mountains in Morocco, some of whom amazed the weary Thunderbirds by walking barefoot in the snow to prove their virility.

"That's a habit they'll get out of in a hurry," commented one man.

The Goums were an exotic sight indeed amid the gray rocks and snow of the Winter Line. They wore brightly striped burnooses and carried long knives, and many had braided pigtails. Since landing in Sicily that summer, they had earned a reputation for savagery in combat and bestial cruelty toward Italian civilians. Whenever they took a village, they promptly raped most of the women. Children and men also became victims if there were not enough females to be sodomized. In some areas, the British had needed to corral women into specially built camps and guard them against the rampaging Goums.

At last, Sparks and his men came down from the mountains. As they trudged and stumbled down the icy trails, many looked more like scarecrows than men, bearded, bleary-eyed, numbed. A few days later, they arrived in a rest camp near Naples to recuperate. There were movies and a special USO show starring Humphrey Bogart, and long nights of uninterrupted sleep. What every man really wanted was to return home.

The respite from fear and death did not last long. In briefings held by Colonel Church, Sparks learned that the rest period would soon end and training would begin again. In just two weeks' time, he would have to lead his men in yet another amphibious invasion.

PART THREE

ANZIO

It's not hard to get promoted in the infantry if you do your job and stay alive. The problem is staying alive.

—FELIX SPARKS

CHAPTER SIX

DANGER AHEAD

Replacements arrive for the 45th Division at Anzio, February 1944. [National Archives]

THE ANZIO-NETTUNO BEACHHEAD, JANUARY 1943

WHILE SPARKS AND HIS MEN had shivered in foxholes above Venafro, Winston Churchill, ever the adventurer, had pushed a bold plan code-named Operation Shingle. It was designed to end the stalemate in Italy, where the Allies were stalled in the Liri Valley and at other key strongpoints along the Winter Line. Mark Clark's Fifth Army would continue to push against the Winter Line but would also land forces at Anzio, some thirty miles north of Monte Cassino and ninety from

Rome. The divisions at Anzio would then link up with Allied forces farther south, finally breaking the deadlock.

There was just one problem: lack of landing craft to ferry troops to the invasion beaches. Most of the craft in the Mediterranean had been dispatched to England in preparation for Overlord—the scheduled spring 1944 invasion of France. The maximum number of troops that could therefore be landed was just two infantry divisions. "Either it was a job for a full army," commented one American naval officer, "or it was no job at all; to attempt it with only two divisions was to send a boy on a man's errand." The decision to go ahead, even after the near disaster at Salerno, was made nevertheless. Again, Mark Clark opted to gamble.

Early on January 22, 1944, the American VI Corps, commanded by Major General John P. Lucas, landed at Anzio and walked ashore with minimal loss of life. The Germans had been taken by total surprise. By midnight, more than thirty-six thousand men and three thousand vehicles were ashore, with the loss of just thirteen men killed and ninety-seven wounded. But then Lucas, commanding the two divisions at Anzio, failed to take advantage of the element of surprise and attack toward Rome.

It was imperative that the Allies at least seize the Alban Hills, some ten miles inland, to prevent the Germans from using the higher ground to pulverize the beachhead with artillery fire. Instead, Lucas ordered his generals to dig in and prepare for a counterattack. "Lucas did not think of Rome," recalled British journalist Alan Whicker, who was with the Fifth Army, recording its advance with a special film unit. "He thought of Gallipoli, Tobruk and Dunkirk, of desperate defeat. In the first forty-eight hours our initial Anzio victory was thrown away."

Why Mark Clark had chosen the timid Lucas remains a hotly debated question to this day. He was certainly no George Patton. During the planning phase, the grandfatherly, pipe-smoking Lucas had noted with ominous precision in his diary: "This whole affair has a strong odor of Gallipoli, and apparently the same amateur [Churchill] is still on the coach's bench."

ANZIO, ITALY, JANUARY 29, 1944

THE TYRRHENIAN SEA off the coast of Anzio was unnervingly calm. The sun shone brightly that morning as Sparks approached the town's harbor. What had happened to the Germans? There was no angry clatter of machine guns, no need to hunch down and flinch at every whistle of a shell. Men scanned the shoreline in disbelief and wondered if the war had in fact ended.

The regiment unloaded almost casually at the dockside in Anzio, once the home of the debauched Roman emperor Caligula and the birthplace of Nero. Men had to step over toppled telephone polls as they moved inland, past stony-faced British troops manning anti-aircraft guns. Ahead lay rolling farmland that stretched inland for fifteen miles toward the first visible high ground, the Alban Hills. A few miles to the north of Anzio, they set up camp near a forest of pine and cork, known as the Padiglione Woods. The nearby Pontine Marshes had been successfully drained by Mussolini but then, in what many considered an act of biological warfare, had been flooded by the Germans to impede the Allies. It didn't take long for the Thunderbirds to realize the marshes were now the source of swarms of mosquitoes.

"Whatever we're going into," said one laconic Thunderbird, "it can't be worse than fighting those damned mountains. The sun's shining, there's no mud, and no hills to climb. Buck up, we got nothin' to worry about."

As Sparks and his men settled down for the night in the Padiglione Woods, they had no idea that General Lucas had failed to seize the initiative and that seventy thousand Germans were headed their way. Sparks in fact believed that the landings had been a great success. He would soon be leading his men victoriously toward Rome.

On their radios in their bivouacs beneath the towering pines, the Thunderbirds heard the German propaganda broadcaster, Axis Sally, read out the names and serial numbers of men who had been taken prisoner. "Easy, boys, there's danger ahead," Sally then purred before playing a recording of "Lili Marlene," a tune so popular that both Axis and Allied troops whistled it throughout Europe.

Two days later, on January 31, 1944, Sparks learned that some Allied troops, fifteen miles inland, at the very edge of the Anzio beachhead, were being hit hard by the Germans. He was then ordered to move his company up to the front and relieve a hard-pressed company of the 36th Engineer Regiment positioned on the left flank of the beachhead, soon to be dubbed the "Bitch-Head" by cynical GIs.

Fearing some of his men might go AWOL as the company moved up to the front lines, Sparks placed E Company's first sergeant and executive officer in the rear.

"Don't let anybody drop out," Sparks told them.

Once a man was allowed to go missing from action, his willpower was smashed for good and he would be useless in combat.

The engineers' positions were a grim spectacle indeed. Dead bodies lay strewn across the shell-holed battlefield nearby. It was equally unsettling to discover that the engineers had been pressed into frontline combat. There was clearly an acute lack of manpower. Sparks began to suspect that all was not well on the beachhead.

Because the Allies had failed to seize the Alban Hills, the Germans were able to look down on every inch of the beachhead. They soon started to pound the landing beaches and then the town of Anzio itself. As artillery zeroed in on key targets in every sector of the beachhead, Albert Kesselring's troops massed for an all-out attack: more than ten divisions of armor and men, several of them crack combat units. Not since the Blitzkrieg of spring 1940, when the Germans had rolled to Paris in less than six weeks, had such a large attacking force gathered to do battle in the West. The key objective was the main road that led from Anzio to Rome, the Via Anziate. If German armor could advance south along it, then Kesselring would be able to push the Allies back into the Tyrrhenian Sea.

Allied intelligence quickly identified the German buildup, and Lucas ordered the 45th Division and other units to shore up defenses to prevent a German breakthrough. On February 14, 1944, Sparks and his men in E Company were therefore ordered to take up new positions. Beneath a bright moon they dug in two miles north of a railroad bridge, dubbed the "Flyover" by GIs, which spanned the vital Via Anziate.

Sparks placed all three of the rifle platoons in his company in a line on either side of the Via Anziate. Two platoons from the regiment's anti-tank company set up behind the riflemen in anticipation of a German strike with tanks. Two tank destroyers also moved in to support them. From briefings, Sparks knew that a mile to his east, beyond higher ground called the Buon Riposo Ridge, stood several abandoned factories. A mile to his rear, to the south, was a labyrinth of large man-made caves, big enough to drive trucks through, reaching far into a shale ridge. Here his regiment's Second Battalion had set up its command post along with an aid station. It was also base for the 158th Artillery's radio crew.

At around 1 A.M. the following day, February 15, Sparks heard the rumble of trucks and the screech and clank of tank treads. The Germans were on the move. A few miles to the north, across a no-man's-land of shallow ditches and draws, thousands of young German soldiers checked their ammunition, wrote last letters, and then began to march to their jump-off positions. They were under orders from Hitler to "lance the abscess below Rome" by charging through the Allies' defensive lines and pushing down the Via Anziate to the sea. Operation Fischfang, aimed at destroying the Allied beachhead, was about to begin.

As soon as he had learned of the Anzio landings, Hitler had ordered they be repelled at all costs. "Fight with bitter hatred an enemy who conducts a ruthless war of annihilation against the German people," he now blustered. "The Führer expects the bitterest struggle for every yard."

CHAPTER SEVEN

HELL BROKE LOOSE

Corporal Roderick Loop, 48 (right), of the 191st Tank Battalion, says good-bye to his son, Private William R. Loop, also of the 191st, after fighting together while attached to the 45th Division at Anzio. [National Archives]

VIA ANZIATE, FEBRUARY 16, 1944

THERE WAS A TOTAL SILENCE. No clanking of tank tracks, no drone of planes, no thunder of distant artillery. All across the beachhead, it was unnervingly quiet, as if the Germans and Allies were taking a deep breath as they sat in their corners, steeling themselves before the clang of a bell and the first round.

Dawn broke, a faint light spreading across the battlefield. And with it came the whine of shells, then a metallic scream followed by the crash and crumple of explosions. The horizon filled with sound, and it seemed that immense trains were hurtling overhead at great speed, then smashing on top of one another. Thunderbirds were bounced around in their foxholes, like dice in a tumbler, from the impact of shell after shell landing throughout the 45th Infantry Division's positions.

Men lay as close as they could to the wet earth at the bases of their dugouts, curled up in balls, or crouched down in shallow trenches, hunched over, their every fiber contracted, helmets knocking their shoulders as millions of hot metal splinters seeded open ground. Dozens died from the concussive effect of shells exploding close by, their lungs burst and muddied field jackets ripped from them. The incessant *crash, crash, crash* could break the hardest. Sparks had already seen one of his junior officers snap and then run away, a whimpering wreck, in the middle of a barrage. Would others do the same?

After an hour, the shelling ceased. There was a stunned silence for a few minutes. The panic-stricken fluttering inside men's ribs disappeared. Hearts thumped with relief. A flare soared into the gray sky and the landscape was bathed in an eerie green. Then the silence was broken and another deafening symphony began, this time of crackling machine guns, rifle fire, and mortars.

Sparks picked up his field glasses and scanned the front. It was not yet fully light and mist hung over the battlefield, littered with splintered trees, scarred by fresh shell holes as if some gargantuan plow had turned over the landscape. He could make out ant-like figures in the distance, moving closer, dressed in long overcoats, swarming into ravines and draws. They were surely the 45th Division's 179th regiment, positioned on his flank. Who else could be so close?

He contacted his battalion headquarters on the radio.

"Are the 179th wearing overcoats?" he asked.

No. They were not.

"Then those are Krauts coming after us."

He heard the clatter and clank of tank tracks. He looked again through his field glasses, peering into the early-morning light. Several spotted gray Mark VI Tiger and Mark V Panther tanks, spewing clouds of bitter exhaust, were about a mile away, trundling down the Via Anziate toward his company's positions. The lumbering twenty-five-ton behemoths of the 3rd Panzergrenadier Division were followed by hundreds more gray-uniformed young men, some drunk and drugged, bellowing orders, blowing whistles, barking encouragement to one another. Some were even singing beer hall songs learned in the Hitler Youth. They belonged to the first wave of assault troops from the experienced 715th Infantry Division. It was part of the German Fourteenth Army commanded by the highly capable General Eberhard von Mackensen, who answered to master strategist Field Marshal Albert Kesselring.

As far as the attacking Germans were concerned, Sparks's position was the crucial *Schwerpunkt*: a place to concentrate their energies in the hopes of breaking through. They had been told that the Americans standing in their way were a National Guard outfit, manned, according to one report, "largely by Red Indians, racially inferior people who had no love of the white man and probably wouldn't fight." They were confident of victory. And they didn't have far to push: Just five miles and the Allies would be ditched back into the Mediterranean.

Sparks peeked out of his foxhole again. The gray hulks of three German Panzer IVs were visible on his left flank. They were avoiding the Via Anziate, their commanders knowing that American artillery fire would zero in and destroy them if they took the road. The tanks were coming fast, only two hundred yards away. With their machine guns blinking streams of bullets, they sliced through one platoon of his men like a scalpel through thin tissue.

Sparks called to two M10 tank destroyers nearby.

"Get them!"

The officer in charge of the tank destroyers hesitated. His head was clearly visible as he stood in the hatch of one of the green M10 vehicles.

"Are those British tanks?" asked the officer.

"Hell, no—they're German tanks!" shouted Sparks. "Shoot them."

The M10s opened fire. Two German tanks exploded, their inch-thick armor blasted to shreds. The third tank pulled back, its commander wisely deciding to retreat before he too was killed.

An M10 moved thirty yards to the east of the Via Anziate and stopped not far from Sparks's foxhole. He figured its commander wanted to gain a better line of fire. There was the scream of a shell. It exploded and the M10 erupted, flames shooting into the sky, killing the crew. Sparks had to jump into another foxhole to avoid being burned.

From his new hole, he again looked to his front, to the north, along the Via Anziate. Hundreds of German soldiers were closing on his positions. He gave the order to open fire. The air filled with bullets. Machine guns snarled. Snipers picked off German officers. There was a constant crackling of M1 rifle fire, interrupted by barely audible pings as magazines emptied. Sparks's machine gunners, led by Sergeant Otto Miller of Lamar, Colorado, soon mowed down most of the first wave. Germans fell in agony, their bodies piling up in some places and obscuring marksmen's views.

A few got through the hail of machine-gun and small-arms fire. Some even managed to close on Sparks's foxhole. He spotted one of his men, a sergeant, who had strapped himself to the .50-caliber machine gun mounted on a tank destroyer. The sergeant opened up on the Germans closing on Sparks, just yards from his hole, killing most of them. But one German, armed with a light machine gun, survived and crawled toward the sergeant manning the machine gun. There was a *brrrrrp* sound. Sparks saw dust fly from the back of his sergeant's field jacket as bullets riddled his chest. A few moments later, one of his men put the German out of action. Several corpses lay close to Sparks's hole. The sergeant had stopped the Germans at its very edge and saved his life.

There were whistles and whines of more incoming shellfire. One of the M10s burst into flames, victim of a direct hit. Explosions ripped through E Company's positions, killing one of Sparks's platoon leaders, an entire rifle squad of twelve men, and knocking out the company's anti-tank guns. More German tanks appeared in the distance and were soon on top of several positions, blowing Sparks's men from their holes at close range.

"Medics!" cried wounded men. "Medics!"

The situation seemed hopeless. Sparks faced a very tough decision. His only realistic hope of survival was to order his own artillery to fire on his positions to stall the German attack. Some of his own men might be killed, but "pulling the chain," as it was called, was his only option. Even so, it was a desperate move.

The 158th Artillery responded with impressive results. Throughout Sparks's company's positions, shells exploded with devastating power. The sky itself seemed to be shrieking, and the noise was all consuming, blotting out thought and reason. Men were probably so terrified they could not see straight, losing depth of perception so that every enemy tank and soldier appeared much closer than in reality. Fragments of shells and ricochets hurtled through the air in all directions, with the ground shaking and jolting men like an earthquake, every near explosion reverberating through their nervous systems, their vision blurring, lungs clogging with smoke, ears ringing, the cries of wounded men and the piercing whine of bullets and shrapnel barely audible. Heart rates soared and some men's motor skills no doubt disappeared under the paralyzing stress, so they could not move, breathe, or think straight, scared speechless and feeling oddly detached, as if the action unfolding around them were a film rather than reality.

Finally, the German tanks and infantry stalled and then withdrew. In other sectors, the enemy continued to advance, breaking through Allied lines. To the west, the 179th Regiment pulled back, unable to hold the rushing waves of Germans. To the east, the British were also forced to withdraw. Sparks and his company, the tip of the Allied spear at Anzio, now risked being cut off. The Germans had only to repeat their attack on his position with tanks and artillery and his decimated company would be quickly wiped out.

At around 11 A.M., something extraordinary happened. Sparks

spotted a German half-track, bearing a white flag, moving toward his position. A German captain dismounted. He clearly wanted to talk with an American counterpart. Sparks pulled himself out of his foxhole and approached the half-track.

"Captain, you have a great number of wounded here and we have a number of wounded," the German officer said in fluent English. "Would you agree to a truce of thirty minutes so we can evacuate our wounded?"

Sparks nodded.

"Yes, that would be all right. Let's get busy."

Sparks shouted orders, telling his men to hold their fire while both sides retrieved their wounded. German litter bearers picked up several wounded and placed them onto a half-track. He decided not to notify any higher headquarters of the brief truce. In all likelihood his superiors would not sanction any pause in the fighting. The Germans now threatened to overwhelm the entire Allied line, all across the Anzio beachhead.

He helped some of his men lift more than twenty wounded men onto a truck. The injured were caked in mud and blood, their faces ghostly pale, shivering badly from the cold, hasty dressings wrapped around their wounds. There was no attempt by either side to recover the many dead bodies lying nearby. It would have taken too long.

Sparks knew that his men could take only so much more. When would he get orders to pull back? Should he request permission to do so? The Germans had thrown at least two battalions, more than a thousand men, at his position already. Hope of holding back another attack faded further when he learned that his last tank destroyer was out of ammunition.

"Get the hell out of here," he told its commander. "You can't do us any more good."

Until he received orders to pull back, he would have to bolster his position as best he could. He radioed his Second Battalion's command post in the caves to his rear and asked if several tanks could be attached to his company. To his relief, he was told that they would be provided. But he would have to wait until darkness.

Even those who had fought at Salerno were shocked at the ferocity and scale of the German assaults that morning. Seven enemy divisions were now pushing south across the Anzio plain, an area that the Italians had ironically called the Campo di Carne—"Field of Meat." The casualties for the Thunderbirds' three regiments were unprecedented and no more so than along the crucial Via Anziate. Sparks had lost more than 100 men from the 230 he had commanded at dawn.

Later that afternoon, as he waited for darkness, he heard the haunting cry of a wounded German who had gotten entangled in barbed wire in no-man's-land.

"My name is Müller. I am wounded."

A few minutes later, the man cried out again.

It was maddening to listen to the man begging for help. But Sparks knew that if a medic went to help the German, there was no telling if he would be shot by the enemy, just as Jack Turner had been gunned down two months before in the mountains.

"My name is Müller. I am wounded."

Someone pulled out a grenade and removed the pin.

"What's your name now, you son of a—"

The grenade exploded and Müller stopped crying.

The awful waiting, the excruciating anticipation was over. Dusk finally settled. Sparks scrambled through several draws and ditches to the caves where he had arranged to meet with a group of four tanks. But when he got there he saw to his dismay that there were just two, not four. Still, they were better than nothing, and he guided them back to his position. At least he now had some real firepower.

He soon needed it. Later that evening, the Germans attacked once more. There were some five hundred of them belonging to the 715th Division's 725th Grenadier Regiment. This time, they did not rush forward, exposing themselves to machine-gun fire. They began to infiltrate

Company E's remaining positions crawling on all fours in the darkness, down the narrow gullies and ravines on either side of the Via Anziate. Shells landed just ahead of them, stunning Sparks's exhausted men, the flashes from the German guns casting a ghastly glow over the battered ground. One by one, men in forward positions were methodically isolated, then overwhelmed and killed or taken prisoner. All of the men in the platoon positioned to the right of the crucial road were lost. Most of those in the platoon to the left of it were also overcome. But then, as dawn approached, at the very point of wiping out Sparks's last positions, the Germans withdrew. There were no more rustling sounds made by crawling storm troopers. Sparks now had just twenty-eight men.

He decided to pull the dozen or so soldiers still left in forward positions back to his command post before the Germans regrouped and attacked once more.

"Send two men forward to the third platoon," he ordered a lieutenant, "and have it withdraw to the command post."

The lieutenant turned to a sergeant called John "Doc" McDermott, a burly Irishman from Caddoa, Colorado.

"Doc," shouted the lieutenant, "take a man and see if you can bring back the third platoon."

"To hell with takin' a man," shouted McDermott, "I'll go myself."

McDermott ran off, down the Via Anziate, toward the third platoon, but it was too late—German tanks had overrun it.

McDermott was never seen again.

ROME, ITALY, FEBRUARY 17, 1944

IN HIS HEADQUARTERS, Kesselring glanced over dispatches and reports from Anzio and noted how fast German artillery stocks and assault units were being used up. "Enemy resistance was strong and determined," stated a Fourteenth Army log. "The enemy prevented a breakthrough. . . . The Panzer Division Hermann Göring gained 1km of ground but it was forced to dig in because of effective defensive fire which caused heavy losses. Combat training units were wiped out."

Kesselring ordered General von Mackensen, in charge of Operation Fischfang, to commit his reserves. It was vital to split the 45th Infantry Division in two. It would be a disaster indeed, he stressed, if he had to inform the Führer of a failure to break through.

An hour before dawn, the Germans fired countless flares and the skies above the Anzio beachhead were suddenly as bright as day. An ominous drone followed, and then men heard the offbeat throb of German bombers' engines. Bombs rained down, followed by jaw-jolting explosions destroying mortar emplacements and machine-gun nests all along the Allied front, some fifteen miles long. The regiment's command post was hit. A house nearby, occupied by headquarters staff, was totally destroyed, severing communications with the Second Battalion in the caves. More German planes wreaked havoc in the rear, dropping thousands of butterfly bombs, notable for their brightly colored fins that whirled in the air.

Kesselring was throwing everything in his arsenal at the battered Allied lines. It was just a matter of time—one more punch, surely—before his forces broke through and pushed the Allies back into the sea.

CHAPTER EIGHT

A BLOOD-DIMMED TIDE

The 45th American Division have had us in an uncomfortable spot. These damned American dogs are bombing us more and more every day. For a few days, a damned American with a Browning automatic has been shooting at us. He has already killed five of our men. If we ever get a hold of this pig we will tear him to pieces.

—LETTER FROM A GERMAN SOLDIER AT HEIGHT OF BATTLE OF ANZIO

A Thunderbird sergeant directs artillery fire at Anzio. [National Archives]

CAMPO DI CARNE, FEBRUARY 17, 1944

THE PANZERS COUGHED TO LIFE, filling the chill early-morning air with black fumes. Men shouldered their machine guns and rifles, and in the dawn light set out along the Via Anziate, determined to destroy what was left of E Company and the Thunderbirds' lines. But to Sparks's astonishment and relief, the Germans did not try to storm his position. Instead, with tanks in support, they moved to his west, where they broke through the 179th Infantry Regiment's lines instead. "They didn't even shell us," he recalled. "But they were [soon] all around us and in back of us. They had already learned that if they did attack, we'd bring in artillery fire. So they gave our position a wide berth."

All that morning of February 17, Germans continued to pour past in a seemingly unstoppable flow of force.

"It looks like a parade," said one man.

What was left of E Company was now stranded.

Around noon, Sparks called over a runner, then sent him back to the caves to inform Colonel Brown, the Second Battalion's recently appointed commander, that it was impossible to hold the current position.

Brown responded: "Withdraw and set up on the battalion right flank on the highway."

There was a small rise some four hundred yards to his rear, down the Via Anziate. Getting to it with the two Sherman tanks would attract enemy fire on Sparks's remaining men. So Sparks ordered the tanks to wait a few minutes, until he and his men had pulled back, and then to make a break for it.

Just as the withdrawal began, he saw a German Mark IV moving along the Via Anziate. It turned and headed down a dirt track, toward his command post. He remembered that his company still had a bazooka. A corporal called George Holt had carried it all the way from Salerno and had never had the opportunity to fire it, much to everyone's amusement.

Here was his chance.

Holt was in a foxhole ten feet away.

"Holt, get that tank!"

Holt fired. His shot missed the tank, landing in front of it—not close enough to do any damage, but stunning the crew. The tank wheeled around, its massive tracks clanking, and pulled back. Sparks shouted for Holt to reload. There was no reply. Had Holt heard him? He sprinted over to the corporal's foxhole. Holt had collapsed. He was blubbering, mumbling incoherently, in shock, useless.

Sparks didn't have time to worry about Holt's mental state. He and eighteen other men, all that was left of E Company, set out south along the shell-holed Via Anziate. They were low on ammunition and had gone without rest for almost thirty hours, enduring immense stress and trauma. They tried to make themselves as inconspicuous as possible but had not gone far when they were spotted. Moments later, fifty Germans attacked them from the rear. Sparks and his men kept moving, kept firing, and were soon down to their last clips of ammunition. Just as they were about to be overwhelmed, the Germans backed off once more. Utterly exhausted, Sparks and his men stumbled up a small rise to the west of the Via Anziate and began to dig in. The badly wounded had to be left behind.

Sparks knew every one of their names.

DUSK SETTLED. One of Sparks's men spotted two hundred heavily armed German soldiers heading toward the Second Battalion command post in the caves, a mile to the rear. Sergeant Fortunato Garcia, from Denver, Colorado, made his way as fast as he could toward the caves as the last of the daylight faded. He managed to get there first, just in time to warn men about the Germans. A few moments later, grenades exploded in the entrances to the caves, killing a soldier and blowing up a radio set. Thunderbirds in positions near the caves opened up with

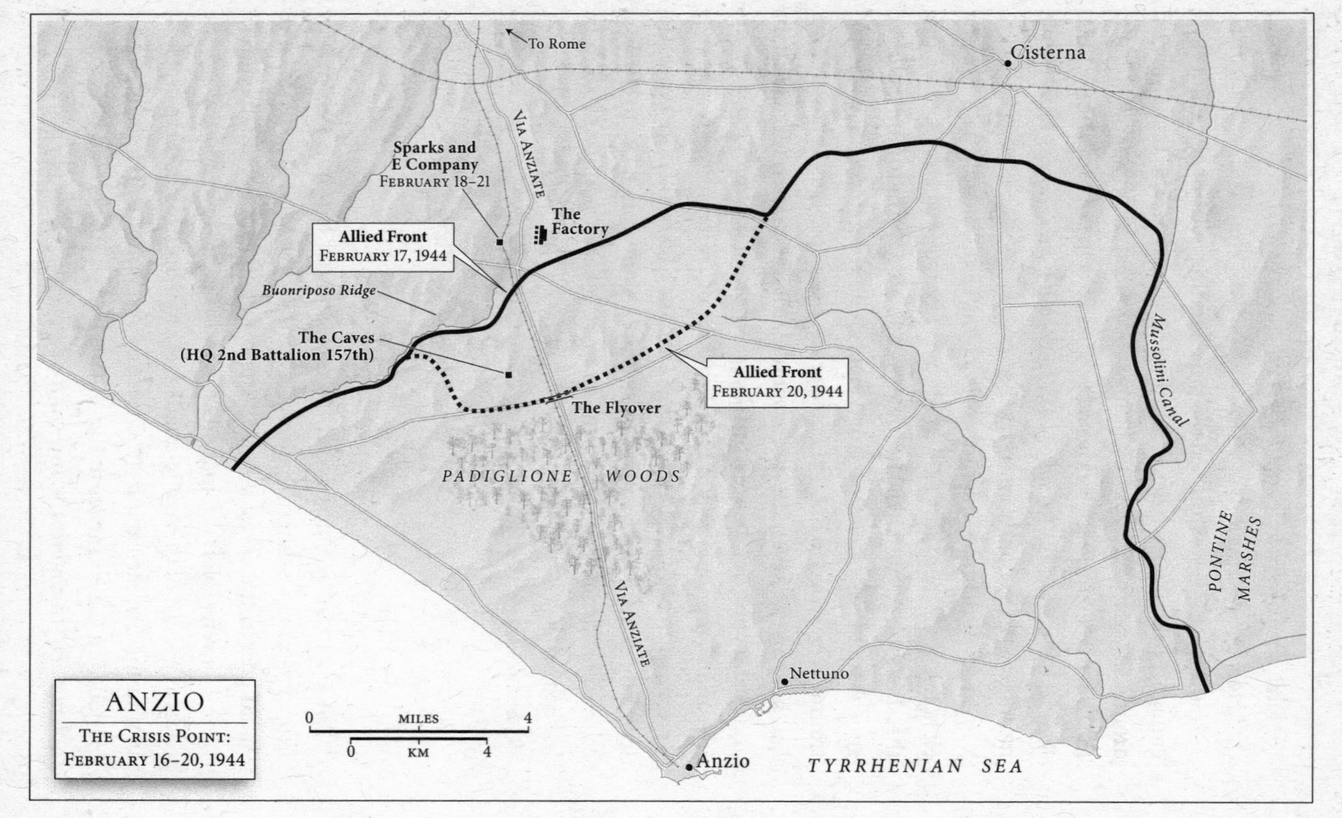

ANZIO
THE CRISIS POINT: FEBRUARY 16–20, 1944
To Rome
Cisterna
Via Anziate
Sparks and E Company February 18–21
The Factory
Allied Front February 17, 1944
Buonriposo Ridge
The Caves (HQ 2nd Battalion 157th)
Allied Front February 20, 1944
The Flyover
Padiglione Woods
Mussolini Canal
Pontine Marshes
Via Anziate
Nettuno
Anzio
Tyrrhenian Sea
0 Miles 4
0 KM 4

M1s and machine guns and some men tossed grenades onto the Germans. Men inside also fired back. Every rifle shot echoed through the underground chambers, sounding like cannon fire. The Germans kept coming, firing at close range with machine pistols and lobbing more grenades into the caves.

The defenders inside were soon so low on ammunition that they filled empty M1 clips by stripping discarded machine-gun belts. In desperation, the battalion's liaison officer for the 158th Artillery, Captain George Hubbert, called in artillery fire on the caves. Minutes later, several batteries opened up. Their gun crews, blackened from cordite powder, almost deafened from the incessant firing, loaded more shells into their howitzers' waist-high breeches, fired them, and then tossed their brass casings onto small hills of spent shells as ginger-colored smoke drifted through nearby trees. Added to the high-explosive rounds were white phosphorous shells that landed for thirty minutes all around the caves, stunning those inside but killing most of the Germans outside. Through the remainder of that night came the cries and moans of dying Germans, surrounded by torn and bullet-riddled comrades.

"*Kamerad, Kamerad!*" cried some of the wounded.

"Don't shoot, I'm your friend," called others in English.

In a defensive position near the caves, a Thunderbird machine gunner spotted a wounded German crawling toward safety.

"There's a Heinie," he told a rifleman close by. "Pick him off."

"I don't see him. Where is he?"

"Gimme your rifle and I'll show you."

The rifleman handed over his M1. The machine gunner aimed and fired.

"Now I see him!" said the rifleman. "He just moved."

"Yeah," said the machine gunner. "I just moved him."

CHAPTER NINE

THE BATTLE OF THE CAVES

German dead at Anzio, February 1944. [National Archives]

ANZIO, ITALY, FEBRUARY 18–20, 1944

AT NOON ON FEBRUARY 18, 3rd Division commander General Lucien Truscott arrived in the wine cellar in Nettuno that was used as the headquarters for the Allied forces at Anzio. General Lucas had called a meeting of his generals. A situation map showed the full extent of the German penetrations. Forty-eight hours had passed since Operation Fischfang had begun. Kesselring was using up his reserves at an alarming rate but had pushed only as far as the Flyover on Via Anziate, two miles to Sparks's rear. In some of the most intense close combat of World War II, the 157th Infantry Regiment's I Company had earned itself a Presidential Unit Citation by preventing the Germans from advancing a yard closer to the sea.

The popular and incisive Truscott, wearing a leather jacket and tanker's boots, examined the map. He could see lines indicating in red the German advances and in blue the Allied positions. They were all smudged, having been redrawn many times. In the center of the map was a blue circle around the caves where the remnants of the 157th Infantry Regiment's Second Battalion were surrounded. Back in America, where the battle filled front pages, the battalion was referred to in some reports as the "Lost Battalion of World War II."

That afternoon, across the fifteen-mile-long perimeter of the Anzio beachhead, the battle raged on. But nowhere was the fighting as savage and critical as it was in the 45th Division's positions astride the Via Anziate. An incredible six hundred rounds of enemy artillery landed around Sparks and his men in their isolated position beside the road to Rome, in one forty-minute spell, with shells exploding every four seconds. Three men were killed, leaving Sparks and just fifteen men huddled in foxholes, their hands no doubt clamped over their ears, hearts racing so fast that some probably had tunnel vision, the noise and concussion from the shells enough to send even the deafened insane.

Perhaps one man above all, General Raymond S. McLain, commander of the 45th Division's artillery, made the greatest impact in blunting Kesselring's attacks. He had a habit of turning up unannounced in critical areas, in a jeep with his equally legendary driver, a former cowboy who drove as if he were on the back of a bucking steer in an Oklahoma rodeo. McLain carried only a Colt .32 automatic, good enough at close range, and appeared at the division command post looking like many a tramp Sparks had avoided in roadside jungles, face caked in sweat and dirt. A few words shouted over his radio led to the sky falling in on the onrushing Germans and their tanks. He constantly swigged a lemonade made from a flavored powder mix in K rations and told Thunderbirds who dared withdraw even a few yards: "The fight's up front, not back there."

All that day, they kept fighting, but even some of the toughest veterans broke under the strain, as Corporal Holt had done, weeping uncontrollably, ashamed beyond words that they could take no more. One Thunderbird sniper finally fell wounded after taking down twenty-five Germans. Medics performed acts of wonder. Others were just as selfless: wiremen who crawled between positions, risking death with every yard, to maintain vital communications; drivers and others bringing supplies to the caves, who were also direct targets. Nowhere was safe from the German shells. The rear areas were just as dangerous as the front lines.

Despite the unrelenting German assault, most Thunderbirds held steady through that endless afternoon of February 18, into the evening, and through the long night. By the following morning of February 19, interlocking American machine-gun fire near the caves had killed so many Germans that their corpses formed a bizarre cross. But it was McLain's artillery and other Allied batteries, which fired ten times more shells than the enemy, that finally halted Kesselring's forces, just as they had at Salerno. Shell-shocked Germans began to surrender in droves. In one sector, German machine-gun and mortar units were ordered to open fire on anyone trying to give up without a fight. When later interrogated, some prisoners confirmed the horror of the Allied shelling. "They [also] told of attacks starting out in battalion strength," recalled one Thunderbird, "being whittled down to less than the size of a platoon by our artillery before reaching our forward positions."

A German in the 715th Division, which went head-to-head with the Thunderbirds, wrote in a letter to his parents: "It's really a wonder I am still alive. What I have seen is probably more than many saw in Russia. I've been lying under artillery barrages like the world has never seen." He was not exaggerating. During twenty-three days of combat in Sicily, artillery units attached to the Thunderbirds had fired almost fifteen thousand rounds. In the last three days alone, since Operation Fischfang had begun on February 16, they had fired four times as many—more than sixty thousand.

THE WOLF'S LAIR, EAST PRUSSIA, FEBRUARY 19, 1944

IN A LARGE map room, surrounded by sycophantic generals, Adolf Hitler seethed with frustration and thumped the briefing table, his face reddening with rage. Operation Fischfang was not going to plan. The Allies had not been pushed back into the sea. The abscess below Rome had yet to be lanced. He began to rant about his generals in Italy. They were the problem, not his brave troops. After a twenty-minute tirade, his voice grew calmer. Another all-out attack might do the trick. And if his useless generals on the ground did not succeed this time, he would consider taking over the command of the battle himself.

VIA ANZIATE, FEBRUARY 20, 1944

HE COULD NOT see his battalion's command post, some five hundred yards to his rear, even with the sky lit up with flares and explosions. But from the small rise, where he had dug in two days before, Sparks had a superb view of the enemy and was able to track his movements and direct his battalion's artillery fire. At 2:55 A.M. on February 20, he reported: "HEAVY EQUIPMENT ROLLING BY. . . . DOESN'T SOUND LIKE TANKS. SOUNDS LIKE TRACTORS PULLING GUNS. MOVEMENT S [South]."

Before dawn, Sparks sent a runner back to the caves to find out what the Second Battalion planned to do next. He could not continue as a forward observer indefinitely. He and his last fifteen men had run out of supplies and were low on water. They had been forced to scavenge abandoned positions nearby for ammunition. When the runner returned, Sparks learned that the British would relieve the Second Battalion the following night of February 21.

To Sparks, it was a crazy idea, one of the "stupidest" things he had ever heard. He and his battalion were surrounded and yet hundreds of British troops were being sent to relieve them. How would any of them get to the caves, let alone hold out once they arrived? The sensible course of action would have been for the battalion to withdraw and reinforce the regiment's new front lines, rather than waste yet more good men on a hopeless position.

The runner also told Sparks that he should be prepare to pull back to the caves. Once the British arrived, he and the rest of the surviving Thunderbirds in the Second Battalion were to break out and try to get back to the regiment's forward lines, some two miles to the rear.

THE BRITISH SET out after dark on February 21, moving anxiously forward, rifles slung, beneath the brilliant green light of enemy chandelier flares that seemed to never go out. A German plane swooped and dropped anti-personnel "butterfly" bombs. They made a hideous popping sound as they exploded in orange and white splashes of blinding light, as if Hitler himself had lit a long string of firecrackers. Dozens of men from the Second Battalion of the Queen's Royal Regiment were killed and more wounded, blood seeping from ears, mouths, and noses, their moans piercing the silence after the plane had passed. By the time the hundred or so survivors reached the caves, they had lost most of their weapons, armor, and supplies. But to the bearded and haggard Thunderbirds' amazement, the shocked British survivors insisted on taking over the Americans' positions.

One Thunderbird, Lieutenant John Cookingham, was soon escorting some brave British troops to a critical defensive position near the caves. A shell exploded nearby and he was hit in the shoulder. Cookingham, who had fought for five days and nights, fending off savage German attacks on the caves with only a few hours' rest, fast lost strength as he was helped back to his foxhole.

"The lieutenant is down," cried some men.

Lieutenant William Beckman rushed to Cookingham's side.

"How ya doing, Cookie?" asked Beckman.

"Not too good, Becky, I'm so tired."

A few seconds later, twenty-two-year-old Cookingham died. He had joined the regiment the previous November on the Winter Line. "His wounds were not life threatening," his younger brother Vincent would later write, "but he [had] stayed up there for many days without sleep, food, and little water and his body was not able to stand the shock." Beckman and others from G Company had to leave Cookingham's body where he died because of the intensity of German fire. As Beckman pulled back, another shell landed close by and he was thrown in the air and knocked unconscious. The next thing he knew, he was lying in a hospital bed in Naples, one of a very fortunate few from the Second Battalion's G Company who would return home after the war.

Later that night, Colonel Brown sent two British rifle squads to relieve Sparks and his men. Less than a dozen traumatized soldiers made it to Sparks's position. Sparks said they could borrow his last machine gun. Clearly, they would need it. But they could only have it for so long. He would come back for it just before he tried to break out. To stand a chance of getting across no-man's-land to American lines, he would need all the firepower he could get.

A few hours later, around dawn on February 22, Sparks set off for the caves with his surviving fifteen men. He had selected one of his last sergeants to lead the way. There was no knowing where the Germans lay in wait. The British had been decimated trying to reach Sparks's position. Would he and his last men from E Company be able to escape detection? The sergeant knew the terrain intimately, having made several trips back to the caves since February 16, and was able to find several ditches and draws that provided excellent cover.

The survivors from E Company made their way to the labyrinthine caves unobserved and unscathed. It was a distressing scene that greeted them inside, a veritable Hades. Men with terrible wounds, who had been heavily drugged to stop their screaming, lay on bloodied stretchers and on the ground in the echoing corridors.

Medics and the battalion surgeon, Captain Peter Graffagnino, worked tirelessly to save as many as they could, but stocks of morphine spikes and bandages and supplies of water were all running desperately low. At some point, First Sergeant Harvey E. Vocke and a few others dared to fetch some water from a nearby stream that was clogged with dozens of decaying German corpses. The Germans opened fire and machine-gun bullets knocked the water cans from his hands. Others were more successful. Though the water was blood red, they filled their canteens and returned to the caves, where they then boiled it and shared it with the wounded.

"I gotta go out there," some wounded men begged as the sound of fierce fighting continued outside the caves. "They need me out there."

In one cave, German wounded and prisoners huddled, rubbing their foreheads and begging for "*Wasser.*" A German officer arrogantly demanded his men be given tea. Another, with a loaded pistol still in his holster, helped Captain Graffagnino tend to the most seriously wounded. Men were as starved as they were thirsty, sharing one meager K ration between three.

Throughout the rest of that day, February 22, 1944, from positions on top of the caves, men fought off repeated German attacks. H Company machine gunner Bill O'Neill had landed at Salerno, having crossed all the way from Africa in a bucking landing craft, and had since seen more than enough combat, but nothing as intense and relentless as that at Anzio. From his foxhole above the caves, he could see a series of low redbrick buildings. Suddenly, he spotted a group of Germans moving toward him from the buildings. They were waving a white flag.

"Piss on them," O'Neill said to a terrified replacement in the hole beside him. "I'm not buying what they're selling."

O'Neill pulled out some tracer rounds, loaded them into his gun, and fired at the white flags. The Germans responded with light mortars, heavy mortars, light artillery, and heavy artillery, and then sent a fighter plane.

O'Neill reached down to grab his field glasses so he could identify the plane just as it dropped a five-hundred-pound bomb. It landed what seemed like only a few yards away. The concussion was stunning, the noise enough to puncture eardrums, but somehow O'Neill remained conscious. He realized that the man sharing the hole with him was reading the Twenty-third Psalm from a Bible.

" 'Yea, though I walk through the valley of the shadow of death . . .' "

O'Neill turned back to face the enemy. He could see a man digging, a hundred yards away.

The German stopped digging.

O'Neill believed the man was a sniper sent up to kill him.

"I'll fix that son of a bitch."

He grabbed his M1 rifle and waited for the German to start digging again. When he did, O'Neill fired over and over, finally hearing a *ping* as the ejected clip signaled his rifle was empty.

"*Bitte* . . . *bitte* . . . *bitte* . . ." moaned the sniper. The only German O'Neill probably knew were the words *Kraut* and *kaput*, preferably used together. *Bitte* sounded like "Peter." He didn't know what it meant.

A Thunderbird lieutenant approached.

"You can come down," said the lieutenant.

O'Neill and his Psalm-reciting compatriot didn't waste any time getting back to the relative safety of the caves, fifty or so feet below them. In a corridor leading to the caves' aid station, a hundred and twenty men lay on litters. "No one had slept," recalled surgeon Peter Graffagnino.

"We were out of plasma, morphine and bandages." Local Italian women who had also taken refuge in the caves helped to nurse the wounded. Others made a thin soup from the handfuls of dried beans and a few chickens they had grabbed as they fled their homes. As candles cast ghoulish shadows across the underground labyrinth's damp walls, white-faced Thunderbirds sipped the soup slowly, not knowing if they would ever eat a decent meal again.

CHAPTER TEN

CROSSING THE LINE

German propaganda leaflet dropped on Thunderbirds at Anzio. [National Archives]

ANZIO, ITALY, FEBRUARY 23, 1944

IT WAS TIME TO move out. At 1:30 A.M., the able-bodied survivors from Sparks's Second Battalion shouldered arms, said last prayers, and formed a line leading to the mouth of the caves. They were a pitiful group, bleary-eyed, bearded, covered in bloodstains and mud, their gaunt faces blackened by grime and cold sweat. The walking wounded and those with trench foot, limping along, brought up the rear. Like Sparks, they had managed just a few minutes of nightmarish sleep between heart-pounding barrages and gut-wrenching close combat. They were numbed and many were stupefied, all at the very limit of their physical and mental endurance, sustained only by last reserves of adrenaline and the determination to live. What lay ahead would be the greatest test of their young lives—crossing German-held territory, dotted with machine-gun nests, for more than two miles.

As Sparks prepared to leave the caves, he heard intense fighting outside. It was time to retrieve the machine gun he had left with the British. Near the entrance to the caves, he found Colonel Brown and told him he was going to get the machine gun.

The battalion's planned escape route led across a bridge that spanned a deep draw.

"I'll meet you at the bridge," he told Brown, and then slipped out of the caves and made his way north through draws and gullies, remembering the route to his old position close to the Via Anziate, around four hundred yards north of the caves. To his shock, there was no one there. The position had been abandoned and his machine gun had disappeared. The British had either been captured or surrendered. Empty-handed and "spooked" by the disappearance of the British, he groped his way back through the darkness and eventually caught up with a group of about fifty men who were trying to break out. He decided to lead the way. Terrified Thunderbirds followed him in single file.

Sparks reached the small bridge over the draw he had mentioned to Colonel Brown and then led some of the men across it. Others lagged behind, slowed by uprooted trees, rocks, and blasted vegetation. He went back to make sure the stragglers, several of them walking wounded, got across the bridge. When he was sure every man in his party had done so, he moved forward once more, heading down a supply trail. He spotted some biscuits and a water-holder that had been dropped by a British soldier. He had not eaten properly in over a week and was ravenous. He stuffed his mouth full of biscuits and washed them down with the clean water.

It was a cold night. Rain fell, soaking his dirty, slicked uniform. Sergeant Fortunato Garcia, Sparks's communications sergeant, who had courageously led the last survivors from E Company to the caves the day before, now volunteered to scout ahead and took off into the darkness. He did not return.*

Sparks heard the rip of a German machine gun. It had a distinct sound, like fabric being torn close to his ear. The gun had opened up on men ahead of him. Then it fell silent. He stood stock-still for a few moments, listening for signs of the enemy before moving forward again. When he caught up with the column, he saw that several men had been cut down and killed, their bodies torn apart by the bullets. Others had scattered. A few were lying, frozen with fear, nearby. The column had stumbled straight into the line of fire of a German machine-gun nest.

A machine gun sounded again.

Bullets cracked through the cold air.

"Fire back, fire back!" Sparks ordered.

Few men did.

"Everybody, follow me!" he shouted.

He crawled forward. He knew there was a canal not far away. It would provide cover. But only a few men still had the courage and strength to follow. The canal's banks were steep, matted with vines and weeds. He dropped into it. Rancid water came up to his shins. Others scrambled down after him. He took a head count. A few minutes ago, he had led a group of around forty men. Now there were just twelve. Not one of them was from E Company. As far as he knew, he was the lone survivor from the two hundred and thirty men he had commanded just six days ago. He figured everyone else had been captured or killed

*Garcia was taken prisoner. He survived the war and was awarded the Distinguished Service Cross for his actions at Anzio.

or had surrendered. He started forward again, moving along the canal, toward German lines. Sensing danger in one direction, he trusted his instinct and led the survivors down another path.

They tried to be as silent as possible as they crawled forward, but they soon heard Germans cry out. Grenades exploded, sending fountains of earth into the sky. But the Germans could not see them and no one was hurt. They scrambled through the German lines and into the no-man's-land beyond. Every one of them had decided he would rather be killed than captured. On they slithered and crawled through the gray mud and scrub, past the detritus of war, shivering from nervous exhaustion, terror, and the cold, unrelenting rain.

Sparks saw men ahead in the darkness. They were British. He did not have a password for them. Would they open fire if he called out? The group of British artillerymen spotted him and, to his astonishment, ran off, horrified by the mud-coated madman emerging from the murk.

"We're Americans!" shouted Sparks as the British fled into nearby woods.

DAWN HAD BROKEN by the time Sparks returned to his regiment. He was the only man to do so from his company. Few men in World War II would endure so much loss and unrelenting violence and come out of it physically unscathed. The former Montana journalist Jack Hallowell was at the regimental command post when Sparks arrived. "He was physically and emotionally done in," recalled Hallowell. "He was a worn-out old boy. He had gone without rest for seven days and nights and had seen horror and death all around him."

Sparks was barely able to stand as he reported to the 157th's commanding officer, Colonel Church, on the Battle of the Caves and the subsequent breakout. Hallowell and others meanwhile dug a hole in the side of a nearby bank. Sparks was still carrying his pistol and another gun when he finally lay down in the hole, where he then slept, undisturbed, for more than twenty-four hours.

Just 225 other men from the Second Battalion, a thousand men at full strength, managed to make it back. They included a man from E Company, a platoon sergeant called Leon Siehr who would return two days after Sparks but would, tragically, be killed later that spring.

Sparks was extraordinarily fortunate to still be alive. But he would never be the same. Other than Siehr, he had lost his whole company, men he had grown to admire and love. No one would ever be able to understand how that felt. It was, in Sparks's words, a "terrible, terrible, terrible blow." Indeed, he had paid the greatest price for getting to know so many of his men by name.

In holding the line at Anzio and preventing a great German victory, the Thunderbirds had been decimated. The regiment's Second Battalion had suffered 75 percent casualties. On February 16, it had numbered 713 enlisted men and 38 officers. When Sparks returned to Allied lines a week later, there were just 162 men and 15 officers left. Ninety of these men had to be hospitalized immediately. Many had lost their hearing because of the constant din of artillery fire and the echo chamber effect of the caves that had amplified every explosion. Several could not walk and had to have legs amputated, so severe were their cases of trench foot.

The British battalion of the Queen's Royal Regiment, which had relieved Sparks's battalion in the caves, fought against all odds for three more days before it was finally destroyed in its entirety. Surgeon Peter Graffagnino and several medics, who had heroically volunteered to stay behind with the wounded in the caves, spent the rest of the war in a POW camp in Germany.

THE THUNDERBIRDS HAD saved the beachhead but had suffered mightily for their heroism. The division had in fact lost half its strength in just thirty-six hours. "[But] the back of the German army had been broken," recalled Jack Hallowell. "First at Stalingrad, now at the plains south of Rome." In Kesselring's own words, Anzio was the Allies' greatest "epic of bravery" in Europe in World War II. Sparks and his fellow soldiers were "*ausgezeichnet*"—"distinguished"—indeed. "We were opposed by equals," recalled arguably the German army's most successful and respected general. "Our enemy was of the highest quality."

Sparks and his fellow Thunderbirds had fought one of the most savage and important battles in the entire history of the American Army, earning praise throughout the Allied high command and also a Presidential Unit Citation. General Truscott, who took over command of Allied forces at Anzio from the weak and indecisive Lucas, was unstinting in his praise: "In the annals of American wars, there are few deeds more gallant than the defense by this gallant battalion."

For his heroism during the Battle of the Caves, Sparks would receive the Silver Star and be promoted to major. But neither the medal nor his promotion would salve his deep emotional wounds. Nothing could compensate for the loss of so many young men who had entrusted him with their lives and fought so courageously for him. He was alive because of them. They had stopped the waves of Germans at the very edge of his foxhole. They had made the ultimate sacrifice and given everything for him. He would never forget their agony as they lay waiting to die. Their cries and groans of desperation, the terror on their young faces, would haunt him for the rest of his life.

CHAPTER ELEVEN

THE BITCH-HEAD

Felix Sparks (left), Naples, 1944. [Courtesy Mary Sparks]

NAPLES, ITALY, MARCH 1944

THE STREETS OF NAPLES bustled with an exotic mix of Allied troops looking for "I & I"—intercourse and intoxication. It was a surreal and frenetic city, covered in a thin film of volcanic ash from the recently erupted Mount Vesuvius, that Sparks visited that March for a few days of sorely needed rest and recuperation. Australians ambled in their wide-brimmed slouch hats; sinister Goums strutted in their brightly colored burnooses; and at every corner, it seemed, feral water-sellers in coats cut from stolen U.S. Army blankets offered a delicious and tangy lemonade, conjuring it up on the spot, wielding enormous iron lemon-squeezers, then adding a pinch of bicarbonate of soda to make the bitter juice fizz. Even the hundreds of sadistic MPs in their bright white helmets, batons tucked under their arms, on the prowl for deserters and violent drunks, swore by the frothing *limonata*. It was the perfect hangover cure.

"Biftek, spaghetti," offered black marketers, profiting from the theft of an estimated third of all supplies landed at Naples, now the busiest port in Europe.

"Verra cheap."

"Good brandy. Only five hundred lire."

On busy streets like the Via Roma pimps and black marketers were almost as numerous as the beggars and emaciated whores. Naples was a vast open-air bordello, it seemed, where everyone and everything was for sale.

"You want nice girl?" asked fathers. "Beautiful signorina."

Every few yards, olive-skinned men would tug on a GI's sleeve, offering yet another temptation. For those with real money, not invasion currency, there were myriad brothels full of women of all ages and body types, dark circles under their eyes, most of them infected with gonorrhea if the warnings plastered on walls along all the approach roads to Naples were to be believed. The Neapolitan strain of gonococcus was in fact so virulent that even the new wonder drug, penicillin, struggled to combat it.

Every Thunderbird, it seemed, was determined not to die a virgin. None had an excuse, given that there were eighty thousand officially registered prostitutes in Naples by that March of 1944. No matter the rank, men fornicated with wild abandon, even if the *bella signora* was clearly middle-aged and pulled up her DDT-sprayed skirt to reveal a wooden leg. In nearby Pompeii, they jumped off trucks dubbed "passion wagons" and headed straight past the famous ruins, along narrow cobblestoned lanes to a brothel reputed to be two thousand years old.

Second Lt. Felix Sparks with his future wife, Mary, before their wedding in Arizona on June 17, 1941. [Courtesy of the Sparks family]

Young lovers. Felix and Mary, students at the University of Arizona, 1940. [Courtesy of Mary Sparks]

Mary Sparks and son Kirk, 1943. Sparks placed this image on the butt of his .45 Colt pistol. [Courtesy of Mary Sparks]

(left) Monty and Patton. The two great Allied generals bid each other farewell, Palermo airport, Sicily, July 28, 1943. [National Archives]

(right) Three and four stars. Eisenhower and Patton, Sicily, 1943. [National Archives]

(bottom) Men of the 157th Infantry Regiment enter Messina, Sicily, August 17, 1943. [National Archives]

Seventh Army soldier receiving plasma from a medic, Sicily, August 9, 1943. [National Archives]

Leaving a meeting on October 22, 1943, in Italy. Left to right: Commander in Chief of Allied Forces Dwight Eisenhower, Major General J. P. Lucas, and Lt. General Mark Clark, commander of the 5th Army. [National Archives]

Thunderbirds from the 157th Infantry Regiment buy flowers from an Italian boy near Caserta, Italy, October 26, 1943. [National Archives]

(top) Men from the 157th Infantry Regiment on patrol, Pozzilli, Italy, January 2, 1944. [National Archives]

(bottom) The 45th Division's chaplain, Lt. Colonel William King, speaks to men during Christmas Day services, 1943. [National Archives]

Dead German officer of the Hermann Goering Division lying in a gulley where Germans had tried to infiltrate Thunderbird lines, March 6, 1944. [National Archives]

Fifth Army soldiers on the march, southern Italy, spring 1944. [National Archives]

Felix Sparks (right) at Anzio. [Courtesy of Jack Hallowell]

Brigadier General Robert Frederick (left), commander of 1st Special Service Force, and Mark Clark, 5th Army commander, after Frederick received DSC at Anzio, spring 1944. [National Archives]

Thunderbird private from E Company 157th Infantry Regiment getting his shoes shined before invasion of southern France, August 7, 1944. [National Archives]

(left) Winston Churchill (left) and Mark Clark (right) aboard a submarine chaser off the coast of Italy, August 19, 1944. [National Archives]

(right) Medics treat wounded GIs, southern France, August 1944. [National Archives]

French police bring in a German prisoner captured by partisans in southern France, August 19, 1944. [National Archives]

Avez vous oeufs? GIs ask French women if they have any eggs, September 4, 1944. [National Archives]

A Thunderbird medic writes out a tag for an officer wounded by shell fire, September 14, 1944, Villersexel, France. [National Archives]

Thunderbirds pause to rest, September 13, 1944, Villersexel, France. [National Archives]

"A massive plaster penis jutted into the street from above the entrance," remembered one man. "A red rag was hung from it when the place was open for business."

Of the tens of thousands of Allied troops having sex in Naples that spring, the Thunderbirds in Sparks's regiment were among the most enthusiastic, judging by the rate of infection with VD, which did not go unnoticed by the top brass, who were outraged that 15 percent of all American hospital beds were now occupied by "clapped-up" GIs. "We were taking more casualties through gonorrhea," recalled the Australian journalist Alan Moorehead, "than we were through enemy action on the whole front-line." Sparks would soon receive an acerbic note from his division commander, forty-nine-year-old Major General William Eagles: "Congratulations Sparks, your men have the highest VD rate in the division."

Sparks was utterly devoted to his young wife, Mary. The bordellos were not for him. He spent his invasion currency elsewhere. Restaurants were well stocked with black-market produce. The gorgeous San Carlo Opera House had not been blemished and was playing superb productions of *Il Trovatore* and *The Barber of Seville* to packed houses of raucous GIs. If Sparks had fancied a few days away from the mainland, he could even have taken a short ferry ride to the nearby isle of Capri, surprisingly unaffected by the war. Instead, he joined other officers in the many bars that lined the most popular streets in Naples.

To block the effects of post-traumatic stress and the memories of death, many turned to the universal anodyne. Alcohol was infuriatingly barred to all noncommissioned men in the U.S. Army, but in the city of kleptomaniacs, where even the children had pockets stuffed with swiped Chesterfields, booze of every imaginable quality and variety was easier to find than clean water. The cheap vermouth and gut-rotting local wine, *asprinio d'aversa*, which tasted like rough cider, blotted out, for a few hours at least, the horror and violence, the screams of terror, the whiz, whistle, whisper, and whir of flying metal that every man knew would kill or wound him sooner or later. Even so, the past had a way of surging back into the present, no matter how much men drank. The guilt and pain survivors tried to bury always broke to the surface, and there was nothing they could do to stop it. Over drinks one night with some fellow officers, when the talk turned away from food, dames, and booze and back to war, Sparks could not hold back his grief. He was said to have cried openly over the loss of all of his men.

Away from the front, thoughts turned more often to families and wives. Men dared to look to the future. One day, maybe, they could touch purity again and hold a woman in their arms without having to pay her. For married men, letters from their wives and children were bittersweet balms reminding them of what they stood to lose or reclaim.

Sparks's wife, Mary, had sent pictures of herself with his son, Kirk, now almost a year old. He managed to respond to her once a week when not in combat, but then a month would go by and she would not hear from him. It made Mary angry, and she would stop writing for a couple of days to remind him not to take her letters for granted. Otherwise, every night before she went to bed, she penned a couple of pages. The photographs of her and Kirk made Sparks smile and chuckle, he wrote his parents, every time he looked at them. They were in fact the most precious things he owned, and he had taken great care not to carry them with him in combat in case he was wounded again and they were destroyed. He kept them in the glove compartment of his jeep or his footlocker instead. After his ordeal at Anzio, the letters and images—one showing dark-haired Kirk sitting on a rocking chair on a porch beside a beaming Mary—distracted him more than anything in Naples from his heartbreak and grief. He had so much to look forward to after the war, if he could stay alive.

THE OBERSALZBERG, BERCHTESGADEN, BAVARIA, MARCH 6, 1944

AT HIS MOUNTAIN retreat near Berchtesgaden, Hitler glared at several maps. As usual, he was far from pleased. At Anzio, his generals had failed him yet again. They had not thrown the Allies back into the sea. The abscess below Rome still festered and made him seethe with bitter resentment every time he looked at his Fourteenth Army's positions. Since he had ordered Operation Fischfang, the German front lines had not moved much more than a mile.

It was not just Hitler who was exasperated by the situation in Italy. In London, Prime Minister Winston Churchill fumed: "I thought we were landing a wild cat that would tear the bowels of the Boche [Germans]. Instead we have stranded a vast whale with its tail flopping about in the water." That March of 1944, the much-desired linkup between the Anzio forces and those battering the Winter Line to the south seemed as distant as ever.

At Monte Cassino, where the ancient monastery had been criminally destroyed on February 15 by fourteen hundred tons of American bombs, the attrition grew ever more desperate and costly by the day. Several divisions and nationalities had been bloodied, then pulverized in Italy's very own Stalingrad, now little more than rubble and rocks. Extraordinarily gallant Poles, flinty New Zealanders, British veterans of Africa and Salerno, and Goums—the only experienced mountain fighters in Italy—had died in their thousands in what was now a veritable international graveyard. There would be fifty-five thousand Allied casualties before Monte Cassino finally fell.

On March 6, 1944, Kesselring's chief of staff, forty-two-year-old *Generalmajor* Siegfried Westphal, arrived at Berchtesgaden. He had traveled all the way from Italy in order to brief Hitler on developments at Anzio. But when he entered the headquarters, fifty-three-year-old Alfred Jodl, chief of the *Wehrmacht* Army General Staff, denied him access to the Führer. Instead, Jodl passed on a written report to Hitler.

Hitler read the report and exploded, his penetrating blue eyes blazing with rage. He insisted on seeing the man who had "slandered" his troops. For more than three hours, Westphal bravely explained to Hitler how it had been impossible to push the Allies back into the sea. To Westphal's surprise, Hitler listened carefully and then expressed sympathy for the German troops at Anzio who had been in intense combat for so long. They must be exhausted. But he also stressed that the German people needed a major victory to bolster their morale, which was no longer possible on the Eastern Front because of lack of resources and troops. The Soviets outnumbered the Germans there by two to one and were growing in strength by the day.

Westphal left the meeting believing his Führer had understood the situation at Anzio clearly. Sixty-two-year-old *Feldmarschall* Wilhelm Keitel, supreme commander of German Armed Forces, met with Westphal as he prepared to return to Italy. Keitel was notorious for his sycophancy, hence his nickname "*Lakeitel*"—"Lackey."

"You were lucky," Keitel told Westphal. "If we old fools had said even half as much, the *Führer* would have had us hanged."

ANZIO, ITALY, APRIL 1944

THEY ARRIVED OFF the boats with long winter coats, looking like nervous high school students before the biggest game of their lives. They were a mere fraction of the fourteen thousand troops brought in to fill the Allied lines that March. When Sparks reported back to his regimental command post after returning from Naples, he was given a hundred and fifty of them and told to create a new E Company.

Some of the new men were shunned or ignored by the regiment's combat veterans, who knew from bitter experience that most replacements did not last long. Why bother to get to know yet another kid who was bound to be killed? That only invited more unnecessary pain. They were not interested in these doomed teenagers unless they shared the same foxhole—not to mention being subjected to their inane chatter about how their hometown was best and their high school sweetheart, the virgin they loved beyond reason, was the most beautiful and loyal.

Worse still, the new boys were woefully unprepared for the horrors that lay ahead. Some could barely salute, and none had any training in how to deal with the psychological trauma of combat. One did not know who Hitler was. Guy Prestia, a machine gunner, remembered an anxious nineteen-year-old who had not even fired an M1. Prestia showed him how one afternoon, stressing the importance of keeping the breach clean to prevent it from jamming in battle. The replacement used his gun for the first time the following night. "He only fired one shot," recalled Prestia. "The one he used to kill himself."

On Easter Sunday 1944, Sparks ordered a group of eight replacements to dig foxholes. But before they had so much as lifted a spade, a German bomb landed nearby with an enormous explosion that killed every one of them. He had witnessed death almost every day in combat, but he was still shocked to the core. The war's immense horror always had a way of exploding back into his psyche and reminding him of its utter unpredictability.

It was a miserable Easter indeed. It rained hard and men battled to stay dry in their foxholes and dugouts, which stank of stale sweat, sweet tobacco, and urine. Living conditions resembled those on the Somme or at Verdun during the trench warfare of World War I. Across the "Bitch-Head," what Churchill had most wanted to avoid—the nightmare of a static war of attrition—was a depressing, enervating reality. Neither side had the power or will to land the knockout blow, so they grappled, punch-drunk, on the ropes.

Thunderbirds likened themselves to rats living in an ocean of mud, where any movement aboveground—day or night—was risky, given the German bombardment. They learned how to walk without standing upright—the "Anzio slouch." The taller men like Sparks looked enviously at their smaller comrades, who took not nearly as long to get their heads below ground level. Others became known as "turtles." Neither the propaganda leaflets dropped by the Germans showing scantily clad

Fräuleins, nor the delivery of hot food and the odd bottle of Coke that men sipped for hours, could persuade them to get out of their holes and stretch their cramped legs.

The inability to escape the danger grated at and finally wore down everyone's nerves. "The jitters were known as 'Anzio anxiety' and 'Nettuno neurosis,'" wrote Ernie Pyle, who was nearly killed when a shell landed on a villa occupied by correspondents in the actual town of Anzio. "A person would hold out his hand and purposely make it tremble, and say, 'See, I'm not nervous.'" But everyone was, from Mark Clark to Sparks on down to the greenest of replacements clasping their shiny new dog tags as if they were rosaries.

One day, Sparks received a letter from a distraught mother in Dayton, Ohio, who had learned that her son, Corporal Robert Fremder, had been missing in action since February 16—the first day of the German attack that had wiped out E Company. "Oh My Dear Captain, why did this war have to be? He was only a boy of nineteen. He would be twenty this coming July. What has happened to him and what has he gone through to make him feel like a man of forty years? . . . Won't you please tell me what happened to my son?"

Sparks did not know what had happened to him. His eyes filled with tears as he read the rest of the letter. It ended with the mother asking him to give the cookies she had baked for her son to his friends in E Company instead, none of whom had returned to Allied lines. Sparks had the courage to face the Germans but lacked the bravery, he recalled, to reply to the mother. What could he possibly say to lessen her anguish? The worst pain, he realized, was not felt on the battlefield. It was not knowing what had happened to someone you loved.*

*Fremder was in fact taken prisoner and would survive the war.

CHAPTER TWELVE

THE BREAKOUT

A Fifth Army GI comforts a badly wounded comrade on the first day of the Allied breakout from Anzio, Mary 23, 1943. [National Archives]

ANZIO, ITALY, MAY 21, 1944

SPRING FINALLY ARRIVED. Nightingales sang above the Via Anziate, where so many Thunderbirds had died. Poppies and other bright flowers dotted the ravaged earth, swaying lazily in the warm breezes, obscuring the scatterings of bullets and rotting corpses. As men pulled back heavy canvas covers and basked in the sunshine in their foxholes, they talked of rumors about a big buildup, this time to punch out of the ring of iron around Anzio.

Patrols became more frequent. Fake artillery pieces made of rubber and wood were spread across some rear areas to distract the German bombers as thousands of real guns were shuttled up to the front line at night. Each day, hundreds of replacements marched from the shattered docks in Anzio to jump-off positions. All through early May, long lines of trucks stretched from the port, carrying men and weapons to the front, lugging new 240mm howitzers, the largest artillery pieces ever used by the U.S. Army, capable of throwing 360 pounds of high explosive over fourteen miles.

On May 21, 1944, Sparks learned that the rumors were true. A massive attack aimed at breaking out of the beachhead, code-named Operation Buffalo, would begin in just forty-eight hours. Newly promoted to major, he was placed second in command of the regiment's Second Battalion, which comprised three companies, and was summoned to the regimental command post to discuss the plan in detail. As Sparks approached the post, he saw several officers standing near the entrance. A lone artillery shell landed close by. Nobody was hurt, but one of the officers, a chaplain, broke down and started screaming. He had been at Anzio for only two weeks. Sparks wondered if he had suddenly lost his faith—his conviction that God would protect him.

The plan of attack, Sparks learned, was simple enough. The six German divisions trapping the Allies on the Anzio beachhead would be bombed and shelled as never before by more guns and planes than had ever been assembled on a European battlefield. Sparks's regiment alone would be supported by ninety-six artillery pieces—four times the usual number. Two extra divisions had been brought in to bolster the Allied forces, bringing the total to 160,000 men, 20,000 more than the Germans. It would be a close-run thing with high casualties guaranteed. There was no easy way to break out of the "Bitch-Head."

To confuse the enemy in the build-up to the attack, men like Bill Lyford, who manned a Browning automatic rifle, were ordered to open fire at different times in what soon became known as "turkey shoots." Lyford at first enjoyed adding tracer rounds to his magazine and watching them gently arc through the sky like long chains of Christmas lights. But suddenly it was as if the whole front pivoted around and every German in Italy was firing back at him. He rolled back into his hole and took out the tracers. Turkey shooting was far more fun from the bottom of a foxhole.

For two days, Sparks and the regiment girded themselves for what Prime Minister Churchill described as "an all-out conquer or die." Thoughts turned once more to life and death. Thunderbirds carefully cut out the red circles at the centers of Lucky Strike cigarette packs and used them as filters for their flashlights, hunkering down to write last letters home, a dim pink flicker illuminating the fading pinups of Hollywood starlets in their humid holes. When they took a shower in an abandoned German blockhouse, they asked themselves if they would ever get clean again. Some hoped they would be hit by shrapnel and be taken off the line. Losing a limb might be better than having to sprint across minefields, carpeted in spring violets and buttercups, while dodging mortar rounds.

Sparks worried too. Most of the men in the Second Battalion were now replacements—many of them just out of high school—who would have to advance into the sights of machine guns for the first time. Just like their forefathers in the Great War in Flanders, they would have to fix bayonets, leave their dugouts, and go "over the top."

Would inexperienced squad and platoon leaders follow his company commanders' orders when the Germans inevitably counterattacked with tanks?

ANZIO, ITALY, MAY 23, 1944

LONG BEFORE DAWN, Thunderbirds boiled instant coffee and smoked Lucky Strike after Lucky Strike. Some spoke in staccato whispers, scared to break the eerie silence. Few felt like eating their K ration breakfasts. Riflemen checked newly oiled M1s, platoon leaders snapped magazines into their tommy guns, BAR gunners like Bill Lyford strapped on leather harnesses holding ammunition and waited for the call of a lieutenant to move out. Dawn cracked on the horizon. Squads filed into gullies, their faces etched with fear, and crept toward no-man's-land. For late May, the weather was unusually brisk and cool.

At a forward observation post, the Fifth Army's Mark Clark joined General Lucian Truscott, who had replaced Lucas as commander of the Anzio forces, to wait for over five hundred artillery pieces to open up on the German positions.

It was 5:40 A.M.

"In about five minutes those Krauts will catch the damndest barrage they ever saw," said an artillery observer. "And after that I wouldn't give two hoots in hell for anybody's chances."

At 5:45 A.M., the horizon filled with flashes and explosions as the Allies launched the greatest barrage of the war to date. Countless thousands of rounds hurtled overhead, and within seconds a dense pall of smoke was spreading across the beachhead. A timid sun peaked over the limestone Lepini Mountains to the west as General Truscott stared into the distance in awe. "A wall of fire appeared as our salvos crashed into the enemy front lines," he recalled, "then tracers wove eerie patterns in streaks of light as hundreds of machine guns of every caliber poured a hail of steel into enemy positions." The din was so great that men had to shout into each other's ears to be heard. It seemed Mark Clark had mustered every howitzer in the Mediterranean in his attempt to blow his way out of Anzio. Not a single Thunderbird complained of profligacy as the ground trembled beneath his feet. To Sparks, it sounded like the "world was coming to an end."

When the shelling ended, teenagers in Sparks's Second Battalion gritted their teeth and fixed sharpened bayonets to their M1s. Platoon leaders snapped orders. Men climbed out of their foxholes and moved toward barbed wire and enemy trenches. They were soon passing through wheat fields at a running crouch, crawling through deep draws, creeping through a cemetery with its broken and shattered headstones,

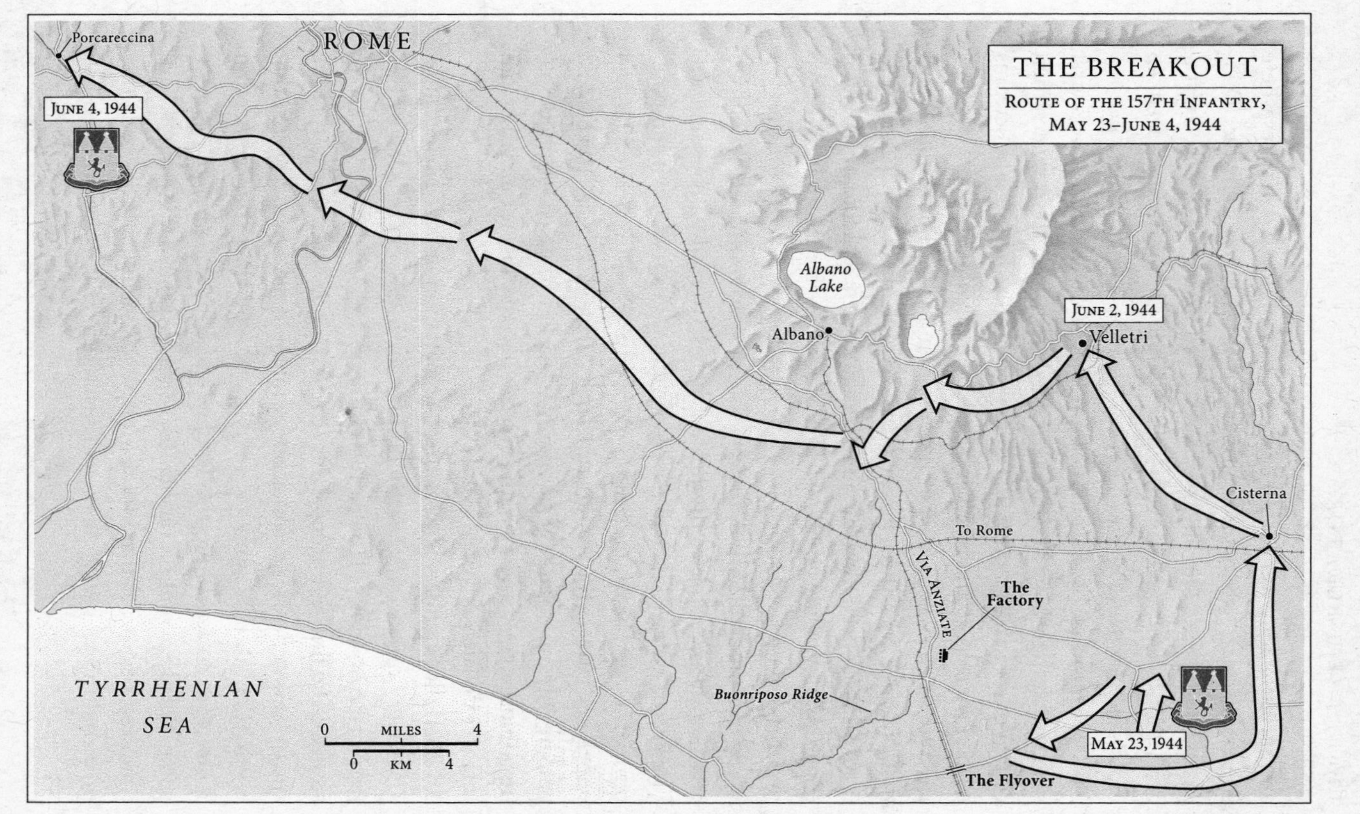
THE BREAKOUT
Route of the 157th Infantry,
May 23–June 4, 1944
Porcareccina
ROME
June 4, 1944
Albano Lake
Albano
June 2, 1944
Velletri
Cisterna
To Rome
Via Anziate
The Factory
Buonriposo Ridge
May 23, 1944
The Flyover
TYRRHENIAN SEA
0 MILES 4
0 KM 4

and sprinting for cover as they closed on the ruins of farmhouses where snipers and artillery observers from the Third Panzergrenadier Division lurked among the piles of bloodstained bricks and cracked terracotta tiles. Men tossed grenades down cellar gratings and sprayed .45 bullets at every window and door.

Open ground lay beyond, leading to the Second Battalion's first objective, a high-banked railroad track close to the Via Anziate. Then came the crunch and crump of mines exploding, followed by screams of men whose legs and feet had been blown off. The Germans had buried mines everywhere, seeding no-man's-land with "Bouncing Betties" that castrated with three hundred and sixty flying ball bearings, "nutcrackers" that fired a single round into the groin, and Shu mines, each containing a quarter pound of TNT, which were buried an inch or two under the sandy ground.

Sparks ordered tank destroyers to clear paths through the mines. His men advanced once more and had reached the railroad by sundown. Elsewhere, Allied units had pushed several miles from their jumping-off points. On the Thunderbirds' right flank, the Third Division had punched its way to the reeking ruins of a village called Cisterna but had paid heavily for a charge across no-man's-land with fixed bayonets, losing almost a thousand men, the greatest one-day loss for an American infantry division in World War II.

The following day, Sparks's Second Battalion attacked once more. The silvery specks of fighters dueled far above. Vapor trails left by Flying Fortress bombers latticed the southern sky. American Piper Cubs, so small and flimsy in comparison, circled like hawks trying to spot the enemy's movements. Early that afternoon of May 24, one reported that twenty-four Mark VI tanks were rolling toward the battalion. Around 3 P.M., they smashed into the Thunderbirds' lines. "I thought we were going to have a rout on our hands," Sparks recalled. "We had a hard time restoring order there for a while. I was yelling at everybody that they couldn't go back." Thanks to several tank destroyers, which had highly effective 90mm guns that fired rounds with a flat trajectory, the German tanks were halted. But it was only when the 158th Artillery also zeroed in on the Mark V and VI giants that the armored counterattack was beaten off.

So it went all along the Anzio front. Kesselring threw everything he had at the advancing Allies, but he no longer had either enough men or artillery shells to stop them. Sparks's battalion stabbed northwest across the Campo di Carne, aiming for the town of Velletri in the Alban Hills, from which the Germans had fired countless shells for more than four months. Regimental commander Colonel John Church pushed Sparks and his other field officers relentlessly toward the vital high ground. Medic Robert "Doc" Franklin was in Church's command post when he learned that I Company commander, Captain J. G. Evans, had dared to question Church's orders to take yet another well-defended German position.

"Take that hill!" snapped Church.

"Colonel, if I take that hill I'll be cut off and captured. I have no flank protection."

"I don't give a damn! Take that hill!"

I Company took the hill, but Evans and others were indeed captured.

In another memorable action, lanky technical sergeant Van T. Barfoot, from Edingburg, Mississippi, earned himself one of just eight Congressional Medals of Honor given to Thunderbirds in World War II. When his platoon was pinned down, he crawled on his belly through a field of wheat until he was around twenty yards from a German machine-gun position. He reached for a grenade, pulled the pin, and tossed it at the Germans. The gun was silenced. There was a slit trench nearby. A rampaging Barfoot jumped into it and opened up with his ten-pound Thompson machine gun, hitting several figures in gray uniforms with .45 rounds. Later that afternoon, after he had reassembled his platoon, he managed to stop a tank with a bazooka, shoot its crew, and disable a German artillery piece. Before the day was over, he had also carried two wounded soldiers to safety.

Other men were as courageous but not as fortunate. By nightfall, there were more than five hundred casualties from the 45th Division—so many that Thunderbirds were forced to share cots with each other in aid stations.

ANZIO, ITALY, MAY 25, 1943

IT WAS AROUND 7:30 A.M. when Captain Ben Souza, leading a platoon of combat engineers, stepped onto a damaged bridge. He looked up to see a jeep speeding toward him. The jeep's driver, Lieutenant Francis Buckley, pulled over and saluted Souza.

"Where the hell do you think you're going?" asked Souza.

"I'm trying to make contact with the Anzio forces," said Buckley.

Souza smiled. "Boy, you've made it."

Buckley belonged to the Fifth Army forces that had finally taken Monte Cassino, broken through the Winter Line with the help of fifteen hundred artillery guns, and then pushed north toward Anzio. There were no longer two fronts in Italy. The long-awaited linkup was finally a reality.

The news relayed from the field kept getting better in Mark Clark's command post. On May 27, several German divisions began to retreat. Thousands of grim-faced but relieved Germans filed along the shell-holed Via Anziate, hands above heads, bound for enormous POW cages in Nettuno. The breakout gathered momentum as Kesselring opted to pull back his remaining forces in the hope of establishing yet another defensive position, aptly named the Hitler Line, north of Rome.

It had taken four days of costly bludgeoning. More than four thousand men had been lost, one every minute. Among the fatalities was Sergeant Leon Siehr, the only man from E Company other than Sparks who had returned from the Battle of the Caves that February. But after 127 days of stalemate, the Allies had finally broken free from Anzio.

VELLETRI, ITALY, JUNE 2, 1944

GRATEFUL LOCALS WELCOMED Sparks and his Second Battalion and plied them with wine as they entered the hill town of Velletri. Unlike Cisterna and every other town on the beachhead below, Velletri had suffered little damage. The Thunderbirds had at long last left the "Bitch-Head" behind. "It was like being freed from the greatest of Nazi concentration camps," recalled an elated Jack Hallowell, who arrived with the regimental headquarters staff. "Men looked down on the old beachhead from the heights they now occupied and wondered how they had survived."

The views were spectacular. The Germans had been able to see everything, every movement, aboveground. Below lay the Campo di Carne, a vast field of broken machines, shell-holes, blackened rubble, and death. The splintered pines and cork trees of the Padiglione Woods, where Sparks had slept the first night he had come ashore, were clearly visible. So was the bare Buonriposo Ridge, near the caves, where he had somehow lived when so many of his men had died.

CHAPTER THIRTEEN

ROME

After fighting through Sicily and at Anzio, a GI visits the Colosseum in Rome on June 9, 1944, with two Italian women. [National Archives]

ROME, ITALY, JUNE 3, 1944

THERE WERE NOW BLUE-AND-WHITE signs for Roma, the Eternal City, at road junctions. The first Axis capital in Europe was tantalizingly close. On June 3, members of the First Special Service Force, an elite American-Canadian paratroop brigade, passed these and other road signs, some of which had been turned to point the wrong way, as they fought their way into the city's ugly southern outskirts.

Leading these "Black Devils," as the Germans respectfully called the men with red spearheads on their shoulder patches, was a truly remarkable leader of men in combat: thirty-seven-year-old Brigadier General Robert Frederick. "He wore a somewhat inconsequential mustache and this, combined with a gentle manner," recalled Major General Lucien Truscott, "gave him more the look of a haberdashery clerk than the first-class fighting man he was."

Frederick would receive eight Purple Hearts by war's end. Lithe and fit as a predatory cat, recalled a fellow officer, he was reputed to have made his first combat jump in slippers after just ten minutes' training. He was without question unnervingly calm under fire and ruthlessly aggressive. At Anzio, his men had crept behind enemy lines and left calling cards beside the corpses of Germans whose throats they slit: "*DAS DICKE ENDE KOMMT NOCH!*"—"THE WORST IS YET TO COME."

Around midday on June 3, 1944, Frederick watched as his men began the final attack into Rome. A jeep approached. Major General Geoffrey Keyes, the fifty-six-year-old II Corps commander, got out of the jeep.

"General Frederick," said Keyes. "What's holding you up here?"

"The Germans, sir."

"How long will it take you to get across the city limits?"

"The rest of the day. There are a couple of guns up there."

"That will not do. General Clark must be across the city limits by four o'clock."

Frederick questioned the sudden imposition of such an arbitrary deadline.

"He has to have a photograph taken."

Frederick tried to hide his contempt.

"Tell the General to give me an hour."

The Allies now enjoyed real momentum for the first time in mainland Italy. But rather than destroy the retreating German divisions of the Tenth Army, Mark Clark had actually disobeyed orders from his immediate superior, the British general Harold Alexander, commander of all Allied forces in Italy. Instead of delivering the knockout blow, he had diverted crucial forces toward Rome, which had little strategic value after it was declared an open city by Kesselring.

The decision to do so was as stupid as it was insubordinate. In opting for a Roman apotheosis over the destruction of the Tenth Army, Clark would end up prolonging the war in Italy for a year, at the cost of tens of thousands of lives. Clark's yearning to be the great liberator of Rome would undermine everything his troops, including Felix Sparks and his fellow Thunderbirds, had fought with such immense sacrifice and suffering to achieve.

It was Montgomery, shortly after the debacle at Salerno, who had advised Clark on how to deal with orders from Alexander: listen, nod agreement, and then do as one saw fit. In any case, Clark believed the honor of liberating the city was his by rights. "We Americans had slogged all the way from Salerno," he recalled, "and I was not going to have this great prize denied me."

At 4 P.M. that day, Clark duly arrived at Frederick's command post accompanied by four staff officers and a large group of press. They found Frederick observing a fierce fight at a roadblock in the distance.

"What's holding up the First Special Force?" asked Clark.

Frederick pulled out a map and indicated German positions.

"I'm holding off the artillery because of civilians."

"I wouldn't hesitate to use it if you need it," replied Clark. "We can't be held up here too long."

Flashbulbs popped as Clark turned toward a nearby road sign that spelled ROMA and asked Frederick to have his picture taken with him standing by it.

"Golly, Bob," Clark said as they were photographed. "I would like that sign as a souvenir. Will you get it for me?"

A grim-looking Frederick asked one of his men, a half-track driver, to get onto a fence and knock the sign down for Clark. Suddenly there was the crack of a shot from a German sniper. Everyone dived into the nearest ditch.

"That's what's holding up the First Special Service Force!" blurted Frederick.

Clark and his entourage withdrew.

Around 6 P.M. that evening, Frederick joined the forward elements of his force as they crossed over the Tiber on the marble-faced San Angelo Bridge, completed in A.D. 134 by the Roman emperor Hadrian. It was starting to get dark when a group of Germans, retreating from the south, suddenly appeared.

"Halt!" shouted Frederick.

The Germans opened fire. Frederick pulled out his .45 and emptied the clip while one of his men cut loose with a tommy gun. Frederick fell to the ground, hit in the right thigh and right arm, and then crawled back across the bridge toward cover, leaving a trail of blood a foot wide behind him. Several minutes later, a GI found him lying on the ground in a pool of blood.

"I'm okay," said Frederick. "I'm okay."

The Germans had meanwhile pulled out. Frederick spotted the half-track he had arrived in. Its driver had been killed. Minutes later, he was being treated at an aid station. A medic pleaded with him to go to a hospital.

"I don't have time," said Frederick.

Despite being in terrible pain and feeling tremendous guilt at the loss of his driver, he continued to issue orders as the battle to secure entry into Rome raged that evening. By 11 P.M., he learned that his men had seized all eight of the bridges across the Tiber that they had been assigned. With the help of his men, he left the aid station and made his way to the headquarters of Major General Alfred Gruenther, the Fifth Army's chief of staff. En route, he noticed a blue-and-white sign, ROMA, similar to the one Clark had earlier requested. He pulled it down and tucked it under his arm. Shortly after, he limped into Gruenther's tented HQ, where he found Charles Saltzman, the Fifth's deputy chief of staff.

Frederick handed him the sign.

"It occurred to me that General Clark might want to add this to his souvenir collection."

Saltzman did not respond to Frederick's thinly veiled sarcasm. "Frederick was continuing on his nerves and whatever painkiller was in him," he recalled. "He said he hadn't slept for sixty hours." Saltzman accompanied Frederick to see the no-nonsense Gruenther, notorious for grilling his generals during debriefings. Frederick impressed Saltzman by answering all of Gruenther's questions accurately. A few hours later, on June 4, he was seated with aides in a hastily commandeered building in central Rome, still refusing to sleep as he examined maps and issued orders.

Reporter and cartoonist Bill Mauldin, who admired Frederick as much as he disdained Clark, found the Black Devils' commander on the morning of June 4 lying in a bed, heavily bandaged. Frederick was angry that his men had been recklessly rushed toward Rome to secure Clark's undying fame, causing avoidable casualties.

THERE WAS PRECIOUS little glory for the Thunderbirds as Rome fell, no celebrating with a raffia-wrapped flagon of cheap Chianti in St. Peter's Square. Sparks could see the Eternal City in the distance, but he had been ordered to move his battalion a few miles to the west. The journey to there was a joyous one, however, even if he didn't get to celebrate in the ancient capital. Ecstatic locals showered him with flowers as he passed through villages toward the regiment's assigned bivouac area.

Later that morning, Clark convened a press conference in the magnificent Palazzo Senatorio overlooking the Piazza del Campidoglio. Thirty-two-year-old CBS news correspondent Eric Sevareid found the general lounging against a balcony, surrounded by correspondents.

"Well, gentlemen, I didn't really expect to have a press conference here," said Clark. "I just called a little meeting."

Newsreel cameras rolled. Flashbulbs popped.

"This is a great day for the Fifth Army," added Clark.

Sevareid was disgusted. "This was the immortal remark of Rome's modern-day conqueror," he later wrote. "It was not, apparently, a great day for the world, for the Allies, for all the suffering people who had desperately looked toward the time of peace." There was no mention of Montgomery's Eighth Army that had fought the Axis since November 17, 1941, in North Africa, accompanied the U.S. Fifth Army across Sicily, and then slogged up the jagged, fatal spine of Italy. No mention of the seven Allied nations whose sons had died in the still smoldering ruins of Monte Cassino. They had suddenly disappeared from history. As Sevareid pushed his way out of the press huddle, he overheard a colleague mutter: "On this historic occasion I feel like vomiting."

ROME'S LIBERATION WAS celebrated around the world. Europe's first Axis capital had fallen. "You have made the American people very happy," Roosevelt cabled Clark. It was a great victory, agreed Stalin. Paris and then Berlin now beckoned.

Chasing the barbarians from the most famous of Italian cities had taken almost a year and cost twenty thousand American lives, with more than one hundred thousand injured. Had it been worth it? Many American strategists were unconvinced. The Italian campaign, they believed, had brought the war no nearer to an end. Churchill himself admitted that these skeptics, which included U.S. Army chief of staff George Marshall, believed he had led them "up the garden path in the Mediterranean." It would have been better to have left Italy well alone and concentrated efforts instead on opening a second front in Normandy. "But what a beautiful path it has proved to be," Churchill added. "They [the Americans] have picked peaches here and nectarines there. How grateful they should be." Understandably, such remarks enraged those who had long since begun to chafe at their British cousins' thinly veiled snobbery and arrogance. "I never at any time considered Italy to be a garden path, and many of the Italian peaches had gonorrhea," recalled Sparks. "As for the nectarines, I never saw any."

ROME, ITALY, JUNE 6, 1944

MARK CLARK ENJOYED worldwide fame for less than forty-eight hours. At 6:30 A.M. on June 6, on "Omaha" and four other beaches in Normandy, Allied forces began to land on what would be remembered by most as the one and only D-Day. Thankfully, Allied planners had learned something from the fiascos of Salerno and Anzio and had decided to land as many divisions as possible over a broad front and then press rapidly inland.

"How do you like that?" said Clark after being woken with the news. "They didn't even let us have the newspaper headlines for the fall of Rome for one day."

The big story was now in France, not the rocky hell of Italy, where the Germans would yet again reassemble, this time north of Rome, and then fight on bitterly to the very end of the war against Mark Clark and his beleaguered Fifth Army. The advance would slow once more to just a few miles a day. According to the journalist Alan Whicker, who had plenty of opportunity to see Clark in action for the rest of his reign in Italy, "He remained the Germans' favorite enemy General: he always gave them an easier time than they expected—and with his strong personality, always got away with it."

As the Allies stormed ashore in Normandy, on the outskirts of Rome the Thunderbirds were finally, after months of mud and horror, laying down their M1s and tommy guns, sitting in the open aboveground without "brain furnaces"—helmets—and basking in the sunshine. In a typically understated letter to his parents, Sparks wrote: "We have been going at a back-breaking clip for the last three weeks. It was really an event for us to finally break through on the Anzio Beachhead although it was no easy job. We are all completely worn out."

That afternoon, the Thunderbirds were able to relax for the first time in four months. Artillery radios were tuned to the BBC. Spirits soared when a news bulletin announced that Allied forces had landed successfully in France and were pushing inland. "Hope returned to the weary infantry," recalled Jack Hallowell. "Morale went sky high. With that beachhead in France, the whole war was almost over. It had to be." That night, for the first time in Italy, men didn't even bother to dig in. Any day now, they would surely be headed home.

ROME, ITALY, JUNE 1944

EVERY THUNDERBIRD HAD the chance to visit Rome. Armed with forty-eight-hour passes and cartons of brand-name cigarettes for barter, they gaped at the Colosseum, whistled at surprisingly stylish Roman girls in silk stockings, and devoured thick and juicy horse steaks at the San Carlo restaurant, a favorite with GIs. Many went to St. Peter's and were blessed by Pope Pius XII. He held daily audiences at 11 A.M., giving benediction to thousands of Allied troops in three languages before graciously holding out his hand so true believers could kneel and kiss his ring finger before visiting the Circus Maximus and the Pantheon, their faith in a benign God temporarily restored.

On June 19, the Thunderbirds boarded trucks and the regiment headed south, back the way it had come, passing an endless caravan of olive-green vehicles. Men stared in silence as the trucks rolled through the ruins of Cisterna and along dusty roads where vengeful Spitfires had obliterated fleeing German convoys. Burned-out Panzers and armored vehicles had been shoved clumsily into ditches; charred corpses swarming with flies marked Kesselring's route of hasty retreat. Finally, they arrived back where they had come ashore, at Paestum, near Salerno. Rumor had it the division was returning to the States. The Thunderbirds had done their part. But then they discovered they were to stay in the area and train for what would be their fourth major invasion, this time of southern France.

Operation Dragoon would land three American divisions, reinforced by the French 1st Armored Division, along the spectacularly scenic Côte d'Azur. At several briefings, Sparks examined extraordinarily detailed photos, taken by OSS agents, of the landing beaches. Planners had attempted to avoid a repeat of Salerno, opting to land where there was no high ground immediately beyond the shoreline. Nevertheless, it was estimated that there would be 20 percent casualties for the entire Seventh Army.

While they waited with dread for yet another D-day, men did their best to enjoy their first extended break from combat in a year. The temptations of Rome and Naples were ever present, the weather glorious, and the USO shows first-class. And there were young American women, serving doughnuts from Red Cross vans, to flirt with at last. "Everyone fell in love simultaneously with the girls and the doughnuts," recalled Jack Hallowell.

As was usual during rest periods, generals visited to make rousing speeches and pin medals on chests. None other than Mark Clark, now referred to as "Marked Time" by some Thunderbirds, arrived to present Distinguished Unit Badges to the Second Battalion for its actions during the Battle of the Caves. Sparks himself was presented with the Silver Star, which he would soon send home to his parents for safekeeping. "I'm not crazy about earning any more!" he told them in a short V-mail.

Another Thunderbird, Technical Sergeant Jim Rutledge of L Company, received a Distinguished Service Cross, America's second highest award for valor.

"Rutledge," said Clark, "I've heard a good deal about you."

"Yes sir," replied a cocky Rutledge. "And I've heard a good deal about you, too."

Clark then made an impassioned speech, vowing that the regiment would stay in Europe to the very end, until the fall of the Third Reich, and share in the glory of defeating Nazism. The speech was not greeted with loud applause. "The 157th had seen too much to be so easily inspired," recalled one bystander. "Given their choices, they would gladly have sat out the march into Germany."

The training grew more intense as the summer went on, as did the urge among the latest batch of replacements to "throw out the first pitch" and lose their virginity. "Have your fun," young Italian men told their sisters. "But when the Americans go we will have nothing to do with you." Few of Salerno's signorinas paid much attention. They swam with Thunderbirds in the blue waters of the Bay of Salerno, visited Virgil's tomb, and held hands with their American boyfriends in the cheap seats at the opera.

On terraces along the waterfront, GIs sat with Italian families, sharing tossed salads and *zuppa di pesce* as they watched the sun set over hundreds of ships gathering in the bay. Some had spent almost a year in Italy and a few had fallen in love with a country they now knew more intimately than many natives. "They had been more steadily in her rain, her snow and her mountains," recalled Thunderbird Paul Cundiff, "and slept longer on and nearer her earth than most Italians." Italy had indeed left its mark. "I have been in Italy so long I feel like a Dago, and probably look like one too," one man wrote. "We speak about half Dago and about half English now, with a lot of Army slang thrown in."

Then came news that the regiment was once again to be called to the boats gathering in the bay, just as Jupiter had summoned the warriors of Virgil's epic *Aeneid* to their destiny. A nearby beach resembled a battlefield of sex as men lined up one last time to "jog their haunches" with a prostitute while others thoughtfully held up sheets to provide a modicum of privacy. They had paid not a bit of notice to the exhortations of the council president of the Mormon Church back in America: "We should say to our boys: come home in purity, or come home not at all." Few would return home unharmed. None would be pure.

In early August, the regiment moved to the deepwater port of Naples. The day before the Thunderbirds were scheduled to load onto boats bound for France, Second Battalion commander Colonel Krieger fell sick with malaria. Sparks was ordered to take his place. Aged just twenty-six, he was now in charge of three rifle companies, E, F, and G, numbering around six hundred men in total, as well as a heavy-weapons company with considerable firepower: eight .30-caliber water-cooled machine guns; six 81mm mortars that could fire fifteen pounds of high explosive over two miles; and several antitank guns. Including his headquarters staff, he would be responsible for the lives of almost a thousand young Americans as the Allies stormed the golden sands of southern France.

PART FOUR

FRANCE

It was just luck. It was just blind luck. There were several times I thought I should have been killed.

—FELIX SPARKS

CHAPTER FOURTEEN

DAY 401

(LEFT) Dead German soldiers lie near a machine-gun emplacement, St. Maxime, France, August 16, 1944. [National Archives]
(RIGHT) Thunderbirds from the 157th Infantry Regiment greeted by citizens in Bourg, southern France. [National Archives]

PROVENCE, SOUTHERN FRANCE, AUGUST 15, 1944

THE RED LIGHT WAS ON. Major General Robert Frederick stood anxiously at the door of the C-47 plane, waiting for the green "GO" light to flash on. His standard-issue paratrooper watch showed the second hand ticking toward 4:40 A.M. He had a .45 on his hip, a white silk scarf at his neck, and a blue flashlight in his hand for signaling once he was on the ground. The plane's engines roared. At 4:40 A.M. precisely, the green light flashed on.

"All right, fellows, follow me," said Frederick.

Chutes soon filled the skies above southern France as five thousand Allied troops floated through the darkness. Frederick shook with fear as he dropped through thick fog. Then the ground rushed up to meet him. He landed badly, colliding against a wall. A ten-inch scar from an old wound opened up. He cut a piece of cord from his parachute and used it as a tourniquet to stop blood from running down his leg into his boots. Then he looked around for other parachutes but didn't see any. Perhaps he had jumped too soon. He pulled out a map and turned on his flashlight. In its blue glow, he tried to figure out where he had landed.

Frederick set off into the darkness. He had gone perhaps fifty yards when he saw what he thought was a German in the early-morning mist. He crept behind the man and then leapt onto him, grabbing him by the throat.

"Jesus Christ!" blurted the man in a thick English accent.

Frederick relaxed his hold. The man belonged to his First Airborne Task Force.

"Who are you?" asked Frederick.

"I'm from the Second British Independent Parachute Brigade."

The paratrooper was as lost as Frederick.

"You'd better be careful. Your helmet in this mist looks like it's German."

Frederick was anxious to link up with others in his unit, code-named Rugby Force, which had jumped into the Argens Valley between the towns of Le Luc and Le Muy. It was critical to secure the valley and prevent the Germans from counterattacking through it. To the south, beyond a range of hills, lay Operation Dragoon's landing beaches near St. Raphael and St. Tropez. The Germans must be denied control of the heights at all costs if the Allies were to avoid heavy casualties as they came ashore.

ST. MAXIME, CÔTE D'AZUR, AUGUST 15, 1944

SPARKS AND HIS men, among fifty thousand VI Corps troops scheduled to land on August 15, crouched down in landing craft as they moved through a haze of gunpowder smoke that clung to the water. They were headed toward a beach near St. Maxime on the Côte d'Azur. There was thick cloud cover. Conditions were perfect for an invasion.

Will I be alive or dead by tonight? wondered BAR carrier Bill Lyford.

A nineteen-year-old held up his sixty-pound flamethrower and called to a friend.

"Hey, Joe. How do you like your Germans, rare or well done?"

For some of the men, it was their fourth D-day.

"Hell," said one grizzled veteran, "I've been on more boats than half the guys in the Navy."

Watching the VI Corps's landing was Prime Minister Winston Churchill. He had fiercely opposed Operation Dragoon, as had Mark Clark, both arguing that it would divert resources from Italy, where the campaign to defeat the Germans dragged on. But now a delighted and excited Churchill chomped on his cigar on board the destroyer *Kimberley*, looking through his field glasses as the first wave prepared to hit the beaches.

There was surprisingly little resistance as the Thunderbirds landed on the sands of St. Maxime. Massive naval bombardment and General Frederick and his men had made sure of that. "The best invasion I ever attended" was how Bill Mauldin, now working for the *Stars and Stripes*, described the landings in southern France, the most successful of the entire war. Not one man from the regiment was killed. Just seven were wounded as they took cover from halfhearted mortar fire and the odd machine-gun burst. By lunchtime Germans were surrendering in droves, filing down from the hillsides before being herded onto the beaches.

That afternoon, as Sparks and his men pushed inland, a Frenchwoman rushed from her house. "From the woman came a torrent of rusty English," remembered Jack Hallowell, "most of which added up to: 'Where in hell you been? We been waiting years for you.'" It was the beginning of what one journalist, welcomed by a waiter carrying a tray stacked with flutes of champagne, would call the Champagne Campaign—a heady advance north from the French Riviera past some of the world's finest vineyards. Fresh flowers were thrown in the Thunderbirds' path, and petals clung to their dusty boots. For the first time, they were truly greeted as liberators. Young women embraced them, planting wet kisses on their cheeks, and presented vintages carefully hidden from the beastly Boche. On they marched beneath parasol pines, feeling the warm sun of the Riviera beating down on their faces, admiring the brightly painted buildings, inhaling the balmy evening air perfumed with mimosa and jasmine.

Sparks's command post that first night in France was in the bucolic village of Plan de la Tour, five miles inland: a very good gain, he felt, for his first day in France. He was delighted his men had gotten off the beach so quickly. The casualty rate had been less than 1 percent rather than the 20 percent predicted. The enemy might be running out of troops, he figured, and could no longer fight effectively on so many fronts.

SPARKS WAS RIGHT. The Germans had expected the landings, but Hitler had not been able to reinforce his Army Group G in southern France, which comprised eleven under-equipped infantry divisions and a badly depleted armored division. He needed every man he could find to hold back the Russians in the east and the Allies in northern France.

In Russia, Operation Bagration had, since June 22, dealt a serious body blow to the Wehrmacht. Two million Red Army soldiers, backed by almost three thousand tanks, had inflicted more than four hundred thousand German casualties—a quarter of Hitler's manpower in the east. Fifty thousand captured German troops were paraded in a rapid

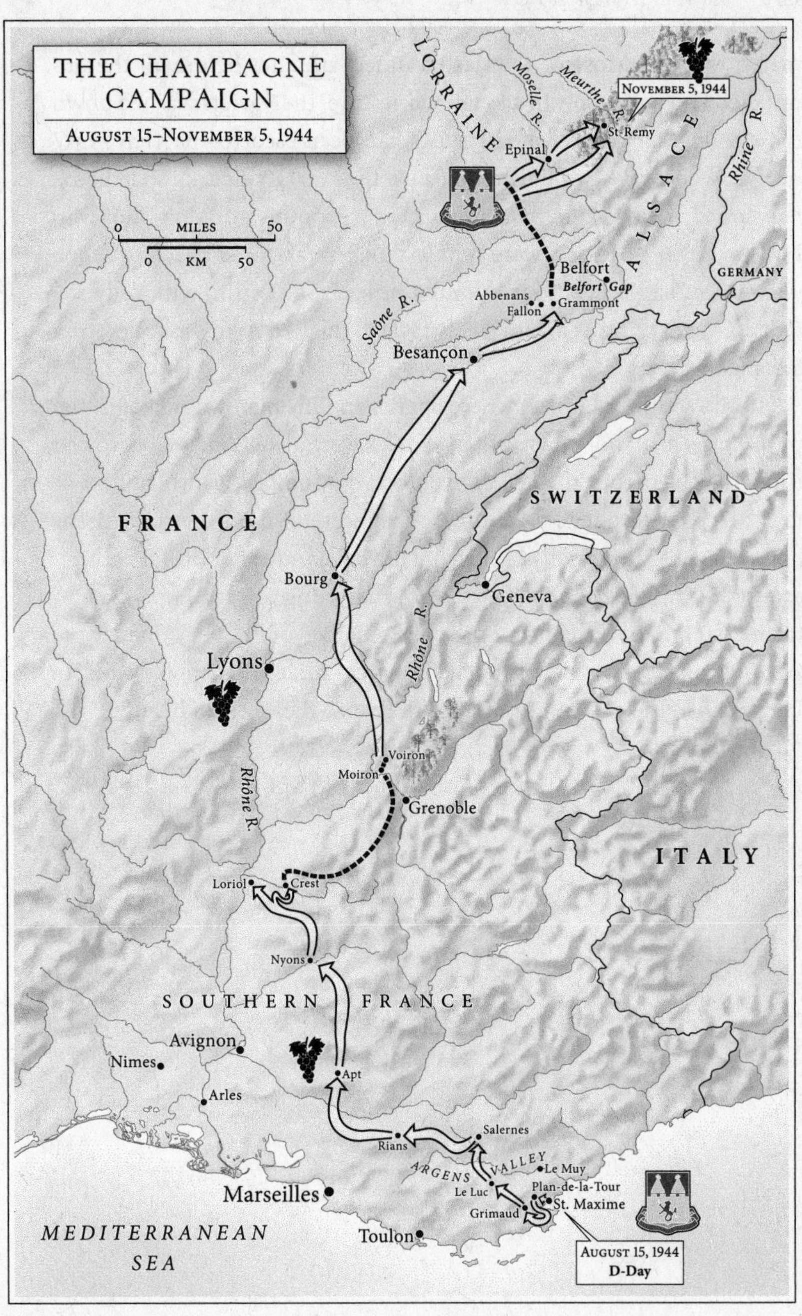
THE CHAMPAGNE CAMPAIGN
AUGUST 15–NOVEMBER 5, 1944
LORRAINE
Moselle R.
Meurthe R.
NOVEMBER 5, 1944
St-Remy
Epinal
ALSACE
Rhine R.
0 MILES 50
0 KM 50
Belfort
Belfort Gap
GERMANY
Abbenans
Fallon
Grammont
Saône R.
Besançon
SWITZERLAND
FRANCE
Bourg
Geneva
Rhône R.
Lyons
Voiron
Moiron
Grenoble
Rhône R.
ITALY
Loriol
Crest
Nyons
SOUTHERN FRANCE
Avignon
Nimes
Apt
Arles
Salernes
Rians
ARGENS VALLEY
Le Muy
Plan-de-la-Tour
Le Luc
St. Maxime
Grimaud
Marseilles
Toulon
MEDITERRANEAN SEA
AUGUST 15, 1944
D-Day

march through Moscow that lasted ninety minutes before all the humiliated had passed by. In a symbolic gesture, the Soviets washed down the streets after the defeated fascists had been escorted back to POW camps, where most would not survive the war. As Sparks snatched a few hours' sleep for the first time in France, on his 401st night of war, Hitler's forces in Russia were now in full retreat, forced back to a line along the Vistula, just four hundred miles from Berlin, with only the Oder River serving as a natural obstacle to the Red Army's accelerating advance.

In the south of France, where Sparks and his men would begin the push north just after dawn, Hitler's forces were also living on borrowed time, fugitives from the law of averages, outnumbered in men and in tanks by four to one. To the north, they were also on the run. Eisenhower's armies had finally broken out of Normandy after brutal fighting around St. Lô and Caen and were now barreling toward Paris, having taken two hundred thousand prisoners, many from Hitler's finest Panzer divisions. Beyond Paris lay the last great prize—Berlin. No wonder Hitler called the day Sparks arrived in France the worst of his life.

CHAPTER FIFTEEN

THE CHAMPAGNE CAMPAIGN

Thunderbirds from the 157th Infantry Regiment take a rest in Pertuis, Provence, on August 21, 1944, after a six-day march in pursuit of the retreating Germans. [National Archives]

PROVENCE, FRANCE, AUGUST 16, 1944

THE THUNDERBIRDS' MARCH TOWARD the Third Reich resumed the next morning shortly after dawn. They pushed farther inland, past seemingly endless vineyards where fat grapes ripened. Despite four years of conflict, the pastel-shaded houses and lovingly tended orchards and gardens gave the impression of a prosperous region little affected by world war.

As they moved north, men started to practice their high school French.

"Avay voo des oeffs?""

"Voolay voo cooshay aveck moi?"

"Avay voo champagne?"

"A la Victoir!"

"And damn toot sweet!"

Villages and towns fell in quick succession as the Thunderbirds conducted their own Provençal blitzkrieg through Salernes along the D561 to Varages, north to Pertuis, and on to Apt below the Grand Luberon Mountains. It was a dreamlike rush through bleached fields dotted with neat bundles of drying lavender, its scent strong in the hot mistral winds, and along dusty roads shaded by plane trees. Photographs taken during the giddy advance showed Thunderbirds ducking their heads into yellow-stoned fountains, surrounded by excited French boys in shorts and sandals. In some villages, partisans greeted them, feverishly smoking sour Turkish tobacco cigarettes, their pomaded hair glinting in the sun, as vengeful crowds gathered to slap and kick black-eyed collaborators and watch the Germans' French mistresses have their heads shaved.

Unlike in Italy, there were no shoeless children begging at the mess tents at chow time. No more widows clad in black scavenging in the dirt with bony hands for cigarette and cigar butts. Local partisans provided key intelligence about the Germans and their movements, and often eagerly joined forces with the Thunderbirds as they advanced, flushing enemy snipers like *sangliers*—wild boars—from cedar forests and gorges of the Luberon Mountains. Some would stay with the regiment until the end of the war.

One day, as he charged deeper into France, Sparks apparently learned from scouts that a key bridge was undefended and decided to check it out. As he approached the bridge, he began to feel distinctly uneasy. It was far too quiet for his liking. Nevertheless, he continued down a hill toward the bridge in his jeep. A dozen Germans suddenly appeared. Sparks put his hands in the air to surrender. A German walked over to the jeep. Then a fist flew. Sparks's driver is said to have knocked the German to the ground and gunned the engine. Before the startled Germans could react, he and Sparks had raced around a corner and disappeared from view.

Sparks joked that he now must hold the record for the shortest time spent as a prisoner in World War II. But the near escape left him determined to be better armed in the future in case he had to blast his way out of trouble. What he really wanted was a shotgun, like the one he'd used to hunt with back in the Arizona. It wasn't long before his men had found an old French farmer, paid him for his buckshot-loaded scattergun, and handed it to a delighted Sparks.

Sparks kept his Colt .45 in a hip holster and carried the shotgun up front in his jeep. In one village, he found a craftsman who replaced the pistol's standard grips with transparent plastic taken from a downed American bomber's windshield. Sparks set a photograph of his son, Kirk, and wife, Mary, under one grip and a favorite pinup under the other. From now on, beauty would be his lucky charm.

THE RHÔNE VALLEY, FRANCE, SEPTEMBER 1944

THE CHARGE THROUGH Provence continued. The 45th Division's exotic caravan, including dozens of requisitioned and hastily improvised vehicles, left a trail of dust and empty wine bottles that stretched as far back as the beaches of St. Maxime. There were battered Dodge trucks with their white stars masked by dust; coughing Renault vans driven by French peasants with FFI (French Forces of the Interior) armbands; jeeps dangerously overloaded with duffel bags stuffed with fresh fruit and bottles of White Lightning, as the local *eau de vie* was called; German vehicles with their white crosses painted over; Sherman tanks with sometimes an entire rifle squad of a dozen men sitting on top smoking Lucky Strikes, beginning and ending every sentence with "fuck," warning the eighteen-year-old replacements with nervous smiles: "Just wait until our lines are overextended."

With a new commander, First World War veteran Colonel Walter O'Brien, leading the charge, the regiment motored a hundred miles northwest in early September, to Grenoble on the Swiss border, and from there due north to Voiron, in the foothills of the Alps, where Carthusian monks made their famous Chartreuse liqueur. The Coloradans in the regiment gazed from the trucks at the snowcapped Alps to their east and at the sturdy dairy cattle in the high pastures, as they talked of Swiss cheese and watches, and felt more homesick than ever.

The next objective was the city of Lyons at the intersection of the rivers Rhône and Saône. There were fears it would be fiercely defended, but as the Thunderbirds approached from the east, an estimated ten thousand German defenders evaded capture by slipping out of the city at night like frightened rats. Even old-timers began to wager that by October the war would be over. News reports indicated that the Allies were advancing fast on all fronts. September would be "victory month," said some. Survive its thirty days and one would survive the war.

Sparks had meanwhile resumed his role as second in command of the First Battalion with the return of Colonel Krieger from the hospital. The regiment's aim now, he learned, was to close the Belfort Gap, a plateau between the northern end of the Jura Mountains and the southernmost Vosges, which provided the last escape route back to the Fatherland for several retreating German divisions in the upper Rhône valley. Lying in wait for the Thunderbirds was the German Nineteenth Army. Walter Bosch, its chief of staff, was a canny tactician, able to get the most from his depleted forces. When he studied the maps, those indicating the 45th Division's path worried him most. To buy time for other forces to pull back through the Belfort Gap, the Thunderbird blitzkrieg had to be stopped. "The thrust of the 45th U.S. Division north was the most dangerous," he recalled, "and most critical potentially for us of all the different attacks launched by the French and the Americans."

On the afternoon of September 11, as it approached the Belfort Gap, the regiment's Third Battalion seized the small village of Abbenans ten miles north of the Rhône River. The Germans counterattacked, determined to delay the American advance. That evening, Sparks learned that Third Battalion commander Major Merle Mitchell and some of his staff had been ambushed while on reconnaissance. Patrols were sent out that night, but they found no trace of the missing men. Two days later, however, scouts stumbled across an abandoned jeep with two working radios. It was a macabre scene: Several helmets and packs had been arranged in a neat pile; and nearby lay a group of dead American officers, among them Major Mitchell.

Sparks moved from the First Battalion and took charge of the Third Battalion. Remembering the example of leadership set by Colonel Ankcorn in Sicily, he made a defining decision that set him apart from many other battalion commanders in World War II. He would stay as close as practically possible to his men, either in a forward command post or in combat with them if necessary, and leave the day-to-day management of the battalion to his second in command. He knew that the closer he got to Germany, the harder the fighting would become. As the battle to break into the Third Reich loomed, he believed he would need to lead the advance if his men were to succeed in taking the next objective, be it a town or a mountain.

THE WESTERN FRONT, SEPTEMBER 1944

THE LOSSES AT Abbenans were repeated throughout eastern France that September. Casualties mounted as the leaves at higher elevations began to fall and winter threatened. Mountains and deep forest stretched along the German border from Switzerland to Holland. As

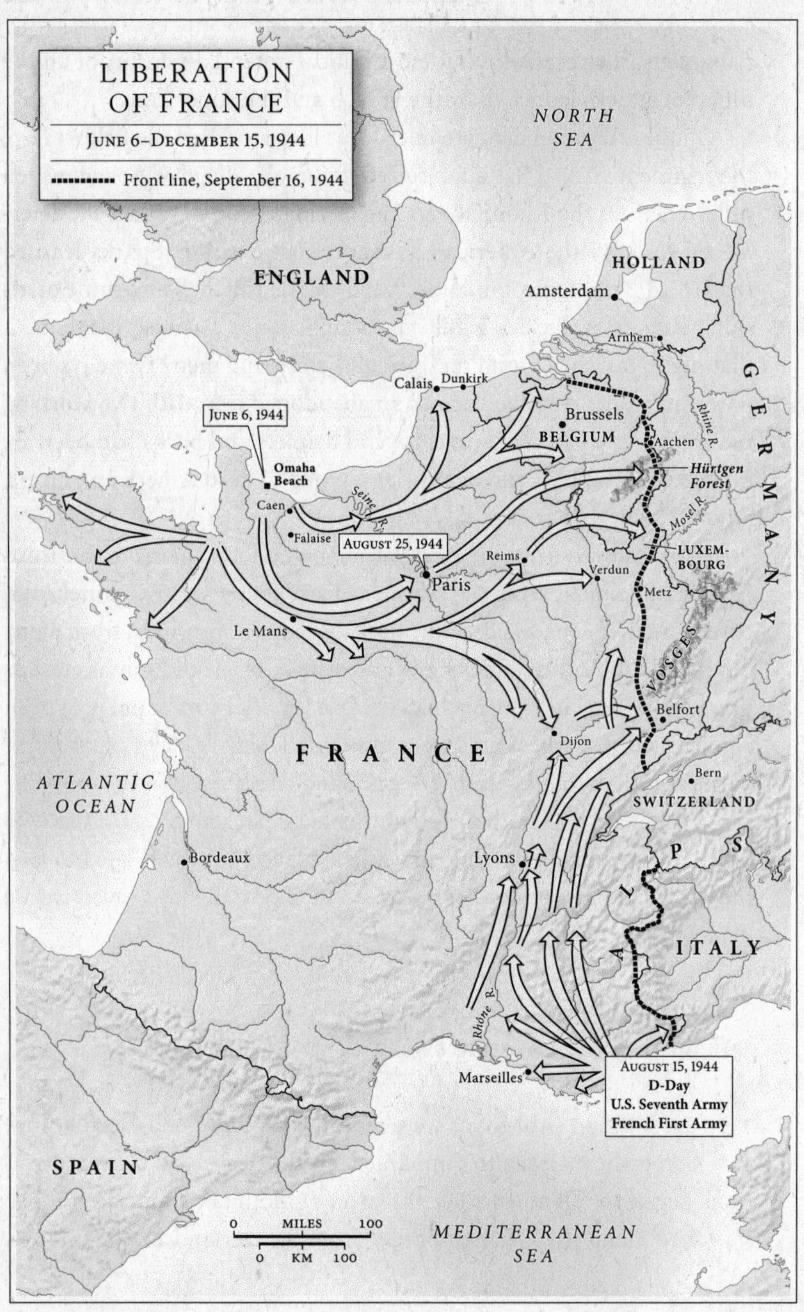

LIBERATION OF FRANCE
JUNE 6–DECEMBER 15, 1944
Front line, September 16, 1944
NORTH SEA
ENGLAND
HOLLAND
Amsterdam
Arnhem
Calais
Dunkirk
Brussels
BELGIUM
Aachen
Rhine R.
GERMANY
JUNE 6, 1944
Omaha Beach
Caen
Seine R.
Falaise
AUGUST 25, 1944
Hürtgen Forest
Mosel R.
LUXEMBOURG
Reims
Verdun
Paris
Metz
Le Mans
VOSGES
Belfort
Dijon
FRANCE
Bern
SWITZERLAND
ATLANTIC OCEAN
Bordeaux
Lyons
ALPS
ITALY
Rhône R.
Marseilles
AUGUST 15, 1944
D-Day
U.S. Seventh Army
French First Army
SPAIN
0 MILES 100
0 KM 100
MEDITERRANEAN SEA

soon as the Allies tried to penetrate this difficult terrain, which afforded precious little mobility, the fighting intensified and turned to bloody attrition—just as it had in Italy.

Allied planners tried to get men and matériel where they were most needed, but supply lines were badly overextended, stretching several hundred miles to Normandy and southern France. When vehicles broke down, they had to be abandoned because of the shortage of spare parts. Gas reserves began to run perilously low. The Allies were consuming more than a million gallons a day. Armies competed for the remaining stockpiles.

At Aachen and Metz and other cities close to or on the German border, the Allied advance ground to a halt. Indeed, from the flooded banks of the Schelde in Holland to the tightly bunched firs of the "Death Factory," as the Huertgen Forest on the Belgian-German border soon became known, the fighting grew more lethal, each yard costing more in men and matériel. Generals like George Patton, who had been rehabilitated after the slapping incident and was now in command of the Third Army, were increasingly frustrated by the situation and quarreled violently over strategy and supply issues. Hopes of victory by Christmas, which both Eisenhower and Montgomery had predicted, began to fade.

One of the greatest problems was manpower. Unlike the Soviets, the Western Allies were running out of cannon fodder, having badly underestimated the number of men needed to defeat Hitler. Field Marshal Bernard Montgomery's failed attempt to cross the Rhine at Arnhem that September—the Allies' only major defeat in Europe—had cost the British six thousand of their finest paratroops. After five years of war, the British Army had, in fact, reached the limit of its human resources, with Americans now outnumbering British soldiers in Europe by almost three to one. Yanks, not Tommies, would do most of the dying from here on out.

An increasingly marginalized Churchill feared his country's immense sacrifice might be forgotten as the United States assumed the dominant role in ending the war in Western Europe. Distant indeed was the summer of 1940, when the British had stood alone, the English Channel being the only barrier separating Hitler from total European domination. How many Englishmen, Churchill asked, had died since 1939? The answer was sobering indeed, even for a legendary tippler like Churchill: 1 in 165 Englishmen and 1 in 135 Londoners had been killed, compared to 1 in 775 Americans.

CHAPTER SIXTEEN

THE VOSGES

Thunderbirds in the Vosges mountains, 1944. [National Archives]

EPINAL, FRANCE, SEPTEMBER 21, 1944

THE MOSELLE RIVER SURGED, high with autumn rains, through the gorges and past the vineyards with their ripe white grapes. Where it crossed through the medieval fortress town of Epinal, at the base of the forested Vosges mountains, the Germans dug in. They blew the stone bridges, mounted machine guns on the northern banks, and then waited to start mowing down Americans.

On September 21, the Thunderbirds attempted to cross the fast-flowing Moselle at Epinal, less than a hundred miles from the German border. All three regiments managed to get across the river, despite its eighty-foot span with steep banks rising twenty feet high in some places. But they suffered heavy casualties. One company lost a fifth of its men. The bloody crossing marked a milestone: The Thunderbirds were now midway between the beaches of France and Hitler's bunker in Berlin. A signpost was placed on a pontoon bridge across the Moselle with arrows pointing in both directions and reading: ST. TROPEZ, 430 MILES; BERLIN, 430 MILES. Sparks had traveled farther in six weeks than he had in almost a year of war in Italy.

Beyond Epinal, he pushed his Third Battalion into the Vosges, mountains thought to be insurmountable in winter, where progress meant mastering a new form of warfare as intense as anything experienced in the dense jungles of the Pacific. The enemy could be inches away and a man would not know it, so closely bunched were the pines trees and so thick were the fogs and mists that clung to the valley floors that fall. "You saw men get killed right beside you every day," recalled G Company's George Courlas. "You soon realized your life was going to be very short."

The thick forests aroused primeval fears in the least superstitious. Scouts could expect to be fired on at any moment. The mere snapping of a twig underfoot could cost a man his life. It took immense sangfroid, nerves of iron, to creep up on enemy positions, footsteps soft in the pine needles beneath towering fir trees. Without a compass, men would get lost for days. Every tree was a possible German strongpoint and every bush could shield a machine gun. "It was sometimes a relief to be fired on," recalled one man, "for fire gave away the location of the enemy."

Others became so tightly wound that they jumped and opened fire at the slightest sound. Men felt they were being watched at all times. They kept their bayonets sharp just in case the next bush, shrouded in mist, suddenly leapt to life. Raindrops sounded uncannily like footsteps, the steady dripping from branches making it seem as if the enemy was creeping closer and closer. At night, the darkness was total. Men could not even see their hands.

Silence was essential to staying alive. Officers and platoon leaders sometimes dared not speak or even whisper commands. It was safest to gesture and blow signals into a field telephone to direct supporting fire. But often it didn't matter how quietly men moved in the trees, whose lower boughs sometimes touched the ground. The enemy would dig in, cover their holes, wait for Americans to creep past, then jump up and fire at them from behind. "You had to get right on top of the goddamn Germans before you got into a firefight," remembered Sparks. "We took more small arms casualties than any other place because it was very close fighting."

Nazi ingenuity and subterfuge reached new heights. One day, a patrol spotted Germans wearing American uniforms and carrying M1 rifles as they booby-trapped a woodpile. The latest latrine joke was that the "Krauts" had stopped surrendering because Americans had started feeding prisoners C rations. Instead, the enemy retreated just far enough to regroup and strike back like a coiled snake. They never failed to leave death hidden in their wake, burying mines and then running over them in tracked vehicles before arming them, so that Sparks's men would see the fresh tracks and assume the roads were safe.

The fir trees, stretching toward the Fatherland, were as lethal as the mines. Artillery fire exploding in their upper branches had a devastating effect on any man cowering in an uncovered foxhole below. Shell fragments and jagged pieces of wood showered down, splitting skulls wide open. The best protection was to stand upright against a tree, exposing only shoulders and helmet, but few had the composure to do so, and instead most flung themselves instinctively to the ground.

Men sometimes had to cross open pastures dotted with dead cows to reach the trees, from which snipers wrapped in camouflaged capes often fired. If Thunderbirds were spotted in the open, just a few seconds might pass before they heard the terrifying sounds of a multiple rocket launcher, the *Nebelwerfer*. It was as if women far in the distance were sobbing their hearts out, then the moaning would grow louder and louder, becoming a banshee-like scream. After a heart-stopping silence, six-inch mortar bombs would land with a deafening racket, spraying shards of metal in every direction.

The unrelenting stress was too much for many men. Even the seemingly unflappable began to break. Stranded one day in a field as bullets cracked a few inches above his head, twenty-year-old Clarence Schmitt, who had been with the regiment a year, realized that his nerves had "snapped": "I'd been one of the lucky bastards who'd never been hit. I just couldn't take any more."

Schmitt ran back to a sergeant in his company.

"I can't take this shit no more."

The sergeant was busy dealing with a sane but terrified private.

"Get your fucking ass back up there," the sergeant shouted at the private.

Then he pointed to Schmitt.

"Can't you see? My men are going crazy."

IT DIDN'T MATTER what rank men were, how tough their upbringing, how calm they appeared before others, when the German 88s began to seed every square yard with lethal shards of hot steel that cauterized as they ripped through flesh. Everyone's nerves snapped sooner or later. According to the U.S. Army surgeon general, all men in rifle battalions became psychiatric casualties after two hundred days in combat. "There aren't any iron men," declared one army psychiatrist. "The strongest personality, subjected to sufficient stress over a sufficient length of time, is going to disintegrate."

The all-important infantrymen, the only forces that could actually defeat Nazism on the ground, comprised just 14 percent of the U.S. Army's overseas numbers. But they suffered three-quarters of its casualties that fall in Europe, with well over a hundred thousand men already pulled off the line for "psychoneurotic" reasons, one of the official euphemisms for combat fatigue. Before they went crazy, more and more young Americans chose to go AWOL. Officially, eighteen thousand American deserters now roamed behind the lines, desperate for the war to end before they got caught and sent back to the front.

The incidence of self-inflicted wounds soared. In the trade-off between life and a big toe, there was no contest. Guy Prestia, in the regiment's E Company, had carried a machine gun all the way from Sicily. He joked with one man in his unit about the man's failure to shoot off his toe. He had kept his boot on and shot himself in the foot, but the bullet had gone between his big toe and the next one. Others were smarter and did it right. They took a loaf of bread and put it on their foot so that when they fired there would be no powder trace. That way, they got away with it.

Most Thunderbirds carried on until they couldn't go a step farther and then suddenly collapsed. One night, Sparks came across a soldier sitting beside a trail through thick woods. The man was crying.

"What's the matter, soldier?" asked Sparks.

When the man didn't reply, Sparks knelt down beside him. Close up, he recognized him. He was one of his company commanders. He had been in combat for more than a year.

Sparks turned to the men beside him.

"Take the captain back to the aid station and you tell the doctor I want this man evacuated permanently. He's not to come back."

Yet another of Sparks's men had finally reached his limit. "You get pounded enough, you're going to break," recalled another of them, Private First Class Adam Przychocki, who had also lived on borrowed time until he too was treated in an evacuation hospital for combat fatigue after enduring one too many bombardments.

How long would his men last, Sparks wondered, in the face of death, with a determined enemy trying to kill them every minute of every day?

Few believed they would survive to see the defeat of Nazi Germany, let alone their families back in America. Yet they kept fighting, carrying out his every command like automatons, no questions asked. They were exactly the kind of soldiers the army wanted: dedicated, hardened, professional killers.

Staying as numb as possible yet still being able to fight was crucial. After Anzio, Sparks had learned how vital it was to cut himself off from his emotions, to stay detached, if he was going to continue to function effectively as a leader. It was all about minimizing pain. He had seen men in foxholes in Italy who understood that if they left their frozen feet alone they would suffer less. If you rubbed them, tried to reanimate them to bring feeling back, you would soon be in agony, unable to stagger down the mountain. You'd have to be carried. No one wanted that.

So long as he stayed numb, Sparks could fight. He could stay sane. He had stopped worrying about getting killed. Only the letters and photos from Mary, the glimpses at her and Kirk in the photos he had placed under Perspex on the butt of his lucky Colt .45, reminded him to care whether he lived or died.

MEURTHE RIVER VALLEY, FRANCE, OCTOBER 1, 1944

SPARKS AND HIS men had arrived in the Alsace-Lorraine region of northeastern France. Many of the signs on roadways here bore German names. Some locals were taciturn and surly, waving halfheartedly at their liberators: It was a far cry from the beaming and joyous French farther south. Many communities had both German and French loyalties, in a region that had passed back and forth between the two countries several times in the last century.

A machine gun snarled. Another joined in. Then there was the hollow sound of German mortars firing, followed by explosions that ripped across a wooded hill. Soon came the whistle and whine of artillery shells. Alarmed by radio reports from his rifle platoons, Sparks set out from his forward command post to join his men who had come under fire. As he crossed an open field, machine-gun bullets snapped overhead. He dived to the ground, crawled back to a radio operator, and called regimental headquarters for reinforcements. When he looked up, he saw a column of half-tracks and a group of tanks in the distance, moving toward him. He was in the open, pinned down with no way to escape.

Sparks began to prepare for the worst—until he noticed that the soldiers in the half-tracks were wearing long woolen coats. He had seen such overcoats before in Italy. To his immense relief, he realized they belonged to Goums, the Moroccan soldiers serving under French command who had relieved him on the Winter Line almost a year ago.

The lead tank trundled forward and stopped thirty feet from Sparks. A small French flag was flying from the tank's radio antenna. He picked himself up and ran over to the tank. An officer jumped down from its turret. Sparks had never been so glad to see a Frenchman. Once again, he had escaped capture or worse. He pointed out where his men and the Germans were. The Frenchman climbed back into his tank and issued orders over his radio, and the tanks moved toward the Germans. Meanwhile, other Goums had jumped down from half-tracks and joined forces with Sparks's men. "The ensuing battle lasted only a few minutes," he recalled. "The surviving Germans, about thirty, were quickly disposed of by the Moroccans. Apparently, they had no use for prisoners."

HOUSSERAS, THE VOSGES, FRANCE, OCTOBER 25, 1944

DAWN WAS ALWAYS the worst time. Heavy dew soaked into boots, the chill air sending shivers down sleepless men's spines. They rubbed their hands together, pulled on beanies to keep their heads warm, checked their rifles, clipped in new magazines, and waited as the somber landscape changed from gray to green.

Chemical mortar rounds landed and large clouds of thick white smoke drifted across a field. Under the billowing screen, Sparks's men moved toward a village called Housseras, northeast of Epinal. It had taken them more than a month to advance a little more than twenty miles, so stubborn was German resistance.

Men's nerves were stretched taut as they stalked the enemy once more. The attack would either be a pushover or very tough going if the Germans chose to counterattack. They had been in continual combat since landing in France on August 15, and most, Sparks knew, were at their limit of endurance. They crept down wet lanes, skirted by bare trees, not knowing if they would see green leaves again. Combat never became less terrifying. It felt as if they were starting from scratch every time they closed on the enemy, cracking feeble jokes to keep their minds off what lay ahead, hearts pounding, stomachs contracting, calves twitching, muscles fluttering in their cheeks, jaws clenched, lips cracked with the dryness of fear.

That October 25, as the Thunderbirds entered woods near Housseras, the Germans opened fire with machine guns and mortars. Several men were killed and wounded. Later, in the quaint village of half-timber houses, a sniper perched in a church steeple stared through the calibrated glass of his high-velocity rifle's sights and moved the crosshairs until they settled on an American. Then came the crack of a bullet, like a dry twig snapping underfoot, and yet another GI fell. By dusk, Sparks's I Company had cleared the town but had lost its second, much-respected commander in less than six weeks, Lieutenant Earl Railsback, whom Sparks had held in high regard. If the killing continued at such a pace, he knew his Third Battalion would soon run out of experienced officers. The Thunderbirds had now been in combat for eighty-eight days straight, without receiving a single replacement.

ST. RÉMY, ALSACE-LORRAINE, FRANCE, NOVEMBER 5, 1944

IN THE LATRINES, rumors began to circulate that finally the Thunderbirds were to be relieved. When they weren't cowering in foxholes under shellfire, trying to keep their feet dry, or defecating in icy slit trenches, men read letters from home and soggy newspaper clippings and laughed bitterly at predictions they would be home by Christmas. Clearly, the American public had not the remotest idea what was happening in Europe.

Early on November 5, Sparks ordered his Third Battalion to seize a village called St. Rémy, a few miles northeast of Housseras. By afternoon he had learned that K Company had come under heavy fire. He left his command post and set out to join his men. As he climbed a hill to reach K Company's location, he recognized a man lying on a stretcher, his leg blown off at the knee. He had known twenty-one-year-old Sergeant Otis Vanderpool since he had been a platoon leader at Fort Sill in Oklahoma in 1941. Finally, the odds had caught up with him.

When Sparks moved closer to the fighting, he spotted Otis's older brother Ervin, thirty-one, a platoon sergeant, but so intense was the firefight up ahead that he wasn't able to tell him about Otis's injury. Ervin had only joined the regiment so he could be keep an eye on Otis. Yet he had since proved to be a superb soldier. At Anzio, he had single-handedly saved his platoon when it came under attack, firing clip after clip from his M1 rifle at an armored car, finally scoring a direct hit and taking out the driver.

That evening, thirty-one-year-old Ervin was shot in the stomach and killed. It was uncanny that both brothers were hit, after so long in the field, on the same day. Perhaps Sparks should have offered Ervin a promotion or at least reassigned him to a noncombat position, as he had done with other men who had fought all the way from Sicily. According to Otis, who would eventually return to Colorado to face his parents alone, Ervin would not have accepted: "He wanted to stay near me."

JUST TWO DAYS after the Vanderpool brothers were hit, the horror and heartbreak finally ended. Sparks and his men were pulled off the line for two weeks of badly needed rest. The forest fighting in the Vosges had pushed them to and beyond the breaking point. It was indeed a twitchy and demoralized battalion that was trucked to a rest area near the spa of Martigny-les-Bains, on a sheltered plateau, famous for its healing waters. Men's jaws finally relaxed, leaving their faces slack, mouths hanging open, after months of tension.

"Who the hell do I see about a discharge?" asked one Thunderbird as he fumbled with trembling fingers to light a cigarette.

There were hot showers and movies. Every radio seemed to play Bing Crosby's hit "White Christmas." Sparks and his men tried to savor every second away from the front, getting dry, catching up on sleep, and writing long-delayed letters to loved ones. Sparks was careful, like every other Thunderbird, to avoid conveying the reality of the war to his parents and Mary back home, for fear of causing undue concern. Letters focused on the mundane, and on birthdays and weddings missed, and that November on Thanksgivings past and the approach of yet another away from home. In 1944 Thanksgiving fell on November 23. Eisenhower had ordered that every man in the European Theater be able to eat some turkey, whether served in a canteen or carried to a remote foxhole in a cold sandwich.

Many Thunderbirds also received forty-eight-hour passes to nearby cities. After being promoted, much to his surprise and delight, on November 14, from major to lieutenant colonel, Sparks is said to have visited a cabaret with a fellow officer. He tried to relax with a beer, only to overhear five enlisted men, who were clearly drunk, making loud and derogatory comments about officers.

"Shut your mouth!" ordered Sparks.

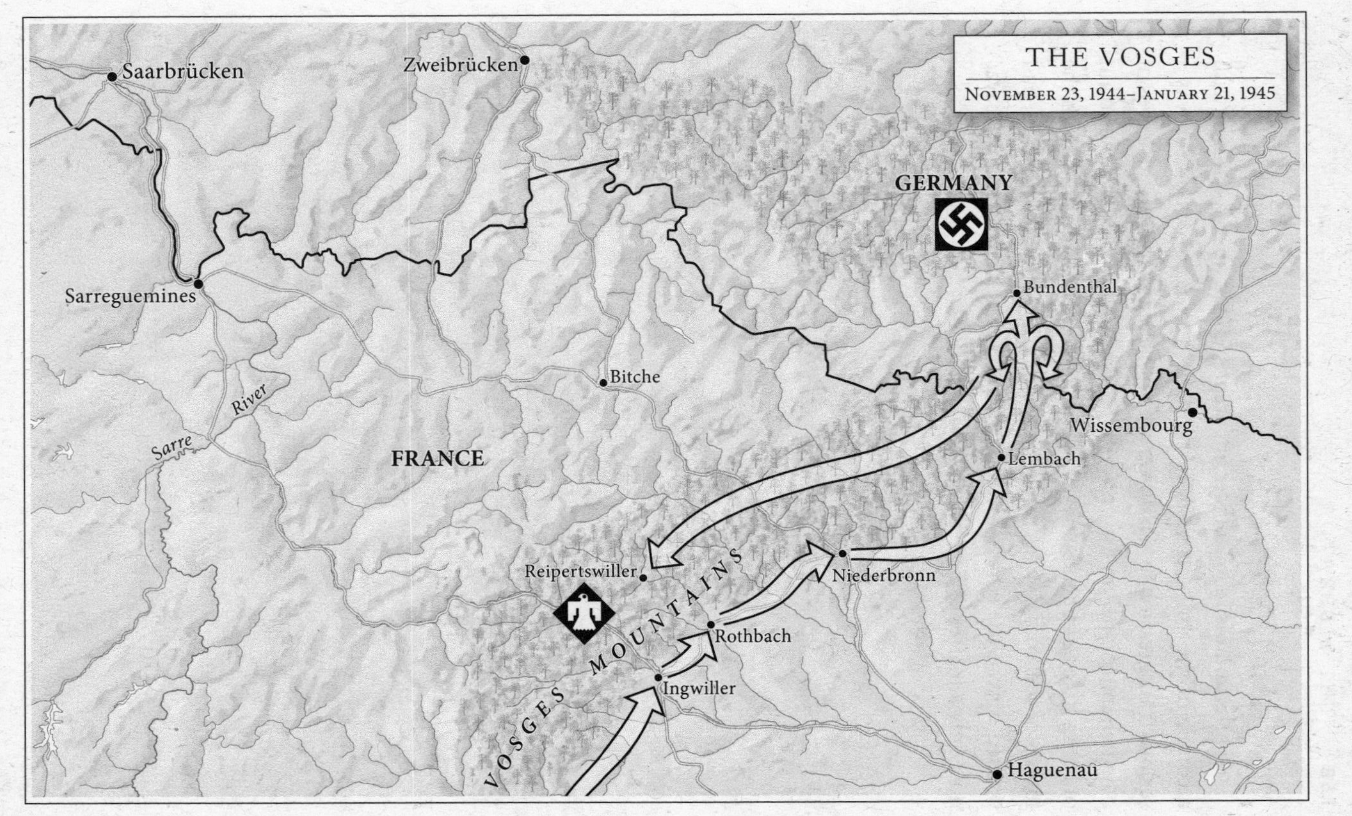
THE VOSGES
November 23, 1944–January 21, 1945
GERMANY
FRANCE
Saarbrücken
Zweibrücken
Sarreguemines
Bitche
Sarre River
Bundenthal
Wissembourg
Lembach
Niederbronn
Reipertswiller
Rothbach
Ingwiller
Haguenau
VOSGES MOUNTAINS

"Go to hell!"

Sparks and his fellow officer apparently ended up in a fistfight with a couple of the enlisted men. Regardless of the provocation, it was a serious transgression for an officer who now had the silver oak leaves of a lieutenant colonel on his uniform. He was finally showing the strain of being so long in combat, even when resting. The close fighting in the forests of the Vosges, where men jumped at the sound of the wind, had pushed him to the edge. As with so many under his command, it was now only a matter of time before he also broke.

PART FIVE

GERMANY

It was a glorious bloodbath, vengeance for our destroyed homeland. Our soldiers still have the old zip. Always advancing and smashing everything. The snow must turn red with American blood.

—GERMAN LIEUTENANT ON THE WESTERN FRONT, DECEMBER 1944

CHAPTER SEVENTEEN

BLACK DECEMBER

Thunderbirds approach a house in Bobenthal, looking for German snipers, December 16, 1944. [National Archives]

SARREBOURG, ALSACE, FRANCE, DECEMBER 3, 1944

THE COMMAND CAR WOUND through the thick pine forests of the Vosges, followed by several vans and a trailer stocked with high-quality liquor. It was December 3 when the car pulled up near the 45th Division's headquarters and thirty-seven-year-old Major General Robert Frederick stepped out of it. He had arrived to replace General Eagles, who had been injured by a mine near Strasbourg on November 30.

It was not a good time for a change of command. The division had returned to combat on Thanksgiving Day and then suffered heavy losses in a nearby town called Sarrebourg, where time bombs left by the Germans had exploded every few hours, causing severe trauma. No one in the division headquarters had slept properly. Everyone was on edge, wondering where and when the next bomb would go off. The Germans had also opened up with 88s on replacements entering combat for the first time and left them splattered on the walls and rafters of a nearby factory.

Frederick's predecessor, Eagles, had been a popular and highly capable figure, and many Thunderbirds were not overjoyed at the news that the thirty-seven-year-old was taking over. The celebrated cartoonist Bill Mauldin, who was covering the 45th Infantry's advance now in the pages of the *Stars and Stripes*, met with Frederick shortly after his arrival. "It will take these men," Frederick confessed to Mauldin, "an inordinately long time to get used to me, partly because of my age, partly because I replaced a well thought of leader."

Frederick had led paratroops with exceptional skill and panache. No less than Winston Churchill believed he was one of America's finest combat leaders of the war: "If we had [had] a dozen men like him, we would have smashed Hitler in 1942. He's the greatest fighting general of all time." However, taking up the reins of a hard-pressed infantry division of more than ten thousand men, just as they tried to break into Germany, was an immense challenge. Did he have sufficient tactical experience to react decisively, like Patton, to fast-moving events, setbacks, and openings? Or would he be hesitant and overwhelmed by the sheer scale and weight of his responsibilities?

WINGEN, ALSACE, FRANCE, DECEMBER 12, 1944

SNOW FELL AS Sparks led his Third Battalion toward the Siegfried Line, the fabled defensive installations stretching along Germany's western border for 630 miles, from Holland to Switzerland.

That evening, Lieutenant Colonel Dwight Funk of the 158th Field Artillery contacted regimental commander Colonel Walter O'Brien.

"Colonel," said Funk, "from where we are now we can put a barrage across the border. Say the word and we can toss a concentration into Germany!"

"What are you waiting for?" O'Brien shouted into the telephone. "Fire away!"

The first man to step into Germany four days later was a muddy Thunderbird who came under fire and took cover behind a stone road sign dated 1826. Machine-gun fire raked the nearby fields. The tired soldier waited for a break in the firing, then rolled to the side, got to his feet, and moved into the Third Reich.

Sparks and his battalion soon followed and set up on a hillside north of the German village of Nothweiler. From his forward command post, Sparks could see the concrete dragon's teeth and pillboxes of the Siegfried Line in the gloomy distance.

THE ARDENNES, DECEMBER 16, 1944

IT WAS JUST after dawn when the uneasy silence ended in the Ardennes Forest, two hundred miles north of Sparks. Along an eighty-mile front, the Germans launched their heaviest barrage of the war in Western Europe. An hour later, a brutal SS spearhead followed by some two hundred thousand Germans pierced the American lines, and dozens of Panzers and Tiger tanks began to storm toward the river Meuse. Hitler's desperate attempt to change the outcome of the war in the west, code-named "Watch on the Rhine," was underway. The Battle of the Bulge had begun.

The German surprise attack was the most serious intelligence failure of the war in Europe for the Allies. The ensuing struggle would rapidly become the largest battle, in terms of participants, ever fought by the United States, with more than eight hundred thousand men involved and almost ninety thousand casualties, including nineteen thousand dead. By nightfall on the first day of the battle, hundreds of German tanks were rolling through Belgium, their commanders hoping to reach the Meuse, cross it before bridges could be blown, and then press on to the strategically vital port of Antwerp, thereby fatally splitting the British and the Americans.

To the south, meanwhile, Sparks and his division had made a significant advance in the opposite direction, into Germany, penetrating over three miles and opening a gap in the German lines four miles wide. The breach had involved fierce fighting by some fifteen thousand men. The *Stars and Stripes* trumpeted: SEVENTH SMASHES INTO GERMANY. But few in the United States would notice. All the major headlines would now be about the fighting farther north. Once again, the Thunderbirds had gotten to their objective, and once more events elsewhere, as in June with D-Day, had robbed them of recognition. The Thunderbirds had been the first Americans to enter Germany from the south. No force in history was thought to have freed so many people and marched so far to do so. But no one back home now knew or cared.

VERDUN, FRANCE, DECEMBER 19, 1944

IT WAS THE most critical meeting during the entire Allied liberation of Europe. Early on Tuesday, December 19, General Dwight Eisenhower, Allied supreme commander, gathered his senior generals in a Maginot Line fortress in Verdun. Fifty miles away, fanatical SS troops were still advancing toward the river Meuse. If they succeeded, Hitler would in theory be in a position to negotiate terms to end the war in the west and then be able to turn all his forces toward the east.

Verdun was indeed a fitting location, being the site of some of the bloodiest carnage and costliest bungling by Allied generals in World War I. The dank, cold atmosphere matched the generals' mood as they sat sullenly nursing their cups of tepid coffee on the second floor of the French barracks. Several tried to hide their embarrassment and shame, knowing their intelligence had failed spectacularly. "The meeting was crowded and atmosphere tense," recalled Sir Kenneth Strong, Eisenhower's chief of intelligence. "The British were worried by events. As so often before, their confidence in the ability of the Americans to deal with the situation was not great. Reports had been reaching them of disorganization behind the American lines, of American headquarters abandoned without notice, and of documents and weapons falling into the hands of the enemy."

Eisenhower entered the room, pale and tense, chain-smoking as usual. He took one look at his despondent staff, huddled in their coats, forced a smile, and then announced confidently: "The present situation is to be regarded as one of opportunity for us and not disaster. There will be only cheerful faces at this conference table."

Eisenhower's career was on the line. He had no option but to buck up his deflated staff. His strategy of advancing into Germany along a broad front, stretching from Holland to Switzerland, now looked like a mistake, as the ever more surly and arrogant General Montgomery had long argued, much to Eisenhower's great irritation.

One of the generals seated in the Maginot Caserne building needed no cheering up: America's last great cavalryman, General George S. Patton. He too had argued that summer against the "broad front strategy," maintaining that a series of bold thrusts at perceived weak points in the German lines would be much more likely to end the war before Christmas, less than a fortnight away.

"Hell," Patton said, "let's have the guts to let the sons of bitches go all the way to Paris. Then we'll really cut 'em up and chew 'em up."

Eisenhower dragged on another Lucky Strike, then turned to face Patton. He had saved Patton's career after the slapping incident in Sicily. Now he needed Patton to return the favor.

"George, I want you to go to Luxembourg and take charge of the battle, making a strong counterattack with at least six divisions. When can you start?"

"As soon as you're through with me."

There was laughter, especially from some of the British officers who believed Patton was being typically brash but also unrealistic. To pull off his counterattack, Patton would need to move 133,179 gasoline-powered vehicles over 1.6 million road miles in atrocious weather.

Patton was not bluffing. He had already drawn up not just one but three plans for a Third Army counterattack in the Ardennes.

"I left my [HQ] in perfect order before I came here," said Patton.

"When will you be able to attack?" Eisenhower asked again.

"The morning of the twenty-first," replied Patton. "With three divisions."

The assembled officers' reaction was now "electric." "There was a stir, a shuffling of feet, as those present straightened their chairs," recalled one aide. "In some faces, skepticism. But through the room the current of excitement leaped like a flame."

"Don't be fatuous, George," said Eisenhower. "If you go that early, you won't have all three divisions ready and you'll go piecemeal. You will start on the twenty-second."

Patton lit a cigar.

"This has nothing to do with being fatuous, sir. I've made my arrangements and my staff are working like beavers at this very moment to shape them up."

Patton outlined his plans and then turned to face fifty-one-year-old General Omar Bradley, commander of the Twelfth Army Group, who had served with him in Sicily.

"Brad, this time the Kraut has stuck his head in a meat grinder."

Patton closed his fist around his cigar, held it aloft, and then made a grinding motion.

"And this time," he added, "I've got hold of the handle!"

Even the dour and increasingly dyspeptic Bradley, whose forces had been split almost in two, now had to laugh.

The conference broke up, the attendees filled with renewed confidence, at around 1 P.M. that December 19, 1944.

As they left the meeting, Eisenhower and Patton shared a few choice words.

Eisenhower mentioned that he had just been given his fifth star.

"Funny thing, George, every time I get a new star I get attacked."

Without missing a beat, Patton fired back: "And every time you get attacked, Ike, I pull you out."

Among others leaving the conference at Verdun was fifty-seven-year-old three-star general Jacob Devers, who commanded the U.S. Sixth Army Group, which included General Sandy Patch's Seventh Army, to which the veteran Thunderbirds belonged. The handsome and highly capable Devers, a classmate of Patton's at West Point, was no favorite of Eisenhower's. In fact Ike, the supreme politician, had unfairly criticized Devers for providing inaccurate evaluations of the fighting in his sector.

Eisenhower now issued Devers fresh orders. His Seventh Army was to abandon its push against the Siegfried Line. Instead, it would now fill in for Patton's divisions heading to the Ardennes. Indeed, the Seventh would replace the Third along Germany's frontier. Eisenhower also told

Devers that he must at all costs prevent the Germans from reentering "those mountains [the Vosges]." If that entailed giving up hard-won ground to hold a firmer defensive line, then so be it. There was to be no repeat of the Ardennes crisis. There could be no second successful German counterattack, not if Eisenhower was to retain the confidence of his political masters.

One can only imagine how Devers felt that cold December day as Eisenhower left Verdun to return to Paris. He had just received extraordinary orders: If the Germans attacked in force in his sector, he was to do what no other American general had yet been asked to do in Europe. He was to retreat. It was a shameful thing for any American soldier, let alone a proud and talented three-star general, to have to contemplate. And in the meantime, Devers would have to make do with just six divisions to man almost a hundred miles of the most difficult terrain on the entire Western Front.

GANDERSHEIM, GERMANY, DECEMBER 24, 1944

THICK FLAKES DRIFTED down, covering the woods and hills outside Gandersheim labor camp in central Germany. Twenty-seven-year-old Robert Antelme, a French writer and resistance worker, made his way to a latrine through the fresh snow. It was now almost six months since Antelme had been arrested in Paris, interrogated by the Gestapo, and then deported into the Reich's vast gulag of labor and concentration camps. He wondered whether he would ever again see his thirty-one-year-old wife, fellow French writer Marguerite Duras.

Antelme walked over to a rail beside a trench and untied the strings holding up his pants. The pants dropped, revealing torn underwear and a sickly mauve coloring on his thighs.

Antelme began to defecate.

Tomorrow it's Christmas. Maybe there'll be a truce for the ovens at Auschwitz tonight?

"Tonight we don't kill. No, not tonight. It's off until tomorrow."

It was too much to hope for and Antelme knew it. It was just wishful thinking. Not until the Americans, British, or Soviets arrived would there be an end to it all. Until they appeared, there would be no reason to hope, no reason to do anything, just suffering and "shit, true shit; true latrines, true ovens; true ashes. . . ."

OBERSTEINBACH, GERMANY, DECEMBER 24, 1944

THREE HUNDRED MILES to the southwest, the snow fell on Sparks's positions dug into the rock-hard soil on a bleak hillside. The leafless hardwoods' topmost limbs were coated in a fine ermine. The whiteness made everything appear fresh and pure.

There were no carols, not even a murmured "Silent Night" that evening. Men shivered, huddled three to a hole, limbs numb, faces drained of color, a crude, snow-crusted canvas cover over them if they were lucky. No playing soccer in no-man's-land with the enemy, no tidings of joy for the men just over the ridge somewhere, waiting to kill or be killed. "We exchanged Christmas greetings with the Germans," recalled Sparks, "in the form of artillery fire."

Sparks knew that his men's morale was at an all-time low. Desertions from the Thunderbird Division and others had never been higher as men endured their second Christmas away from family and loved ones, sharing cigarette butts and defecating into their helmets in freezing mountain foxholes all along the Western Front, from the besieged Bastogne in the Ardennes, to northern Italy, where men now cursed whenever they heard Mark Clark's name. "I sure wish I could see my darling wife so I could cry on her shoulders," wrote one Thunderbird to his family. "There are only a handful of us 'old fellows' left. Maybe my luck will change for 'better,' let's not even think of worse."

Another Thunderbird recalled how the living now shared that Christmas with the dead: Frozen American and German bodies were piled high on trucks near one command post, stacked on top of one another like so many uniformed boards. Everyone swore about the Germans, the Allied generals, and the press, and scoffed bitterly at the flag-waving back home and at the politicians' false promises made to keep a naïve American public buying war bonds. "I don't owe my country a damned thing" was one refrain. Hope had given way to the universal foxhole religion of cynicism, marked in the most devout by outbursts of piercing black humor. The optimistic rallying call "HOME IN FORTY-FOUR" had become "STAY ALIVE IN FORTY-FIVE."

The day after Christmas, Sparks was on the move again. His Third Battalion seized two towns, Niedersteinbach and then Obersteinbach, where they dug in and awaited further orders. He knew his men were increasingly vulnerable and they knew it too. It didn't take a military genius to wonder what might happen if the Germans launched a fierce counterattack as they had to the north, in the Ardennes. Sparks had fewer than a thousand men to patrol and defend a front that stretched almost ten miles. It was a job for a division, numbering ten times more men, not a depleted and demoralized battalion.

When Sparks walked through his positions near Obersteinbach, within striking distance of the Siegfried Line, he could sense his men's growing anxiety. To break the tension a little, he announced that they were all to fire their weapons at the stroke of midnight on New Year's Eve. Sparks himself would fire first, opening up with his trusted shotgun to mark the beginning of his third year at war in Europe. His entire battalion would follow suit, shattering the frozen silence.

ALDERHORST, GERMANY, DECEMBER 28, 1944

HITLER WAS UNDERGROUND once more, in his latest headquarters, colored crayons in shaking hands, beside a map table. Increasingly, he spent his days strung out on amphetamines, needing to be brought down by sedatives to be able to sleep. He had withdrawn from public life, having made his last speech before a crowd in 1943. He refused to visit bombed areas as he moved from one troglodyte's lair to another, preferring fevered fantasy to reality. He could not even bear to look at his own troops, ordering his valet to pull down the blinds in his carriage when his train passed them.

The Battle of the Bulge was still raging, but the German attack had been stalled. Hitler's forces in the Ardennes were, in some places, being pushed back toward the Fatherland. Yet the Führer was not downcast, even though his "last great gamble" had clearly not paid off. Instead, he was convinced that one more surprise strike at the Allied lines, this time in the Vosges, would decisively change the course of the entire war. The German First and Nineteenth Armies were to strike in three days' time, break through the lines of the U.S. Seventh Army and the French First Army in Alsace, and then destroy them before taking on Patton's Third Army and wiping it out.

Before Hitler ended the day with his standard post-midnight snack of tea and cream buns, he addressed a group of field commanders.

"This is a decisive operation," stressed the Führer. "Your success will knock out half the enemy forces on the Western Front. We will yet be masters of our fate."

Operation Northwind, the last major German attack in the west, was about to begin.

THE ISLE OF FYNN, NORWAY, NEW YEAR'S EVE, 1944

THE SONGS GREW louder and more drunken as midnight approached. The young men in gray uniforms, the symbol of a black Edelweiss mountain flower on their caps, SS runes on their lapels, sang along to the radio and tried to forget the war for one night at least. Among them was twenty-year-old Johann Voss, a machine-gun squad leader in SS Mountain Infantry Regiment 11, "Reinhard Heydrich."*

Having joined the SS at age seventeen and fought in Finland against the Soviets, Voss had spent the last few days wandering the Norwegian island, stealing kisses in a barn from a skinny blue-eyed farm girl, and learning how to operate his unit's new MG42 machine guns. "I remember us singing more and more loudly," Voss recalled, "and that at midnight [a comrade] fired a whole box of tracer ammunition in the air with the new MG42 he had mounted in an anti-aircraft position. We switched off the radio when we heard some Party big shot speechifying. We wanted none of that."

Voss was one of more than four million German soldiers sworn to support Adolf Hitler and to defend their homes and families that winter. He and his comrades had not fought for four years simply to lay down their weapons at the borders of the Reich. Despite heavy losses, Voss and his fellow German soldiers were far from physical and moral collapse: There were still 168 infantry and 25 Panzer divisions intact. The Waffen SS, to which Voss belonged, could boast twenty-three well-equipped divisions, seven of them armored. All were supplied with superb weapons, like the MP40 submachine gun, manufactured in huge quantities from stamped steel and ideal for use in forested terrain like the Vosges.

Voss and his comrades in his Black Edelweiss Regiment had long become inured to the empty phrases of politicians, just as Sparks had long since stopped paying attention to the jingoism that was interspersed with radio broadcasts of Tommy Dorsey and Glenn Miller tunes. But that did not mean that men like Voss, having spent their entire adolescence in the golden years of the Third Reich, were not still fiercely committed to Hitler and, more importantly, to one another. In fact 62 percent of captured Wehrmacht soldiers still professed loyalty to their Führer. The percentage among the SS, who had sworn a solemn blood oath of allegiance to Hitler, was higher still.

*Voss is a pseudonym.

LONDON, NEW YEAR'S EVE, 1944

THE SNOW FELL on the drunken revelers, on Buckingham Palace, and on Nelson's Column at the heart of Trafalgar Square. Standing among the throngs, counting down the last seconds to 1945 was twenty-four-year-old American reporter Marguerite Higgins, hoping she might finally get to the front lines before the war was over. She would in fact do so, encountering Sparks in the most extraordinary circumstances, but as bells rang out across London that night the prospect of filing even one decent story seemed remote. For months now, the talk back in America had been of the war ending in Europe.

The ambitious Higgins had arrived in London from New York a few weeks before aboard the *Queen Mary.* Among other reporters crossing the Atlantic had been the *New Yorker*'s Janet Flanner, who vividly recalled Higgins's arrival on board. Higgins had missed the sailing and reached the *Queen Mary* as it actually steamed out of New York Harbor. Flanner had watched as a ladder was dropped to a tugboat and then a slim, blue-eyed woman in army uniform climbed onto the deck, her helmet falling back to release a cascade of blond hair. "She looked so sweet and innocent," recalled Flanner. "I immediately thought of Goldilocks and wanted to protect her."

The headlines that New Year made Higgins even more aware that she was missing the "Big Show": U.S. FLYERS BLAST NAZI ARMOR FLEEING BULGE. BRITISH IN GERMANY, 29 MILES FROM DUSSELDORF. TWIN DRIVES IN HOLLAND BREAK NAZI LINE. BRITISH LAND IN GREECE, NAZIS WITHDRAWING. 3RD ARMY SMASHES THROUGH SIEGFRIED LINE.

THERE WERE ALSO stories about the Red Army on the front pages. It had stalled in late 1944 in its advance toward Berlin but by New Year's Day was advancing once more. As it did so, it liberated concentration camps hastily abandoned by the SS in the face of the Soviet onslaught. Few prisoners were found alive. Most had been killed or were being marched west, ahead of the Soviet advance, deeper into the gulag of six-hundred-odd camps in the Reich, where seven hundred thousand people still languished, caught between life and death.

Twenty-one-year-old Jack Goldman was one of fifty-eight thousand Auschwitz prisoners marched west from Poland, where some four million European Jews had been exterminated in the Final Solution, including most of Goldman's German family. His father had in fact been shot in front of him in retaliation for the assassination of SS general Reinhard Heydrich in Prague in May 1942.

To avoid Allied planes, the SS made Goldman walk at night in the cold and snow. He and his fellow survivors, marching in rows of five abreast, sometimes managed a few minutes of sleep, held up by the men around them. Then they were ordered into open freight cars and taken to a transit camp in Germany, where Goldman was placed in a barrack that looked to him to be no bigger than a doll's house but which was soon home to fourteen other men. Fifteen thousand of his fellow prisoners from Auschwitz had not survived the journey to Germany.

Soon after, Goldman fell ill with typhoid fever and became delirious. One day, the SS ordered him and his fellow survivors to get ready to march once more, and Goldman could not move. He was too weak.

A German guard approached him.

"Shoot me," said Goldman. "Do what you want."

"Get up!"

The German hit him with his rifle butt.

"Go!" said the German.

Goldman somehow found the strength to get up. Those who couldn't were shot.

GOLDMAN AND OTHERS being forcibly removed from the territories closest to the Soviet advance were joined that winter by hundreds of thousands of German civilians fleeing the Red Army, clogging the iced roads with their carts loaded with meager possessions, desperate to find sanctuary from "Ivan," the murderous Slav rapist invoked by Nazi propaganda.

The Red Army liberated mostly women as it swept into eastern Germany that January—the men were either dead or away fighting. "Women, mothers and their children," noted one Soviet officer, "lie to the right and left along the route, and in front of each of them stands a raucous armada of men with their trousers down. The women who are bleeding or losing consciousness get shoved to one side, and our men shoot the ones who try to save their children."

The mass rape often ended with the victims being mutilated and bludgeoned to death. Such was the indiscriminate vengeance of Stalin's warriors. "We are taking revenge for everything," wrote one Soviet soldier to his parents. "Fire for fire, blood for blood, death for death."

No wonder that at least fifty thousand traumatized refugees were arriving in Berlin each day—a pathetic fraction of the eight million civilians fleeing west, their future dependent on the speed of the Western Allies' advance. Indeed, the faster Sparks and his battalion pushed forward, the more women and children they would be able to save from rape and enslavement under Stalinism. The quicker they destroyed all German resistance in their path, the more Jews like Jack Goldman and other victims of the Nazi terror like Robert Antelme might survive. Every setback and delay now cost more than ever.

ON NEW YEAR'S Day 1945, Johann Voss and his regiment, part of the 6th SS Division "Nord," sailed for the mainland of Norway and the following day left by train for Germany. He and his fellow SS were about to face their greatest test yet. The last of Hitler's elite, they were headed to fight in familiar winter conditions, this time in the mountains of the Vosges, where an increasingly nervous Sparks and his men were huddled, trying their best to fend off frostbite, in their dugouts and foxholes.

CHAPTER EIGHTEEN

THE BREAKING POINT

Every man has a breaking point.

—FELIX SPARKS

American shells land on the village of Reipertswiller, January 1945. [National Archives]

REIPERTSWILLER, THE VOSGES, FRANCE, JANUARY 1, 1945

DAWN BROKE ON THE first day of 1945. The sun pierced the heavy mist and dark clouds but then quickly disappeared. All along the thinly held Seventh Army lines, shells whistled and screamed. Operation Northwind had begun. By sundown, eight German divisions, including more than thirty thousand SS, were storming west through the high mountain passes and valleys of the Vosges, headed toward Strasbourg.

Along with the rest of the 45th Division, Sparks and his battalion retreated to defensive positions ten miles to their rear. There was little panic even though heavy Germany shelling continued as they withdrew in trucks to Reipertswiller, a small village in France. It was painful to pass through ruined towns that had been so hard-won and were now to be ceded back to the enemy. Thunderbirds cursed bitterly. Having to turn their backs and return to France without putting up a fight felt wrong. "It is getting hard to know who wants to keep us from reaching the Rhine," complained their new division commander, General Frederick. "Ike or the Krauts." In some of the villages that had to be abandoned, bewildered French children threw icy snowballs at the departing Thunderbirds.

For the next ten days fighting raged in the Vosges as more than one hundred thousand enemy troops fought to break through the Seventh Army's defenses. General Frederick faced his first great challenge as a division commander: stopping the rampaging SS from rolling over the Thunderbirds, who held the critical center of the Allied line. With the Seventh Army fighting on three sides, and Eisenhower fearing it might soon be destroyed, all manner of reinforcements were rushed to help bolster the front, including French soldiers from General Leclerc's 2nd French Armored Division and green troops from the U.S. 70th Division.

The Thunderbirds stood firm but not without significant loss. In Sparks's regiment, fifty men were injured as they held off the German attacks. They included popular medic Joe Medina, who was wounded and knocked unconscious by shell fire and days after being hit woke in a hospital in France. Medina was possibly the last medic from the regiment to have known Sparks before the war. They had come a long way together, the soft-spoken Mexican-American shepherd's son and the lieutenant colonel who had joined the "Eager for Duty" regiment at Fort Sill on February 6, 1941. Medina had since tended scores of badly wounded men under Sparks's command, in every battle since Sicily, and had been treated by Sparks with real warmth, like a good friend, until this, his third serious wound, finally took him off the line for good.

REIPERTSWILLER, FRANCE, JANUARY 14, 1945

IN THE HILLS north of Reipertswiller it was 8:30 A.M. when German shells began to explode and shards of hot steel flew in every direction. The rate of fire was so quick it sounded as if the 88mm guns were in fact machine pistols, the shrill whistles of shells becoming a constant scream, the crump and thud of explosions a steady drumming.

The Thunderbirds were striking back, pushing the German forces in Operation Northwind toward Germany. But the Nazis were in no mood to give up without a fight. At Reipertswiller and in many other villages and nameless mountain passes, Seventh Army units were meeting truly stunning resistance.

Even after the ordeal of Anzio, Sparks was surprised by the intensity of the German shelling. He knew that without massive counterfire and armored support his Third Battalion could not advance much farther. Later that morning of January 14, he set out to join the forward elements of his Third Battalion. He was with three other men: a translator, nineteen-year-old German-born Karl Mann, who had joined the regiment as a replacement at Anzio; a much-trusted driver, Albert Turk; and a runner, Carleton Johnson. Sparks and Turk were up front.

Karl Mann sat in the backseat beside Johnson. Mann had first seen combat as an ammunition carrier for a water-cooled .30-caliber machine gun in the battalion's heavy-weapons company, before being asked by Sparks the previous November to become his interpreter. Despite Mann spending most days in Sparks's company, the twenty-seven-year-old Third Battalion commander remained a distant, inscrutable figure to him. Colonel Sparks was not one for small talk or sharing his feelings and never mentioned his family back home, unlike some officers. With the often curt, no-nonsense "Shotgun" Sparks, it was all business all the time.

The jeep sped down a paved road. It had snowed the previous night, and two to three inches of fresh powder coated the ground. All of a sudden there was a loud explosion and Sparks was thrown into the air, several yards clear of the jeep. He was alive, though badly bruised and in shock. His left knee and right finger were cut. He lay sprawled in the snow, stunned, blood seeping from his wounds into the whiteness.

Mann was also in shock but otherwise unharmed. The sleeping bag he'd been sitting on had absorbed much of the blast. He climbed out of the jeep and saw that its back wheel was actually resting on top of a mine, an inch from the detonator. There were dozens of other mines laid out across the road in an extended W pattern, mostly hidden by the snow. One of the jeep's front wheels had run over and detonated one of them.

No one but Sparks was hurt. While he was being tended to in an aid station, Captain John L. McGinnis, the Third Battalion's executive officer, took over command of the Third Battalion as it began to push farther into the hills north of Reipertswiller. The German artillery fire was still so intense that Captain McGinnis himself was soon wounded and carried into the Third Battalion's aid station, joining a fast-growing number of other men.

Sparks had little choice but to return to his post and resume command of his battalion. It had yet to reach its objectives, and his men would need him if they were to succeed. Back at the front line he gave orders to strike farther north into thickly wooded hills. By 3 P.M., his battalion's three companies had managed to advance almost a mile despite the ferocious enemy fire.

As darkness approached, Sparks ordered a halt. It was 6:10 P.M. when he received an urgent message from regimental headquarters. Intelligence reports predicted an imminent SS counterattack involving at least three thousand troops. It was vital that Sparks's battalion, numbering fewer than a thousand men, seize a ridge before the German offensive began. Early the following morning, Sparks ordered his battalion to attack once more. Around 9 A.M., it came under accurate fire from mortar and artillery and men were forced to take cover. By 1 P.M., K and L Companies had nonetheless reached the critical ridge, suffering fewer than a dozen casualties. Soon I Company also arrived and took up position between K and L Companies. Now the battalion ran in a line some eight hundred yards long, east to west, in the forested mountains north of Reipertswiller.

Sparks's men had carried out his orders successfully. But the regiment's other battalions had not managed to seize ridges on either side of Third Battalion's, which meant that the Third Battalion was isolated, without support, its positions dangerously exposed. "We were the only God-damn battalion in the division who took our objective," remembered Sparks. "We were sitting up there all on our own."

That afternoon, Sparks walked up a trail through the dense forest, to the positions his men had taken. He found them well dug in. He told his company commanders they would need to be extra vigilant. He then returned to his forward command post near Reipertswiller, at the base of a supply trail, while it was still light. At 4:15 P.M., as darkness began to settle, he received an urgent radio report from Company K. Enemy troops were advancing and occupying a ridge to the left of the battalion. They then probed Sparks's battalion's positions but were pushed back by heavy machine-gun fire.

Later that evening, L Company detected another German probe and opened fire. The Germans quickly pulled back, leaving their dead behind. When several stiffening bodies were later examined, it was learned from pay-books that the Germans were from the 6th SS Nord Division. By now, the SS on the Western Front had a fearsome reputation for brutality and indiscriminate violence: A widely reported massacre of American POWs on December 17 at Malmédy, during the Ardennes offensive, had sent a chill through the entire U.S. Army in Europe and inflamed long-standing hatred for Hitler's most fanatical warriors. Sparks's men knew they could expect little mercy if they had to surrender.

Sparks ordered every able-bodied man who could wield an M1 onto the line to defend his battalion's position, hoping reinforcements would arrive in time to repel another German strike.

REIPERTSWILLER, FRANCE, JANUARY 17, 1945

THE TROOPS FROM the 11th SS Mountain Infantry Regiment crept forward. They then set up positions in the woods overlooking a trail and opened fire with mortars and machine guns on Thunderbirds who were advancing along it, quickly pushing them back. The SS now controlled the main supply route that led to the Third Battalion's positions. Meanwhile other German units moved through the thick forest and effectively surrounded Sparks's men, seizing high ground on all sides of the ridge.

Among the enemy troops was twenty-year-old Johann Voss. He was fighting the "Amis," as the Germans called the Americans, for the first time and learning that they were just as tough and persistent as the Russians and Finns he had encountered in the North, and far better supported by artillery fire. Voss and his comrades were grimly determined experts in mountain fighting, having long since adapted their weapons and tactics to the terrain. Armed with *Panzerfausts*, they were

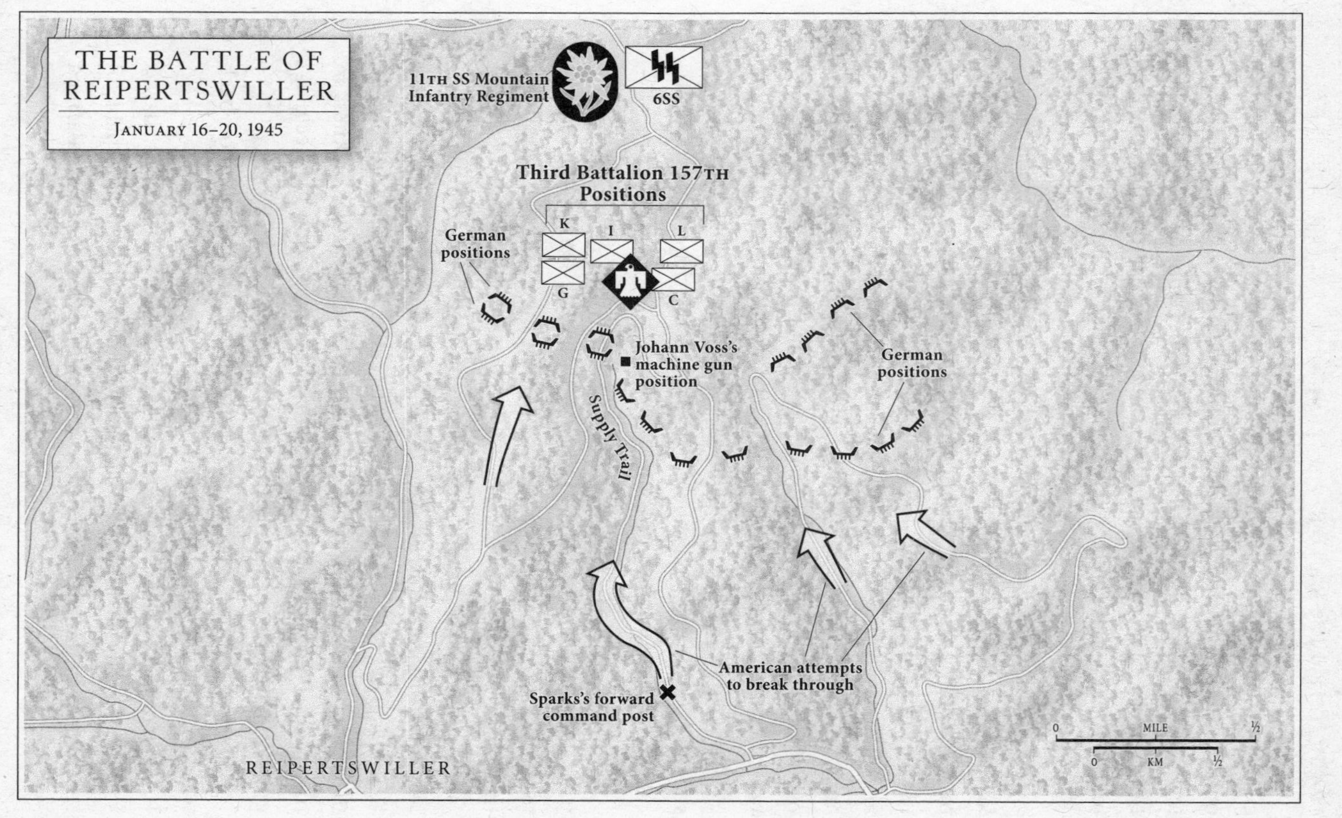
THE BATTLE OF
REIPERTSWILLER
JANUARY 16–20, 1945
11TH SS Mountain
Infantry Regiment
6SS
Third Battalion 157TH
Positions
K
I
L
G
C
German
positions
Johann Voss's
machine gun
position
Supply Trail
German
positions
American attempts
to break through
Sparks's forward
command post
0
MILE
½
0
KM
½
REIPERTSWILLER

crucially far more mobile than the Thunderbirds, having fitted machine guns and even *Nebelwerfer* rocket launchers to sleds. Voss and his fellow SS also had excellent artillery support; their morale was far higher than that of Sparks's men; and they were determined to fight to the end to defend their homeland. The odds were in fact very much against the Americans.

At his forward command post, an increasingly concerned Sparks learned that the key supply trail to his men had been cut off. It had to be reopened or his entire battalion could be overrun. Swift and intense use of force was essential. Above all, Sparks was determined to avoid another tragedy like that at Anzio, when his men had been surrounded and then gradually wiped out over several days. The lesson of the Battle of the Caves had been to hold at all costs, but only if the stakes warranted the resulting sacrifice in young men's lives. The current situation, as Sparks saw it, did not necessitate a prolonged, stubborn resistance. As soon as possible, his men should be pulled off the ridge, using the critical supply trail as an escape route.

Sparks consulted with regimental commander Colonel O'Brien, who shared his views. O'Brien contacted the Division G-3, in charge of operations, and asked permission to pull the Third Battalion from the ridge. The G-3 then conferred with the 45th's commander, General Frederick, who saw the situation differently. Sparks's men must remain in their positions. More lives would be lost and the Allied front would be under greater threat if the SS seized the ridge. Frederick's orders were to "hold the line as long as possible to keep from creating weakness in the front." Frederick wasn't about to risk his reputation for steely aggression by giving up ground this late in the war.

The response to O'Brien's request to pull the Third Battalion back was emphatic: "Permission denied."

When Sparks learned of Frederick's order, he was furious. It was sheer stupidity. Frederick was clearly way out of his depth, incapable of reading the battle correctly. Sparks was as incensed as he was alarmed by Frederick's belligerence. From crackling radio messages, he knew his men were weak and getting weaker by the minute, running low on ammunition, their positions being methodically picked off by superb SS troops. This was no time to stand and hold as Americans had at Bastogne that Christmas when the outcome of a much greater battle was in the balance. If the SS wanted Reipertswiller so badly, let them have it.

REIPERTSWILLER, FRANCE, JANUARY 18, 1945

IT WAS JUST after midnight when General Frederick's second in command, Colonel Paul Adams, contacted Colonel O'Brien's regimental headquarters. He wanted to know if any men had managed to open the vital supply trail and get through to Sparks's stranded companies.

Major Carroll, the regimental S-3, did not know.

Adams was far from pleased.

What the hell was going on? What was the holdup?

"Will you find out why Third Battalion hasn't tried to use light tanks to contact the companies before this?" Adams asked Carroll.

"They have tried to contact them before," replied Carroll. "They were not successful. They ran into automatic fire and rifle grenades."

The thirty-eight-year-old Alabama-born Adams, who had previously served as General Frederick's executive officer, had been with the division for only a fortnight. Like so many senior officers in the American Army that January, he had been rapidly promoted and lacked critical combat experience.

Adams angrily demanded to know why Sparks had been "fooling around all evening." Why hadn't he been able to reach his men?

Carroll handed the telephone receiver to Colonel O'Brien. Adams vented his frustration at O'Brien, then added: "Tell Colonel Sparks to get the lead out of his ass and get up to the companies!"

It was a gross, inexcusable insult to one of his regiment's finest officers. Clearly, Adams didn't have a clue about Sparks or the severity of the fast-deteriorating situation on the ground. All he could see was lines on a map.

O'Brien managed to control his temper, but only just.

"You'd better watch your language and what you're saying!" he told Adams. "Colonel Sparks is more courageous and eager to get the job done than anyone I know of!"

The conversation ended abruptly.

THIRD BATTALION'S POSITIONS, two hills with a saddle between them, were utterly devastated, dotted with hundreds of shell holes. German and American corpses littered the churned and bloodstained ground. The trees that had previously provided cover looked like so many snapped matchsticks. The surrounding ridges controlled by the SS were just as apocalyptic due to the unprecedented heavy fire of the 158th Artillery, which had landed an astonishing five thousand shells on the Germans the previous day.

Sparks was in constant communication with his battalion through a radio in his forward command post. Every urgent message compounded his frustration and concern. Casualties had mounted through the long night, bringing the total over three days to 118, a quarter of his battalion. The SS had dug in behind and to the front of them and had them completely pinned down. Whenever a Thunderbird showed his head aboveground, he was seemingly greeted by machine-gun fire, followed soon after by the hiss and scream of a *Nebelwerfer* rocket launcher. Observers lurked behind rocks and trees on the high ground around the battalion's positions. The crosshairs of SS sniper rifles had settled on American foxholes all across the ridge.

To his relief, around 6 A.M. on January 18, a sleepless and ever more anguished Sparks got what he needed to attempt a breakthrough: Three M8 reconnaissance vehicles arrived at his command post. It was dark as he greeted the young officers of the armored vehicles. At first light, they would set out to reopen the supply trail to his stranded battalion.

Time was running out. The SS were, remembered one Thunderbird, "close to the kill and they knew it." In the hills surrounding the battalion, they strapped on the twin fuel tanks of flamethrowers, shouldered MG42 machine guns, ammunition belts hanging around their necks, and picked up their recoilless grenade launchers called *Panzerfausts*. They then began to move through the forest from several directions toward the ridge held by Sparks's men. Their primary target was Lieutenant Osterholt's G Company, closest to the supply trail, now down to just sixty-eight men, many of them wounded.

Dawn was breaking as the two hundred SS troops, in winter camouflage, crept closer toward G Company, trailing small sleds on which MG42 machine guns had been mounted, ready to be fired. Then the SS crouched down and checked their machine pistols, flamethrowers, and "potato-masher" grenades, waiting for the order to attack. A few minutes later, there was a shrill blast of a whistle: the signal to attack. Soon the white-helmeted SS were on top of Lieutenant Osterholt's G Company, tossing stick grenades into foxholes and dugouts and letting rip with machine pistols, which made a *b-r-r-r-r-r-p* sound due to their high rate of fire.

The sled-mounted MG42s raked G Company's positions, firing fifteen hundred rounds a minute, green and white tracers ripping through the murky forest, ricocheting off rocks and shattering already smashed tree limbs. Snow, fragments of bark, and lethal splinters from tree bursts filled the air. Flares soared and cruelly lit the killing field below as the SS moved in on Sparks's men, squirting jets of roaring yellow flame at the most stubborn defenders.

It was not just G Company that came under attack. The SS probed all across the Third Battalion's positions. From every one of Sparks's five stranded companies came radio calls of distress. Fewer than thirty men from G Company escaped the German infiltration. The other forty in the unit were either killed or captured. Those who somehow got clear of the jets of burning gasoline and hails of bullets staggered to K Company's positions, fifty yards to the north on the benighted ridge.

In G Company's seized positions, the SS searched for food and weapons. Among the abandoned equipment they found an SCR-300 radio. It was still working, much to the delight of the SS men's commanding officer, *Standartenführer* Helmut Raithel, who had it brought to him in his command post. The quick-thinking Raithel sent for an English-speaking rifleman in another SS battalion. The soldier was in fact fluent, having lived in Chicago before the war. It wasn't long before he was translating the curt messages he heard over the radio.

The SS now knew the Americans' every move.

AT SPARKS'S FORWARD command post, the two-hundred-pound, dark green SCR-694 radio set delivered more bad news.

"G Company is captured! Something has to be done quick!"

The SS began to shell the battalion's positions mercilessly. More shells landed in rapid succession on the Thunderbirds than anywhere else in the previous four hundred days of war, even at Anzio. Shards of white-hot steel seeded almost every yard of the Americans' positions. "No aid could be given to the wounded," recalled one Thunderbird. "When hit, men sank in their holes and tended their wounds as best they could." An astonishing three out of four men were injured by the flying shrapnel.

When the barrage finally ended later that morning, the armored vehicles at Sparks's command post set out, accompanied by three squads of infantrymen. It was miserable weather, even for January in northern Europe. There was a steady lashing rain that considerably reduced visibility as the rescue party moved toward the vital supply trail.

Twenty-two-year-old Sergeant Bernard Fleming and his rifle squad of twelve men moved cautiously through woods beside the trail. He heard intense small-arms fire close by. The other rifle squads in the rescue party were knocking out German machine guns overlooking the trail. Then silence. Fleming continued up the trail, believing his fellow Thunderbirds had successfully broken through the German cordon around the battalion.

He was mistaken. Waiting in ambush up ahead were more SS machine gunners, well dug in and concealed, their new MG42 guns fully loaded and positioned to lay down deadly fire on the supply trail as it crossed a small bridge. A few minutes later, as Fleming and his squad approached the bridge, the SS opened up with the machine guns. Several men fell in agony, badly wounded in their legs—the only parts of their bodies that had been visible to the SS from their holes below the tightly bunched firs.

Sergeant Bernard Fleming looked around for cover. He was close to a large hole in the ground caused by a fallen tree.

"Come on," he shouted at his men. "Get over here."

Fleming and his men jumped into the hole.

Not long after, two men from another squad appeared and jumped into the hole with Fleming and his men.

"We got orders to withdraw," one of them said. "But I couldn't get out. I heard you guys firing down here, so I came down."

The SS opened fire again. Fleming and the others were pinned down. Indeed, the rescuers now needed saving. Their only hope was to get word back to Sparks's command post.

A young radio operator, Private Emmett L. Neff volunteered: "I'll go."

Neff took off running through the woods, dodging trunks and branches, skirting the trail, headed for the American lines, but after twenty-five yards he fell in agony, shot through the ankles.

Neff shouted that he'd been hit.

"I'm going out there to get him," said Fleming. "Give me a lot of fire."

The men in the hole all did so. Fleming ran over to Neff, dragged him back to the hole, and began to pull off Neff's bloodied boots so he could examine his wounds.

"I'm gonna go," said Private Lawrence S. Mathiason.

"Wait a minute now," said Fleming. "They already got one guy. They're going to watch us."

Mathiason ran off anyway. He hadn't made it ten yards when the Germans "drilled" him with machine-gun and rifle fire.

Fleming took off his heavy ammunition belt and handed his tommy gun to one of his men. He didn't need the extra weight.

"You guys stay here," he said. "I'm going to get help."

Fleming sprinted from the hole then dropped down beside Mathiason. He was dead. Fleming continued running. The SS had him in their sights. Bullets cracked overhead. One passed through his trousers but he wasn't hit. He made it to the bottom of the trail, where he found Sparks in the Third Battalion's forward command post.

Fleming told Sparks of the failed rescue mission. Now there were more men, stranded near the supply trail, who needed help.

Sparks could not stand to stay in his command post, listening to his men being killed, for a minute longer. He decided he would lead the next attempt to break through. He owed his men no less. But he wasn't about to get himself killed in some crazy suicide mission. Armored cars clearly weren't capable of punching through the German positions on the trail. Real firepower would be needed.

He picked up his field telephone and called regimental headquarters.

Major Carroll answered.

"[We] have to clear the hill," said Sparks. "If you send tanks I will take [one] and fire at the positions myself."

Sparks then put a call through to Lieutenant Curtis of K Company. They were fast running out of ammunition and in dire risk of being overrun, just as G Company had been earlier.

"Help on the way," said Sparks.

To soften up German positions overlooking the supply trail, the 158th Artillery began to fire high-explosive shells. Soon, one was landing every six seconds—a truly astonishing rate of fire—in the steep draw through which the supply trail climbed. One SS machine gunner, in a position overlooking the trail, hunkered down, listening to the continuous bursting of shells, not daring to imagine how many of his friends were being killed.

Around 9 A.M., two Sherman tanks arrived at Sparks's command post. He had little faith in the tanks' ability to withstand a direct hit from a German 88mm shell. They were nicknamed "Ronson Lighters" because of their tendency when struck to "brew up" and explode with a giant jet of flame, just like their namesake, which the manufacturer boasted always "lights first time." But they had powerful 76mm guns and their armor could stop machine-gun bullets and mortar fragments.

Sparks briefed their crews and then climbed into one of the eleven-foot-high vehicles. He did not close the hatch, knowing his view would be severely restricted if he did so. Instead, he stood up in the turret, put on a pair of headphones, and began to give orders to the driver and three other men, including a gunner and wireless operator. In doing so, he crossed a line—officers of his rank were not supposed to commandeer tanks, let alone lead their crews in combat.

Engines revved up. The tank crews went to work in their steel hulks, surrounded by levers and handles and set on top of ninety gallons of fuel, beside stores of high- explosive shells. Both tanks lurched forward, tracks grinding the ground, and headed up the supply trail.

Sparks hadn't gone far when Colonel O'Brien contacted his command post.

"What is the score with Colonel Sparks?" asked O'Brien.

"He is taking a couple of medium tanks to try to clear out the draw again," replied one of Sparks's officers.

"Tell him to hold where he is. A battalion of the 179th [Infantry Regiment] is coming up to attack."

Sparks was directing the lead tank, still standing in its turret, when the message from O'Brien was relayed to him. He ignored it and instead told the tank's wireless operator to send a message to K Company.

"Help is fighting to get to you."

O'Brien was still on the line back at the Third Battalion command post.

"Colonel Sparks says he will try to get up to his companies with the tanks," said one of Sparks's officers.

O'Brien chose to let Sparks continue. He could ill afford to lose his finest battalion commander, but he knew from experience that the young colonel could be infuriatingly stubborn when he set his mind to something. Given his men's desperate situation, he would in all likelihood ignore a direct order to pull back, even if Eisenhower made it, and if anyone could get through, it would surely be Sparks. Under O'Brien's command, he had never failed to take an objective.

The Sherman tanks trundled up the supply trail, the rubber treads and steel cleats of their tracks struggling for grip. Sparks dismounted a couple of times to reconnoiter ahead and then moved forward again in the lead tank. Suddenly there was the angry rip of a machine gun and a sharp pinging as MG42 bullets ricocheted off the lead tank. Sparks returned fire with the tank's .30-caliber machine gun, squeezing off short bursts to avoid burning out its air-cooled barrel, sweeping the trees and rocks on either side of the trail, hoping to hit any men lurking with *Panzerfausts*.

He also barked instructions through his headset to the men operating his tank's 76mm cannon. A loader tugged a shell from a bracket and closed the breech, then the gunner fired, the cannon's violent recoil just inches from his face. The sound was like an immense, deafening bark. Because the 76mm fired at a very high velocity, it made far more noise than an artillery piece. With his clattering machine gun, which could cut trees in two, and the cannon, which could blow a log dugout to smithereens, Sparks managed to pin down the SS overlooking the trail. Several men from Bernard Fleming's rescue party who were hiding along the trail were able to pull back to safer positions.

Sparks ordered the tanks forward again. The trail steepened and narrowed as it approached the bridge where Fleming and his men had earlier run into an ambush. The tanks' engines were gunned. It was ever more difficult to gain traction. The drivers peered through narrow slits as they operated sluggish controls. The wireless radio blared. Sparks shouted orders. The turret trainer whirred and guns rattled.

It was a terrifying experience to be inside a Sherman tank during combat. Every man knew that at any second an enemy shell could hit. If lucky, he would see a bright red bruise to the tank's metal that faded seconds after impact. Then he would have to clamber to the turret, scraping elbows on sharp edges, and get the hell out before the enemy had time to fire a second time. Just as often, the fuel and high-explosive shells would ignite and then flames would rip through the iron tomb, leaving men looking like little black dolls, two-foot-tall blocks of charcoal.

Sparks approached the bridge. Some fifty yards away, concealed on the hillside, was twenty-year-old SS veteran Johann Voss. He watched as Sparks closed on the bridge, still firing bursts from the tank's machine gun. "If [he] could pass the bridge unharmed," recalled Voss, "we only had a slim chance in a duel. Our bullets would only scratch their armor."

The tracks on Sparks's lead tank spun on the steep, icy ground and then lost traction. The tank slid sideways, exposing its right flank. A *Panzerfaust* sounded. There was a loud explosion as a shell hit Sparks's tank at the base of the turret. The sound would have reverberated through the tank as if it were a drum. The impact knocked out the 76mm cannon. Sparks and the crew were unharmed. Crucially, the tank and the machine gun were still operable.

Sparks stood in the turret and looked around.

Several Thunderbirds lay bleeding on the ground beside the supply trail.

One man cowered behind trees.

"Can I come out?" he shouted.

"Make a break for it," shouted Sparks.

The soldier had gone only a few yards when Sparks heard the rattle of a machine gun. Another of his men had been mercilessly gunned down. It was as if something snapped deep inside him. Days of excruciating tension and frustration and very little sleep had pushed him beyond his breaking point. He looked around at his wounded men. Not for a second longer would he stand by as they slowly bled to death. He had lost his entire company at Anzio. He would rather die than lose all his men again. All that mattered was doing something to save some of them.

Sparks climbed out of the tank's hatch and jumped to the ground.

SS corporal Johann Voss stood beside a machine gunner in his squad, watching Sparks through field glasses.

The gunner had his finger on his trigger.

Voss saw Sparks move toward his injured men.

"Wait a minute," said Voss. "Let's see what happens."

Voss and his fellow SS held their fire.

Sparks ran to the man farthest from him, some fifty yards away. The man had been shot through the chest. He was a heavy kid and Sparks was not strong enough to carry him on his back. So he dragged him across the icy ground. Still, the SS stood and watched. There was no honor to be gained, recalled Voss, by drilling a brave officer with 7.92mm bullets as he tried to help his wounded men. Indeed, there was a silent understanding among the SS watching Sparks. Killing him would be wrong.

Sparks lifted the heavy kid onto the tank. Two other wounded men were not far away. He got to them and helped them onto the tank too. Incredibly, the SS still held their fire.

Voss could still see Sparks clearly through his field glasses. Never had he witnessed such an act of courage by the enemy. There was no way he was going to open fire on the wounded lying on the tank. He watched as Sparks got back into the lead tank. The rescue had lasted no more than eight minutes.

Sparks ordered both tanks to return to American lines. It was impossible to continue up the trail. The tanks' treads were worthless on the steep ice. He did his best to make the injured comfortable, tending to their wounds as the tanks backed down the trail. One had a broken leg, and he was able to make a splint, securing it with an ammunition belt.

Voss and his nearest comrades held their fire, but others several hundred yards down the trail, who had not witnessed the rescue, did not. There was a hollow sound—the *tonk* of a mortar being fired. Then the SS opened up with what seemed like everything they had. Bullets pinged and ricocheted off the metal of Commander Joseph Crowley's number two tank, which followed behind Sparks's, shredding most of the material attached to it. But neither tank was knocked out. They both continued down the supply trail as fast as possible.

It was 1:30 P.M. when an utterly drained Sparks arrived back at his forward command post. The front of his tank was charred black and part of the cannon had broken loose. The machine gun was almost burned-out. Sparks had fired an incredible five thousand rounds.

Word of the attempted breakthrough spread fast. Sergeant Bernard Fleming, whose wounded squad members had been rescued, later remembered that Sparks's actions "buoyed the morale of all who were aware of his gallantry that day. Our commander had proved *once again* that he valued his soldiers' lives and was willing to take large risks on their behalf."

Sparks couldn't have cared less what the men he had rescued thought. He had not been able to break through. What was left of his battalion was still stranded, being picked off by fanatical Nazis. He had not reached his men on the ridge. He had not saved any of them.

He had failed. Yet he had survived.

He had not cared if he got killed. In fact, he had expected to die when he got out of the tank.

Why hadn't the SS riddled him with bullets?

Why? he wondered. *Why didn't they shoot me?*

CHAPTER NINETEEN

DEFEAT

Brigadier General Robert Frederick, commander of the 45th Infantry Division. [National Archives]

REIPERTSWILLER, JANUARY 18, 1945

THE LAST RADIOS IN use on the ridge hissed and crackled as their batteries and crystals began to fade. In his command post beside the supply trail, Sparks checked on his men and helped organize further efforts to break through. Two companies from the 179th Infantry Regiment arrived and tried later that afternoon of January 18, but both failed to reach his men. The conditions on the ridge were horrific. "The wounded men were put in holes with unwounded men so that they could be cared for properly," recalled Private First Class Benjamin Melton, one of the few remaining men able to stand and fight. "Some were severely wounded and needed tourniquets. We made those out of belts and had to loosen them every thirty minutes. We had no medical supplies, no food and no heat to melt the snow for water."

The SS noose closed still tighter on the Third Battalion, whose plight had not gone unnoticed at the very highest levels in the Third Reich. It was announced in the *Wehrmachtbericht*, an information bulletin issued by the headquarters of the *Wehrmacht*: "*Gebirgsjäger* of the 6th Mountain SS Division 'Nord' have . . . encircled an American battle group and relief attempts have been unsuccessful."

At seven o'clock that evening, the regiment's command post received a pitiful message from L Company, five hundred yards to the east of K Company on the ridge. It was now facing a fourth night of attacks by SS troops. The enemy was so persistent that men dared not nod off even for a few seconds in case they woke to find Germans slitting their throats. The badly wounded could not last much longer without plasma and proper attention.

"Will [medical supplies] get here tonight?" asked a man from L Company.

The reply was brutally honest.

"Impossible to get there."

The following day, January 19, 1945, it also proved impossible. Plans were made to drop supplies by air, and planes were loaded with medicine, rations, and ammunition, but the weather closed in and pilots were forced to sit on the runways, waiting for an opening in the heavy, snow-laden clouds. The break did not arrive.

Meanwhile, the SS continued to tighten the noose.

"We are being attacked," reported one of the decimated companies.

One can only imagine the frustration and heartbreak Sparks felt as hopes of reaching his men began to fade along with the voices of his young officers on the radio. Unlike at Anzio, he could not list every private's name. But he knew all of his five company commanders and his many platoon leaders well. He could vividly imagine their horrific ordeal, having survived the Battle of the Caves.

On January 20, driving sleet mixed with snow made visibility worse. The planned airlift was called off, and yet, despite entreaties over loud-hailers from the Germans that they surrender, Sparks's last men stubbornly held out in the hope of being rescued. On two occasions, a German soldier appeared with a white flag asking for Sparks's men to give up. The German came under fire both times.

Later on the morning of January 20, Richard Baron, who belonged to a machine-gun platoon stranded on the ridge, heard the clanking of tracks and the grinding of gears. German tanks were moving in. The end was near. SS officers under a white flag appeared. A small group of Americans, including Captain Byrd Curtis, the commander of K Company, and the SS officers were soon huddled in the driving snow and sleet discussing terms of surrender. The SS promised Curtis that if he surrendered with his men under a white flag they would be given the best treatment possible.

For a few minutes, Baron and others were able to get out of their holes and stretch stiff limbs. As he stood in the open, trying to keep warm, Baron looked at his fellow survivors. They were shivering, drenched, with hollow eyes and drawn features, every one of them taxed to the very limit of his endurance.

Then came an ultimatum. Two senior German officers, one of them thought to be battalion commander SS *Haupsturmführer* Guenter Degen, demanded the Americans give up by 5 P.M. If not, they would be slaughtered. The SS officers had maps with them and indicated their positions to prove that the Americans were hopelessly surrounded. They again promised they would not mistreat any prisoners, then returned to their positions.

The Thunderbirds on the ridge took a vote. None opted to surrender. The Third Battalion's last able-bodied survivors, around a hundred men, were still determined to hold the ridge. They knew they had not yet been abandoned from radio communication with Sparks.

Rescue efforts continued. The Second Battalion of the 411th Infantry Regiment of the 103rd Infantry Division attacked during a heavy snowstorm. The snow provided cover, but even so, the battalion was cut down. If a force of several hundred men could not get through, there seemed little point in trying to hold the ridge any longer. Despite the fact that it was now far too late, General Frederick finally agreed to pull Sparks's Third Battalion off the ridge.

At 1:30 P.M., Colonel O'Brien ordered the surviving men to try to break out.

At 4:15 P.M., K Company replied: "We are following thru, give us everything you can for the next ten minutes."

The 158th Artillery gladly obliged. It had fired more than five thousand rounds in forty-eight hours. Yet more shells now rained down on the Germans. The barrage was intended to pin down the enemy and surround the survivors from Sparks's battalion with a protective ring of fire, which would shift as the men made their way back to friendly lines. The method had worked with great success the previous month in allowing stranded men in a town called Bundenthal to break out. But that was before winter had truly set in. Now poor visibility and the difficult terrain led to artillery hits on the desperate Americans rather than the Germans surrounding them.

The SS responded with a savage barrage of their own. Forward artillery observers were hidden under rocks on nearby slopes and were, in contrast to the Americans, able to direct fire with pinpoint accuracy. I Company's Private Benjamin Melton saw one of his officers receive a direct hit and simply disappear. Another I Company rifleman, Joe Early, and others made a run for it. "As soon as we got out of our foxholes," he recalled, "they let us have it with mortars, crossfire machine guns. I fortunately got back to my hole and gave up." Other men trying to break out began to throw down their weapons and put their hands in the air.

It was around 4:30 P.M. when K Company on the hill sent a last message. They could not find a way through the German lines. There was nothing more Sparks could do to help them. It was agonizing all the same to learn of his men's final communication. Finally, as dusk fell, the receivers on the stranded battalion's last radios became too weak for men to hear what Sparks or anybody else was saying.

As the SS's 5 P.M. deadline neared, an officer told Private Melton and others in I Company to lay down their guns. Some attached white handkerchiefs to the stocks of their M1s and then stuck them muzzle down into the bloodstained snow. Melton was not one of them. "I was damned if I was gonna stay there," he recalled, "and be killed in cold blood." He joined another private, Walter Bruce, and a third man, and tried to get back to American lines. They had not gone far when a machine gun opened up on them and killed the third man. Melton and Bruce kept running, avoiding paths and trails. They came across some tracks in the snow and followed them. Then they saw a dugout. "We laid low until a GI looked out from beneath it," recalled Melton. "You can imagine how glad we were to see that guy."

Long after dark, at 5:40 P.M., the fortunate pair from I Company arrived at Sparks's command post. They were barely able to stand and were quickly taken to an aid station, suffering from nervous exhaustion. Only they had made it off the hill. Everyone else, as far as they knew, had been captured or killed.

THE SS APPROACHED, aiming machine pistols. The survivors from the Third Battalion put their hands in the air. The first moments of captivity were always the most dangerous. Emotions ran high. The enemy was at its most unpredictable. Dead SS men lay nearby, more than sufficient reason for instant vengeance. Would there be a repeat of the Malmédy massacre on December 17, when more than a hundred American POWs had been slaughtered in cold blood by SS troops? It was anyone's guess.

The SS did not line them up and aim MG42 machine guns at them. Instead, they formed an honor guard as more than four hundred battered and shivering Thunderbirds walked, stumbled, or were carried on litters off the ridge. Twenty-five officers were taken to regimental headquarters and asked to pass through the SS mess tent and share what rations the SS had, a rare honor indeed. "Rumor had it that all the men were handed a box of Scho-Ka-Kola each, a fine gesture by our commander," remembered Johann Voss, "although I heard some grumbling that there weren't any boxes [containing chocolate] left for us."

Sparks's men were not the hopeless half-breeds of Goebbels's propaganda rants. They had fought like lions to the very end. The SS were duly impressed by their "resilience," as Voss put it, during arguably the most heroic last stand by U.S. infantrymen that winter in Europe. Before Sparks's men began their march to the rear as POWs, they were praised by no less than *Generalmajor* Gerhard Franz, commander of the 256th *Volksgrenadier* Division.

Franz stood in his staff car and formally addressed his brave opponents, both officers and men, before they set off on a five-day journey to Stalag 12A. The survivors were put on a train, seventy to a boxcar. They couldn't all lie down at the same time, so they took turns standing and sitting. There was a bucket in the middle of one boxcar for a toilet. It leaked. But few cared. All that mattered was that they were alive, unlike two hundred of their friends whose stiff corpses dotted the ridge. According to SS records, the survivors numbered 456 enlisted men and 26 officers, most of them wounded.

For Johann Voss and his fellow SS, there was no exaltation in victory. They had lost twenty-six comrades. One hundred and twenty-seven were wounded and twelve were listed as missing. Voss felt a deep joy that he had survived but a growing horror as he walked along the silent ridge and saw the devastation, the bodies of dead young Americans, covered in a white shroud of snow. Even though he held little hope of eventual victory in the war, he was proud he and his fellow SS had succeeded in dealing a major setback to the Americans in Operation Northwind, the last great strike at the Allies in the west. He had the satisfaction of knowing his Black Edelweiss regiment had won a battle if not the war.

THE FOLLOWING DAY, January 21, 1945, was the darkest in the Thunderbirds' long and distinguished history. Defeated for the first time, the 157th Infantry Regiment was ordered off the line. The raw facts of the disaster were impossible to accept. Sparks struggled to come to terms with the enormity of the tragedy as snow fell on the fatal ridge above his command post. First at Anzio, now at Reipertswiller, he had lost almost all of his men. "My most tortured memory is of the Battle of Reipertswiller," he would write decades later. "It is still difficult for me to believe that it happened."

On the ridge, the falling snow covered the shell-strewn dugouts where Sparks's men had fought so courageously, the black stains of shell impacts, the smashed trees, and the bundles of two hundred fallen GIs. There was utter quiet. Nothing moved. It was as if the landscape itself were stunned, frozen in mourning.

The wind whipped the snow into a blizzard that hounded what was left of the battered regiment as it fell back to a rest area not far from Reipertswiller. The wind and snow turned to sleet, soaking the men, biting at them, scolding them, taunting them, it seemed. The temperature dropped as the men boarded trucks. Sleet became freezing rain. Roads were soon strips of ice. Thunderbirds cursed as the trucks slipped into ditches. They were moving back, away from the SS, away from death, but for the second time in less than a month they were passing through towns that they had captured with great loss and pain.

The roads grew even icier, the snow deeper, as the remnants of the 157th Infantry Regiment moved to a nearby village called Metting. For the third time since landing in Sicily in 1943, the regiment was then completely reorganized. Over three days, more than a thousand replacements were brought in, including thirty new officers. They were full of questions and energy, a stark contrast to the men who had come down from the mountains utterly exhausted and depressed.

METTING, FRANCE, LATE JANUARY 1945

NOT LONG AFTER the battle, Frederick met with Sparks as he tried to re-form his battalion in the town of Metting. Wracked by survivor's guilt and humiliated by defeat for the first time, Sparks was in no mood to gloss over what had happened at Reipertswiller. He was "hurt badly." Had Frederick given the order to pull back, as had been requested, two hundred of Sparks's men would still be alive. Frederick had made an unforgivable mistake.

They discussed what had happened at Reipertswiller. It was quickly evident that the scale of the loss was too much for Sparks to even begin to absorb: seven company commanders, thirty platoon leaders, and six hundred brave men killed, wounded, or captured. He began to cry, tears streaming down his cheeks. Perhaps Frederick lit the fuse paper. Or maybe Sparks provoked Frederick. What's certain is that Sparks failed to control his anger.

"If I had it to do over," said Sparks, "I'd go against your orders and pull the battalion out while I could."

Frederick lost his temper. Harsh words were exchanged. After a few minutes, he was seen leaving Sparks's command post, visibly angry. Sparks knew he had made an enemy. Generals didn't appreciate being insulted and taken down a peg or two by a lieutenant colonel. But he didn't care. As far as Sparks was concerned, Frederick wasn't "worth a damn."

It was not just Frederick who suffered a tongue-lashing. Sparks also had a confrontation with the assistant division commander, General Paul Adams. And to make matters worse, he did more than show his contempt for his superiors face-to-face. In late January he went an extraordinary step further, formally requesting that the inspector general investigate the division staff's mishandling of the battle, in particular their failure to allow the withdrawal of his troops. It was an astonishing act, as courageous and perhaps foolhardy as anything he had done on the battlefield. Having finally passed the breaking point at Reipertswiller, an utterly drained yet still iron-willed Sparks didn't care if his actions imperiled his chances for promotion or further honors.

There was no excuse for what had happened at Reipertswiller. Other officers in the regiment agreed. Captain Anse Speairs had recently returned from leave in the States to discover that he had lost every man in his company. "Frederick didn't see the situation," he recalled. "Sparks did."

Frederick must have deeply resented Sparks's call for an investigation, though he had little reason to worry about censure, given senior Allied generals' demand during the battle for him to not yield a yard. His reaction to Sparks's request for an investigation was harsh and swift. In a confidential letter, sent from 45th Infantry Division HQ on January 29, only a few days after Sparks had upbraided him in person, he had his revenge, stating that he did not concur with a January 24 recommendation, made by Colonel O'Brien, that a Distinguished Service Cross be awarded to Sparks. "The circumstances surrounding the capture of elements of Lieutenant Colonel Sparks' battalion are now under investigation," wrote Frederick. "The actions for which he is cited . . . are considered to have been the normal actions of any commander in this situation and do not constitute extraordinary heroism for which the Distinguished Service Cross is awarded."

Frederick had nixed Sparks's DSC recommendation, despite three officers' providing evidence of Sparks's extraordinary heroism. But he thrust the knife far deeper by then adding: "He [Sparks] was ordered by his Headquarters to assemble available personnel of his battalion and . . . join his battalion." Frederick's implication was obvious: Sparks had been partly responsible for his men's capture and deaths because he had not been with them when they were surrounded. As a result of Frederick's actions, Sparks would never gain due recognition for his heroism on January 18, when he had saved at least some of his men. Instead, he would receive a silver star in the mail—four years later.

CHAPTER TWENTY

THE RIVER

I do not suppose that at any moment of history has the agony of the world been so great or widespread. Tonight the sun goes down on more suffering than ever before in the world.

—WINSTON CHURCHILL, FEBRUARY 6, 1945, YALTA

GIs take a cigarette break during the fight to break into Nazi Germany. [National Archives]

PARIS, FEBRUARY 1945

THEY WERE GORGEOUS. They wore hats piled high on their heads, like wastebaskets turned upside down and coated with flowers and feathers, black silk stockings provided by their many officer boyfriends working at SHAEF headquarters, and bright dresses they had made from offcut fabric. Despite severe rationing, these chic *midinettes* who worked in the fashion industry mercifully brightened the streets and bars of Paris in the dead of winter. All of Europe was hungry, especially Paris, but the young and old, and above all the *midinettes*, could still find the esprit and energy to fill the *bals publics*, the dance halls, around the Place de Bastille. Their wooden-soled shoes—the Germans had seized all leather stocks during the occupation—sounded like a frenzied clacking after a few glasses of the strong, brassy wine that GIs couldn't get enough of.

Sparks was there that gray February, drowning his sorrows and seeing the sights. Early that month, he had received a seventy-two-hour pass to Paris, where he was able to meet with his brother, Earl, a captain serving in the Army Air Forces. Earl was two years younger and close to Sparks. Before the war, they had spent many a winter's day hunting and laying traps in the desert around Miami, Arizona. Now they went on the prowl for booze and a good time. It was a relief to walk down streets without having to look out for mines. In the American Officers' Club, after enduring months of bowel-blocking field rations, Sparks could gorge on fresh vegetables and T-bone steaks doused in thick gravy.

He wrote his parents that he had managed to "get around to see the Eiffel Tower, Notre Dame Cathedral, Napoleon's Tomb and other places of historical interest." He added that he found Paris "quite interesting," but by now, after almost two years away from home, he was heartily sick of Europe. "To me it was just like any other European city," he continued. "Any American city has it beat a mile."

When Sparks returned from Paris, he resumed his command of the Third Battalion. He had not been demoted or disciplined after confronting his two most senior officers, Adams and Frederick, about the loss of his battalion at Reipertswiller. They needed field commanders like him to finish the war. As Frederick knew only too well after three years in combat, such highly experienced and effective officers, however maverick and insubordinate, were utterly indispensable and increasingly rare.

After the bitter disappointments and setbacks of late 1944, the Allies were now back on the offensive, poised to break deep into Germany once they had crossed the Rhine. The SS had been repelled late that January in the Vosges, Johann Voss's unit and others forced to retreat into the Fatherland along with tens of thousands of their comrades from the Ardennes, where the Allies had also succeeded in regaining lost ground. The battle for Germany was about to begin.

The Thunderbirds would play their part. But first they had to be brought back to full strength. Green officers came in from the States, some were transferred from other units, and Sparks was given just three weeks to reconstitute a battalion of about nine hundred and fifty men. Many of his new lieutenants were ninety-day wonders who had never fired a shot in anger. Because men with at least some combat experience were essential, other divisions in the Seventh Army had been scoured for sergeants to help lead the instant infantry that now replaced Sparks's lost Third Battalion.

Private Dan Dougherty was one of hundreds of young men rushed in from other units to fill the gaping holes in the regiment's ranks. His first sergeant had told him: "Dougherty, you are now a staff sergeant in the 45th Division." There was a jeep waiting and he didn't even get the chance to say good-bye to the men he had known for ten months. Dougherty and the new men constituting Sparks's Third Battalion hoped and prayed they would see out the rest of the war, but they knew the odds of surviving unscathed were slim. Twenty thousand Americans had died in Europe that January—more than in any other month of the war.

There was still no sign of any imminent Nazi collapse. Many more like Dougherty—"reinforcements," as the U.S. Army preferred to call replacements—would be needed before all of Nazi Germany was subdued. In Berlin, Hitler was calling for the *Gauleiters*—regional Nazi Party leaders—to instill in the German people a "Teutonic rage." Only by rising to the challenge of fighting the invaders, he stressed, would the German people discover their true worth. The Führer's implication was clear: If the Germans did not stop the Allied advance, they were not deserving of the Third Reich or of ultimate victory in the great racial struggle that would determine all of Europe's future. Therefore, like all inferior races, they were expendable. "Should the German people give up," Hitler warned, "then this would demonstrate that they had no moral worth, and in that case they would deserve destruction. That would be the rightful judgment of history and providence."

Hitler went further in an angry aside to Albert Speer, his amoral armaments minister, who dared express the hope that some of Germany's industrial base might be saved rather than incinerated. "If the war is lost," snapped Hitler, "the people will be lost also. It is not necessary to worry about what the German people will need for elemental survival. On the contrary, it is best for us to destroy even these things. For the nation has proved to be the weaker, and the future belongs solely to the stronger. In any case only those who are inferior will remain after this struggle, for the good have already been killed."

REMAGEN, GERMANY, MARCH 7, 1945

IT WAS AROUND 4 P.M. when Lieutenant Karl Timmerman and men from the 27th Armored Infantry of the 9th Division reached the approaches to the Ludendorff railway bridge near Remagen, fifty miles east of the French border near Bonn. To their surprise, the Americans saw that the bridge was still standing. Since September 1944, some seven months before, the Allies had been fighting to reach and then cross the river only to be repelled in Holland and stalled all along Germany's borders. Every other bridge across the Rhine had been destroyed. Seizing

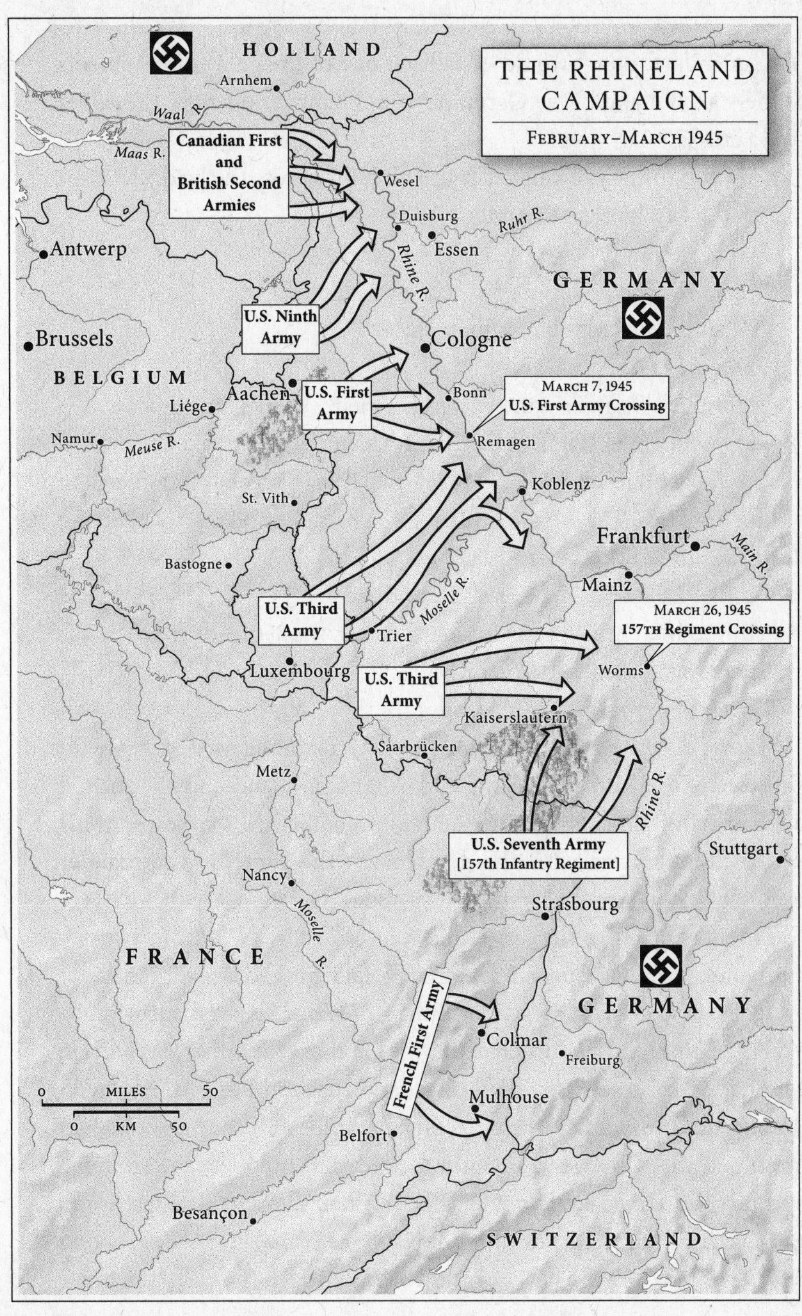
THE RHINELAND CAMPAIGN
FEBRUARY–MARCH 1945
HOLLAND
Arnhem
Waal R.
Maas R.
Canadian First and British Second Armies
Wesel
Duisburg
Ruhr R.
Essen
Antwerp
Rhine R.
GERMANY
U.S. Ninth Army
Brussels
Cologne
BELGIUM
Aachen
U.S. First Army
Bonn
MARCH 7, 1945
U.S. First Army Crossing
Liége
Namur
Meuse R.
Remagen
Koblenz
St. Vith
Frankfurt
Main R.
Bastogne
Mainz
Moselle R.
U.S. Third Army
MARCH 26, 1945
157TH Regiment Crossing
Trier
Worms
Luxembourg
U.S. Third Army
Kaiserslautern
Saarbrücken
Metz
Rhine R.
U.S. Seventh Army
[157th Infantry Regiment]
Stuttgart
Nancy
Strasbourg
Moselle R.
FRANCE
GERMANY
French First Army
Colmar
Freiburg
0 MILES 50
0 KM 50
Mulhouse
Belfort
Besançon
SWITZERLAND

the Ludendorff intact would constitute one of the great achievements of the war. But surely the Germans would blow it up before the Allies could cross?

"Do you think you can get your company across the bridge?" Timmerman's battalion commander asked.

"Well, we can try it, sir."

"Go ahead."

"What if the bridge blows in my face?"

There was no reply.

"All right," Timmerman ordered his men. "We're going across."

Sure enough, as Timmerman and his company neared the bridge, there was a huge explosion. When the debris settled, Timmerman picked himself up and looked through the smoke and dust, expecting the bridge to have collapsed.

"Look," he shouted. "She's still standing."

Timmerman ordered his company across the 350-yard span.

There was some hesitation so he decided to lead the way.

"Get going, you guys, get going."

They got going, dodging holes in the planking that gave awful glimpses of the Rhine's swirling eddies far below, and quickly secured the bridge. When General Omar Bradley contacted Eisenhower at his Reims headquarters with the good news, the supreme commander could barely believe it. "Hold on to it, Brad. Get across with whatever you need—but make sure you hold that bridgehead." Within twenty-four hours, eight thousand Americans had poured across. The first bridgehead on the eastern banks of the Rhine had been established.

Hitler immediately ordered the trial and execution of five officers who had failed to destroy the bridge, and replaced Field Marshal von Rundstedt, commander in chief west, with Albert Kesselring, who had frustrated the Allies so brilliantly in Italy. But not even the supreme optimist Kesselring could hold back the Allied tide. On all sides, as the spring thaw arrived, the enemies of National Socialism were thrusting relentlessly toward the heart of the Third Reich. In the east, a massive

January offensive had been spectacularly successful; more than two million Soviet troops were closing on Berlin itself, less than a hundred miles from the Reichstag. The only hope of prolonging the war for Hitler lay in grinding down the Allies in street fighting in cities designated as fortresses all across what was left of the Third Reich—which he had boasted would last a thousand years.

FEW SOCIETIES IN history have fought to the point of utter destruction. The question that vexed many was why the Germans fought on so fiercely, dying in their thousands each day, even when it was clear that the war was lost. The Allied demand for unconditional surrender may have been a factor, although Churchill himself rejected the notion out of hand—the Allies' conditions for a negotiated surrender, he noted, "looked so terrible when set forth on paper, and so far exceeded what was in fact done, that their publication would have only stimulated German resistance."

Nazi propaganda was not a critical factor either. Highly effective until the cataclysmic defeat at Stalingrad in February 1943, Goebbels's hysterical diatribes swayed only the very young and willfully gullible by spring 1945. "I wish I had a pistol to kill all of you," a captured twelve-year-old Hitler Youth leader, born the year Hitler had taken power, told his American interrogators. "Do not hope ever to eradicate our National Socialist ideals or ideas. There are enough of us left to continue the fight as long as we live."

Nor did Hitler's popularity explain why the Germans kept on fighting. By now, many reviled him. Very few, however, dared openly express their disdain for him and his party, lest they be executed by one of the many roving kangaroo courts, which doled out instant discipline. Some ten thousand Germans would be killed without trial in the last days of the Third Reich. "German soldiers were told to fight, to do their duty," recalled Thunderbird Sergeant Rex Raney, "or they'd be machine gunned in the back. That's why the Germans held out so long: there was a hard core of 'crazy men' that put the fear of God into their countrymen."

At the front lines, many German officers had long since become disillusioned with Hitler's leadership. "Is there nobody there who will restrain the madman and call a halt?" wrote one embittered junior officer on the Western Front. "Are they still generals? No, they are shitbags . . . cowards! Not the ordinary soldier." Cowards indeed. After the July 1944 assassination plot, Hitler had purged Germany of any potentially effective counterforce. There wasn't a single general left who dared question the rush toward Armageddon.

Terror, the central dynamic of Nazism, explained a great deal. Fear of the truly barbaric Soviets, who would rape a woman every three minutes in Vienna and at an even faster rate in Berlin; fear of maniacal Nazis in the SS and the Gestapo; fear of the invader and loss of one's homeland—all were key factors in explaining the scale of the final Götterdämmerung now enveloping the German people from all sides. But not even terror kept so many fighting, with real enthusiasm and skill, when it was clear that all was lost. In the end, it all came down to Hitler. He had diabolically trapped Germans in a vortex of escalating nihilism. So long as he breathed, the rush toward annihilation gathered pace. He was still head of state, the armed forces, the party, the apparatus of terror. Every institution, from the civil service to the judiciary, had been radicalized and brought under his total control. Until his death or capture, there could be no release for the German people. Nor would there be any respite for Felix Sparks and his men.

CHAPTER TWENTY-ONE

THE SIEGFRIED LINE

The famous dragon's teeth of the Siegfried Line. [National Archives]

THE SIEGFRIED LINE, MARCH 15, 1945

NIGHT WAS DAY. Huge batteries of American searchlights shone on the clouds that reflected an eerie glow on the landscape below. They illuminated the dragon's teeth tank traps, the four-foot-thick concrete bunkers, and the faces of frightened young Thunderbirds on the attack once more. Heading back into combat never got any easier, even for veterans like Sparks, who had made the transition from rest to fighting more than twelve times since Sicily.

It was 1 A.M. as Sparks led his battalion from the French border town of Sarreguemines, ten miles due south of the German city of Saarbrücken, toward the much-fabled Siegfried Line, the major bulwark stretching from Switzerland to Holland. He had first set eyes on it the previous December but had been ordered to pull back during Operation Northwind. Now he would have to overcome its formidable defenses, bathed in the eerie reflected light, before pushing on into Germany. In briefings, he had been told it might take several weeks to breach them.

The Siegfried Line's bunkers, numbering some thirty-five hundred, were the key strongpoints. Seizing those in the sector assigned to the Third Battalion was Sparks's immediate objective. It soon proved to be a deadly and laborious process. Air strikes, artillery fire, and blasting with anti-tank guns were effective, but Thunderbirds still had to brave machine-gun and mortar fire to get close enough to aim their M1s at embrasures and drop phosphorous grenades through air vents. Any Germans inside then usually panicked as choking and blinding white smoke filled the bunker. The phosphorous was highly effective. Pellets burrowed into uniforms and then seared through flesh down to the bone.

Flushed from their concrete death traps, the enemy either surrendered or were killed in a hail of machine-gun fire. Others pulled back before they could be cornered, then regrouped and counterattacked. Cranston Rogers, a staff sergeant and platoon guide in G Company, got pinned down during a three-hour firefight when the Germans struck back later that morning of March 15, 1945. Two platoon leaders out of three in his rifle company were killed. Rogers assumed command of one platoon, contacted regimental headquarters, and gave his position. Around 1 P.M., he detected a friendly unit moving toward him. A young officer led the force. He introduced himself as Colonel Felix Sparks. It was the only time in Rogers's 183 days of combat that he witnessed an officer of Sparks's rank at the actual front.

The gains that first day were steady but costly. Thirty pillboxes were taken and the first German defense line had been broken, but five men in Sparks's regiment were killed and more than forty wounded, mostly by artillery fire. The following day was even more deadly, with fifteen men killed. But resistance weakened by the hour and Germans began to give up in droves, more than a hundred and fifty by nightfall. Three hundred surrendered to the regiment two days later, on March 20, when Sparks finally led his Third Battalion through the last of the Siegfried Line's pillboxes and tank traps into open country beyond. "It had taken the enemy nine years to prepare the Siegfried defenses," stated one report. "The 157th and other Seventh Army units over-ran it in less than a week."

THE RHINELAND, MARCH 21, 1945

IT WAS A spectacular advance. Sparks's battalion took to trucks once more and sped toward the mighty Rhine, eighty miles due east through mostly flat farmland. The Thunderbirds were now on Nazi soil. Unlike in France, where their artillery had been careful to avoid civilian casualties, few cared who got hurt so long as the charge into Germany, day and night, did not stall. They could sense that the war was almost at an end. The faster they advanced, the more savage their response to any delay, the more "Krauts" they killed—the better their own odds of survival. "Every time you killed one," recalled Captain Anse Speairs, "you were one step closer to Berlin."

The Allied Air Force had almost complete control of the air, so there was little chance of being strafed by Messerschmitts as the Thunderbird convoy hurtled down main roads. Reconnaissance cars led the way, followed by alert infantrymen wielding bazookas and machine guns, who rode on tank destroyers and Shermans, with Sparks's heavy-weapons company a few hundred yards behind. As soon as reconnaissance cars ran into a roadblock, enemy fire, or snipers in houses, word quickly passed down the line and the tank destroyers and tanks blasted the resistance mercilessly. Then men remounted their vehicles, reloaded, and rolled on once more.

Wednesday, March 21, was officially the first day of spring. Spirits soared as the Thunderbirds roared through quiet villages and towns where crocuses and daffodils bloomed and a ragtag group of defenders chose to surrender rather than fight on. "Straggling Germans, still wearing their grey-green uniforms and surrender caps," recalled one Thunderbird, "wandered aimlessly about, watching in dazed amazement the flood of troops, supplies and equipment sweeping past them toward the west bank of the Rhine River." In some homes that flew white flags, locals huddled close to their radios, hoping the Americans would quickly pass by, and listened between newscasts to the latest hit song: "This Will Be a Spring Without End."

Sparks's first command post beyond the Siegfried Line was in Homburg, thirty miles inside Germany and sixty from the Rhine. Fires had consumed much of the city and corpses lay in every ruined street. Traumatized young German women begged for food and offered themselves in exchange. "For an extra bar of chocolate I could have had her mother too!" boasted one soldier.

"It is difficult to describe the devastation which [air strikes] have wrought," General Frederick wrote from his command post in the shattered Homburger Hotel. "So intense has been the attack that scarcely a man-made thing exists: it is even difficult to find buildings suitable for command posts. This is the scorched earth."

OPPENHEIM, GERMANY, MARCH 24, 1945

BENEATH CLEAR SKIES, General George S. Patton walked, head held high, onto a pontoon bridge across the Rhine near Oppenheim. The incomparable Napoleon, whom Patton idolized, had once crossed the river just a few miles away.

Patton was in an ebullient mood. Two days earlier, his Third Army had beaten Bernard Montgomery's forces to the river by a matter of hours. He had outmaneuvered the "little fart" yet again.

Patton sauntered with his senior aides toward the middle of the Rhine. "Time out for a short halt," he said.

Patton grinned as he strolled to the edge of the pontoon bridge, undid his fly, and urinated into the river. He turned toward his aides, doing up his fly, and said: "I have been looking forward to this for a long time."

On the eastern bank of the river, in imitation of William the Conqueror, he knelt down, scooped up two fistfuls of Nazi soil, and then let it fall through his fingers.

"Thus, William the Conqueror!"

JUST AFTER MIDNIGHT two days later, the Thunderbirds' 179th and 180th infantry regiments began to cross the Rhine in boats. There was no supporting artillery barrage in the hopes of surprising German defenders on the eastern bank. It proved a costly mistake. Men were greeted by intense machine-gun fire, with the 180th losing half the boats in its second and third waves. But there was now no stopping the Americans—those who made it across the river sprinted for cover, fixed bayonets, and then quickly stormed the German positions.

Sparks's Third Battalion crossed on March 26 near the cathedral city of Worms and met comparatively little resistance. Many were disappointed when they finally saw the fabled river that had held up the Allied advance since Montgomery's disastrous attempt to cross it at Arnhem in Holland the previous September. "It was small compared to the Hudson," recalled Private First Class Vincent Presutti of M Company. "Nonetheless it was no picnic because we had no cover as we crossed."

"Call that thing a river?" said one Thunderbird seated in the back of a truck. "Why, we've got mill streams bigger than that back home."

Beyond the river, the advance once again gathered pace. Sparks knew the war would not last much longer, perhaps a month at most. The last great obstacles blocking the path to victory had been crossed. The grass was turning green. Each day was warmer than the last. Men no longer huddled together in foxholes at night to stay warm. The worst was surely over. There was even time, as Sparks passed through villages and towns that had hastily surrendered, to collect a few spoils of war. Nazi flags were popular items, but the most sought after were weapons, and in particular daggers, especially those belonging to the SS. One day, he found a black SS jacket with a single bullet hole in the chest over the heart, complete with lurid red armband, and an SS dagger with a double-edged blade that had an officer's name inscribed on it.

On March 27, as Sparks pressed toward the river Main, forty miles to the southeast of Worms, he received new orders. He was to take his Third Battalion and cross the river at Aschaffenburg. The city had already been cleared by elements of Patton's Third Army. It would be a simple, routine mission, another day's easy rolling past white sheets dangling from yet more windows. The remainder of the Thunderbirds would soon follow.

By nightfall on March 27, Sparks had reached the western bank of the Main. His men dug in for the night. At around 9:30 P.M., they heard the unsettling sound of women screaming. Somewhere on the eastern bank of the river, Germans were playing at psychological warfare. Loudspeakers blared *"Achtung, Achtung"* as the piercing screams continued.

Most of Sparks's men paid little or no attention to the eerie wails. They had become indifferent to the increasingly pathetic German attempts to unnerve them. Indeed, the "Krauts" were simply up to their usual tricks again. Few if any asked themselves why the Germans would try to intimidate them if Patton's Third Army had already cleared the area—what would be the point?

A FEW MILES to the east that night, in a fortified command post at the center of Aschaffenburg, a gray-haired and bespectacled Major von Lamberth issued crisp orders and waited, confident he had done all he could to turn Aschaffenburg into a death trap. Hours earlier, he had issued a proclamation:

SOLDIERS, MEN OF THE *WEHRMACHT*, COMRADES—THE FORTRESS OF ASCHAFFENBURG WILL BE DEFENDED TO THE LAST MAN. AS LONG AS THE ENEMY GIVES US TIME WE WILL PREPARE AND EMPLOY OUR TROOPS TO OUR BEST ADVANTAGE. THIS MEANS . . . FIGHT! ERECT DUGOUTS! MAKE BARRIERS! GET SUPPLIES! AND WIN! . . . AS OF TODAY, EVERYONE IS TO GIVE TO HIS LAST. I ORDER THAT NO ONE SHALL REST MORE THAN THREE HOURS OUT OF TWENTY. I FORBID ANY SITTING AROUND OR LOAFING. OUR BELIEF IS THAT IT IS OUR MISSION TO GIVE THE CURSED ENEMY THE GREATEST RESISTANCE AND TO SEND AS MANY AS POSSIBLE OF THEM TO THE DEVIL.

Lamberth was a formidable foe, chosen by the German high command to lead the defense of the city because he was deemed most capable, even though several of his fellow officers outranked him. His resolve had only increased when he saw a message from the Supreme Command of the German Armed Forces in the west. It instructed him and his men to fight to the last bullet. He had fought in World War I, on the Eastern Front, and was determined to do precisely as ordered: kill as many Americans as he possibly could.

Concrete bunkers and pillboxes had been heavily fortified, mines laid in all critical areas, and buildings strewn with countless booby traps. But it had been the troops' psyches that Lamberth had taken most care to bolster, bearing in mind Napoleon's dictum that the "moral is to the physical as three is to one." To ensure loyalty and obedience in the ranks—*pour encourager les autres*—Lamberth even had a man hanged in public, a lieutenant called Friedl Heymann, a highly decorated combat veteran who had been recovering from serious wounds in the city. When Heymann had not joined a reserve unit as ordered, Lamberth's men had seized him from the home he shared with his young wife, whom he had recently married. He was quickly tried, convicted of "*Fahnenflucht*"—"fleeing the flag"—and then executed in a public square on Lamberth's orders.

A sign was attached to Heymann's dangling corpse: DEATH TO ALL TRAITORS.

CHAPTER TWENTY-TWO

CASSINO ON THE MAIN

Icy-eyed GI's darted through the flaming streets, killing the vicious German troops like mad dogs.

—PAUL HOLLISTER, "THUNDERBIRDS OF THE ETO," IN OLECK, ED., *EYE WITNESS WORLD WAR II BATTLES*

Thunderbirds fight through the ruins of Aschaffenburg, Germany, March 1945. [National Archives]

ASCHAFFENBURG, GERMANY, MARCH 28, 1945

THE THIRD BATTALION BOARDED trucks and was driven toward Aschaffenburg, with Sparks following in his jeep. After two hours, the convoy neared the Nilkheim railway bridge across the Main. At a ridgeline, Sparks stopped the trucks. He wanted to take a good look at Aschaffenburg, lying below him on the eastern banks of the river.

The city rested on a bluff some forty miles upriver from Frankfurt. Forested foothills of the Spessart Mountains rose to the north, east, and south. Through his field glasses, Sparks could make out two main landmarks: the Schloss Joahnnesburg, a seventeenth-century castle, and the tenth-century Stiftskirche, a Roman Catholic basilica that sat atop the city's highest point, the Dahlberg. To his surprise, he could not see any American troops in the city. There was no movement at all.

Something's wrong. If the Third Army took that place, there should be some Third Army troops.

He looked down again at the railroad bridge. All was quiet. There was no sign of the enemy. The bridge had been covered with planks to allow troops across. But he felt uneasy all the same. He ordered his men off the trucks and then reconnoitered ahead on foot with his runner Johnson and a few other men until he got to within a mile of the bridge. Again the area was deserted. Around 2 P.M., Sparks ordered a platoon of around forty men to cross the bridge. The silence continued until a full company of two hundred had crossed the bridge and begun to move into streets on the eastern side. Then Sparks heard the unmistakable sounds of German small-arms fire and mortars in the distance. His men scattered, looking for shelter.

What the goddamn hell?

Sparks was furious. He had been told that Patton's Third Army had secured the city. Clearly, that was not the case. Fearing a German counterattack, he ordered his three companies to set up defensive positions across the bridge, on the eastern bank of the Main, in the outskirts of the city that had supposedly been made safe. As his men set up machine-gun positions and mortars, Sparks made contact with a reconnaissance troop of around a hundred men from the 4th Armored Division, which belonged to Patton's Third Army. They were dug in near the bank of the river, upstream from the bridge, and led by a young captain.

"Colonel," said the captain, "I'm glad to see you."

"What's going on here?"

"Well, Colonel, there's a hell of a lot of Germans still here. German civilians tell us there's at least five thousand."

Five thousand?

That was five times the strength of Sparks's battalion. Most of his privates were replacements, and all of his men were less than eager to engage the enemy in fierce close combat, especially so near to the end of the war. In recent weeks they had encountered far more civilians waving white flags than they had enemy soldiers with guns. Indeed, they had assumed the war was all but over.

The captain gathered his men and prepared to leave. He clearly had no stomach for the fierce fighting he knew lay ahead.

"I was ordered to stay here until relieved and guard the bridge," he explained to Sparks.

"I guess you're relieved," said a caustic Sparks.

Sparks then radioed back to the division.

"There's no way I can take this area with one battalion."

Sparks was told that the rest of the regiment would arrive the next morning. He was to hold his position through the night.

As dusk settled, there was considerable bitterness among Sparks's men. They felt they had been cruelly deceived. Yet again, they had been given the rough end of the deal. It was supposed to have been a SNAFU (Situation Normal, All Fucked Up) as GI slang had it, not a FUBAR (Fucked Up Beyond All Recognition). Elements of the 4th Armored, Task Force Baum, had in fact passed through the area but had not stopped to secure it. Instead they had been bound for Hammelburg prison camp, some seventy miles away, on a highly secretive mission to free George Patton's son-in-law, Colonel John Waters, who had been captured in Tunisia in February 1943. The foolhardy rescue attempt, ordered by a reckless Patton, would fail catastrophically within a matter of hours, with all but fifteen of the three-hundred-man force captured, killed, or wounded. From start to finish, the whole exercise was a tragic fiasco. The suicidal "Hammelburg Raid," as it was called, was far less forgivable than slapping shell-shocked GIs. It would certainly have cost Patton his career had it not been quickly covered up and its survivors sworn to silence.

The city had not been taken—far from it. Task Force Baum had passed by in the night but had not gone unnoticed. *Festung Aschaffenburg* (Fortress Aschaffenburg), like a hornet's nest, had merely been tapped unnecessarily with a flimsy stick. Now Lamberth's most fanatical troops were stirring.

There was, however, some good news that evening. Captain Anse Speairs, the regimental adjutant, had made an extraordinary discovery a few miles from the Nilkheim Bridge: a huge warehouse of more than a million bottles of fine wine and liquor that had been seized from all over occupied France. He returned to the regiment's mobile headquarters—where the staff was preparing to reinforce Third Battalion the following morning—with a jeep loaded with twenty-three cases of the finest French brandy he had ever seen. Soon, every available truck in the regiment was dispatched to the warehouse to liberate more cases of brandy, at least 640 cases of vintage wine, as well as countless other bottles of assorted liquor and champagne.

"You've got a problem," Speairs told regimental commander Colonel O'Brien. "Do you want the wine or the cognac?"

There was only so much room in O'Brien's trailer. He couldn't take it all.

"Let's get rid of the wine."

What O'Brien couldn't take was quickly shared throughout the regiment that night. One battalion issued twenty-six cases of brandy to each company—more than one bottle to each Thunderbird. Ever inventive, a thirsty GI quickly devised a potent new cocktail, the soon-to-be-famous

"157th Zombie," consisting of cognac, Bénédictine, and Cointreau; most men agreed it was best followed by a champagne chaser. It would be several days before some canteens actually carried water rather than wine.

If it was Dutch courage the Thunderbirds needed, they now had plenty of it. In a supply run, cases of booze were apparently delivered to the Third Battalion that night as it guarded the Nilkheim Bridge. The uneasy silence was split not by machine-gun fire but by the sound of popping champagne corks. Some Thunderbirds got blind drunk, but others opted to stay sober, anxiously awaiting the dawn. They didn't want to have to fight the Germans with a hangover.

Cranston Rogers in G Company was ordered to take his platoon and cover the railroad bridge's southern approach that night. In his entire six months in combat, he had never been so scared. According to his company commander, a division of German troops, more than ten thousand men, was gathering a few miles away before heading to retake the bridge. Sparks and his battalion would be outnumbered ten to one.

ASCHAFFENBURG, GERMANY, MARCH 29, 1945

IT WAS A relief to see the trucks cross the Nilkheim Bridge at first light, and Thunderbirds from the regiment's First and Second Battalions form into squads and platoons. As promised, the rest of the regiment had arrived. After a sleepless night, Cranston Rogers, the platoon guide in G Company, was equally relieved that the story about the German division coming to attack in the night had turned out to be a false alarm.

In almost five hundred days of combat, the Thunderbirds had not been ordered to clear a heavily defended urban area. Doing so was always costly, for it meant engaging the enemy at close quarters by clearing houses room by room. Resentful Thunderbirds from all three of the regiment's battalions now prepared for the worst. Officers checked their pistols. Rifle squads armed themselves with extra grenades, sharpened knives, grabbed crowbars and axes for breaking through doors, and organized themselves into "search groups" of up to six men. One or two men in each group would enter a building first, covered by the others, and then try to kill any defenders without being hit first.

Having come so far, it was agonizing for Sparks to have to commit his men to a form of attrition that made no strategic sense whatsoever—the German high command had nothing to gain from Aschaffenburg's defense. That morning, under a murky sky, his battalion made very slow progress. By lunchtime, the advance had become infuriatingly costly and tough going. It seemed as if snipers' crosshairs covered every open window and rubble-strewn crossroads. To his shock, Sparks learned that in the suburb of Schweinheim, Company L had attacked across open fields and lost all of its officers in just five minutes. Not since Anzio had so many men fallen so fast, more than fifty wounded from the regiment in only a few hours. By late afternoon, his entire battalion had stalled. He ordered his men to dig in while the 158th Artillery tried to soften up defenses.

That evening, unsettling rumors began to spread that some civilians were fighting alongside the uniformed German defenders. According to one report, young girls were hurling grenades from roofs, and wounded soldiers from a military hospital had even joined the fray, egged on by both Major von Lamberth and a local Nazi Party ideologue, *Kreisleiter* Wohlgemuth, who had recently issued a proclamation: "Whoever remains in the city belongs to a battle group which will not know any selfishness, but will know only the unlimited hatred for this cursed enemy of ours."

"*Nun Volk steh auf und Sturm brich los!*" declared Aschaffenburg's most fanatical defenders. "Now the people stand up and the storm breaks loose!"

FESTUNG ASCHAFFENBURG (FORTRESS ASCHAFFENBURG), GERMANY, MARCH 30, 1945

THEY ATTACKED AGAIN at dawn—all three battalions in the regiment. "It was tough, tough, tough, tough," recalled Sparks. It appeared that Germans were hidden behind every window and door. He could not use artillery in some areas because his men were often just yards from the enemy. In some rooms, they were only inches away from Hitler's last stalwarts, forced to kill or be killed with daggers and pistols. At one point, his men came under fire from one of their own tanks that had been captured and hastily repainted and identified with the German white cross. Sparks ordered his accompanying tank destroyers to eliminate the seized Sherman. They did so, but not long after, the leader of the tank destroyer platoon and Sparks's operations officer were both hit and had to be taken back to an aid station, joining fifty-nine other men from the regiment wounded that day.

Later that afternoon, Sparks went in search of somewhere to set up a command post. Karl Mann sat in the back of a jeep with Sparks's runner Johnson, behind Turk and Sparks, as they reconnoitered a deserted street. At a crossroads, Turk stopped close to a Sherman tank and Sparks spoke with its crew. Soon after, recalled Mann, Sparks found a cute little dog in a deserted house nearby and decided to keep it. They then returned to the crossroads. In their absence, the Germans had shelled it and several of the tank crew had been wounded. Mann wondered what might have happened had they stayed just a few minutes longer at that crossroads.

As night fell, the costs of securing *Festung Aschaffenburg* became depressingly clear: The regiment's aid station recorded its highest daily casualty count so far. From the top to the bottom of the division, frustration and a hardening anger set in. The only good news that night for some officers was that Captain Anse Speairs, whose job it was to scout out potential command posts, had yet again found a safe and comfortable headquarters for the regiment—a hotel that had been abandoned in a rush by the pregnant wives and girlfriends of SS troops. "There was a good supply of baby bottles and nipples," recalled Speairs, "some Swiss chocolate and the bar still had beer on tap."

Meanwhile, the Germans tried to cut off the American forces by destroying the Nilkheim Bridge across the river Main. Two of the world's first combat fighter jets—formidable Me-262s*—attacked the bridge but failed to destroy it. German Navy frogmen also attempted to blow it up by placing a torpedo against its sandstone center support, but they were spotted by sentries as they floated down the river toward the bridge. Mortars opened up and one round landed among the four intrepid frogmen, detonating the mine they were carrying and killing them all.

ASCHAFFENBURG, GERMANY, MARCH 31, 1945

BY DAYLIGHT, THE entire division had been committed to the battle—three regiments numbering over five thousand riflemen. Yet casualties continued to mount. Sparks ordered his men to employ direct fire from heavy-caliber weapons as they tried to clear out German positions. Every mobile piece available was quickly deployed. The M36 tank destroyer had a highly effective 90mm gun and proved particularly effective, as did the M4A3 tank with its 76mm gun. Sparks watched as these vehicles blasted away, often at point-blank range. Then Thunderbirds stormed the positions. The Germans answered round for round, landing hundreds of mortars on Sparks's battalion. In one fifteen-minute spell, more than two hundred rounds fell on his men, one every five seconds, sounding like a vicious hailstorm.

As far as Captain Anse Speairs at regimental headquarters was concerned, it was time to offer an ultimatum to the Germans in the hope of saving lives. He suggested to regimental commander Colonel O'Brien that he drop on the town from a plane some leaflets demanding surren-

*The Me-262 could fly at 528 mph—ninety more than any Allied plane in the ETO.

der or else the city would be completely flattened. Speairs finally managed to get approval at division level.

That afternoon, he found himself sitting in a Piper Cub spotter plane above the city.

Speairs opened a window and dropped two hundred leaflets on the Germans. "Your situation is hopeless," read the handfuls of mimeographed leaflets, addressed politely to The Commandant of the City of Aschaffenburg. "Our superiority in men and material is overpowering. You are offered herewith the opportunity, by accepting unconditional surrender, to save the lives of countless civilians. . . . Should you refuse to accept these conditions, we shall be forced to level Aschaffenburg."

Lamberth ignored the offer.

Sparks's men reached the strongest points of resistance by late that afternoon, penetrating as far as the artillery barracks, the *Artillerie Kaserne*, in central Aschaffenburg. By nightfall, they had split the city in two but were struggling to hold their gains because of German infiltration. Snipers would crawl through rubble and sewers into buildings that had been cleared by Sparks's men and then open fire on them from behind.

Mopping up such resistance usually meant sudden death for either an American or a German. Thunderbirds kicked in doors, lobbed in grenades, ran inside to see who was still alive, who wanted to surrender, and who wanted to die. Then they yelled upstairs for others to come down and give up. If nobody answered, they had to creep upstairs to check, hoping there weren't more Germans waiting with grenades in a bedroom or the toilet.

When running from one house to another, or across a street, it was safest to do so in squads, each man a few yards from the next. Snipers didn't usually fire at groups, preferring the lone soldier. Squads had a tendency, if they lost a man, to hunt down the sniper with a vengeance. As was the case throughout Germany that spring, not many snipers, recognizable by the bruises on their faces from a rifle's recoil, were taken alive.

Just like killing, surviving this kind of warfare required one to act counterintuitively. When bullets started buzzing past, Sparks's men instinctively wanted to drop their heads and kiss the rubble. But if they all did so and then clustered, they provided an ideal target, especially to an MG42 machine gunner. The experienced men knew they should always hold their heads up with their eyes open and stay on the attack. It was the best way to stay alive.

In some streets, recalled First Sergeant Cranston "Chan" Rogers, the G Company platoon guide, he had to fight against a curtain of small-arms fire. It was the utter randomness of the killing—the feeling it induced that any man could die unfairly at any second—that would still haunt him many years later. Ordered by his company commander to take a schoolhouse, Rogers joined a young lieutenant and others from his platoon in a frontal assault on the schoolhouse held by a hundred Germans.

"Let's go," ordered the lieutenant.

Rogers scrambled up a pile of rubble. He stumbled and fell flat on his face. His helmet came off as he dropped his rifle. He was stunned for a moment. The lieutenant and his runner kept going. They were both cut down by a machine gun and killed. Had he not stumbled, Rogers too would have been dead.

The fighting only intensified as the Thunderbirds tried to eliminate German strongholds in the center of the city. In the Bois-Brule Barracks on Würzburger Strasse, Sparks's men wounded or killed every German defender. Unprecedented quantities of white phosphorous were fired into cellars to smoke the enemy out. Explosions ripped at the eardrums every few seconds, the constant barrage sounding to stunned defenders as if a gigantic machine gun had opened up on them. Any building or high point in the city from which German fire could be directed was quickly destroyed, including the Roman Catholic basilica's steeple, the highest point in the city, which was demolished by twenty-five artillery rounds. Nothing was sacred. Only God knew when it would end.

Lieutenant Van T. Barfoot (right) near Epinal, France, after receiving the Medal of Honor, September 28, 1944. [National Archives]

(left) Lieutenant Earl Railsback, one of Sparks's finest young officers, killed in the Vosges, fall 1944. [National Archives]

(center) Karl Mann, Sparks's German-born interpreter. [Courtesy of Karl Mann]

(right) Johann Voss, SS Black Edelweiss machine gun squad leader. [Courtesy of Johann Voss]

(top) Medics take a German prisoner (left) and an American to an aid station near Aschaffenburg, March 31, 1945. [National Archives]

(bottom) Tanks attached to 157th Infantry Regiment clear buildings of snipers in Aschaffenburg. [National Archives]

(top) Barricades created by Germans in Aschaffenburg, March 1945. [National Archives]

(bottom) German civilians flee their homes, which have been set on fire by Thunderbird tanks trying to eliminate snipers in Aschaffenburg, March 28, 1945. [National Archives]

American tanks roll through ruins of Nuremberg, April 20, 1945. [National Archives]

German troops captured in Nuremberg, April 20, 1945. [National Archives]

American tanks take to one of Hitler's famous autobahns, April 1945. [National Archives]

Thunderbirds from 157th Infantry Regiment cross the Danube on April 26, 1945. [National Archives]

The infamous "death train" containing about 2,000 dead people, which Sparks and his men discovered near the entrance to Dachau on April 29, 1945. [National Archives]

Sparks's men in I Company run toward the shelter of woods near the entrance to Dachau, April 29, 1945. [National Archives]

Entrance to the Dachau complex, shortly after liberation. [National Archives]

Dachau inmates assault an SS guard in the coal yard on April 29, 1945. [National Archives]

GIs inspect boxcars at Dachau shortly after liberation. [National Archives]

Sparks's men rounding up German soldiers in Dachau. [National Archives]

SS guards killed by American liberators lie beside a guard tower at Dachau concentration camp. [National Archives]

Robert Frederick, 45th Division commander (center), arrives at Dachau, the afternoon of April 29, 1945. [National Archives]

Robert Frederick being shown the crematorium at Dachau by an inmate. [National Archives]

Three of 32,000 inmates liberated from Dachau, photographed on April 30, 1945. [National Archives]

Sparks's 157th Infantry regiment comes to attention in Munich for decoration ceremonies, May 24, 1945. [National Archives]

Felix Sparks, commanding general, Colorado National Guard, 1960s. [Courtesy of the Sparks family]

ASCHAFFENBURG, GERMANY, EASTER SUNDAY, APRIL 1, 1945

THE LOW-LYING CLOUD above Aschaffenburg cleared on the fourth day of the battle, April 1, 1945, and an increasingly frustrated General Frederick was able to call in air support. A P-47 fighter-bomber squadron attacked using .50-caliber ammunition because of fears that bombing might kill Americans below in the burning and shattered city. But the strafing runs were ineffective, and so the P-47s were instructed to bomb specific targets such as the Gestapo headquarters. Fighter-bombers were soon flouting curtains of 20mm anti-aircraft flak and striking all across the city where resistance was strongest.

Around a thousand Germans kept on fighting. Lamberth's overall strategy—*Auftragstaktik*—to hold off the Americans for as long as possible was proving agonizingly effective. Then, for the first time in Europe in World War II, it was reportedly decided to use napalm on a civilian area. The napalm, essentially jellied petroleum, added a particularly deadly fuel to flames that engulfed more and more of the city.

The air strikes seemed to make no difference, nor did the napalm, the phosphorous that burned to the bone, the tons of high explosives, the thousands of artillery rounds aimed at strongpoints each day. Still the Nazis held out. So stubborn in fact was the resistance that Allied Supreme Command even considered issuing a directive, eerily like Lamberth's, that any German civilian would be shot without trial on the spot if found bearing arms.

Four times that Easter Sunday, Lamberth's fanatics were dislodged from their hiding places in ruins yet managed to creep back through sewers and the skeletons of buildings into Thunderbird positions in the town's center and inflict casualties. Aschaffenburg was indeed what one newspaper described as a "half-destroyed city of death."

"Hate is our prayer," announced *Deutschlander* radio in a national broadcast that day. "Revenge is our battle cry."

LAMBERTH AND HIS men clearly still possessed the energy and obedience that had made the Wehrmacht so hard to destroy, from Sicily to Anzio, from the Vosges to the river Main. But they were not, after all, Supermen. Finally, that evening, facing another long night of close combat and relentless shelling, cornered in hopeless positions, low on ammunition and out of water, some of the defenders began to surrender.

Sparks was surprised how old some of Lamberth's warriors were: over fifty in some cases. The German Army was clearly running low on manpower, however fanatical its resistance. Others who wandered toward the Thunderbirds' lines in tearful dazes, arms above their dirty faces, wore uniforms several sizes too big. They were mere boys, yet to grow stubble or taste alcohol. That March of 1945, sixty thousand German sixteen- and seventeen-year-olds were sent into battle, often with just a few days' training.

Late on Easter Sunday, Sparks reached Aschaffenburg's central square. A gruesome scene awaited him. Two German soldiers, executed on Lamberth's orders, had been hanged from a gallows with signs pinned on each of them: THIS IS THE REWARD FOR COWARDS.

WORN DOWN BY the constant shelling, hundreds more Germans began to throw down their weapons and wave white flags. The most eager to escape the American onslaught were traumatized women and children, some three thousand of whom still remained in the shattered city, cowering in cellars and bomb shelters.

As the Thunderbirds closed on the last SS holdouts in the city, many civilians tried to break out of *Festung Aschaffenburg*, much to the displeasure of the more fanatical defenders. One young Thunderbird,

Harry Eisner, caught sight of a crowd of around a hundred moving toward him. Some were walking and others running. Then he heard rifle shots and saw civilians fall dead, fired upon by their own countrymen. Others kept on, walking and running, undeterred.

Eisner spotted a pretty schoolgirl. Her pale arms were folded tightly across her stomach. Her socks drooped around her ankles. She had an ashen face.

She was a laughing child once.

The girl looked so terribly sad. Eisner would never forget that she wore a faded blue dress and had a pigtail. Soon, she stood right in front of him and he saw a thin red line across her stomach. He realized that she was bleeding. He tried to move her arms from her stomach. She resisted, keeping them firmly in place. He opened the collar of her dress and saw that she had been badly wounded. Her arms were all that were keeping her from being disemboweled.

Eisner picked her up and held her tenderly. He was determined to save her. He no longer felt tired. Adrenaline coursed through him as he turned to other Thunderbirds for help. They too were galvanized by the girl's plight and were soon clearing the nearby road so that a medic in a jeep could get to her. Killing Krauts did not matter now. All that counted was saving this one child, preserving a life rather than taking one. Finally, the medic arrived. Eisner felt his heart pounding as the medic tended to the child, injecting her with fluid. She still had her eyes open. Their steady gaze never left Eisner as the medic carried her to the jeep and then placed her gently in it. She kept looking at Eisner, even as the jeep pulled away.

ASCHAFFENBURG, GERMANY, APRIL 3, 1945

THE THUNDERBIRD WAS with a German captain when he arrived at Colonel O'Brien's command post. He had been captured in fierce combat and had been allowed to return to his own lines with the German, who bore a note from Aschaffenburg's military commander. It was excellent news: Lamberth was finally prepared to surrender if the Americans would send someone to his headquarters to negotiate terms.

Colonel O'Brien was, however, in no mood to negotiate and refused Lamberth's offer. Instead, he told the German officer to tell Lamberth to surrender at once or air strikes would intensify and the entire city center, as well as its outskirts, would be pulverized. There would be unconditional surrender or total destruction, consistent with the broader Allied approach in subjugating Nazi Germany.

A brave German-speaking American lieutenant accompanied Lamberth's officer back to the German headquarters. Thankfully, Lamberth agreed to O'Brien's demand, but he would not himself surrender to a mere lieutenant. Sparks was the most senior officer available in the vicinity of the Old City where von Lamberth was holed up, and so he was instructed to take Lamberth's surrender in person.

Sparks, his interpreter Karl Mann, and his runner Johnson arrived at Lamberth's headquarters later that morning. Lamberth emerged, holding his pistol belt and holster in one hand. With the other, he saluted Sparks before handing over his gun. Then he ordered all of his fellow officers to give up. Soon, they had all dropped their pistols at Sparks's feet. To the end of his life, Sparks would prize Lamberth's Luger.

Sparks knew Germans were still holding out in several places. So he turned to Karl Mann, his interpreter.

"Tell the major he's got to go with me," said Sparks. "We're going to all these remaining strong points."

Lamberth rode on the hood of the jeep, holding a bullhorn, and ordered his men to give up. His defense of the city had been totally pointless. Sparks had only contempt for him. His devotion to Hitler had cost thousands of lives and reduced a beautiful, ancient city to a vast field of rubble. He had executed honorable men for suggesting surrender, and yet here he was, walking from one shattered building to another, holding a white flag, ordering boys and old men to lay down their weapons.

At last, silence descended on *Festung Aschaffenburg*. When the last

Germans had given up, Sparks turned Lamberth over to officers who took him back across the river Main, where he formally surrendered to Colonel O'Brien. I Company medic Robert Franklin watched as other Germans were escorted from strongpoints to be processed into POW camps, the so-called cages, which now swelled throughout Germany with hundreds of thousands of vanquished Nazis. Even in defeat, some were full of spit and vinegar, astonishingly arrogant. Franklin saw a German officer marching alongside his captured men, shouting abuse at an American officer. The American walked over to the German and kicked him hard in the backside. The German looked humiliated and fell silent.

Then the looting began. Some Thunderbirds smashed windows of a jewelry store and pocketed everything in display cabinets. Franklin also saw men from his own I Company, now commanded by a Lieutenant Bill Walsh, enter a German headquarters and break into a safe containing a large amount of German payroll. One of the thieves handed Franklin a handful of several hundred thousand marks. Franklin gave most of the banknotes to other men in his unit as souvenirs, not realizing that the money could actually be used. "Had I known it was good," he recalled, "I would have bought some hotels and cafes and other property in Aschaffenburg."

In the defense of Aschaffenburg, the Germans had suffered more than 5,000 casualties. At least 1,000 were killed. It was a heavy price to pay for useless ground, but a mere fraction of the 284,000 fatalities suffered by the German armed forces that March of 1945. The regiment had lost 200 men, 90 from Sparks's battalion alone. Eleven officers had been killed.

Lamberth's fanatical resistance had shocked not only the Thunderbirds but also the American high command. No less than secretary of war Henry L. Stimson had learned of the intensity of the siege and soon told reporters: "Nazi fanatics used the visible threat of two hangings to compel German soldiers and civilians to fight for a week." Such behavior meant he must now make it clear to the German people that their "only choice is immediate surrender or the destruction of the Reich city by city."

SOUTHERN GERMANY, APRIL 4, 1945

IT WAS BEHIND him now, the "Cassino on the Main," its smoldering ruins and fires receding into the distance. Sparks pressed on, heading south toward Bavaria, the birthplace of Nazism. Shaken by the fanatical resistance in Aschaffenburg, some of his men riding in trucks believed rumors of a Nazi suicide mission to stall the advance once more. Thankfully, the counterattack failed to materialize and the Thunderbird caravan rolled on, smashing through "sixty-one minute" barricades hastily placed in streets by the increasingly pathetic *Volksturm* and other half-hearted resisters. "Sixty minutes to build them," Thunderbirds joked, "and one minute to knock 'em down!"

In the savage close combat at Aschaffenburg, many of the men had passed a point of no return. "I didn't feel sorry for any Germans after Aschaffenburg," recalled Sergeant Rex Raney, who had fought all the way from Sicily. "When women and kids hold you off, war takes on a different atmosphere." Raney had accidentally stepped on part of a blown-up German soldier in the city and tried everything to clean his boots but wasn't able to get rid of the stench of death, even though his sense of smell had been severely impaired at Anzio. "My boots stunk so bad—death walked with me for about five days before I got a new pair. I left the old ones for some Frenchman."

The Thunderbird convoy built up speed as it made toward the Danube River. Spirits rose. The confidence of conquerors returned. Men pulled out bottles and began to drink. There had been little time to savor the wonders of France during the long march to Germany. At last some of the old-timers discovered what the ripening grapes they had seen were capable of producing—the best wines in the world.

There had been so much booze stashed in the liquor warehouse that the Thunderbirds had not been able to bring it all with them. So Sparks and others had decided to bury some of the bottles, vowing to return for the hidden caches. On they rolled, through villages where from every window there seemed to hang crisp white sheets. Men opened more bottles and toasted the imminent fall of the Third Reich. A few undoubtedly sipped the vintages with hearts full of hate, determined to wreak vengeance. They had lost their best friends for no good reason, so close to the end.

CHAPTER TWENTY-THREE

DOWNFALL

Everyone now has a chance to choose the part which he will play in the film a hundred years hence.

—JOSEPH GOEBBELS, APRIL 17, 1945

One of tens of thousands of German boy soldiers captured in spring 1945. [National Archives]

BAVARIA, APRIL 13, 1945

THE NEXT OBJECTIVE WAS Nuremberg, venue of the famous Nazi rallies of the 1930s. Even the old-timers under Sparks's command dared hope they might survive to the very end as the division stormed south toward the Bavarian city where Hitler had basked in the adulation of vast, torch-bearing crowds at the height of his popularity and power. Reports from all across Germany were ever more heartening for the Thunderbirds. The Nazis and Hitler were doomed, the *Wehrmacht* in disarray, resistance collapsing on many fronts. Stalin's rampaging Red Army was closing the vise on Berlin, eager to strike the final stake into the heart of German fascism.

Some of the less experienced Thunderbirds began to talk of the end being a few days away.

"The shooting's all over. . . ."

"Hitler's suing for peace. . . ."

"The war's ended, but they haven't announced it yet."

"Yeah," replied one veteran, "the war's over just the way it was before Aschaffenburg!"

German troops were few and far between as both the 45th and 3rd divisions raced toward Nuremberg, their commanding generals, Frederick and "Iron Mike" O'Daniel, eager to claim the kudos that would come from capturing the city.

On April 13, Frederick was being driven along a road lined with troops when he heard some of them call out to him.

"Roosevelt died!"

Frederick was a die-hard Republican but was deeply saddened as well as concerned by the news of the sixty-three-year-old Roosevelt's death the previous day. Would the new U.S. president, Harry Truman, be able to fill Roosevelt's shoes?

There was barely a single GI who did not mourn their commander in chief's passing. An editorial in the *New York Times* declared: "Men will thank God on their knees a hundred years from now that Franklin D. Roosevelt was in the White House."

In Berlin, by contrast, Dr. Joseph Goebbels ordered his staff to bring out the best champagne.

SS chief Heinrich Himmler telephoned Hitler in his bunker.

"*Mein Führer,*" Himmler said excitedly. "I congratulate you!

Roosevelt is dead. It is written in the stars that the second half of April will be the turning point for us. This is Friday, April Thirteenth! Fate has laid low your greatest enemy. God has not abandoned us. Twice he has saved you from assassins. Death, which the enemy aimed at you in 1939 and 1944, has now struck down our most dangerous enemy. It is a miracle."

When armaments minister Albert Speer visited Hitler's bunker later that Friday the 13th, he was surprised to see Hitler rushing toward him, brandishing a newspaper clipping.

"Here, read it!" exclaimed Hitler. "Here! You never wanted to believe it! Here it is! Here we have the miracle I always predicted. Who was right? The war isn't lost. Read it! Roosevelt is dead!"

NUREMBERG, GERMANY, APRIL 17, 1945

THEY WERE ON the outskirts, pressing through the first streets, crouching behind piles of rubble, hoping they were not in the crosshairs of an SS sniper. Sparks's men began to probe the suburbs of Nuremberg. Would the city, which Hitler described as the most German of all, be another Aschaffenburg, only on a greater scale?

The Germans tried to stall the advance, relying mostly on MG42 machine guns and snipers concealed in the mile after mile of huge piles of rubble that now made up most of the city. The scale of destruction of Germany's industrial cities and towns was now abundantly clear. Nuremberg itself was a vast ruin. Sparks could stand in some places and see for miles without a single building blocking his sight.

On January 2, under a rising moon, thousands of tons of incendiary and explosive devices had been dropped by the RAF, and the city's ancient center had been quickly destroyed. The famous Rathaus castle, almost all of the churches, and about two thousand medieval houses had gone up in flames. Four hundred and fifteen industrial sites had been obliterated. The raid had in fact been a "near-perfect example of area bombing," as an RAF source would later describe it.

Nuremberg was but one of many Bomber Command successes. Across Germany, ten million civilians were now homeless. More than six hundred thousand had been killed and eight hundred thousand badly injured in the Allies' five-year-old bombing campaign, the ferocity and scale of which even Churchill, its primary architect, had come to regret. The airborne destruction, which had cost the lives of fifty-five thousand Bomber Command crewmen—more than the total of British Army officers lost in the First World War—in fact sickened the increasingly tired and dispirited warlord who urged Sir Arthur "Bomber" Harris, head of RAF Bomber Command, to concentrate on strategic targets rather than German cities: "Otherwise what will lie between the white snows of Russia and white cliffs of Dover?"

Hidden in the skeletons of apartment buildings, armed with *Panzerfausts*, the SS were of particular concern to Sparks after the ordeals at Reipertswiller and then Aschaffenburg. Himmler, although desperately trying to do a deal with the Allies to save his own neck, had ordered the more than one million men in the *Waffen*-SS and *Allgemeine*-SS to never capitulate even if they faced, in Hitler's words, an apparently hopeless situation. From bitter experience, Sparks knew the SS could be counted on to do so.

But still he could not despise them. Unlike his supreme commander, Dwight Eisenhower, he felt no hatred for the men trying to kill him, even the hawk-faced diehards of the SS, despite losing his battalion to them. In fact, he respected some of them. They were very good soldiers. There were sons of bitches to be sure. But most were just following orders. Like their American foe, the Germans had no choice but to fight. They were caught in the Nazi machine. They were told to fight, so they fought.

In Nuremberg, in the last days of World War II, not many of Hitler's most loyal warriors were given a chance to capitulate. The Seventh

Army, to which the 45th Division still belonged, had been granted full resources for the first time. Sparks was able to call in tank support and kill the last remaining SS by simply blasting the buildings from under their feet.

So it went in dozens of other cities and towns in what was left of the Third Reich as Hitler's birthday, on April 20, approached.

NUREMBERG, GERMANY, APRIL 19, 1945

SPARKS CONSULTED HIS MAP. He was not far from a prominent landmark: the 1905 Opera House in the center of Nuremberg, a cradle of culture and civilization from medieval times, home to the artist Dürer and others who had once made Germany world renowned as a country of great poets and philosophers.

It was April 19, the day before Hitler's birthday. That morning, Sparks's Third Battalion had encountered its stiffest resistance yet in Nuremberg, coming under intense fire near a railroad embankment. Sparks had deployed two companies and now followed close behind in a jeep, driven as usual by Turk, and with his runner Johnson and interpreter Karl Mann in the backseat. Yet again, he wanted to be as close as possible to the front lines. But it was difficult to find a path through the endless acres of rubble. Turk drove slowly as Sparks tried to spot street signs amid the blocks that had all but disappeared. Then he saw the Opera House with its enormous green roof.

Sparks turned to his driver, Turk.

"Uh, oh. I think we've gone too far."

Turk pulled up. Sparks realized that he had not only caught up with his companies but had in fact overshot them. Once more, he looked at his map, which he usually spread out on the hood of the jeep in front of him. Then, from the high dome of the Opera House, a German machine gunner fired a burst at Sparks and his group. The rounds passed between Sparks and his driver and between the legs of the men in the

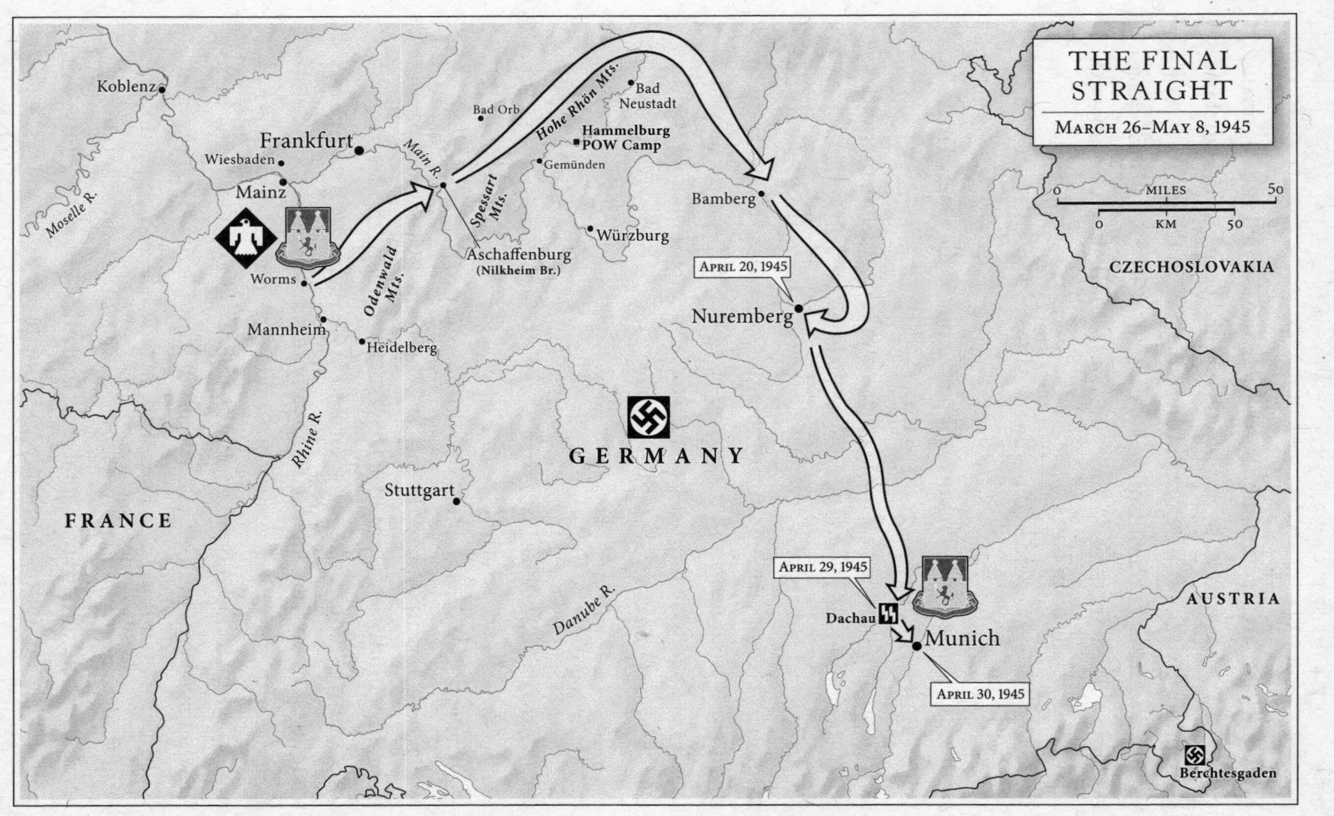
THE FINAL STRAIGHT
MARCH 26–MAY 8, 1945
0
MILES
50
0
KM
50
CZECHOSLOVAKIA
AUSTRIA
GERMANY
FRANCE
Koblenz
Moselle R.
Frankfurt
Wiesbaden
Mainz
Worms
Mannheim
Heidelberg
Rhine R.
Odenwald Mts.
Main R.
Spessart Mts.
Aschaffenburg
(Nilkheim Br.)
Bad Orb
Hohe Rhön Mts.
Gemünden
Hammelburg
POW Camp
Bad Neustadt
Würzburg
Bamberg
APRIL 20, 1945
Nuremberg
Stuttgart
Danube R.
APRIL 29, 1945
Dachau
Munich
APRIL 30, 1945
Berchtesgaden

backseat. They abandoned the jeep, which also carried the command radio and the radio code. Incredibly, no one had been hit. The burst had gone under Sparks's arm before putting a big hole in the jeep.

Sparks and the other men ran for cover in the nearest shell-holed buildings. Then they made their way back until they met up with Sparks's lead rifle company.

"Move it!" Sparks ordered his men. "Move it! Move it! We gotta get my jeep."

It was too late. The Germans had pulled out of the Opera House in the meantime, taking Sparks's jeep with them.

"Goddamn it. It had all my personal gear in there, letters from my wife. The sons of bitches got away with my jeep."

Sparks had put his photographs of Mary and his year-old son, Kirk, in the glove compartment, not wanting to keep them on his body in case he was wounded and the photos got damaged. Now his only mementos of them were the pictures he had placed on the butt of his lucky Colt .45, holstered at his waist.

THE THIRD REICH, APRIL 20, 1945

BY DUSK ON April 20, 1945—Hitler's fifty-sixth birthday—all of Nuremberg was in American hands. "The ruined city was a present from the Thunderbirds," recalled Sparks. The regiment had lost twenty-three men, the highest one-day total since Aschaffenburg. But there was some consolation. That night, G Company's Cranston Rogers and fellow Thunderbirds discovered a six-story cold storage warehouse that had miraculously not been bombed. It was full of frozen food. Many men treated themselves to a celebratory feast of strawberries and ice cream.

In Berlin, the Royal Air Force had already left its own gift for the Führer in the early hours: thousands of tons of yet more incendiary bombs. It had not been a good day in Hitler's final lair, fifty feet beneath the ground at Number 77 Wilhelmstrasse—the Isle of the

Departed—as forty-year-old Albert Speer described it. Speer himself had been shocked to see how far his idol had now fallen: "His complexion was sallow, his face swollen, his uniform, which had been scrupulously neat, was neglected and stained by the food he had eaten with a shaking hand."

There had been no foreign dignitaries to celebrate Hitler's fifty-sixth birthday. No honor guard of supermen to present arms. For once, however, Hitler had ventured, albeit briefly, into the Chancellery garden, where pallid teenage boys—Hitler Youth who had fought heroically—had been presented to him. Hitler had patted a few on the cheek and then shuffled back belowground. "Probably he sensed that his only convincing role," recalled Speer, "was as an object of pity."

The Slavic hordes Hitler so despised, and now feared, were almost at his doorstep. A Soviet force of 2.5 million men and women, backed by 42,000 artillery pieces and mortars, was storming toward him, smashing through Berlin's outer suburbs, accompanied by an incredible 6,250 tanks—the greatest attacking armored force in history.

NUREMBERG, GERMANY, APRIL 21, 1945

THE TOP BRASS was in the mood to celebrate. To Sparks's irritation, the 45th Division decided to hold a parade. Selected men from the 157th gathered the next day, April 21, in the ruins of the city where Hitler had bewitched his followers at massive annual rallies. For newsreel cameras, a huge concrete Nazi eagle, atop the stadium where Hitler had ranted and mesmerized, was blown up and then the Stars and Stripes was shown fluttering in the sky above the famous parade ground. Fittingly, the men given the honor of destroying the emblem belonged to a Thunderbird unit that had been booed in public before the war for wearing the 45th Division's old patch—a swastika.

The parade commenced that April 21 with columns of men marching across Nuremberg's massive central square, Adolf Hitler Plaza.

Sparks thought the whole spectacle a waste of time, but in any case he had sent his Third Battalion's L Company. After the parade, as the company returned to its assembly area, one of Sparks's men fell dead from a single sniper shot. The sniper died not long after, hunted down by enraged Thunderbirds. What Sparks regarded as unnecessary grandstanding by General Frederick and others for the world's press had cost a good man's life.

BERLIN, APRIL 22, 1945

THE END WAS close. In Berlin, the Soviets were drawing nearer to the Chancellery and history's greatest criminal, Adolf Hitler. The yellow-brown stone of the L-shaped building contrasted with the piles of dark rubble that surrounded it. The golden eagles above its entrances, clutching swastikas in their talons, looked sad and pathetic. A pall of black smoke rose above the famous Unter der Linden, where the trees were bare—firebombing had seared spring buds to the soot-stained branches. The Brandenburg Gate stood defiant, however, its twelve massive Doric columns pockmarked by shrapnel and bullet holes. Children in cellars were dying in ever greater numbers from starvation. Between bombing raids and barrages, the old could be seen eating new grass like foraging animals. Yet it was a glorious spring. "Clouds of lilac perfume drift over from untended gardens," one Berliner noted in her diary, "and waft through the charred ruins of apartment houses."

That afternoon, with the Soviet front lines just a few miles away, the Führer held a final conference with his most senior generals. It would be the last time many would see Hitler alive. The news he relayed was, for the first time, stripped of all fantasy and optimism. The Reich was almost at an end. Berlin would be encircled in a matter of hours. Defeat was inevitable. But it was not Hitler's fault. Then began a wild stream of invective and crude abuse. His generals, his people, and his soldiers had failed him.

DEFEATING GERMANY
Spring, 1945
American, British, and French forces
Russian forces
NORTH SEA
DENMARK
BALTIC SEA
HOLLAND
ENGLAND
London
English Channel
BELGIUM
LUXEMBOURG
Paris
FRANCE
SWITZERLAND
GERMANY
POLAND
CZECHOSLOVAKIA
AUSTRIA
HUNGARY
Elbe River
Oder River
Vistula River
Rhine River
Danube River
April 22–May 2, 1945
Berlin
Potsdam
Hannover
April 25, 1945
Soviets and Americans first link
Torgau
Dresden
Breslau
Frankfurt
157th Infantry Regiment
Aschaffenburg
Coburg
Mannheim
Nuremberg
April 20, 1945
Prague
Pilsen
Stuttgart
Dachau
Munich
April 29, 1945
April 30, 1945
Linz
Vienna
Berchtesgaden
Innsbruck
0 MILES 100
0 KM 100

The generals reassured Hitler that the war was not yet lost. He was needed more than ever. Among the most morally repugnant of them, sixty-three-year-old field marshal Wilhelm Keitel, insisted his Führer leave on a plane for the Alpine redoubt of Berchtesgaden, some 150 miles southeast of Munich.

"I shall not leave Berlin," said Hitler. "I shall defend the city to the end. Either I win this battle for the Reich's capital or I shall fall as a symbol of the Reich."

Keitel thought Hitler had totally lost his senses. The German Army could not be commanded effectively from Berlin. Millions of men would be abandoned to chaos and anarchy if Hitler did not leave Berlin and set up his headquarters elsewhere.

"I must insist," Keitel told Hitler, "that you leave for Berchtesgaden this very night."

Hitler ignored him.

"In seven years," Keitel blustered, "I have never refused to carry out an order from you . . . You can't leave the *Wehrmacht* in the lurch."

"I'm staying here," said Hitler. "That is certain."

NUREMBERG, GERMANY, APRIL 23, 1945

ONCE NUREMBERG HAD fallen, the route to Munich ninety miles farther south was wide open. The end of the Thunderbirds' two-thousand-odd-mile odyssey across enemy-occupied Europe was tantalizingly close, just over the horizon. The exultant rat race, as some GIs now called the advance, began once more, the men's actions and mood increasingly those of conquerors eager to pick up booty and get to the end with minimal loss of life.

Beyond Munich, there loomed the Bavarian Alps and, for Sparks and his men, he discovered, a fitting final mission. Designated a task force commander, Sparks was to lead his men to Munich and then push on to Hitler's mountain residence, the Berghof, near Berchtesgaden.

Once again, when the division had to achieve crucial objectives, Sparks was the man senior commanders turned to. Clearly, General Frederick had not harbored a lasting grudge toward Sparks for his actions following Reipertswiller. As the war progressed, the animosity between them had cooled, perhaps as each had grown to respect the other.

Allied intelligence believed that Hitler was about to flee for the Berghof, where he would make a last stand. Sparks was given a whole battalion of tanks, fifty-four in total, two battalions of artillery, and two engineer companies. He was to seize bridges and move as fast as he could toward the Alpine redoubt, smashing through all obstacles. The race was on to get to Berchtesgaden before Hitler could turn it into the ultimate Nazi fortress.

"Move as rapidly as possible," Sparks was ordered. "Bypass opposition if serious."

He made excellent progress, as much as fifty miles on some days. Finally, he was on the last straight. "Smiles returned to the faces of soldiers who had lived through a second winter of war," remembered one of Sparks's men, "and animated conversation replaced the dry humor for which veteran Thunderbirds were everywhere known." The task force encountered some small-arms fire but no real opposition, according to G Company's Cranston Rogers. But now he and others were more cautious than ever as they flushed out mostly teenagers and old men from hastily prepared defenses. No one wanted to be the last man to get killed.

The advance sped up as Sparks's task force then took to one of Hitler's famous autobahns. Me-262 jets and other planes had been hidden in woods along the straight four-lane highway leading to the Alps—there were no airstrips left to land on. Occasionally, what remained of the Luftwaffe managed to stall the task force but only for a few hours at most. At one crossroads, the Thunderbirds encountered a particularly ugly scene. A bomb had exploded close to an antiaircraft position nearby. "Men or parts of men were lying on the highway," remembered one eyewitness, "and on terraces built up by stone walls men's bodies, stripped naked by concussion, were hanging with their bleeding heads downward."

GANSHEIM, BAVARIA, APRIL 25, 1945

SPARKS WAS WITHIN striking distance of the Danube River. But his task force was moving too far, too fast, and beginning to outrun supply lines; his tanks were low on fuel. It was getting dark when he halted his column. After refueling, Sparks ordered his men to seize a bridge near the town of Gansheim. As he neared the bridge later that evening, there was a massive explosion. The sky turned red. The Germans had blown the bridge. But by dawn he had his men moving again. Several platoons crossed over in boats. Engineers then quickly built a pontoon bridge, enabling Sparks to get the rest of the Third Battalion across.

The following day, April 27, Sparks spotted a group of American tank destroyers some three hundred yards in the distance. Two rifle companies from his battalion were moving ahead of him, behind his tanks. Suddenly, one of the distant tank destroyers fired at one of Sparks's tanks and it went up in flames, its crew killed instantly. He was incensed. Five good men died a horrible and senseless death. He raced over to the tank destroyer. There followed a short, one-sided conversation with a lieutenant from the 42nd Infantry Division.

Sparks's impression of the division did not improve later that day when he came across a battalion that had strayed into his task force's assigned sector. The battalion was sprawled along a highway and looked totally disorganized. He managed to find its commander resting under a tree, waiting for further orders. He pulled out a map and showed the officer that he was far from his division's assigned sector. The officer didn't appear to care. In disgust, Sparks moved ahead, leaving the men from the 42nd Division sitting around as though they were taking a lunch break on a weekend hike back in the States.

It was late on April 28, 1945, when he finally ordered his men to stop and dig in for the night less than forty miles from Munich. Once Munich fell, they would roll up into the Alps to take on Hitler himself. He was looking forward to what would surely be the war's last act. While he felt no enmity toward the German people, he loathed Nazism with a passion, having seen its unprecedented destruction. If he managed to get to Hitler first, he would gladly "cut his throat slowly with a knife."

PART SIX

THE HEART OF DARKNESS

Above all I charge the leaders of the nation and those under them to scrupulous observance of the laws of race and to merciless opposition to the universal poisoner of all peoples, international Jewry.

—LAST LINES OF ADOLF HITLER'S FINAL TESTAMENT, SIGNED 4 A.M., APRIL 29, 1945

CHAPTER TWENTY-FOUR

THE DAY OF THE AMERICANS

Medics examine bodies found in boxcars at Dachau. [National Archives]

BAVARIA, APRIL 29, 1945

UNDER GRAY SKIES, Sparks was moving south again. At 9:22 A.M., he received a message from division level ordering him to secure what was described as a "concentration camp." It was located on the outskirts of a town called Dachau, some ten miles north of Munich.

"S-3 to all battalions," read the message. "Upon capture of Dachau, post air-tight guard and allow no one to enter or leave."

The order was infuriating. Sparks would not be able to get to Munich as soon as he had hoped. He had "absolutely no idea" what a concentration camp was, but in any case he would have bypassed it. Even though it was in his zone of attack, he didn't consider it a military objective.

The weather was unusually cold as he looked at his map and then reluctantly split his task force in two. He would lead one half into Dachau, utilizing his battalion's reserve, while the remainder of his force pushed on toward Munich. If either group ran into serious opposition, there would be no spare rifle company for him to call in as backup. That worried him. It was not good tactics. It was asking for trouble.

Sparks set out for the camp, figuring it probably contained Allied POWs. There was sporadic small-arms fire as he and his men neared Dachau but otherwise very little resistance.

HE COULD SEE a pale dawn through a window as he lay on a bunk. Twenty-eight-year-old French writer and resistance worker Robert Antelme looked around him. The daylight washed across the barrack full of dying and terribly malnourished men. The lice had sucked on him all night but no longer. Did they know something was about to happen? Two days ago, on April 27, he had seen the silhouettes of SS guards in watchtowers, manning MG42 machine guns. But this morning there was no sign of the SS near his barrack. There was no roll call.

Time has stopped dead. No orders. No forecasts. Not free.

Everything is ripe: ripe for dying, ripe for freeing . . . ripe for the end.

IT WAS ALSO early that morning when the reporter Marguerite Higgins arrived at the 42nd Division's 222nd Regiment's headquarters. Unlike Sparks, she knew what a concentration camp was; Buchenwald had already been liberated by the Americans on April 11 and made international headlines. Determined to get the first report on the liberation of Dachau, she had arranged to accompany the 42nd Division's assistant commander, Brigadier General Linden, and his men as they moved into the camp that day.

Since its opening as Nazi Germany's first concentration camp on March 22, 1933, just fifty-one days after Hitler took power, more than two hundred thousand "undesirable elements" had passed through Dachau and at least thirty thousand had died inside, more than thirteen thousand in 1945 alone. As Higgins set out for the camp with General Linden and a group of his men, Robert Antelme and some thirty-two thousand inmates waited inside anxiously, hoping the SS would not massacre them.

IT WAS AROUND noon when Sparks radioed I Company commander Lieutenant Bill Walsh and gave him the coordinates for a nearby road junction. Soon after, twenty-five-year-old Walsh, a tall and imposing figure with a chowder-thick accent from Newton, Massachusetts, arrived at the junction with I Company, which had earned the presidential unit citation for its actions at Anzio. Most men in the unit were now replacements, desperate for it all to end.

Sparks consulted a map he kept in his jacket pocket. The camp was around a mile to his east, on the edge of the city of Dachau, which had a stated population of around thirty thousand. On the map, Sparks could see that a river, the Amper, ran through the town.

"I don't know what the hell we're running into," Sparks told Walsh. "I'll give you an extra machine gun platoon. A heavy weapons company will go with you."

I Company set off with its attached firepower. Sparks followed behind in his jeep. On the outskirts of the town of Dachau, scouts engaged in a brief firefight with a small group of Germans defending a bridge leading into the town. They were also slowed by friendly fire from the 42nd "Rainbow" Division on their right flank.

Sparks and I Company moved forward cautiously into the town itself, on the lookout for booby traps and snipers. The sky was overcast. Snow threatened. There were some white sheets hanging from windows, signaling surrender. It was eerily quiet, as if the entire town were holding its breath in anticipation of their arrival. Dachau was as pretty as any other town the Thunderbirds had seen in Bavaria: cobbled streets skirted by timber-framed homes with brightly painted shutters. There were fresh beds of spring flowers.

I Company arrived at some railroad tracks. The tracks led toward the southern perimeter of the sprawling Dachau complex, which included the concentration camp as well as several barracks and factories. Sparks still followed I Company in his jeep. His interpreter, Karl Mann, seated in the back of the jeep, noticed that some I Company men had captured a tall and burly German who was wearing an SS uniform with a Red Cross armband. He was being pushed around by some GIs and, finally, made a break for it. Several shots were fired and he fell to the ground, dead.

Sparks then caught sight of the Dachau complex for the first time. It resembled some kind of garrison surrounded by a ten-foot-high brick wall. He did not know that the actual concentration camp, *Konzentrationslager* [KZ] Dachau, was relatively small, around five acres, compared to the much larger SS barracks and complex, which was around twenty.

Sparks could see a street, called "Avenue of the SS," that led to the Dachau complex's main entrance, marked by a large gate that was closed. A giant concrete eagle with Nazi insignia at its base towered above the gate. If the SS were going to put up a fight, they would do so as Sparks and his men approached this main entrance, which they were certain to have guarded. Sparks decided to split his men into two groups and enter the complex from two different directions.

He conferred with Walsh.

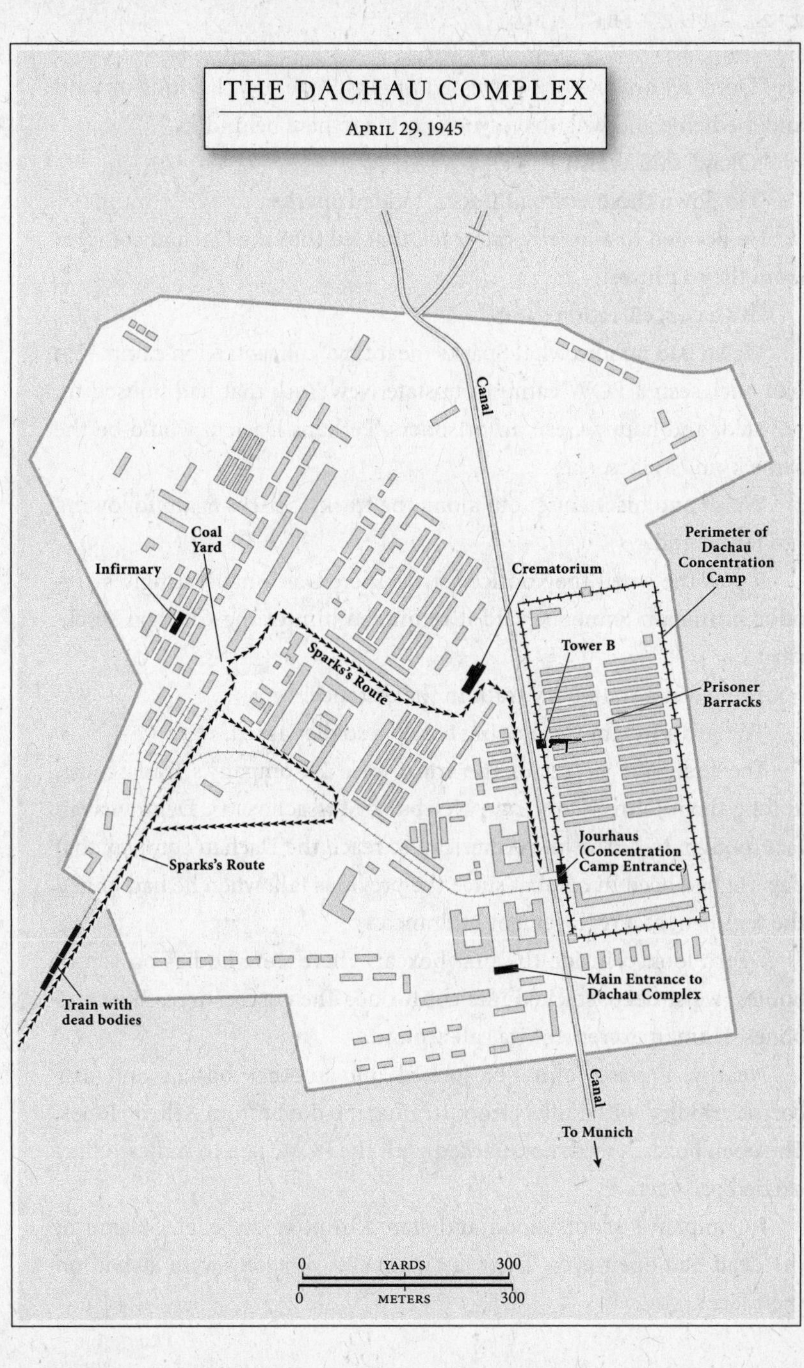

THE DACHAU COMPLEX
April 29, 1945
Canal
Perimeter of Dachau Concentration Camp
Coal Yard
Infirmary
Crematorium
Tower B
Sparks's Route
Prisoner Barracks
Jourhaus (Concentration Camp Entrance)
Sparks's Route
Main Entrance to Dachau Complex
Train with dead bodies
Canal
To Munich
0 YARDS 300
0 METERS 300

"Don't let anyone out," stressed Sparks. "We got all kinds of food and medicine and what-have-you coming in here behind us."

"Okay," said Walsh.

"Go down these railroad tracks," added Sparks.

He pointed to a nearby rail track that led into the Dachau complex from the southwest.

"It's a concentration camp."

Walsh had no idea what Sparks meant by "concentration camp." He had once seen a POW camp in upstate New York that had housed fit, well-fed, and happy German prisoners. Perhaps Dachau would be the same kind of place.

Walsh and his men set out along the tracks, Sparks again following not far behind.

It was the smell they noticed first. There was a nauseatingly sweet odor in the air. Someone said it reminded him of the Chicago stock-yards.

There was a stationary train in the distance.

"What's a freight train doing here?" a soldier asked.

The first men to get to the train were I Company's lead scouts, among them John Degro from Newbury, Massachusetts. Degro was in fact thought to be the first American to reach the Dachau complex that day. He had been in combat since the previous fall, when he had joined the regiment as a replacement in France.

Degro looked inside the first boxcar. There were bodies on top of bodies, waist-deep, stacked like cordwood. The corpses were skin and bones. Human excrement was all around.

Nearby, Private John Lee looked into another boxcar and saw corpses riddled with bullets from strafing, no doubt from Allied planes. The open boxcars were not marked with the POW sign to indicate they carried prisoners.

I Company's scouts stood and stared in utter disbelief. Several of the dead had open eyes. Their last moments of agony were etched on their faces.

It was as if others were staring at the Thunderbirds, remembered one scout, and with accusing looks asking: "What took you so long?"

Many of the victims were naked. Some had been whipped. In one car, a dead man lay on bodies, his face frozen in agony, having cut off his gangrenous leg with his own hands. The stump was covered in dirty paper.

There were thirty-nine boxcars in all, containing some two thousand corpses. The train had left Buchenwald with around forty-eight hundred prisoners some three weeks earlier. It had first stopped so that hundreds could be shot. The SS that cruelest of springs had been overwhelmed, confused, and exasperated by the sheer numbers of their victims and, under orders not to let any prisoners fall into the hands of the Allies, had killed with clinical efficiency. On April 21, when the train halted for the second time, thirty-one hundred severely malnourished and dehydrated people on board were still alive. Six days later, when the train pulled into Dachau at night, there were just eight hundred. The dead were left to rot on the train.

I Company commander Bill Walsh arrived at the boxcars. At first, he thought the skeletal people were sleeping.

What the hell is this?

Sparks was next on the scene, having left his jeep in a nearby side street, along with his shotgun and radio. His only weapon now was his Colt .45, holstered at his hip. At first, as were many of his men, he was paralyzed by what he saw. The sights and smells robbed the mind of reason.

Then Sparks saw a girl. He would never forget her face. She lay on top of a pile of bodies, her eyes wide open, imploring. It was as if she were looking into the skies, searching for an answer: "Why?"

Sparks spotted two dead inmates on the ground nearby. They had been killed in the most bestial way. All he could do was stand and stare. Then he vomited. One of the victims had had enough strength to crawl out of one of the boxcars. But then a German had crushed his skull with a rifle butt. His brains were splattered over the ground.

Sparks's men also saw the corpse with the crushed skull. Some began to cry. Others cussed. Most were dumbstruck. They couldn't believe what they were seeing. It was unreal. Maggots. The smell. Naked people stacked in heaps.

What place was this? What had happened at Dachau? How could human beings commit such evil?

Disbelief and shock turned to rage.

"Take no prisoners," someone said.

"Let's kill every one of these bastards."

"Don't take any SS alive!"

Sparks ordered his men to check to see if any people were alive. None were. Then he told them to keep going toward the camp, a hundred yards in the distance.

Bill Walsh still looked stunned.

"Okay, move!" Sparks ordered Walsh.

Walsh and I Company began to move past more railroad cars, down the tracks that led into the Dachau complex.

Sparks followed behind, passing more open boxcars filled with bodies, boxcars like the ones he had ridden in across America ten years before. Ahead of him, some of his men were boiling with rage, eager to avenge the SS crimes. I Company scout Private John Lee had never seen his fellow Thunderbirds so unhinged.

Sparks heard men screaming and cursing.

"Let's get these Nazi dogs."

It was all too much. His men were losing their minds. Lieutenant Walsh set the tone, ranting and raving about SS sons of bitches. He and others had been pushed past the breaking point. The army had trained them to fight. It had not prepared them for this kind of psychological shock. Nothing could. They had come across a tragedy beyond comprehension. "Every man in the outfit who saw those boxcars," recalled one of Sparks's men, "felt [like] meting out death as punishment to the Germans who were responsible."

Sparks snapped commands and tried to regain control of his men. It took several minutes.

"Okay," he finally said when I Company had calmed down enough for him to make himself clearly understood. "We're going in the camp."

Sparks led the way over a perimeter wall with one group of men while Lieutenant Walsh advanced with another group from I Company. On the other side of the wall, Sparks found himself in the neat garden of a pleasant home, one of several used by families of the SS officers within the Dachau complex.

Roses were blooming. It was all so utterly surreal. Sparks was in a daze, barely thinking straight. He struggled for a few moments to clear his head and get a grip on his emotions. Then he entered the back door of the brick house and walked into a kitchen. He told his men to be careful—there might be booby traps. He and others quickly looked around the house. There were three or four bedrooms. He walked into a child's room. Wooden toys were scattered on the floor. The child and its family had clearly left in a hurry.

KZ Dachau had been guarded by several hundred SS but most had fled in the last few days. Commandant Eduard Weiter had also tried to disappear before the Americans arrived, knowing he would be tried, convicted, and hanged for crimes against humanity. Before he could be brought to justice, he would shoot himself to death on May 6 at Schloss Itter, one of the more than two hundred sub-camps in the Dachau gulag in Bavaria.

MEANWHILE, WALSH AND his party came across four SS men who had their hands on their heads. Walsh took them into one of the boxcars and called for a machine gun. Then he changed his mind and fired his pistol at them. But he did not kill them all. Other I Company men could hear the survivors' cries of pain. A private called Pruitt entered the boxcar and lifted his M1 rifle and fired, killing the wounded men with eight or nine clinical shots. "They were suffering and taking on and I figured there was no use letting them suffer, so I finished them off," Pruitt later testified. "I never like to see anybody suffer."

Walsh's men carried on, moving beyond the rail tracks into the Dachau complex itself.

CHAPTER TWENTY-FIVE

THE HOUNDS OF HELL

The effect of it just opened up a flood of raw emotions.

—FELIX SPARKS

The kennels at Dachau on April 29, 1945. [National Archives]

SPARKS SAW MANICURED LAWNS and rosebushes in full bloom, clearly well tended. To his left there was the sound of firing. He and his men carried on, keeping close to doorways in case of snipers, not bunching. He reached a central building with a large lobby. At one end were glass cases containing antique firearms. He again heard firing. He left the building but could not see where the shots were coming from. Poplar trees in spring bud and buildings obscured his view. Then he saw Lieutenant Bill Walsh emerge from between a couple of buildings. He was chasing a German.

"You sons of bitches," Walsh was screaming repeatedly.

Walsh began to beat the German over the head with the barrel of his carbine.

"Bastards. Bastards. Bastards."

Sparks ordered Walsh to stop, but Walsh ignored him. So Sparks pulled out his .45 and clubbed Walsh on the head with its butt, stunning him and knocking him to the ground.

Walsh lay there, crying hysterically.

"I'm taking over command of the company," yelled Sparks.

One of Walsh's men, Sidney C. Horn, recalled that seven men were needed to take a hysterical Walsh into a room and "get him quieted down. He really lost it there." Walsh had gone "crazy," as Sparks would later put it, overwhelmed like many of his men by the scenes of atrocity. Walsh later confessed: "I'll be honest with you. I broke down. I started crying. The whole thing was getting to me. This was the culmination of something that I had never been trained for."

A FEW HUNDRED yards away, Robert Antelme, the courageous French writer and resistance worker, still lay in his lice-infested cot, close to death. His barrack, one of thirty-four in KZ Dachau, had been designed for around two hundred and fifty people but now contained more than a thousand. He had been at the mercy of the Gestapo and then the SS since July 1944, having arrived at Dachau from Buchenwald on the same train, it is thought, that the Thunderbirds had just discovered.

There was the sound of gunfire not far from his barrack.

"They're here!" someone cried.

Antelme found the strength to sit up. He glimpsed a green helmet out of the window. An American was walking past. Antelme propped himself up on his elbows. His internal organs were visible through his parchment-thin skin. He listened to his fellow inmates as they figured out what was happening.

The barrack soon filled with mad voices.

A man screamed.

Another clutched his head.

"Don't you understand?" he cried. "We're free! We're free!"

Over and over, the man clutching his head shouted that they were free. Then he screamed and stamped his feet on the floor. Antelme saw more American helmets pass by outside. There was an old man lying beside him. Antelme was determined that he should glimpse freedom—an American helmet—before he died.

Antelme kicked at the old man's feet.

"We're free! Look, will you! Look!"

Antelme hit the man's foot again, this time as hard as he could. The old dying man had to see freedom. He must see the Americans' green helmets.

The man managed to move his head and turn toward the window. But it was too late. Sparks's men had passed by.

Antelme fell back on his bunk. He knew he was dying. He had no strength, nothing left in reserve now. He was too weak to sing like the others, too emaciated to even crawl toward his liberators and embrace them. But at least he had seen it. He had seen freedom. He had glimpsed the green helmets of Felix Sparks's men.

SCOUTS FROM I COMPANY discovered a building at the center of the Dachau complex. It was a hospital of some kind. A red cross had been painted on its roof. The scouts pushed their way into the building and discovered it was an infirmary for SS guards and soldiers, not for camp inmates. It was maddening to see well-cared-for SS men lying on clean white sheets.

Lead scout John Degro and others ordered the Germans lying in beds to get outside, where many soon cowered, hands in the air, some still bandaged. Then Degro and others hustled the SS men toward a nearby coal yard. "We kicked all the Germans into the yard," recalled Degro. One of the men taken from the infirmary was Hans Linberger, a *Waffen*-SS veteran who had been wounded in a battle near Kiev when an anti-tank gun shell had exploded and blown off his left arm. He had also suffered shrapnel wounds, his fourth serious injury in combat, before arriving at the Dachau infirmary on March 9, six weeks before.

After hearing gunshots, Linberger would later claim, he had taken a Red Cross flag and gone to the infirmary's entrance to tell the Americans it was undefended. A GI had stuck a gun to his chest, Linberger would also tell the German Red Cross, and then hit him in the face. Then the Americans had emptied the hospital and separated the SS from other Germans.

Linberger now stood with other SS against a stucco wall in the coal yard, adjacent to the Dachau complex's heating plant. The men rounded up with Linberger were indeed SS, but few, if any, had served in a concentration camp—they did not belong to the SS-*Totenkopfverbande* (SS-TV) that administered camps in the Third Reich. In fact, very few of KZ Dachau's actual guards were now in the Dachau complex—the vast majority had fled the day before, leaving other SS men quartered nearby to surrender the camp.

As far as I Company's men were concerned, Linberger and the young men holding their hands above their heads were SS-*Schutzstaffel*, the "Protection Squadron," their insignia of two lightning bolts indicating they were Hitler's most fanatical troops. That was all that mattered. They had massacred defenseless GIs at Malmédy. They had ruthlessly employed flamethrowers to scorch the men's fellow Thunderbirds to death at Reipertswiller that January. Always, they had fought hardest to kill the Americans, to slow their advance, most recently in Aschaffenburg and Nuremberg. They had, it appeared to the Thunderbirds, also overseen the unimaginable atrocities at Dachau.

SPARKS MOVED DEEPER into the Dachau complex. He and the platoon with him were "extremely cautious," he recalled, as they searched every building. He heard rifle shots punctuating the strained silence with an almost reassuring familiarity. Then he discovered the source of the firing: His men were shooting guard dogs in a nearby kennel, which had at one time held as many as 122 "hounds from hell." Other than Alsatians and Dobermans, there were Great Danes, boxers, and wolfhounds. Sparks's men killed two dozen of the dogs that a former camp commandant, Egon Zill, had trained to attack inmates tied to metal poles. The SS had made prisoners strip at gunpoint, tied them to the poles, and then tapped the men's testicles with sticks and urged the dogs to jump up and rip them off. When the victims had been neutered, the SS roared with laughter and rewarded their hounds with red meat.

The dogs died quickly, howling and whimpering as the Thunderbirds gunned them down. A soldier apparently used a dagger to cut a dog's throat after it had been shot but stubbornly did not die. Just one of the dogs would survive, to be found a week later with a bullet wound, hiding in an SS barracks.

The dogs' corpses now joined human ones littering the camp. Due to a shortage of coal, the SS had not been able to cremate the recent dead. So blue- and green-tinged carcasses lay piled in their scores outside barracks and, to Sparks's utter horror, stacked to the ceilings in rooms near a crematorium. Hundreds had died in the last few days. "Since all the many bodies were in various stages of decomposition," recalled Sparks, "the stench of death was overpowering."

AGAIN THERE WAS a haunting silence. There were no more gunshots. Finally, the tens of thousands of inmates realized that the Americans had liberated the camp. The SS had clearly been dealt with. At last, it was safe to venture from their barracks. A prisoner called Kupfer-Koberwitz lay wounded in the inmates' sick quarters and noted the reactions of his fellow survivors in a secret diary: "Everyone starts to move—the sick leave their beds, the nearly well and [others] jump out of the windows, climb over the wooden walls. Everyone runs to the roll-call place. One hears yelling and cheers of hooray. . . ."

The camp then erupted. Inmates began to shout and scream, producing a spine-chilling roar, a sound Sparks would never forget.

Inmates soon surrounded some of Sparks's men. A Pole called Walenty Lenarczyk, inmate no. 39272 at Dachau, helped others grab Thunderbirds and lift them up. There were soon more than a hundred prisoners clustered around the Americans, trying to kiss their hands and their uniforms with the soft felt Thunderbird patches on their shoulders. "All we could think about were Americans," recalled Walenty. "For the past six years we had waited for the Americans, and at this moment the SS were nothing. It was truly our second birthday."

Lenarczyk saw four German SS guards making a run for it. The Americans could not open fire because prisoners surrounded them. Other inmates swarmed around the fleeing SS men, one of whom elbowed a prisoner out of his way. The inmates then attacked en masse and the SS men were killed, in all likelihood stamped to death.

Elsewhere in the camp, victims suddenly became victimizers and in several instances beat other SS men, their *Kapos* and informers, to pulps with fists, sticks, and shovels. It was as if with every stabbing action, every limb broken, every punch and kick, they were repaying each day of suffering. The Thunderbirds did little to intervene, turning their backs on two inmates beating a German guard to death with a shovel. The German, it was later learned, had castrated a prisoner. In another incident, Russian prisoners grabbed a German by his legs and tore him apart, his bones cracking loudly.

TWENTY-FIVE-YEAR-OLD MARGUERITE HIGGINS and men from the 42nd Rainbow Division arrived that afternoon from a different direction to the Thunderbirds'. At the main entrance to the Dachau complex, they encountered tall and slim SS Second Lieutenant Heinrich Wicker of the *Totenkopfverbande*. Twenty-three-year-old Wicker had earlier that morning met with his mother, sister, fiancée, and two-year-old son inside the Dachau complex. They would never see him again.

Accompanied by Victor Maurer, a Red Cross representative, Wicker formally surrendered the Dachau complex to Brigadier General Henning Linden, the 42nd Infantry Division's assistant division commander. It is assumed that Wicker was killed later that afternoon, either by inmates or by the liberators he had surrendered to.

Linden and his party then entered the complex itself. Higgins later described in a world exclusive how inmates called out to her in several different languages.

"Are you Americans?" asked one.

Higgins nodded.

Starving men, many in tears, swept forward.

"Long live America!" they cried.

Some were too weak to walk, so they crawled toward Higgins.

The first to reach her was a Polish Catholic priest. He threw his arms around her neck and kissed her several times. She did not resist. Then she stepped back and pulled off her helmet and goggles. Her blond hair fell free. Her pretty young face with its slightly snub nose was visible.

"My God! My God! It's a woman. Pardon, Madame!"

CHAPTER TWENTY-SIX

THE COAL YARD

To me belongeth vengeance and recompense; their foot shall slide in due time: for the day of their calamity is at hand and the things that shall come upon them make haste.

—DEUTERONOMY 32:35

Men from I Company, 157th Infantry Regiment, 45th Division, shortly after SS soldiers were shot in the coal yard at Dachau. [National Archives]

SPARKS DID NOT KNOW that Higgins and soldiers from the 42nd Infantry Division had entered the Dachau complex. Buildings and barracks blocked his view as he made his way to the coal yard where his men had lined up SS men against an eight-foot-high stucco wall. Lieutenant Bill Walsh was present, having calmed down somewhat and been restored to his command by Sparks. I Company's Lieutenant Daniel Drain set up a machine gun. A corporal, Martin J. Sedler, stood next to the gun. Nineteen-year-old Private William C. Curtin lay down behind the gun and aimed it at around a hundred SS men standing against the stucco wall.

To Sparks, the situation now seemed to be firmly under control. The SS were under guard. Others were being rounded up elsewhere. Thunderbirds had been posted at various places around KZ Dachau to prevent anyone getting in or out, including at the main gate.

A private approached Sparks.

"Colonel, you should see what we found," said the private.

Sparks left with the soldier.

Once Sparks had departed, time seemed to speed up as if in a dream, according to one of the I Company officers in the coal yard, twenty-five-year-old Lieutenant Jack Busheyhead, a Cherokee Indian.

Lieutenant Walsh ordered a private to keep his BAR machine gun trained on the SS troops lined up at the wall. If they didn't stay back, the private was to open up on them. Some of the SS arrogantly refused to stay back against the wall, another Thunderbird recalled, and to keep their hands above their heads.

Others muttered in German.

"Keep your goddamn hands up and stay back," someone shouted.

Lieutenant Walsh then lined up riflemen and called for tommy gunners.

Private Curtin began to feed the belt into his machine gun. He pulled back a lever to cock it. It was ready to fire.

"Let them have it," said Walsh.

Walsh opened up with his pistol.

Curtin fired three bursts, he later claimed, maybe fifty rounds in all. Then his machine gun jammed.

A medic called Peter Galary spotted an SS man, clearly an officer, who had not been hit.

"Drop to the ground," shouted the SS officer.

Most of the SS did so, but three still remained standing, utterly defiant.

Galary grabbed for a fellow Thunderbird's gun.

"Fire it over here."

Galary wanted to kill the SS officer because he seemed to be the leader, but Galary's fellow Thunderbird wouldn't let go of his gun.

The firing continued.

Lieutenant Busheyhead also opened up on the SS, spraying them with his carbine. The firing lasted probably no more than a few seconds but it seemed like much longer. The Thunderbirds fired from left to right and from right to left.

An SS man beside Hans Linberger fell on top of him.

"The pigs are shooting at my stomach," the man cried.

Blood from the man covered Linberger's face.

An SS officer called Weiss was not far away.

"Stay calm, we die for Germany," he said.

Sparks was by now around ten yards beyond the stucco wall. At the sound of gunfire, he wheeled around and ran back toward the coal yard. It took him perhaps five seconds to realize what was going on. Meanwhile, Arland B. Musser from the 163rd Signal Photo Corps snapped photographs. A film cameraman, Henry Gerzen, was also present and also recorded Sparks as he ran to the middle of the coal yard, pulled his .45 from his holster, thrust out his palm, shouted for his men to stop, and fired shots into the air.

The firing got everyone's attention and stopped the shooting.

Sparks's men looked at him.

"There will be no more firing," said Sparks, "unless I give the order."

He saw Curtin behind the machine gun. He ran over and kicked him in the back, knocking him forward onto the coal-dusted ground. Then he grabbed him by the collar and pulled him away from the gun.

"What the hell are you doing?" shouted Sparks.

Curtin began to cry.

"Colonel," he blurted, "they were trying to get away."

There were a few moments of silence.

Sparks turned to Lieutenant Drain. He was in charge of the machine-gun squad and now stood nearby in a state of shock.

"Lieutenant," said Sparks, "let's not have any more firing here."

The Germans lay in piles at the wall. At least seventeen had been killed. As many as seventy-five men were on the ground, and many looked badly wounded. A Thunderbird ordered the surviving SS to stand up. Most were able to get to their feet. A private standing in the coal yard could not understand how they had survived with so many shots fired. Only now did other bystanders realize the enormity of what had just happened. It was wrong to shoot the Germans as they stood with their hands in the air, no matter what they had or had not done.

Corporal Henry Mills, standing nearby, was sickened by the killings.

I've been here too long. I've to go home now. . . . I want to see my mom.

Twenty-two-year-old Mills had not seen his mother for three years.

We came over here to stop this bullshit, and now here we got somebody doing the same thing.

It was not the American way of fighting.

Sparks ordered his men to help the wounded get to the infirmary. Some men began to do so. Others did not. They included medic Peter Galary, who later admitted that he refused to patch up the Germans who had been shot. Colonel Howard Buechner, the battalion surgeon, also failed to treat any of the wounded, according to a subsequent investigation.

Among the SS, a man named Jager asked Hans Linberger if he had been hit.

No, said Linberger, he had not.

Jager had been shot in his forearm.

Linberger gave Jager some chocolate. He was convinced they were about to be finished off. Then a Thunderbird medic, claimed Linberger, threw some razor blades toward him and others.

"There, finish it yourself," the medic said.

Jager took a blade and slit his jugular vein.

LEAVING HIS MEN to deal with the wounded SS, Sparks moved on toward KZ Dachau's confinement area with Johnson and Mann. After several minutes, they reached the area's wire fence. Beyond it, thousands of inmates were cheering the Americans.

In a nearby barrack, twenty-one-year-old Jack Goldman listened to the commotion. When the Americans came, he did not have any clothing, just a soiled blanket he wrapped around himself to try to fend off the cold. He knew English, but when he tried to talk he couldn't say a word. He was mute, too affected to speak. He saw a young Jewish Hungarian woman take off her shirt, pull out a needle and thread, and begin to sew it into a pair of underpants for him, his first clothes as a free man. More than four hundred thousand of her fellow Hungarian Jews had been killed in less than two months in 1944 alone.

Sparks's men would later bring Goldman and others some scraps of food they found in a nearby warehouse. Goldman was also handed a discarded *Waffen*-SS uniform to put over his underpants. He refused to take the black jacket and trousers. So they found him a green uniform. That felt a lot better.

Goldman and his fellow inmates were no longer considered vermin. Sparks's men asked him his name. He was no longer a number. He was a human being.

MEANWHILE, LIEUTENANT WALSH and other Thunderbirds from I Company had left the coal yard and moved toward the entrance to KZ

Dachau. They found the main gates closed and guarded by other men from I Company. An inmate called Albert Guerisse, who represented the camp's International Prisoners Committee, was standing near the entrance when Walsh approached. Guerisse was in fact a thirty-three-year-old Belgian resistance member who had operated an escape line, under the alias Patrick Albert "Pat" O'Leary, for downed Allied pilots until he had been betrayed to the Gestapo in March 1943.

Walsh was introduced to Guerisse.

"Are there any Americans in here?" asked Walsh.

"I don't know," replied Guerisse. "I think so, but there may be only one or two."

"I can't open the gates," said Walsh, "but I want you to know there's all kinds of medical supplies and doctors and food and stuff like this coming behind us, and they're going to take care of you."

"I want you to come in here," replied Guerisse. "I want you to see what was going on."

Guerisse was insistent.

"Okay, I'll go in," Walsh finally agreed.

He walked toward the gate with Lieutenant Busheyhead, the Cherokee Indian with dark swept-back hair, and a sergeant from I Company. The gate was partly opened and they squeezed through. Walsh followed Guerisse. He saw two or three men, perhaps *Kapos* or guards, who were surrounded by inmates and being battered to death with shovels. Walsh did not stop the killings.

Guerisse took Walsh to an area where the Germans, including the infamous Dr. Sigmund Rascher, had performed fatal medical experiments, testing hundreds of inmates for reactions to exposure, frostbite, and high altitude. Bodies were laid out on a walkway outside the building. They entered a barrack. Walsh saw an old man on the second tier of a bunk. He had a cigarette, a German one. It had water stains.

The man offered it to Walsh.

"Oh, no, *you* keep it."

Hundreds of men were now staring at Walsh from their bunks.

"Take it," said Guerisse. "That's the only thing that guy owns in this whole world. That's his everything . . . a cigarette. Take it."

Walsh did so.

A FEW HUNDRED yards away, Colonel Felix Sparks walked toward the entrance of KZ Dachau, passing a guard tower at the edge of the confinement area. The tower was later identified as "Tower B" in an official investigation into the killing of guards that day. Sparks saw several bodies of SS guards, laid neatly in a row. They had been shot. Other SS men's corpses floated in a nearby moat on the outside of the confinement area's electrified fences.

Sparks finally reached the *Jourhaus*, a building at the actual concentration camp's entrance, whose famous wrought-iron gate had a sign above it—*Arbeit Macht Frei* (Work Sets You Free). He saw that inmates were crying, laughing, singing their national anthems—there were more than forty nationalities in Dachau—and dancing with joy.

"America!"

"America!"

"Hurrah for the United States!"

Some were pushing against the barbed-wire fence. Hundreds climbed onto the roofs of barracks and other buildings and waved. A few were utterly dazed, others looked vacant, too overcome with emotion to even speak. Then Sparks saw scores of dirty, emaciated hands—clawing maniacally at other prisoners, ripping them apart.

Bodies flew through the air, prisoners tearing at them.

Sparks asked Mann to find out what was happening.

Mann returned a few minutes later. "They're killing the informers."

Sparks told Mann to tell the inmates to send their leaders to the fence.

"You must remain here," Sparks told them. "We're bringing food, water, and medical attention to you as rapidly as possible."

Sparks was relieved when they listened to his instructions.

Some of Sparks's men, taking pity on the inmates, began to throw them food. Sparks figured the starving survivors would soon begin to fight over the scraps.

"Don't throw them any food!" he yelled.

A man appeared at the gate and said he was an American. Sparks's men allowed him to exit. The man explained that he was in fact Major Rene Guiraud, an American OSS agent, one of an estimated seven Americans in the camp. Guiraud told Sparks that he had been captured on a secret mission and sentenced to death as a spy, but the Germans had not got around to carrying out the sentence. Guiraud was one of 31,432 people still alive inside KZ Dachau. The largest contingents of survivors were Polish (9,082) and Russian (4,258). There were more than 1,000 Catholic priests and 2,539 Jews. Hundreds of their fellow inmates, most of them victims of a typhus epidemic that had raged since the previous fall, had been left to rot in piles and pits.

Some of these corpses would later be buried, recalled Sparks, with the "forced assistance" of the people of Dachau, who had been indifferent to the suffering just downwind from them for more than twelve years. A few of these Germans would actually be made to handle the bodies. They all claimed they did not know what was going on inside the camp. This willful blindness would be the subject of much debate among shocked and nauseated correspondents who would visit the camp in the coming days and weeks. One even reported seeing locals scurrying past the thirty-nine boxcars packed with putrefying corpses, toward the SS barracks, where they stole what supplies they could find. Young children cycled past the rotting corpses, chattering away, excited, looted SS clothing hanging from their handlebars.

CHAPTER TWENTY-SEVEN

THE LINDEN INCIDENT

ES GIBT EINEM WEG ZUR FREIHEIT. SEINE MEILENSTEINE HEISSEN: GEHORSAMKEIT, SAUBERKEIT, NUCHTERNHEIT UND FLEISS. (THERE IS A ROAD TO FREEDOM. ITS MILESTONES ARE: OBEDIENCE, CLEANLINESS, SOBRIETY, INDUSTRY.) —MESSAGE ON A SIGN AT DACHAU

An inmate helps GIs pull a dead German soldier from a canal at Dachau. [National Archives]

SPARKS STOOD NEAR KZ Dachau's gated entrance. It was now about an hour after he had arrived at the camp. Three jeeps carrying 42nd Division personnel appeared and pulled up a few yards from Sparks. In the first was General Henning Linden, the 42nd Division's fifty-three-year-old assistant commander. In the second was reporter Marguerite Higgins, described by an inmate as "carrying the faintest hint of perfume among the smells, the disease . . . a miracle very difficult to accept." Her blond hair was held in a scarf.

Higgins's report of that day's events in a front-page world exclusive for the *New York Herald Tribune* would be the greatest coup of her career. "It was one of the most terrible and wonderful days of the war," she recalled. "It was the first and the worst concentration camp in Germany." To avoid embarrassment and censure, however, her vivid account would make no mention of what happened next.

Linden and Higgins got out of their jeeps.

Linden was a short, rather chubby man and was carrying a riding stick. He walked over to Sparks.

"This lady would like to interview some of the prisoners," said Linden. "She wants to go in there."

Sparks looked at Higgins. She had a pretty face and large eyes. He had not seen an attractive American woman for quite some time.

"No," Sparks said. "She can't open that gate."

Linden far outranked Sparks and was twice his age. He didn't like this Thunderbird officer's attitude one bit.

"I'll take responsibility," said Linden.

"General," replied Sparks, "you're not in your area of responsibility. You're out of your combat zone. This is my area. I take my orders from my commanding general."

Who the hell did Sparks think he was talking to?

"Colonel, there are some famous people in there," Higgins explained. She named the Lutheran pastor Martin Niemöller and the French premier Léon Blum. She had a list with her of what the Germans called *Prominenten*—"famous prisoners."

"Lady, I don't give a damn who's in there."

Higgins persisted.

Were any of the people on her list inside?

"I don't know whether they're here or not."

It had been a long, emotionally exhausting day. Sparks was dead tired and fast losing his patience.

Higgins wouldn't take no for an answer.

"Look at all those people pressing against the gate," explained Sparks. "You can't go in there."

Linden had heard enough. He began to argue with Sparks, stating that he had greater authority because of his rank. Besides, he had earlier accepted the formal surrender of the entire Dachau complex from SS second lieutenant Wicker.

Sparks said his orders were to let no one in or out. He certainly wasn't going to make an exception for a pompous general escorting a journalist, no matter how pushy and attractive she was.

"That woman's not going to open that gate."

To Sparks it seemed that Linden was only with Higgins so he could get his name and that of the Rainbow Division in the headlines. Sparks had lost good men because of the division's actions and must have deeply resented Linden interfering in his sector of command. That very morning, I Company had reported being fired on accidentally by Linden's men.

Sparks was now red in the face. In more than six months with Sparks, his interpreter Karl Mann had never seen this. He had never lost his temper, not once, although there had been plenty of reason to do so.

Linden and Sparks started to shout at each other. "There was a brigadier and a colonel arguing," recalled one eyewitness, "ready to shoot each other over who had liberated Dachau first." Sparks and his men had entered the complex first, but Linden and his party had accepted its surrender, hence the confusion and now violent disagreement over jurisdiction and command.

As Linden and Sparks shouted at each other, Higgins seized her chance. She ran toward the gate and then started to pull it open.

There was pandemonium. Prisoners surged forward.

"Shoot over their heads!" Sparks ordered his men. "Shoot over their heads!"

They did so.

"Charge the gate and close it!" added Sparks.

Again his men did as ordered.

Higgins ran back to her jeep in fear.

Sparks turned to Linden.

"General, collect your party and get out of here."

"I'm relieving you," replied Linden.

"No, you're not," said Sparks. "You don't have the authority to relieve me. I'm in my territory."

At a loss for words, Linden apparently then shook his fist at Sparks.

Sparks turned to one of his privates. "Escort the general and his party out of here."

The private hesitated before he stepped forward and then raised his rifle.

Linden was understandably outraged. As Sparks recalled: "[He] had this little riding crop, carried I guess as his badge of authority. He whacked the kid over his helmet with it. Didn't hurt the kid, rang his bell a little bit." The blow was more than enough, however, to send Sparks over the edge: "That did it, I just exploded."

Sparks drew his .45 and pointed it at Linden.

"You son of a bitch! You touch another one of my men, I'll kill you right here."

Sparks aimed at Linden's head.

"If you don't get the fuck out of here," said Sparks, "I'm going to blow your brains out."

Linden sat down in his jeep.

"All right," he seethed. "I'll leave, but I'll see you before a general court-martial."

"Go ahead."

Linden left with Higgins.

An officer in Linden's party, Lieutenant Colonel Walter Fellenz, then approached Sparks and began to argue with him.

"I'll see you after the war," threatened Fellenz.

"You son of a bitch," Sparks shot back. "What's the matter with right now?"

Fellenz backed off, returned to his jeep, and left, following behind Linden and Higgins.

Once Sparks had regained his composure, he issued further orders and made certain the concentration camp was secure as he had been ordered. Then he walked with Mann and Johnson to where his driver, Turk, was waiting nearby in their jeep.

Sparks got on the radio.

"We need food and medicine up here quick," Sparks said. "Quick. Quick."

At 4:35 P.M., Sparks also contacted his regiment and informed Colonel O'Brien that he had set up a command post in an administrative building inside the camp. Not long after, one of Sparks's men entered the command post and said an officer was requesting Sparks's presence. Sparks left his command post and in a nearby room met with a lieutenant colonel who told Sparks he was from the inspector general's office with the Seventh Army. He wanted to question Sparks about his altercation with Linden.

There was a large crash. A soldier from an artillery unit attached to Sparks's regiment had smashed a glass case holding antique weapons nearby.

Sparks angrily turned on the man.

"Get your ass out of here!" shouted Sparks.

"Can't you control your own men?" said the officer.

Sparks said the man wasn't under his direct command.

"Colonel, I want you to explain to me what happened with General Linden."

"I don't have time to sit around here," Sparks shot back, "and gossip with you."

Sparks returned to his command post. Later that afternoon, he met with General Frederick and Colonel O'Brien. Frederick was dressed in a winter combat jacket with a fur-lined collar. The sky was still gray. There was a chill in the air as Sparks gave his commanding officers a tour of Dachau. A Polish inmate explained some of the more notable sights.

The first stop was the dog pen. In an adjacent kitchen, guards had prepared meals for the camp's canines. The meals were of far greater nutritional value than the thin cabbage soup and lumps of sawdust bread given to the inmates.

The Thunderbird commanders moved on to the next sight—the crematorium.

"Here, about one hundred to one hundred and fifty men were put to death each day," the Pole explained. "Workers with grappling hooks dragged them into a waiting room next to the furnaces. There they waited to be cremated."

The Pole then moved on to some gravel pits. Countless enemies of the Reich had been shot here, he explained. Not far away was an embankment, and along its base was a ditch covered by a wooden grating.

"Men were forced to kneel like this," said the Pole as he knelt down to demonstrate, "and then be shot. Their blood drained into the ditch."

Some of the victims that spring had been German officers suspected of plotting against Hitler. They had been dispatched with a single shot in the back of the head.

As they toured the camp, Sparks explained to Frederick what had happened earlier that day at the coal yard. He also told him about the confrontation with General Linden.

"Don't worry about it," said Frederick. "I'll take care of that."

Sparks took Frederick at his word.

CHAPTER TWENTY-EIGHT

THE LONG DAY CLOSES

We live in a free world today because in 1945 the forces of imperfect goodness defeated the forces of near-perfect evil.

—MICHAEL DIPAULO, FRENCH CONSULATE STAFF MEMBER, ADDRESSING U.S. VETERANS IN 2001

Dachau inmates celebrate their liberation. [National Archives]

DARKNESS FELL ON DACHAU. At 7.03 P.M., Sparks learned that other companies from the regiment were moving toward the camp. He and his men would soon be relieved, and he would then be able to re-form his task force and push on to Munich.

Later that same evening, General Frederick's chief of staff, Kenneth Wickham, heard mention of Dachau at a briefing.

"What is Dachau?" Wickham asked Frederick.

Frederick didn't reply.

"Well, what did you see?" Wickham persisted.

Frederick did not answer because to describe what had happened there might lead to him breaking down. He did not want that, not after seeing so much. There was nothing that could excuse what the Germans had done there. That was all that could be said.

Back at Dachau, as the long day finally drew to a close, nineteen-year-old Dan Dougherty of C Company was one of many Thunderbirds who struggled to make sense of the horrors that day: "We knew we had seen something mind-boggling." That afternoon, Dougherty had entered the coal yard and discovered the bodies of the SS men who had been killed. One of the sergeants in his platoon had crawled over a "mound of corpses two or three feet high and fifteen feet across" and whipped out a hunting knife and cut off a finger. "He wanted an SS ring for a souvenir."

It would be a cold and sleepless night for other Thunderbirds, "the most sickening and devastating we had ever experienced," remembered Private John Lee. "The stench, the smell of death . . . permeated the air to the point that no one could eat his rations."

Lee's squad was assigned that night to guarding the camp's bakery to prevent any hunger-crazed inmates from raiding it. He was sick all night. "I don't think there was a guy who slept that night," he recalled, "and I don't think there was a guy who didn't cry openly that night."

Now, at least, Lee and his fellow Thunderbirds knew what they had been fighting for. As the *45th Infantry Division News* would soon declare in a headline above gruesome pictures: THIS IS WHY WE FOUGHT.

Unlike thousands of others who had died on the long journey to Germany, Sparks and his men had seen why the sacrifice had been necessary. "I've been in the army for 39 months," a Thunderbird would tell a reporter. "I've been overseas in combat for 23. I'd gladly go through it all again if I knew that things like this would be stopped."

DACHAU, APRIL 30, 1945

THE FOLLOWING MORNING, trucks loaded with food and medical supplies entered the camp, sent from Seventh Army supply depots. The piles of dead bodies had not been removed and were green- and yellow-skinned, rotting in the crisp spring air. Tears flowed from many who saw the camp that day. "We cried not merely tears of sorrow," recalled rabbi David Eichhorn, who also arrived that morning. "We cried tears of hate. Combat-hardened soldiers, Gentile and Jew, black and white, cried tears of hate."

By midmorning, Sparks had left Dachau and was again leading his task force toward Munich. On a narrow trail through a dense forest, he came across a group of German forward observers. They pointed their rifles at him and the other men in Sparks's jeep.

"Don't move," Sparks told his men.

Sparks had to think fast.

"Hands *haut*!" ordered Sparks.

A German lieutenant stared at Sparks.

Anxious moments passed.

The Germans put their bolt-action guns down. "They knew it was over," recalled Sparks. "Turned out they were lost."

Sparks and his men pressed on, past orchards where the first buds appeared on fruit trees, the Tyrol Mountains looming to the south, the first flowers showing in pastures, the peaks a jagged white, far higher than Webster Mountain and others to the north of Miami, Arizona, when Sparks was a boy. Then it was on into the suburbs of Munich.

Jack Hallowell, traveling with the regimental headquarters staff, recalled how many Thunderbirds now felt as they entered the birthplace of Nazism: "They wanted to kill. Probably for the first time they realized the full evil of the thing they were fighting. . . . The urge for revenge was in each man's trigger finger." It was just as well that Munich was not fiercely defended, as Aschaffenburg and Nuremberg had been, "for the resulting slaughter would have been historic if the feelings of the riflemen were any guide."

BERLIN, 3:30 P.M., APRIL 30, 1945

ADOLF HITLER TOOK one of his two Walther PPK pistols, sat down at a table, placed the barrel to his right temple, and squeezed the trigger. On the wall behind him was an oil painting of Frederick the Great, whose great military feats Hitler had invoked to inspire his generals in the last months of the war. The air was heavy with the scent of bitter almond—cyanide that Hitler's wife of just a day, Eva Braun, had just swallowed. She lay dead on a couch a few feet from her husband, her eyes open, wearing a blue dress with white collar and cuff.

Throughout the bunker, the news soon spread:

"*Der Chef ist tot!*" ("The chief is dead!")

MUNICH, APRIL 30, 1945

IN CENTRAL MUNICH that evening, the Thunderbirds finally reached the end of their long, bloody march across Nazi-occupied Europe. Sparks commandeered an apartment building for his last command post of the war. It began to snow as the guns fell silent that evening. Soon, a three-inch blanket covered the fields of rubble in the city where Nazism had been conceived. With an eye to history, Captain Anse Speairs, the regiment's roving adjutant, managed to find an apt place for a headquarters that night of April 30: the famous Munich beer hall, the Hofbräuhaus, scene of Hitler's failed attempt at revolution, the "Beer Hall Putsch," that had occurred in November 1923.

A white sign was jauntily daubed above the Hofbräuhaus in large letters so all could see: CP—157TH INFANTRY.

PART SEVEN

LAST BATTLES

CHAPTER TWENTY-NINE

THE LAST DAYS

German civilians in Munich loot warehouses on the second day of the Allied occupation, May 1, 1945. [National Archives]

DACHAU, MAY 1, 1945

IT WAS UNUSUALLY COLD that spring of 1945 in southern Germany. Marcus J. Smith, an American doctor working at Dachau, wrote in his diary on May 1: "Snow falling. Trying to keep warm, ambulatory inmates huddle over small fires on which they heat pots and bowls filled with scraps of food."

Later that day, the future French president, twenty-nine-year-old François Mitterrand, who had worked with Robert Antelme in the

French resistance, arrived in Dachau with a group of French observers and politicians. Mitterrand later claimed that he was crossing between barracks when he heard someone call out his name. It was Antelme.

Mitterrand rushed to his friend's side and helped him to stand up. With the voice of a dying man, Antelme begged Mitterrand to get him out of the camp, but the American officers accompanying Mitterrand's group forbade it. They were still under strict orders, as Sparks had been, not to let any of the inmates out, for fear of spreading typhus and other rampant diseases.

Mitterrand had no option but to return to Paris, leaving Antelme to surely die. It was an agonizing farewell, one never to be forgotten by any of those present. Antelme somehow summoned the strength to write a moving note to his wife back in Paris, the writer Marguerite Duras: "My darling, a stolen letter. Stolen from time, from the misery of the world, from suffering. A love letter. . . . Goodbye, Marguerite, you can't imagine how painful your name is to me."

As soon as he could, Mitterrand found a working telephone and managed to put a call through to Duras in Paris.

"Listen carefully," said Mitterrand. "Robert's alive."

Duras was stunned.

"Now keep calm," said Mitterrand. "He's in Dachau."

Duras had received news a fortnight before that Antelme had been seen alive, but then there had been no further word.

"Listen very, very carefully," stressed Mitterrand. "Robert is very weak, so weak you can't imagine."

Mitterrand had held a man weighing less than eighty pounds in his arms.

"It's a question of hours," Mitterrand added. "He may live for another three days but no more."

Mitterrand told Duras that two of his most trusted contacts were about to set out from Paris and try to spring Antelme from the camp. There was no knowing if her husband would be alive by the time they got there.

MUNICH, MAY 1, 1945

THE AMERICAN COMMAND car maneuvered past MPs and roadblocks, through shell-holed streets and past bullet-riddled buildings plastered with the insignia of the Thunderbirds and other liberating American units. General Frederick was headed from his division command post to the Haufbräuhaus in the center of the city. On one wall, someone had scrawled: "I AM ASHAMED TO BE A GERMAN."

Long lines of German POWs now streamed out of Germany's third largest city toward massive holding areas, the "cages."

"Where are we supposed to put them all?" asked Frederick.

Other Thunderbirds, by contrast, smiled as they watched Hitler's fabled "supermen" trudge by, en route to join some 125,000 POWs held in 45th Division enclosures at the war's end. Frederick's men were in good spirits, enjoying the spring sunshine as they flirted with local fräuleins looking for food, chocolate, and cigarettes. "Someone remarked that the German women seemed to have even better looking legs than the French women," recalled Jack Hallowell. "Then someone said there wasn't supposed to be any fraternizing. Then everyone laughed."

General Frederick arrived at the Hofbräuhaus, where he met with his maverick field commander, Colonel Felix Sparks. It was a grand setting. High vaulted windows flooded the 157th's new headquarters with bright spring light. Much of the building had been destroyed in intensive bombing on April 25, 1944, but several hundred beer steins had been found intact in the cellars. Before long, they would be put to good use.

"Things are heating up for you," said Frederick. "General Linden is causing a big stink. I'm going to send you on back home. Our division has been selected to make the invasion of Japan. We're going to re-equip and retrain and then we'll invade. You go on ahead, take a leave. You can rejoin us in the States."

The stink had in fact nothing to do with Linden, who did not press court-martial charges. It was about the shootings in the coal yard. Two

Signal Corps men, Arland Musser, a stills photographer, and Henry Gerzen, a film cameraman, had recorded the massacre. Their images had been developed and reviewed on April 30, the day after the liberation of the camp, and had been so shocking that they had been quickly sent up the chain of command to Seventh Army's chief of staff, Major General Arthur A. White. He was now considering an investigation into the shootings.

But Sparks knew none of this. As he saw the situation, Frederick was trying to protect him from court-martial because he had snapped and pointed his gun at Linden, not because some of his men had killed unarmed SS prisoners.

"I'm going to send a command car down in the morning to pick you up and take you to Le Havre, France," added Frederick. "There will be orders for you there to go home."

The next day, May 2, Sparks gathered his Third Battalion's company commanders at the Hofbräuhaus and informed them he was being sent back to the United States. It must have been a wrenching experience for him. He had fought all the way from the beaches of Sicily only to be relieved of his command with the war almost at an end. Sparks asked his three company commanders to tell his men he was leaving. In a log, one of his men noted later that day with deadpan understatement: "[Sparks] feels badly about leaving this unit."

As promised, a command car was put at Sparks's disposal. Three men left Munich with Sparks—his most trusted soldiers: Albert Turk, his driver; Karl Mann, his interpreter; and his runner, Carlton Johnson. By two o'clock that afternoon, they were motoring toward the French border.

DACHAU, MAY 3, 1945

WHILE SPARKS HEADED for home, friends of Robert Antelme drove in the exact opposite direction—toward Dachau—perhaps even passing Sparks's car on the way. One of the rescuers, a man called Beauchamp, recalled that when they arrived at the camp it was a beautiful spring day. They spent several hours searching for Antelme before finding him in an alley between barracks.

They dressed him in a French officer's uniform, propped him up, and walked him out of the camp. "As we passed the SS huts," one of his rescuers recalled, "Robert wanted to raise his cap and salute as he'd done as a detainee. We waited for [a] patrol to pass, then ran to the car with Robert in our arms." As they drove toward the French border, Antelme could not stop talking: "Death itself was quite obviously no longer important because of the urgent necessity it imposed to say everything."

They stopped in Pforzheim and tried to have something to eat in a French mess. The officers there looked away from Antelme, little more than a shuffling skeleton. They continued, driving across the border into France at night. "Although he thought he was going to die," recalled one of his rescuers, "there was no despair. He was happy to have this moment of freedom." In Verdun, a doctor examined Antelme and told the rescuers to drive slowly because a single jolt might cause his heart to fail.

A call was put through to Marguerite Duras: "I'm ringing to warn you that it's more terrible than anything we've imagined." They finally arrived in Paris and pulled up outside Duras's apartment in the rue Saint Benoit. Neighbors and the building's concierge were there to welcome Antelme. Duras rushed to the landing on her first floor, but at the sight of him she ran horrified back into her apartment, screaming.

It would be many hours before Duras was able to find the courage to look at her husband. Then she began to valiantly nurse Antelme, spoon-feeding him every few hours, terrified to sleep in case he died when she was unconscious. He had been a big man, over two hundred pounds in his prime, before the Gestapo and the SS had gone to work on him. Now he weighed just seventy-seven pounds. "The fight with death started very soon," recalled Duras in the most moving of all her many books, a memoir called *The War*. His temperature was soon 104.5 degrees, then 106. Through his wafer-thin chest, Duras could see his heart vibrate like a violin string. But it did not stop. It kept beating, defying the predictions of several doctors. "For seventeen days," wrote Duras, who nursed Antelme around the clock, "we hid from him his own legs and feet and whole unbelievable body."

Duras dared not tell Antelme she had fallen in love with another man—the news would kill him. Antelme's mind was as fragile as his body, which could not process anything but the thinnest soup: "We gave him gruel that was golden yellow, gruel for infants, and it came out of him dark green like slime from a swamp."

LE HAVRE, FRANCE, MAY 1945

IT TOOK SPARKS several days to get to Le Havre. After possibly stopping in Aschaffenburg to pick up bottles from the "Nazi liquor warehouse" that he had buried, Sparks crossed the border into France. He ordered Mann and Turk back to Munich and continued on with Johnson in the command car, through a devastated country where more than six hundred thousand had died during the war, four hundred thousand of them civilians. In retreat, the Germans had callously felled the long avenues of elms and ash that had once elegantly shaded most main roads, leaving countless ugly stumps. Some villages and crossroads were clogged with POWs and displaced people. The advancing Allies and retreating Germans had blown up many bridges. "It was a long way, six to seven hundred miles to Le Havre," recalled Sparks. "We went by Paris and got drunk one night. I wasn't in any hurry."

In Le Havre, Sparks reported at an office on a dockside.

An MP wearing a white helmet approached.

"Sergeant, I'm Colonel Sparks. I have orders to report here and I understand there are orders here for me to get on a ship to go back to the United States."

"Yes, Colonel, we're expecting you. I'll call my commander."

That sounded odd to Sparks.

What the hell is he calling his lieutenant for? he thought.

It wasn't long before an MP lieutenant arrived.

"Sorry, Colonel," said the MP politely, "I have orders to take you back to Seventh Army headquarters in Munich."

General Frederick had not been able to smooth things over after all. Had he even tried? Who had tipped off the military police?

"Well, I'll go back," said Sparks, "but you're not gonna take me."

Sparks's runner, Carlton Johnson, stood menacingly nearby.

The MP hesitated.

"You give me your word, Colonel?"

"Yes, I give you my word."

"Okay."

Sparks returned to his command car and headed back the way he had come.

PULLACH, MUNICH, MAY 4, 1945

IN BAVARIA, A Lieutenant Colonel Joseph M. Whitaker had begun a painstaking investigation into the shootings at Dachau. Twenty-three officers and enlisted men would soon give sworn testimony. On May 4, Lieutenant Bill Walsh found himself sitting in an office in Pullach, a suburb to the south of Munich, opposite Whitaker, the Seventh Army's assistant inspector general. Walsh had killed several defenseless SS men in Dachau, but he wasn't about to admit it. He'd fought too long and hard, seen too much, to go home with his head hung in shame.

What did Whitaker know? What had others said? Had any of his men talked?

"Please state your name, rank, serial number and organization."

"Lt. William P. Walsh, 0-414901, Company I, 157th Infantry."

Walsh was fully advised of his rights under the 24th Article of War.

"Did you have any serious fight in taking this camp?"

"There was a fight, yes, sir. Scattered resistance all through it."

After answering several more questions, Walsh explained what had happened in the coal yard: "I segregated the SS troopers from the regular army soldiers, put them in a yard. I ordered a machine gun [squad] to come inside and hold them back. . . . If they didn't stay back, fire at them. . . . I told the machine gun to fire to hold them back."

"How many were shot in the yard?

"I don't know, sir. There weren't many because we only fired one burst."

"With what weapon were you armed that day?"

"A carbine. I had a forty-five also."

Whitaker then picked up a photograph and handed it to Walsh. It showed his men in the coal yard and a machine gun pointing at SS guards lined up against a wall. It was one of several photographs taken by the Signal Corps that day which Whitaker had obtained. Walsh could not have known what else had been captured in stills or on film—there had also been a newsreel cameraman in the coal yard.

"Where were you when this picture was taken?"

"I am not in that that I can see. I am quite sure I am not in the picture."

"You were present when this picture was taken?"

"I will be frank, I don't know who took it or when it was taken, but I was around there when the shooting started."

"Were there any of your superior officers present when this shooting took place?"

"No, sir."

Had Walsh consulted Sparks or any other superior before the shooting "about what to do with the SS troopers"?

"No, sir."

"Did you intend to execute these SS men when you put them in the yard?"

"No, sir."

Over the next few days, Whitaker interviewed more than a dozen of Walsh's men in I Company. "Rumor had it that we were going to be sent to Leavenworth [a maximum security prison]," recalled one of them. Whitaker also went to the camp and examined the coal yard. Very little had changed. The bodies of the SS had not even been removed. Whitaker later reported finding seventeen dead Germans and dozens of brass casings from spent bullets in the coal dust. He found blood and pieces of flesh splattered onto the coal yard's wall, and counted twelve bullet holes.

Whitaker called more men to testify. When nineteen-year-old Private John Lee entered Whitaker's office, he saw to his shock that Whitaker had photographs of the shooting. Lee's name was written in pencil on the back of one of the photographs. "Somebody had already identified me," he recalled. "I was scared to death."

Whitaker quickly got down to business.

"Did the prisoners make any effort to move away from the wall?"

"When [we] got ready to fire a lot started to move forward toward us," said Lee.

"After the firing stopped were some of the men still standing?"

"Most of them I don't believe were shot at all but fell to the ground and hid under each other or tried to hide. That is why I believe they moved forward—so that they would have room to fall on their face."

"When I examined some of these bodies I observed that some had their skulls crushed in, the foreheads smashed back. Did you see any of that?"

"No, sir. I didn't see any of that."

Lee was also asked if Sparks was present during the shooting.

"No, I don't believe he was present."

Whitaker also asked another eyewitness, Private Harry Crouse, where Sparks had been during the shooting.

"By the railroad."

"Did he see this shooting?"

"I wouldn't say that he saw it. It might have been that his back was to it, but he certainly heard it."

"Did you see Colonel Sparks shoot any Germans that day?"

"No, sir."

So far, not one of Sparks's men had said anything that could incriminate him. But then Whitaker questioned a Private Fred Randolph, a rifleman in I Company.

"Did you see SS men and other Germans killed by American soldiers?"

"Yes, sir. I did."

"What was the first such incident you saw?"

"When we first entered. Four Jerries came walking down with their hands on their heads and surrendered to Lieutenant Walsh. Walsh was quite angry and upset and took them into one of those wagons and called for a machine gun, then he changed his mind and took them into a boxcar and fired his pistol at them, and one of the GIs climbed in after Lieutenant Walsh got through and fired his gun at bodies of half dead Germans I guess. Fired about eight or nine shots."

"Do you know the name of that GI?"

"Pruitt."

"After the incident with Walsh at the boxcar when next did you see some Germans shot?"

Randolph's answer was explosive.

"At about the same time one German was already shot once I think, and was lying near the railroad tracks, and Colonel Sparks fired at him with his pistol, about two or three shots."

If Randolph's statement could be supported, Sparks would possibly face court-martial. And if he could be linked to the coal yard killings too, then he would without doubt be held responsible for his men's actions at Dachau. Lieutenant Walsh was the key to a prosecution if there was to be one. Under further questioning, would he incriminate Sparks, his commanding officer?

Walsh was called back. He did not implicate Sparks. He did, however, admit that he himself had given the order to open fire, but only after the SS had made a move toward his men. Whitaker did not believe that the SS had done so. He concluded that seventeen SS men had in fact been "summarily executed" on Walsh's orders and that Walsh and others "participated in the execution of the seventeen."

PARIS, MAY 1945

PARIS HAD LOST none of its charms. After navigating the appalling roads from Le Havre to the capital, Sparks could not resist sampling the delights of the City of Light for another couple of days, probably visiting the hugely popular "Pig Alley," the Place Pigalle, where thousands of rowdy GIs congregated in search of booze and a good time. Sparks got drunk again and then set out for Germany, crossing pontoon bridges, now-silent mountains in the Vosges, and endless streams of displaced people. He finally found Seventh Army headquarters not far from Munich, in a small town.

Sparks reported to the Seventh Army's chief of personnel.

"Well, Colonel," the chief said, "General Patton's Third Army has taken over these headquarters as of today and we're being shipped to Austria."

"Well, where's General Patton's headquarters?"

"Bad Tölz, fifteen or twenty miles outside of Munich."

"Okay, I'll go there."

Sparks set off once more with Johnson in the command car, headed for Patton's headquarters. Patton was now the newly appointed military governor of Bavaria. He was tired after three years of war, needed a long rest, and was impatient to get back to the United States to bask in the glory he knew was his. Under his leadership, the Third Army had captured more enemy prisoners, liberated more territory, and advanced farther in less time than any other American armored force.

The war was just days from ending and Patton was far from happy about it. "This business of not having to fight is rather an inglorious ending for a great experience," Patton wrote. He was hopeful, however, of getting an opportunity to fight the Japanese.

It was late afternoon when Sparks arrived at Third Army headquarters, a grim-looking *Waffen*-SS barracks with some nine hundred rooms, in the foothills of the Alps. He reported to the Third Army's chief of staff, who was rude and angry. He told Sparks that he was facing court-martial for allowing German prisoners to be killed unlawfully.

The charges were so serious that General Patton himself was going to handle the matter.

"General Patton's out now," the chief of staff added, "but he'll be back in the morning. Come and report to him at nine o'clock tomorrow morning."

The next morning, a worried Sparks arrived for his meeting.

"Colonel, sit here," a captain told Sparks and then left to find Patton, who was staying in a nearby mansion once owned by the wealthy publisher of *Mein Kampf*.

Sparks sat waiting for an hour, he later recalled, growing increasingly anxious and impatient.

"When's the captain coming back?" he asked.

"I don't think he's coming back today."

"When he comes back," an exasperated Sparks snapped, "you tell him to go to hell."

Sparks was asked to wait just a little longer. Finally, he was shown into a small office, no more than ten feet square, just big enough for two chairs and a desk.

Behind the desk sat the four-star legend, George S. Patton.

Sparks saluted.

"Sir, I'm Colonel Sparks. I have orders to report to you."

"Oh, yes, Colonel Sparks," said Patton in his strangely high-pitched voice. "I have some serious court-martial charges against you and some of your men here on my desk."

Sparks looked over at the papers on Patton's desk.

"Didn't you serve under me in Africa and Sicily?"

"Yes, sir, I did. I would like to explain about what happened at Dachau."

"There is no point in an explanation. I have already had these charges investigated, and they are a bunch of crap. I'm going to tear up these goddamn papers on you and your men."

Sparks would later remember that it was with a characteristically dramatic flourish that Patton did indeed tear up the papers on his desk before dumping them in a wastebasket.

"You have been a damn fine soldier," added Patton. "Now go home."

The interview had lasted less than two minutes.

Sparks saluted and left.

GEORGE PATTON WAS happy to sweep the whole incident at Dachau under the carpet, just as he had done with other unsavory episodes concerning the Thunderbirds, whom he had once praised as the "Killer Division." According to biographer Carlo D'Este: "Patton was soft on those who achieved great deeds in battle, and the petty charges against Sparks fell under the heading of 'chickenshit.' Unless their crimes were heinous, such men who served under him received medals and praise, not court-martials."

An army judge advocate had read Whitaker's report on the shootings and believed there were grounds to bring murder charges against Lieutenants Walsh and Busheyhead, and Private Pruitt, who had finished off Walsh's victims. But the commander of the Seventh Army, Wade Haislip, decided not to carry out the recommended court-martial because the initial investigation had, he argued, not taken into account the emotional state of the men. Besides, no one wanted an American atrocity, a "war crime" in SS veteran Johann Voss's words, reported at the end of the war, when the victors were understandably at their most morally self-righteous.

The crimes of the Nazis, not American heroes, were what the top brass were keen to investigate and publicize. According to the 45th

Division's chief of staff, Kenneth Wickham: "General Patton, who had taken over the Army area, kind of said, 'To hell with it [the I.G. investigation],' and that was it. We didn't go further into it and General Frederick wasn't concerned much one way or the other. He was just kind of annoyed by it."

After a lengthy investigation of the treatment of all German POWs, in late 1945 Colonel Charles L. Decker, an acting deputy judge advocate, concluded that at Dachau there had probably been a violation of international law because the SS had been shot without trial. "But in the light of the conditions which greeted the eyes of the first combat troops," he added, "it is not believed that justice or equity demand that the difficult and perhaps impossible task of fixing individual responsibility now be undertaken."

IN A LATER WAR, Lieutenant Walsh might have been tried for murder. But after helping defeat Hitler, he returned as a hero to Massachusetts, attended Northeastern University on the GI Bill, enjoyed a long and successful career as an engineer, and was honored at several Holocaust commemoration events in his final years. At the dedication of the U.S. Holocaust Museum in 1993, he was a "special honoree," and at the fiftieth anniversary of D-Day, a year later, he was again treated as a "VIP hero" at the Capitol, where he was helped to stand during the televised ceremony, because of weakening legs, by none other than Senator Bob Dole from Kansas, who had been badly wounded while serving with the 10th Mountain Division in Italy in April 1945.

A proud Thunderbird to his last breath, Bill Walsh died aged seventy-eight in July 1998. He was remembered, according to the *Boston Globe*, as a gentle and kind man who loved to play golf and be with his children. There is no evidence that Walsh had ever expressed or felt any guilt, let alone regret, about his actions at Dachau.

"Some goddamned day," Walsh had said in 1990, "when I go to hell with the rest of the SS, I'm going to ask them how the hell they could do it. I don't think there was any SS guy that was shot or killed in the defense of Dachau who wondered why he was killed, or couldn't figure it out. I think they all knew goddamned-well-right why some of them were killed, goddamned-well-right."

CHAPTER THIRTY

VICTORY IN EUROPE

In the United States of America, in the city of Philadelphia, upon the exact spot where 169 years ago a group of brave Americans met and decided to fight for American independence, there stands a marker upon which is written these very same words: "Proclaim freedom throughout the world to the inhabitants thereof."

—RABBI DAVID EICHHORN, SABBATH SERVICE, DACHAU CONCENTRATION CAMP, MAY 6, 1945

GIs read about Hitler's death in the Stars and Stripes. *[National Archives]*

REIMS, FRANCE, MAY 7, 1945

THE GERMANS WALKED INTO the Ecole Professionnelle et Technique de Garçons, a redbrick three-story building in Reims, and then strode along a corridor to a classroom on the ground floor. Fifty-four-year-old Alfred Jodl and Admiral Hans-Georg von Friedeburg then stopped and squinted, momentarily blinded by the arc lights set up for a bank of film cameras in the crowded classroom.

The sharp-featured Jodl was one of Hitler's most despicable generals, certainly no man of honor. Just one example of his venality was his signing of the infamous "Commando Order" of October 28, 1942, declaring that Allied commandos and partisans were to be shot rather than treated as POWs.

Jodl was told that the documents on a table before him were ready for his signature. It was 2:41 A.M. as he signed the formal surrender documents with a Sheaffer pen.

"I want to say a word," said Jodl.

"Yes, of course," replied Eisenhower's chief of staff, fifty-year-old American general Walter Bedell Smith.

"With this signature," stated Jodl, "the German people and the German armed forces are, for better or worse, delivered into the victor's hands. In this war, which has lasted more than five years, both have achieved and suffered more than any other people in the world. In this hour I can only express the hope that the victor will treat them with generosity."

They would be treated with immense generosity. But Jodl himself would not. He would be hanged for crimes against humanity in October 1946.

Not far from the classroom, General Dwight Eisenhower paced back and forth in his secretary's office. Bedell Smith strode into the room. The surrender had been signed. Jodl and Friedeburg entered and walked to the middle of the room, clicked their heels, and saluted the Allied supreme commander.

Eisenhower stood stiffly. He had sworn that he would never shake hands with a Nazi and saw no reason to start doing so now.

"Do you understand the terms of the document of surrender you have just signed?"

"*Ja, ja,*" said Jodl.

"You will get details and instructions at a later date. And you will be expected to carry them out faithfully."

Jodl nodded.

"That is all."

Jodl bowed, saluted, and then marched out of the office.

Eisenhower was suddenly all smiles.

"Come on, let's all have a picture!"

Later that morning, he sent a message to his bosses in Washington, the Combined Chiefs of Staff: "THE MISSION OF THIS ALLIED FORCE WAS FULFILLED AT 0241, LOCAL TIME, MAY 7, 1945, EISENHOWER."

LONDON, MAY 8, 1945

THE FOLLOWING DAY, May 8, 1945, the world learned of the German final surrender. There were intense and prolonged celebrations in many capitals to mark the end the most destructive war in human history. The men of evil, Churchill told the British nation, "are now prostrate before us." Later that afternoon, after having lunched with the king at Buckingham Palace, Churchill was driven to Whitehall. When he stepped onto a balcony at the Ministry of Health, he could barely hear himself speak, so loud were the cheers of the crowds.

"This is your victory," he shouted. "It is the victory of the cause of freedom in every land. In all our long history we have never seen a greater day than this."

BAVARIA, MAY 8, 1945

WHILE CIVILIANS EMBRACED, kissed total strangers, and took to streets around the globe in euphoria, many infantrymen in Europe, brutalized and broken, sat alone with their grief or paced their rest areas in mournful silence. "There is V-E Day without but no peace within," wrote the war's most decorated infantrymen, Audie Murphy, of the 3rd Division, which had fought at the Thunderbirds' shoulder all the way from Sicily. "People were damaged," remembered Thunderbird Guy Prestia. "It was like we'd been in a car crash. There was trauma. It takes a while to get over that."

News of the surrender reached the Thunderbirds that evening of May 8. "There was great relief," recalled Sparks, "but no celebrations." Although many of Sparks's men had kept booze seized from the warehouse in Aschaffenburg, it was not a night of popping champagne corks and knocking back the best cognac. It was hard to believe, hard to accept that the killing and dying were finally over. There would be no more Anzios, Salernos, or Reipertswillers. Finally, after the death of 135,576 young Americans, Europe was free.

Few had fought so long and hard during the war, indeed any war, as Lieutenant Colonel Felix Sparks. "Boy I was goddamn glad when it was over," he remembered. "I only weighed about 130 pounds. I was just skin and bones."

Sparks had seen too much and waited too long for the end. For four years, he had planned for this day and had often wondered if he would ever see it. So many of his men were not there with him: The regiment had suffered 20,251 casualties since landing in Sicily. A total of 1,449 of his fellow Thunderbirds in the 157th Infantry Regiment had laid down their lives to liberate Europe from the greatest evil of modern times.

SALZBURG, AUSTRIA, MAY 8, 1945

MARGUERITE HIGGINS LEARNED of the German surrender as she was interviewing 3rd Division troops in Salzburg, seventy miles south of Munich. "We all went out on a balcony to see artillery guns of the division flash in celebration into the sky," she recalled. "Red and blue flares, tracer bullets, ack-ack guns, tank guns, fired into the midnight sky for the last time on this front."

The noise echoed throughout the valley below, the explosions illuminating a jet-black sky, casting bright splashes on the mountain peaks and the deep valleys around Berchtesgaden, Hitler's mountain retreat. There were tears in Higgins's eyes.

The first woman to win a Pulitzer for foreign reporting, Higgins would later remember her World War II experiences with great affection, writing of the "human closeness and magnificence of character that danger sometimes provokes. . . . I have witnessed the awesomeness of man tried beyond endurance."

ROMMILLY-SUR-SEINE, FRANCE, MAY 8, 1945

"*WAS IST AUS uns geworden?*"

"What has become of us?"

That was the question a relieved twenty-year-old SS Corporal Johann Voss asked after the final fluttering roll of MG42s had sounded in Europe. The silver runes he had worn so proudly were now a "symbol of all wickedness." Voss languished along with a staggering five million other Axis prisoners under Allied control in one of the many POW enclosures that dotted liberated Europe: an archipelago that was almost as vast as Hitler's web of labor and concentration camps, where more than ten million civilians had died, including more than a million Jewish children, and where hundreds of thousands now struggled to recover from extreme malnutrition. "Our world has perished," wrote Voss while in captivity. "A new world dawns, one in which our values are utterly discredited, and we will be met with hatred or distinct reserve for our past."

The SS had committed staggering acts of atrocity. But they had not all been monsters. Voss's unit, for example, would not be charged with a single war crime. His comrades in the 6th SS-Mountain Division, which had defeated Sparks and his men at Reipertswiller, had fought at the end to defend their country. Like their fellow Germans, they had paid a high price for their attraction to Hitler. The Fatherland lay in ruins; the dreams of a Germany restored to world power had been torched; most of their comrades had died.

In one Berlin suburb, women now outnumbered men by more than ten to one. Total losses, civilian and military, approached 10 percent of the 1939 population. More than five million German dead littered the battlefields of a devastated Europe, especially in the east. Ninety percent of all German combat deaths had in fact occurred fighting the Soviets, who had suffered and sacrificed most to defeat Hitler: an astounding 65 percent of all Allied fatalities.

Like many of his fellow SS warriors, Voss would never accept the International Military Tribunal's declaration that the SS was a criminal organization. "The whole idea of considering a combat unit as a criminal gang is preposterous," he would write. "It can only be seen as an act of revenge—by adding dishonor to the defeat. It also shows much ignorance of the spirit of the *Waffen*-SS." The verdict, Voss believed, was "meant to rob us of our honor, the very last value of which a defeated enemy can be deprived. '*Ehre verloren, alles verloren.*' ('Honor lost, all lost.') Unconditional surrender was not enough: humiliation had to be added to make the victory complete."

Voss would be released from a POW camp in December 1946 and rejoin his immediate family, all of whom had survived the war. He was lucky indeed: He had never received an SS blood group tattoo in his armpit and was therefore not physically branded as a criminal for life.

PARIS, MAY 1945

EUROPEANS BEGAN THE painful process of healing, grieving, and dealing with the psychological trauma of so many days of war. Never had so many people been killed so quickly—more than nineteen million civilians in Europe alone. In Paris, one of Nazism's ravaged survivors, Robert Antelme, slowly began to regain weight. Later that May, when his wife, Marguerite Duras, felt he was strong enough, she broke the news to him that his twenty-four-year-old sister, Marie-Louise, had died at the hands of the Nazis in Ravensbrück just days from the end of the war, one of about fifty thousand women who had succumbed there to despair, overwork, disease, and starvation. Later that summer, Duras also finally admitted that she was in love with another man. "I told him we had to get a divorce," she recalled. "He asked if one day we might be together again. I said no." Antelme still could not stop loving her. He was incapable now of hate.

Antelme had been but one of countless people caught up in the "crazy, hysterical madness" of World War II in Europe, in John Steinbeck's words. He would later write one of the most powerful accounts of the war, *The Human Race*, about his time in captivity. It was his only book. There was no need for another. He died aged seventy-three in 1990 after a long illness, one of more than thirty thousand Europeans liberated from hell by Sparks and his men in 1945. "The world goes on being awash in wickedness, arrogance, mediocrity," wrote one of his many friends. "But Antelme showed us that the business of living may be accomplished with goodness, with modesty, and with nobility."

KÖNIGSPLATZ, MUNICH, MEMORIAL DAY, MAY 30, 1945

THEY DID NOT want it to resemble a Nazi parade, here where Hitler had addressed hundreds of thousands of hysterical followers at the height of his power. So they turned the microphone low. The colors of the Thunderbirds' three regiments flapped gently in the breeze under bright sunshine as Protestant, Jewish, and Catholic chaplains addressed the five perfect rectangles of men filling only half of the vast King's Plaza in Munich, flanked by eight tanks. A few hundred Germans watched from near a pile of rubble that had been cleared from the square. Then General Robert Frederick walked to a platform set up before the rows of Thunderbirds.

So few had lived to see the end. Nine out of ten men who had left America with the division had been wounded, killed, or taken prisoner by the time the guns fell silent in Europe for the second time in the twentieth century. The division's initial number of men had been replaced seven times since July 10, 1943, when it had first landed in Sicily.

No American division had fought harder to liberate Europe. And the top brass knew it. General Alexander Patch, Seventh Army commander, described the Thunderbirds as the "best damned outfit in the U.S. Army." The Germans also had great respect, having dubbed the National Guard unit the "Falcon Division." Only at Reipertswiller had they managed to defeat it. High praise also came from none other than Field Marshal Albert Kesselring, arguably Germany's finest World War II field commander: "The 45th is one of the two best Divisions I have ever encountered." The other was the 3rd Division, which had fought so often at the Thunderbirds' side, and had lost more men than any other division in Europe.

Few people would ever be aware of what the Thunderbirds had achieved or the extent of their losses: 3,650 men killed in action, 13,729 men wounded in action, and an astonishing 41,647 non-battle casualties—62,907 in all during their 511 days at war. Much of the glory and headlines in Europe had been grabbed by Patton's Third Army after D-Day, June 6, and by other celebrated units, such as the 101st Airborne. The horrors of Anzio and Salerno had been forgotten in favor of the heroism of Omaha Beach and the American grit at the Battle of the Bulge. The disasters and bloody attrition of Italy and the Vosges did not square with the more reassuring narrative of inevitable victory.

Even senior Pentagon officials, visiting Munich that May of 1945, knew astonishingly little about the American division that had, in the words of historian Carlo D'Este, "distinguished itself as the most combat-experienced division in the US Army." One such bureaucrat, a colonel, even made the mistake of asking a veteran which beach he had "come over," assuming it had been in Normandy.

"Sir," the insulted Thunderbird replied, "my outfit hit so many beaches that we forgot their names. One soldier out of my old company is still alive. The rest are buried at Salerno and Anzio and the Siegfried Line. Sir, I never saw Omaha or Utah beach. We were busy killing krauts. Anything else, sir?"

It is not known how the official reacted or whether he even stayed in Munich long enough that May to watch General Frederick address the entire 45th Division, gathered on Memorial Day in the King's Plaza, the vast square at the center of the city.

"Today," said Frederick, "in the very heart of a conquered Germany, we pause to pay tribute to our comrades who gave the fullest measure of the sacrifice for their country. We cannot bring them back, but we can do our part to insure the endurance of those principals for which they died."*

As Frederick left the platform, he came across his chief of staff, Kenneth Wickham, who noticed there were tears in Frederick's eyes.

"Oh God, how I hate war," said Frederick.

*Frederick spent 551 days in combat and was decorated with twenty-eight U.S. and six foreign medals.

CHAPTER THIRTY-ONE

PEACE BREAKS OUT

A pretty girl is like a melody. But the melody of a pretty German girl is your death march. She hates you, just like her brother who fought against you. . . . Don't fraternize!

—AMERICAN FORCES NETWORK RADIO BROADCAST, 1945

Children play in the ruins of Nazi Germany, 1945. [National Archives]

BAVARIA, JUNE–JULY 1945

NO ONE KNEW WHEN the call would come to return to the boats, this time to go home. It was excruciating having to wait, especially for Sparks, who had yet to set eyes on his son. When his men weren't plotting which farm to buy back home or which high school classmate to ask out on a date, they traded sweet-smelling Lucky Strikes and long-necked bottles of Coca-Cola from the PX for local beer and indeed fräuleins, who outnumbered local men by three to one. Some Thunderbirds still wanted to "kick the Germans in the teeth," but the vast majority could distinguish between the ordinary German soldier and the Nazi regime, and very few held grudges. In fact, there was extraordinarily little enmity left toward their vanquished foe.

Thunderbirds played with hungry German children and showered them with Hershey's chocolate and gum. (The children's daily calorie intake was half of what it had been before the war, and elsewhere malnutrition and attendant diseases were rampant.) They also shared gasoline with the fathers of girls they dated, washed down endless steins of Bavarian beer as they danced to brassy folk music, and didn't give a damn what the U.S. Army, which had scandalously underpaid them for four years, thought of it all. Thunderbird Paul Cundiff dated a German refugee from Aschaffenburg that summer and believed in all seriousness that his and other Thunderbirds' "response to the peace in Germany was one of the greatest demonstrations of democracy the world had ever known."

Sparks recalled with typically laconic understatement that there was "some non-fraternization with the German Fräuleins, the latter in compliance with specific army orders. However, noncompliance was widespread." Fraternization was in fact so common among the sixty-one U.S. divisions in occupied Germany at the end of the war that the army's inspector general in Washington sent squads of prurient "chickenshit" busybodies to investigate. They were far from welcome in Munich. General Frederick, for one, was incensed by their officious lack of sensitivity to the reality of occupation duties. Young German women in the hundreds were by now dating Thunderbirds, even marrying some of them, and he was much more concerned with restoring order and basic services to the ruined city than clamping down on fraternization.

"Why do you allow your men to date German girls?" Frederick was asked.

"Rubbish!" he snorted. "I asked men suspected of that if the girls were German and they said, 'No, displaced girls from Poland.' It's easy to differentiate because German girls wear silk undergarments and the Poles wear burlap."

The inspectors seemed to be satisfied with that and left Munich. "And had they asked one more question," Frederick recalled, "they would have left on stretchers." A week or so later, after his remarks had been reported in a U.S. newspaper, Frederick received a letter from his wife.

"How do you know," she asked, "what underwear girls have on?"

REIMS, FRANCE, JULY 1945

IT WAS NOW more than two years since Sparks had landed in Sicily. To his great frustration, instead of returning home he was assigned late that June to a new command in Reims, where the German surrender had taken place. As "Commandant of the Sweep Sub Area," he was to oversee the transport of tens of thousands of impatient GIs back to the United States. Liberty ships would arrive at several Channel ports, and Sparks would determine how many and which soldiers should then board for the return to the States. Understandably, as he saw more and more men with far less combat experience going home, he soon grew to detest his new assignment. "I got goddamn tired of it," he recalled. "I had a wife back in the States, a kid who was two and a half years old that I'd never seen." He knew it would take another year at least to ship every American soldier out of Europe.

"I'll be damned if I'm going to stay here another year," he vowed.

Sparks had a full staff and an adjutant. Ever the maverick, one day he ordered his adjutant to list his name as the troop commander on the next ship that had no officers aboard who were above Sparks's rank. A few days later, his adjutant told Sparks there was a ship scheduled to leave from Antwerp with mostly Air Corps men. The commanding officer was listed as a major.

"Eliminate his name and put mine there," Sparks ordered.

Sparks set off for Antwerp and boarded the ship bound for New York as its troop commander. "Nobody said a word. I had my own stateroom and I got to eat with the captain." The voyage across the Atlantic seemed to last forever. "It took three weeks for Christ sake! The captain and I and a couple others played bridge the whole time."

Sparks's fellow Thunderbirds also returned that summer, aboard the SS *Marine Devil* and the SS *Sea Owl*. "On board," remembered one man, "the relief was as deep as the sea itself, for only when land faded would many believe that they were actually homeward bound." After 827 days overseas, the Old World was now finally in their wake. The division's artillery had left behind almost a million shell casings for scrap metal merchants from Sicily to Munich to remember them by. The Thunderbirds approached New York after eight days of "hominy grits" for breakfast and "smoke corned shoulder" for dinner.

Young American women waved from small boats that plowed up the Hudson River abreast of the troopship. Somehow, they were so much more beautiful than the European ladies they'd loved and now left far behind. To the Thunderbirds' immense delight, one group of women, a river band, began to play "Beer Barrel Polka." It got better. An inspection officer boarded and broke the news that all the Thunderbirds were to be treated to steak dinners. Then he apologized for the mist and rain that had greeted them.

"What do you mean, rain?" cried one Thunderbird. "It's the most beautiful day we've ever seen."

NEW YORK HARBOR, AUGUST 1945

SHE STOOD TALL, 151 feet to be exact, at the center of Liberty Island, unblemished by the war, in her flowing pale turquoise robes, holding up a torch, representing Libertas, the Roman goddess of freedom, a broken chain lying at her feet. Sparks would never forget first setting eyes on her as he stood on the deck of a troopship, about to set foot on American soil for the first time in more than two years. To his right, across the busy New York Harbor, he saw New York City for the first time, the Manhattan skyline, the Empire State Building most prominent, towering above the streets crowded with honking yellow cabs and countless frisky military personnel.

Almost as soon as Sparks arrived at Camp Kilmer across the Hudson River in New Jersey, he managed to place a call to his wife, Mary, back in Arizona. It was the first time they had spoken in more than two years. Sparks had left her as a twenty-four-year-old second lieutenant and was now a world-weary lieutenant colonel, as well as a father who had yet to hold his two-year-old son, Kirk, in his arms. "He said he'd been put in charge of a troop train," Mary recalled more than sixty years later. "He was headed out west but it would take him a few days."

Sparks had had enough of the army by the time he arrived in baking hot San Antonio several days later. Told he could be discharged at Fort Bliss, the army base near El Paso, he called Mary again. He couldn't wait a day longer to see her and wanted to be alone with her before returning home to Miami, Arizona, where his family were eager to welcome him.

"Come to El Paso," Sparks told Mary, "and get a hotel room."

She took her father's car, dressed in her best, a striped pantsuit, her strawberry-blond hair done up as was the style at the time, and set out from Tucson, through the empty desert, alone, wondering how he might look, how he might have changed, as excited as she had ever been. She booked into a hotel, parked the car, and went to her room fifteen floors above downtown El Paso, the Rio Grande just to the south, Mexico beyond. She had waited two years to see Sparks again, and every minute more was agonizing. The last time he had held her close, their baby Kirk had been inside her, kicking. She had prayed every day he would survive and that her son would have a father. She had shown Kirk pictures of Felix and read his letters out loud to him. She wanted nothing more in her life than for him to see his father and be held by him.

EL PASO, TEXAS, AUGUST 15, 1945

AT 7 P.M., radios across the city and indeed America announced that the Japanese emperor Hirohito had made a public broadcast for the first time. He had in fact declared that the Japanese would "treat with the enemy" after it had employed a "new and most cruel" weapon—the uranium 235 atomic bomb, dropped on Hiroshima on August 6, killing some eighty thousand civilians, and then on Nagasaki on August 9, incinerating a further twenty-five thousand.

World War II was finally over.

Some 416,000 Americans out of 16,000,000 in military service had died since Pearl Harbor, at least 200,000 fewer than during the Civil War. Almost twice as many had died in Europe as had died in the Pacific. Three-quarters had served in the army, whose losses dwarfed those of the combined navy and fabled Marine Corps by a factor of four. The Japanese had lost around 1.2 million men in battle, more than a tenth of their military personnel.

Never again would America enjoy such prestige or economic clout around the globe. The nation of 140 million people had arguably suffered least of all the main belligerents yet had gained most from victory, its industrial productivity now greater than the rest of the world combined. Average wages had increased by more than 50 percent and the catastrophic unemployment of the thirties had disappeared. By contrast, the Soviets had lost more than six million men in battle, and a further fourteen million were wounded. Many of its cities and much of its agricultural land had been laid to waste. An estimated ten million Soviet civilians were also killed, part of the final butcher's bill for World War II—"the Great Patriotic War," as Russians still call it—of well over fifty million lives.

It was indeed America's greatest achievement: Two highly advanced forces of immense inhumanity and destruction had been defeated in less than four years. There was plenty, finally, to celebrate, and all across the nation people went wild with relief and delight, streaming from homes, workplaces, and bars into the streets.

THAT NIGHT OF V-J Day, Mary sat on her own, feeling terribly lonely, listening to drunken revelers crowding downtown El Paso. She had left Kirk in the care of her parents back in Tucson. The following morning, she heard a knock on the door. She opened it. Her husband was finally within reach, standing there, thin and gaunt, around 140 pounds, in his lieutenant colonel's uniform, a felt Thunderbird patch and silver oak leaves on his shoulders, same gorgeous black hair, a great smile on his face, joy in the dark brown eyes. Then, at last, he was holding her in his arms. There was no need for words. It was the happiest day of her life.

They had saved themselves for each other. She was real, not an image, so pure, an angel, a goddess; full of stories of Miami, his three sisters, the now booming mines, and of his son, two-year-old Kirk, walking, talking, able to say "Papa." The thought of being with Mary again one day had sustained him through the darkest hours, times when he might otherwise have given up hope like so many other young men who lay in graveyards from North Africa to the Alps. At last she was beside him, fifteen floors above the dry, dusty city, its streets filled with happy voices, drunks in peacetime.

To mark the end of the war, all businesses in El Paso closed, even the restaurants. But the streets were full of cars, horns hooting and honking, and with people hollering. Sparks and Mary went hungry, but couldn't have cared less. The following day, they climbed into the car and drove a couple of miles north, toward the boulder-strewn Franklin Mountains. At Fort Bliss, Sparks found an adjutant.

"I want to get out of the army," said Sparks. "I was in college when I got drafted and I want to go back."

"I'm sorry, Colonel. I don't have any orders to release anybody."

"The war is over and I want to get out."

"I'm sorry, Colonel, we don't have any orders or authority . . . but we anticipate we will."

"Well, as soon as you get authority," said Sparks, "you send me a telegram."

Sparks gave him Mary's address in Tucson and then climbed back into her father's car and set out on the four-hundred-mile journey across the desert to their homes in Arizona, the Chiricahua Mountains looming to the south, the Gila wilderness rising to the north near Silver City. There was plenty of time to catch up and get to know each other again. But Sparks said nothing about what he had really been through while he had been away. That would have to wait another thirty years. In Tucson, their car pulled up in front of Mary's parents' home. Sparks was soon walking into the house, to the room where his child was waiting. Mary would never forget seeing him hold their son for the first time. Kirk recognized his father from photographs, but it would be several weeks before he grew accustomed to the tall stranger who had suddenly entered his life. It was difficult to forge a bond at first. "He was two-and-a-half years old," recalled Sparks. "I had never seen him. He didn't take to me very well."

Sparks then drove a hundred and twenty miles north with Mary and Kirk, through the Sonoran Desert and the Tonto National Forest with its towering Ponderosa pines and bald eagles, to Miami, Arizona. The copper mines were busy again; the reassuring growl of machinery beneath the ground had returned. There was no party to welcome him, just close hugs from his sisters and parents.

A few days later, Sparks received a telegram announcing that he could in fact be discharged. He had fought in eight campaigns and earned two Silver Stars, two Purple Hearts, and the Croix de Guerre, among many other honors. But now his career in the U.S. Army, one of the most distinguished of any American in combat in World War II, was finally over.

COLORADO, LATE 1940S

HE DIVED TO the ground, lying flat. Would the shrapnel miss? But there was no hot metal and, when he looked up, no screaming men with stomachs gouged, limbs missing, jagged bones showing. There was just a power line buzzing above his head.

Other than diving to the ground under power lines, Sparks showed remarkably few outward signs of being damaged by the war. Yet emotionally he had been profoundly affected, and it had been partly his fault: He had gotten to know his men too well, and so their deaths had left him more wounded than most. There had been so many men killed under his command. In particular, he remembered the senseless gunning down in Italy of his medic Jack Turner, from Lamar, Colorado; and the losses of Sergeant Vanderpool and Lieutenant Railsback near Epinal a year later. Turner's death seemed to torment him most. He would never forget seeing him cut in half by machine-gun fire, lying in the open, bullet-riddled, with a red-cross armband, "deader than hell."

During the war, Sparks had enjoyed listening to men like Turner wax lyrical about their hometowns, the Rockies and Colorado in general. "I got to thinking about it," he recalled. "I had served with all these men from Colorado and [yet] I had never been in Colorado." In early September 1945, eager to complete his law degree, Sparks called the registrar at the University of Colorado and learned that he could attend the fall semester, which started the following week. He and Mary packed a few bags and with their son took a bus from Arizona to Boulder, Colorado, a thousand miles to the north. Their first home as a family was in a trailer park, dubbed "Vetsville," near Boulder Creek. "The trailer was a little bit primitive—we didn't have a bathroom or water," remembered Sparks. At last, he was back at school, back with his family. Just a few months ago, he had been confronting immense loss and horror. Now he had a future. He had survived.

SPARKS HAD BEEN attending classes for less than a month when he received a letter from the governor of Colorado, John Vivian: "I've discovered you were one of the senior officers in your regiment and have returned to Colorado." Vivian went on to ask Sparks to help reorganize the state's National Guard. "There were still a lot of problems in the world," Sparks later explained, "and the Army was getting frantic because it didn't have any soldiers."

Sparks had no desire whatsoever to resume a full-time military career, but he strongly supported the National Guard and its traditions and was glad to help revive it in Colorado. But it would take at least two months of his time, and he was busy studying for a law degree. He went to ask permission from his dean, a man named Ed King. "You're a good student," said King. "Just take the final exam." Sparks took two months' leave and, with a military vehicle and gasoline credit card, set off around the state, discovering its immense majesty as he visited the hometowns of many of the men who had served under him.

In Lamar, on the Arkansas River in southeastern Colorado, Sparks sat with the parents of Jack Turner, the medic whose death had affected him so much. It was from this small town on the old Santa Fe Trail, more than three thousand feet above sea level, that Company E, which Sparks had so fondly commanded, had originally been drawn. Sparks told Turner's parents that their son had been "a good man."

In the rich farmland on the eastern plains of Colorado, in Fort Morgan, home to Glenn Miller and K Company before the war, Sparks visited a young widow called Rose. "She had two kids in rapid succession, and then her husband was killed. I was sitting in the living room, and the two little kids were there. She said, 'This man knows Daddy.' Two little tiny kids. They didn't know what the hell she was talking about. That really got to me. . . . 'This man knows Daddy.'"

Getting the National Guard back up and running was a tremendous challenge, given that so few men wanted to return to service, but Sparks succeeded nevertheless in laying the foundations for the state's present-day force, and still found time for his studies. Two years later, in 1947, thanks in part to the GI Bill, he finally achieved what he himself described as his greatest goal in life: a law degree. He then passed his bar exam with ease and decided to set up his own practice in Delta, a small town in southwest Colorado, near the Continental Divide, that had been home to Company C, and where he knew the hunting and fishing along the banks of the Gunnison River were as fine as any in Colorado. Indeed, the town lay at the very heart of arguably the most stunning scenery in the American West. There were bighorn sheep, desert cottontails, and collared lizards in the surrounding forests. The Black Canyon of the Gunnison National Park plunged just to the north, the Gunnison River flowing bright green from the sunlight reflecting off its sediment-rich waters, at the base of vertical walls of gray and purple rock crisscrossed with pink granite.

Sparks rented an office for $15 a month from a World War I veteran, bought some secondhand furniture and an old typewriter, asked his wife, Mary, to work part-time as his secretary, and took whatever business he could find. He had sacrificed five years of his life to fighting a war far away in Europe and was determined to make up for lost time.

Now he gave free rein to his ambitions, working very long hours to establish his reputation as a lawyer and becoming active in local politics. Like others who had come back from the hell of so long in combat, he wanted to squeeze everything he could from life, as if doing less might in some way dishonor those who had not survived.

In 1948, Sparks "campaigned to beat hell" as a Democrat "with no fat in his talk" and was elected district attorney, serving four years. He began to make waves in statewide politics, notably by attacking Colorado senator Ed Johnson, a prominent isolationist before the war who had voted against aid to the British when they stood alone in 1941, failed to support the New Deal, and yet had found time to introduce legislation requiring the "licensing of movie performers based on their morality." In Johnson's jaundiced eyes, the luminous Ingrid Bergman, a favorite among former GIs, was nothing more than an "apostle of degradation."

In an open letter to fellow veterans of the 157th Infantry Regiment, Sparks claimed that Johnson had led a "small but powerful group of men who did everything in their power to reduce the military strength of this country to impotency." Sparks added that while in combat he had "sworn a thousand times that if I lived to return home again the people who were responsible for our unpreparedness would not go unnoticed."

Sparks himself certainly did not go unnoticed by the powerful in Colorado. One day in 1952, he got a call from a reporter with the *Rocky Mountain News*. "Judge, how do you feel about being appointed?" What? "The governor just appointed you to the Supreme Court." Sparks immediately called the governor and asked why he had not been consulted, but he agreed to take the position. Utterly incorruptible, he would quickly come to regret the decision: "I was extremely disappointed. Matter of fact I was quite bitter about it before I was through. . . . There were some rotten things that went on in that court—very rotten."

Sparks's first assignment was to serve on an admissions committee. His first day on the committee, a judge appeared in his office. "Here, sign these," the judge told Sparks. "I've checked them over and they're all right." Sparks said he wanted to look at what he was signing. He did so and realized the papers admitted men who had in fact failed the bar exam not once but three times.

"These guys flunked the bar three times," Sparks told the judge when he returned. "How can they be admitted?"

"They're Democratic . . . you'll need them for the election."

Sparks refused to sign. The judge apparently never forgave him. Far too blunt and honest to go far in politics, he would never break the habit of speaking truth to power, whether to a four-star general or a state's governor. He served just two years before leaving the court in disgust, then returned to Delta, to the cottonwood-lined Gunnison River and the peaks of Grand Mesa, to resume his old practice. Eventually, a specialization in water law led to him serving as director of the Colorado Water Conservation Board for twenty-one years. Sparks's colleagues savored like "fine wine" his sometimes fierce but always witty memos. Until he retired from his law practice in 1979, he always fought "for the little guy," according to his son Kirk, and against corruption, corporate malpractice, polluters, and other powerful interests, and was especially determined to preserve Colorado water rights for the state and to protect its natural resources. "Colorado can never repay [Sparks]," recalled former governor Dick Lamm, "for the way he protected Colorado water. I think he would have fought a duel to save Colorado water for Coloradans."

LAMAR, COLORADO, 1970S

THE PAST WOULD not die. Sparks could not forget the war. As the decades passed, he felt the need to commemorate the men who had died under his command. He also wanted to spend time with those who had survived. They alone understood what he had endured. Only they knew the cauldron of war that had forged him more than anything in his life, far more than the bitter poverty and unemployment of his youth. In the seventies, he began to attend Company E reunions in Lamar, sharing long-repressed memories and drinks with men like the Montana journalist Jack Hallowell, who had also survived the long journey from Sicily to Dachau. "Sparks had known every man in the company on a first name basis," recalled Hallowell, "whether they were married, how many kids they had, what they liked for breakfast." Now Sparks was no longer Captain Sparks or Colonel but Felix or simply Sparks or even "Sparky." "If there was a piano," added Hallowell, "I'd play the German song everybody knew—'Lili Marlene.' Sparks would boom out the verses, even the questionable ones."

The bond between Sparks and the men who had carried out his orders had been something holy, and it would never weaken. As Irwin Rommel's troops said of him: "*Er hat die Strapazen mitgemacht*"—"He shared the shit." Sparks had certainly done that and more. "When the regiment had wanted an objective taken, Sparks was frequently first choice," remembered Hallowell. "If you were with him, you knew your unit would be leading the assault. If the unit got in a jam, he'd take personal risks trying to help his men get out of it. I don't know what guardian angel kept watch over him, but one certainly did."

In the early eighties, Sparks organized his regiment's first reunion and then dedicated himself to preserving its history, publishing newsletters and encouraging the men he had once commanded to also honor their fallen comrades. "He was a lawyer and had deep pockets," recalled Anse "Eddie" Speairs, who had liberated the liquor warehouse in Aschaffenburg. "He didn't hesitate to spend his money on his hobby—the 157th Infantry." Speairs had gone on to serve in Korea and Vietnam: "I volunteered for it all. It gets in your blood. . . . It's like dope—you get accustomed to it and you love it."

Among those who attended the first reunion was K Company medic Joe Medina, who had served under Sparks for almost four years and later became one of his best friends from the regiment. Medina had retreated into the mountains of Colorado and tended his family's sheep herd for years after he returned from Europe, finding the remote solitude the most effective balm for his post-traumatic stress.

"You remember that time you gave me first aid?" Joe was often asked at reunions.

"No, I don't remember," Joe would reply. "I treated so many."

Another stalwart over the years was Rex Raney, who had also returned to Colorado after the war and actually lived several blocks from Sparks in Delta. In fact, his mother-in-law had worked for a time as Sparks's secretary. It wasn't until he had been married for twenty years that Raney, who became a teacher, realized how much the war had affected him. He had, like Sparks, gone all the way, from Sicily to Dachau, convinced he would never again see his parents, let alone the United States or Colorado. As with many of the veterans at reunions, he had struggled to "put the pieces back together" when he returned, suffering terribly from post-traumatic stress, especially at night, when the past that he tried so hard to forget returned in full, vivid force. "My wife told me the first fifteen years were not the best," he recalled. "I guess things happened at night. She's had a little peace for the last twenty or so."

Just as he had done during combat, Sparks remembered every man's name, and also the name of each man's wife, and sometimes the names of his children. During one reunion, Vincent Stigliani, who had served in E Company until captured, turned up some forty years after the war and surprised Sparks. "You don't remember me, do you?" asked Stigliani, who was fluent in Italian and had often sought out chickens and fresh food for Sparks.

"It's Vinnie!" cried Sparks. "The chicken guy!"

Sparks was back in his element, surrounded by soldiers once more, concerned about them again, determined they should receive the recognition they were due. In 1982, he learned that some men at a reunion had not received medals he had recommended them for in January 1945, after the battle of Reipertswiller. These men had been with him that terrible day, January 18, when he had led two tanks toward his surrounded battalion. In fact, none had received so much as a Bronze Star. The investigation Sparks had requested into the battle at the time had in fact recommended that Sparks's entire battalion also receive some sort of official honor. No action had been taken. Sparks immediately set about remedying this, and three years later, in 1985, the tanks' crews finally received the medals he had first recommended them for forty years earlier.

ONE DAY, ABOVE all others, from more than five hundred at war, still haunted Sparks. The events of April 29 at Dachau had cast a long shadow over his life. According to his son Kirk, he was greatly pained by the notion that he had not acted honorably and humanely that day. He had stopped the madness, the slaughter. The idea that others might think otherwise nagged at him like an old wound, no matter how many accolades and medals he received in recognition of his service and sacrifice.

At a reunion in the early nineties, the talk was of an inspector general's report into the shootings at Dachau, titled *Investigation of Alleged Mistreatment of German Guards at Dachau*, which was finally declassified in 1987 and then discovered in the National Archives by a researcher in 1991. There had been rumors and innuendo for decades about Sparks and his men's actions at the camp in the first hours after liberation. Brazenly false accounts of what had happened had stained their reputations.

One of Sparks's fellow Thunderbirds had, sadly, done the most harm. According to the largely mendacious book *Dachau—Hour of the Avenger* by former battalion doctor Howard Buechner, published in 1986, Sparks's men had killed more than five hundred Germans in cold blood. It was an utterly shameful falsehood, with serious implications. At a reunion shortly after the book's release, some men were even overheard talking about how much jail time they were going to have to serve—indeed, whether they would have to die in prison.

In 1945, Buechner had actually admitted under oath that he refused to treat the wounded SS men after the shooting and that he had seen 15 or 16 dead and injured SS men on the ground along the coal yard wall. The number was far less than the 520 who he claimed in his book had been executed that day, of which 346 were, he added, machine-gunned by I Company's Lieutenant Jack Busheyhead, a former good friend of Buechner's who was no longer alive to defend himself.

Neo-Nazis and Holocaust deniers have predictably seized on Buechner's fiction ever since—particularly on the Internet—in an attempt to diminish the crimes committed by the SS at Dachau by equating the actions of the SS with Sparks's and his men's: Both were guilty of atrocity. Indeed, the SS had been victims too. But the declassified inspector general's report finally set the record straight.

LT. COLONEL FELIX L. SPARKS, 0-386497, WAS IN COMMAND OF THE 3RD BATTALION, 157TH INFANTRY, DURING THE DACHAU OPERATION. . . . ACCORDING TO THE TESTIMONY [HE] WAS THE ONE WHO STOPPED THE SHOOTING OF THOSE SEGREGATED. THE INSPECTOR WAS UNABLE TO FIND ANY CONFIRMATION OF THE STATEMENT OF ONE WITNESS THAT LT. COLONEL SPARKS FIRED HIS PISTOL [AT A GERMAN]; THERE IS NO PROOF THAT HE HAD ACTUAL KNOWLEDGE OF THE BOX CAR SHOOTING ALTHOUGH NEARBY; NOR THAT HE KNEW OF THE SEGREGATION OF THE SS MEN OR THE PURPOSE THEREOF.

The report concluded that because Sparks had not been questioned, it could not make any "conclusions as to his responsibility." Sparks had long wondered why he had not been called to testify, given that he had in fact been in Europe during the investigation. No one had wanted to hear his side of the story, reasoned Sparks, because he would have contradicted evidence given by General Linden, a West Pointer. Under oath, Sparks would also have revealed why the 42nd Division general and his party had been at Dachau in the first place—to escort the reporter Marguerite Higgins and thereby garner headlines. "It didn't look good," said Sparks, "for an assistant division commander to go out of his area with a nice-looking babe to someone else's territory so she could conduct interviews."

In the early nineties, a Jewish World War II veteran named David Israel, who had visited Dachau after the liberation, began to research the events of April 29, 1945. Israel was fascinated by the many conflicting and dramatic accounts of what American soldiers had done that day. He learned that a group of photographers had been with the 45th Division, the 3rd Division, and the 42nd Division as they sped toward Dachau, Munich, and Berchtesgaden to the south. The film crews and the 163rd Signal Corps men were assigned to these units in the hope they would get the scoop of the war—shots of Hitler being captured.

Israel contacted members of the corps, hoping that perhaps they might be able to tell him more about what had really happened at Dachau. They were not under Sparks's command, so they would have little incentive to lie or cover up. He discovered that one man, Robert Goebel, had been at Dachau but had never spoken about events there. In early 1994, Israel tracked him down to an intensive cardiac care unit in Buffalo, New York, where he was recovering from heart surgery.

"We were in the army together," said Israel over the telephone. "I'm doing some research about the war."

"Are you crazy, calling me here? I can't remember that long ago."

"How about one day? Dachau, April 29, when Germans were lined up against a wall?"

"I remember that. . . . I took pictures there. Never developed some of them; matter of fact they're still in a can, back in my garage in New Jersey. . . . Look, if I recover, I'll send you the negatives."

Israel knew from others in the 163rd Signal Corps that motion picture film of the killings in the coal yard had been destroyed in London, along with other images, after senior figures had ordered it never be seen again. Clearly, some images had escaped destruction, but would the negatives reveal anything? After fifty years, would they have survived in a fit state to be developed?

Goebel did live and did send the negatives, which were spotted and damaged. Israel had them developed carefully. He was stunned by what he saw in four shots, shown in sequence on the negative. At the next reunion of the regiment, Israel appeared and pulled out the images. The four clearly showed Sparks thrusting his hand out, firing his pistol, shouting for his men to stop. Taken a split second apart, they showed beyond any doubt what Sparks and his men had sworn to be true: He had not ordered the killings. He had stopped them.

Sparks looked at the images in astonishment.

"Yes, that's me. There's the map in my pocket."

According to Israel, Sparks "choked up," deeply moved. Finally, he felt he had been proved innocent.

CHAPTER THIRTY-TWO

THE LAST BATTLE

The content of your character is your choice. Day by day, what you choose, what you think, what you do—is who you become. Your integrity is your destiny . . . it is the light that guides your way.

—HERACLITUS

Felix Sparks, the successful lawyer, 1950s. [Courtesy of the Sparks family]

DENVER, COLORADO, MARCH 15, 1993

THE FIFTEEN-YEAR-OLD pulled out a 9mm semiautomatic and then pulled the trigger, aiming at a car full of teenagers. One of the bullets went through a rear window and hit sixteen-year-old Lee Pumroy in the back of the head. Lee's twin brother was beside him in the backseat and held him as he died in his arms. The shooter, it was later reported, had been intent on hitting John Vigil, a sixteen-year-old passenger in Pumroy's car, but had ended up killing Felix Sparks's grandson instead.

It was a shattering blow to an old man who had already experienced far too much death and tragedy. Indeed, Lee Pumroy's killing wounded Sparks more than any other loss, both during the war and in the almost fifty years since the guns had fallen silent in Europe. He was particularly close to Lee and his twin brother. They had lived for a while with Sparks after their mother Kim, one of Sparks's three children, had divorced.

Sparks's eldest son, Kirk, had only seen his father cry once before, when Kirk's mother had been diagnosed with breast cancer, which thankfully she had survived. Sparks had once scolded Kirk himself for crying in public. But now the tears came in torrents. According to grandson Blair Lee Sparks, a Denver police officer, the killing opened a floodgate of suppressed grief. The heartache at losing so many men, hidden for more than fifty years, and now the pain of losing a loved one to the gun, was finally too much for any man to bear.

The grief could have easily killed Sparks. He was recovering from his third heart operation when he learned his grandson had been killed. Incredibly, he had been in Miami, Arizona, attending his ninety-five-year-old mother's funeral, when he was told of the fatal shooting. At least he had been spared having to break the news to her. Days later, at his grandson's funeral, he told mourners it was just not right that grandparents should outlive their grandchildren, and he began to weep once more.

The only other time grandson Blair had seen Sparks lose his composure was when a burglar had broken into Blair's home. Sparks had heard about the burglary, grabbed his Colt .45, the same pistol he'd fired at Dachau, and turned up late at night in his pajamas. No one was going to hurt his family. The Denver police had finally managed to calm him down. "They were like: 'Who's this old guy from World War II in pajamas with a .45 strapped on?'"

Not long after the funeral, Sparks wrote to his friend Jack Hallowell, who now lived close by in Denver: "May God bless you for thinking of us in our time of grief and tragedy. Friends like you help us bear the pain of our broken hearts. While the funeral for our beloved grandson is over, the battle has just begun in hopes of sparing others from similar grief and tragedy. It will be my last battle."

Seventy-six-year-old Sparks was not content to mourn and grieve. As was in his nature, he would strike back. He was determined to stop the senseless slaughter of children on American streets by changing the law. At the ensuing trial, the teenage shooter, sixteen-year-old Phillip Trujillo, was convicted of murder. Sparks then devoted every waking moment to a campaign to change the gun laws in Colorado. "I'm not the type to sit back and grieve, though we grieve a lot," he said. Yet he was surely fighting an impossible battle in Colorado, where the right to carry a gun, whatever one's age, had been considered a birthright since the state was admitted to the Union in 1876.

Sparks formed a pressure group comprising people who had lost loved ones. "Elect me your president," he told one meeting of bereaved Denver parents. "I'll put in $50,000, or whatever is required. I'll work full time." Sparks duly became the leader of PUNCH: People United No Children's Handguns. To fight his case in the courts, he got himself readmitted to the bar in Colorado. Soon, the story of a highly decorated combat veteran railing against gun violence started to draw state and then nationwide attention. "It's difficult to talk about this but I have to for the other kids," Sparks told one reporter. "It was the other grandson who got me started because he was threatening to get everybody who had anything to do with it. I told him he couldn't do that and he said: 'Grandpa, I can get a gun anywhere.'"

In the same interview, Sparks admitted that it wasn't until he had started attending reunions in the seventies that he had been able to talk about his time in combat. "The thing about war is it can give you a pretty low opinion of mankind," Sparks added. "I don't have a low opinion of mankind, but sometimes we sure do some stupid things."

Sparks called on friends, on both sides of the political divide in Colorado, and other influential figures to lend their support, distributed leaflets, and placed ads in newspapers. At the height of his campaign, he told another reporter, his phone rang off the hook. Others provided almost $10,000 to support his cause. Among his backers were 132 men who had served with him in the 157th Infantry Regiment in World War II. "Just within the past few weeks," Sparks informed them on June 30, 1993, "several children have died or been seriously wounded by handguns in the hands of other children in the Denver area, including the deaths of two young boys who were in the 7th grade. A ten-month-old baby and a five year old were also shot."

Sparks now encountered an enemy just as determined and canny as any he had faced in Europe—the NRA. "They figure everybody should be carrying a gun," he declared. As he tried to rally support for a change in gun laws, he discovered that the NRA had secured the backing of politicians in Colorado and across America. Sparks decided to do some lobbying of his own. He was a former Colorado State Supreme Court justice. He had commanded the Army National Guard in Colorado. After reestablishing the Colorado National Guard in the forties, Sparks had continued his service, returning to active duty in 1962 during the Cuban Missile Crisis and becoming commanding general for ten years before retiring as a brigadier general in 1977.

Eventually, the governor of Colorado, Roy Romer, agreed to a special session of the legislature, which would only consider what the governor placed on the call—legislation that Sparks had written banning handgun possession for minors. Sparks believed that "religion has been responsible for more deaths than any other factor in history." He had not seen much evidence of God at work during the war. Nevertheless, he organized a prayer vigil the night before the legislature met to vote on his proposed law. He also called for a rally on the steps of the capitol the day of the vote. Among those who attended was permanently disabled Jim Brady, the press secretary who had been wounded by a handgun during the attempted assassination of President Reagan in 1981. Sparks's followers turned out in force and crowded into the capitol's galleries. The "goddamn NRA" had relentlessly fought Sparks and his efforts "every step of the way" and had given money to no fewer than thirty-five Colorado legislators. But Sparks's proposed law passed all the same, such was the public mood and outcry over children killing other children with guns. The law banned anyone under the age of eighteen from carrying a handgun. It remains on the books to this day. Before it was passed, a sixth grader could walk into a classroom with a handgun in a backpack and nobody could do anything about it.

"We rolled right over that NRA," said a victorious Sparks. "They didn't know what hit them."

As Sparks left the capitol in Denver to go celebrate victory in his last battle, a woman called out to him: "Mr. Sparks."

Sparks turned to her.

"I have two teenage boys," said the woman. "I've been up here just watching. I know some of the things you've done, but I think this might be the most important job you've had."

"It's not finished yet," he answered. "Just call me Felix."

Sparks's efforts and those of many others across the United States saw a steady decline in teenage homicide from handguns through the nineties. But Saturday night specials and other cheap handguns were no longer the only threats. Six years later, on April 20, 1999, between 11 A.M. and noon, just a few miles from where Lee Pumroy was gunned down, teenagers Eric Harris and Dylan Klebold used pump-action shotguns and submachine guns, more powerful than those used by Sparks and his men in combat, to slaughter thirteen classmates and injure twenty-four others at Columbine High School. Sparks's calls for far stricter gun laws had been tragically vindicated.

To the end of his life, Sparks would continue to decry the easy access to guns in America, which have claimed more lives than all the wars fought by Americans throughout the nation's history. More young Americans had died from gun violence in the year his grandson was shot than had died under his command throughout the Second World War—when death was a daily occurrence. "We've got nuts and plenty of weapons," said Sparks. "This business of letting everybody carry a concealed weapon is a form of insanity."

DENVER, COLORADO, 2001

THE DISPLAY SHOWED a green helmet and his lucky Colt .45 pistol, with its cold blue glint of steel. The gun was the same one Sparks had fired to stop the killing of SS men in Dachau. Standing near the display was a German-born Jew, seventy-seven-year-old Jack Goldman. He could still vividly remember April 29, 1945, when Felix Sparks and his men had arrived just in time to save him. After migrating to the United States and serving in Korea, he had settled in Denver. In 2001, to mark the dedication of Colorado's Centennial National Guard Armory, named in Sparks's honor, he was finally able to look his liberator in the eye and tell him what he thought of him in public, before his family and peers.

Goldman stood at a rostrum and looked over at eighty-four-year-old Felix Sparks with his heavy jowls, thinning hair, and weak heart.

"Thank you very much."

In the nineties, Sparks had loudly condemned Holocaust denial. "To say it never happened," he had stressed, "is the height of viciousness and stupidity. I'll fight those kinds of people until my last breath." Dachau had been "the most terrible lesson you could get in discrimination." Ignoring hate mail, he had spoken out at Holocaust remembrance ceremonies and in synagogues, challenging deniers to tell him that what he had seen inside Dachau hadn't happened.

"Tell that to my face," he had declared. "I was there!"

Also present at the dedication of the armory was Colonel Van T. Barfoot, the 157th Infantry Regiment's sole living recipient of the Medal of Honor. "There were very few officers who had the concern for his men that Colonel Sparks did," said Barfoot. "He has shown the epitome of leadership. He has advanced America."

Barfoot had, like Captain Anse "Eddie" Speairs, gone on to serve his country in both Korea and Vietnam. In 2009, he would make national news for refusing to take down a prominent flagpole from which he had raised Old Glory each morning outside his home in Virginia. A housing association deemed that ninety-year-old Barfoot could not fly the flag for "aesthetic reasons." "There's never been a day in my life," Barfoot protested, "or a place I've lived in my life that you couldn't fly the American flag." After a national outcry, Barfoot was allowed to fly the Stars and Stripes from his flagpole once more. Until his death in 2012, he raised Old Glory every morning and then lowered the flag each evening.

Sparks's son Kirk, who looked exactly like his father had in middle age, also spoke at the ceremony. As with all of Sparks's children, he had followed his father's example and served in the military.

"The most influential force in my father's life has been the military," Kirk said. "Dad doesn't say much. He just goes into action."

Sparks was deeply moved. He told some funny stories and then brought the focus back to his men.

"If you're going to be a successful commander," he said, "you've got to have good men behind you."

SPARKS HAD NEVER received that Distinguished Service Cross in 1945 for saving some of his men. Surely, before he died, the U.S. Army could put this to rights? Following the dedication of the National Guard Armory in 2001, some of Sparks's men campaigned to have him finally awarded the medal that General Frederick had denied him for his actions at Reipertswiller.

As a result of the campaign, Sparks learned that Johann Voss, the SS veteran who had Sparks in his sights in 1945, was still alive. He had always wondered why the SS had not killed him that afternoon as he tried to save his men. Why had Voss and his fellow machine gunners not opened fire? Sparks did not ask Voss for an answer. He did not have to: Voss told the *Rocky Mountain News* that it had been impossible to shoot such a courageous officer in the act of trying to save his men.

Sadly, the campaign to have Sparks's bravery recognized did not succeed. But awards had in any case never meant much to him. "Medals, what are they?" Sparks asked. "I don't need any more." He did not display them in his home or wear them to reunions. It was only when Mary searched his office one day that she found a large collection tossed into the drawer of a dresser. It was as if he'd deliberately hidden them there. His most prized memento of his war years was not a medal but the felt Thunderbird shoulder patch he had worn, etched with the regiment's motto: "Eager for Duty."

ST. ANTHONY CENTRAL HOSPITAL, DENVER, SEPTEMBER 24, 2007

MARY SPARKS DIDN'T know if she was reaching him, if he knew what she was saying, if she was getting through.

"I love you."

She said it over and over, but he was so far gone she could not tell if he could hear. He could not speak. The world was receding. His last words had been to ask his family if they had been happy with their lives.

She was there, at his bedside, at 1 P.M. that Monday when he died of pneumonia. He had fought hard to the last breath. It was only days before a planned reunion with his men in Colorado. On hearing of Sparks's death, Governor Bill Ritter ordered all Colorado and U.S. flags in the state to be lowered to half-staff. Days later, at Sparks's funeral at the Arvada Center for the Arts and Humanities in Denver, mourners included his six grandchildren. They passed a collage on a wall that showed Sparks's life in black-and-white: from the skinny young man who had ridden the rods to find work in the Depression, to the great-grandfather of seven: a lifelong warrior who had first enlisted in 1936 and gone to war with the NRA sixty years later and won. Also on view was his lucky Colt .45 pistol, the one he had fired to stop the murder of SS men at Dachau. It still had the photographs of his wife and first child, Kirk, on its grip. There was also the insignia of the organization he had loved more than any other—the 157th Infantry Regiment.

Many people gave eulogies to Sparks, a "giant of Colorado," according to former governor Dick Lamm.

"When my father was in the Army," said his son Kirk, "there was only one thing that was important to him. It wasn't home, mom or apple pie or flag or country. He just cared about his men—keeping them alive, taking care of them."

After the service, several of those men and other mourners gathered at the Crown Hill Cemetery in central Denver. The sun shone and the flags flapped in a brisk wind as the 101st Army Band marched ahead of Sparks's hearse. According to tradition, a horse without a rider, carrying boots facing backward and with a saber hanging from its right side, followed the hearse to the gravesite. A Pack 75 howitzer fired eleven times. Then there was a twenty-one-gun salute and taps was played. Finally, Mary Sparks was given the flag that had draped her husband's coffin.

Felix Sparks had never recovered from the loss of his grandson. The victory over the NRA had not dulled the pain. "[It] doesn't bring my grandson back," Sparks had said. "Got shot through the head. That hurt. Still hurts." He had lived by the gun. He knew what immense damage it could do, on and off the battlefield. Given the choice of being buried with full honors in Arlington National Cemetery or in the city he had made his home, he chose a windswept graveyard where coyotes sometimes roam.

Felix Sparks lies beside his slain grandson.

ACKNOWLEDGMENTS

OVER THE FIVE years I have worked on this book, many people have helped me enormously. I was first able to meet with General Felix Sparks and his family thanks to the remarkable Jack Hallowell, a fine warrior, journalist, and friend. He introduced me to Sparks and many others, including Jack Goldman, one of thirty-two thousand inmates at Dachau when Sparks liberated the camp. This book is dedicated to Jack Hallowell, a true Thunderbird.

In Vermont, I owe a great debt to Amy Watson, who transcribed dozens of hours of videotaped interviews and, more than anyone, watched the men in this book unburden themselves. In Denver, Dave Schmidt, erstwhile historian for the Colorado National Guard, was most generous in handing over hours of interviews and other materials. Jeffrey Hilton was also most helpful and also conducted several hours of interviews that I have drawn on.

The amazing Rick Crandall in Denver first introduced me to Regis University's Professor Dan Clayton, director of the Center for the Study of War Experience, who conducted several lengthy interviews with Felix Sparks, which were absolutely essential to this book. I can never thank Rick or Dan enough for their wonderful support and generosity. Dan has done more to promote a true understanding of the war than any other scholar in the United States. Phil Stinemates of Omni

Services was also very considerate in granting permission to use his recordings of Sparks. Nate Matlock at Regis also helped me interview several veterans in Denver, and provided several recordings of Sparks, and I am most grateful to him for all his help, friendship, and support as well as comments on the manuscript.

Historian Colonel Hugh Foster was just as considerate, and I am very grateful to him for all his many years of work with the regiment, a group of men very close to his heart. He kindly answered countless queries and contacted many men and proved a formidable fact-checker. If there are any mistakes in the book, they are entirely my fault and not his. I am indebted to him also for putting me in touch with Johann Voss, who answered many questions with grace and eloquence. I would also like to thank Jim Sheeler for all his sterling work on the regiment over the years. The Thunderbirds could not have found a better journalist to commemorate the finest.

Lynn Bush was also most helpful, providing liaison, great company, and a tremendous amount of information over several years. I will always cherish our time with Jack Hallowell. Thanks also to the best chronicler of the 45th Infantry Division, Flint Whitlock, in Denver. Two other invaluable guides were Mike Gonzales and Allen M. Beckett at the 45th Infantry Division Museum in Oklahoma.

The National World War II Museum's Seth Paridon was also enormously generous with his time. I am also grateful for the support of the museum's Nick Mueller, as well as Keith Huxen, Stephen Watson, Tommy Lofton, Larry Decuers, Jeremy Collins, and others. I would also like to thank Karen Jensen and Gene Santoro at *World War II* magazine.

The Colorado National Guard's Robert W. Redding, commander of the 157th Infantry Regiment, was most helpful and supportive, as were Jean Schjodt and others in Denver, such as Steve Judish, Marie Valenzuela, and Kris Johnson. Chris Miskimon provided valuable help and great company. The ace researcher Dave Kerr sent many documents and photos from the National Archives, many of which I have used. David Israel kindly provided photographs of Sparks at Dachau. Congressman Ed Perlmutter, who has served Coloradans with great distinction and was a good friend of Felix Sparks, was also most helpful. I am also grateful to Bill Holden and Vincent Cookingham.

I would also like to thank the following veterans of the 157th Infantry Regiment, many of whom spoke to me at length: Cranston Rogers, Vinnie Stigliani, Warren Wall, Joe Early, Adam Przychocki, Vincent Presutti, Les Alexander, Dan Dougherty, Bill Lyford, Edward Peppler, Bernie Kaczorowski, Van T. Barfoot, Karl Mann, who welcomed me to his home, Guy Prestia, John Piazza, George Courlas, Bill O'Neill, Ed Speairs, Joe Medina, Rex Raney, Don Thompson, Clarence Schmitt, and Oren Scott.

I am also indebted to the Sparks family—particularly Felix Sparks's son Kirk, wife Mary, brother Earl, and grandson Blair, and several other relatives and grandchildren who kindly sent me a few photographs.

Yet again, I owe a massive debt to the amazing and gracious staff in the Sawyer Library at Williams College, who provided me yet again with a home to write another book, in particular David Pilachowski.

I am also grateful to my incisive and endlessly patient editor, Charlie Conrad, his assistant Miriam Chotiner-Gardner, and many others at Crown Publishers in New York. They are all consummate professionals.

John Snowdon again provided wonderful help and company, and took fantastic portraits. Thanks also to Rob Kraitt in London and Liza Wachter in Los Angeles for all the great years of collaboration.

This book would not have been possible without my friend/agent/fellow author, Jim Hornfischer, the best in the business.

My wonderfully talented wife, Robin, who read the manuscript at a critical stage, and photo-researcher/filmmaker son, Felix, again provided all the support one could possibly want. I am also grateful to my family on both sides of the Atlantic.

NOTES

PROLOGUE—THE GRAVES

1 **They lay beneath perfect:** Felix Sparks, 157th Infantry Regiment Association newsletter, September 1, 1989.

1 **They had died near:** Buechner, *Sparks: The Combat Diary of a Battalion Commander (Rifle) WWII*, p. 81.

1 **Seventy-two thousand men:** Ibid., p. 94.

2 **It was hard to:** Felix Sparks, interview with author.

2 **Every time, they had:** Felix Sparks, Regis University interview.

2 **It was this spirit:** Felix Sparks, Regis University lecture, "Stories from Wartime."

2 **The American soldiers under:** Ibid.

2 **His great grandfather had:** Felix Sparks, Regis University interview.

3 **On the German border:** Ibid.

3 **His men's foxholes were:** *Rocky Mountain News*, March 10, 2007.

3 **He had never gotten:** Ibid.

3 **Thirty platoon leaders:** Karl Mann, written report on World War II provided to the author, p. 14.

3 **Why hadn't it been:** Felix Sparks, Regis University lecture.

3 **Events that day:** Felix Sparks, interviewed by James Strong, *The Liberation of KZ Dachau*, documentary, 1990.

4 **The rumors festered still:** David Israel, interview with author.

4 **The cost had been:** Buechner, *Sparks*, p. 94.

PART ONE—THE DUST BOWL
CHAPTER ONE—THE WEST

7 **He pulled on his:** Felix Sparks, Regis University lecture.
8 **But none of it:** Earl Sparks, interview with author.
9 **His mother was a:** Felix Sparks, Colorado National Guard oral history.
9 **His passion was military:** Blair Lee Sparks, interview with author.
9 **He hoped someday:** Earl Sparks, interview with author.
10 **The hobo warned Sparks:** Felix Sparks, Colorado National Guard oral history.
11 **"If they catch you":** Ibid.
12 **"Yeah, I do":** Ibid.
12 **"No, I'm not kidding":** *Colorado Lawyer* 27, no. 10 (October 1998).
14 **He put it all:** Felix Sparks, Colorado National Guard oral history.
15 **He was going somewhere:** Mary Sparks, interview with author.
16 **Local bars posted:** Joe Medina, interview with Nate Matlock.
16 **In September 1940:** Allen Beckett, interview with author.
17 **On the killing fields:** Felix Sparks, Colorado National Guard oral history.

CHAPTER TWO—OFF TO WAR

19 **"Let's get married":** Mary Sparks, interview with author.
19 **Annoyed she had not:** Ibid.
19 **But then, in November:** Mike Gonzales, *A Brief History of the 45th Infantry Division in the Second World War*, 45th Infantry Division Museum.
20 **Sparks and his fellow:** Buechner, *Sparks*, p. 63.
20 **What would happen to:** Felix Sparks, interview with author.
20 **He would be back:** Felix Sparks, letter to his parents, May 19, 1943. Quoted courtesy of Blair Lee Sparks.
21 **Some felt strangely empty:** Hallowell et al., *Eager for Duty*, p. 17.
21 **"It's 'The Last Roundup'":** Buechner, *Sparks*, p. 65.
21 **After two weeks:** Felix Sparks, Shoah Foundation interview.
21 **Dolphins played in the:** Franklin, *Medic*, p. 5.
22 **Sparks was among:** Felix Sparks, Colorado National Guard oral history.
22 **You can stick:** Felix Sparks, Regis University interview.
22 **But if they didn't:** Ibid.
23 **Among the fifteen hundred Apache:** Paul Hollister, "Thunderbirds of E.T.O.," in *Eye-Witness World War II Battles,* compiled by Major Howard

Oleck, Belmont Books, New York, 1963, p. 133. "In the American southwest, the Indians had long venerated the Thunderbird. It was the mythical giver of rain to parched lands—bringer of freedom and hope to the perishing. And it brought its gifts with crashing thunder and bolts of lightning. Vast and powerful, the Thunderbird was awesome to evil men, and a potent friend to good men."

23 **But it was also:** Cundiff, *45th Infantry CP*, p. 121.

PART TWO—ITALY
CHAPTER THREE—SICILY

28 **Operation Husky was:** Orange, *Tedder*, p. 225.

28 **The answer is in:** Eisenhower, *Letters to Mamie*, pp. 134–35.

29 **"I think I'll signal":** Shapiro, *They Left the Back Door Open*, p. 118.

30 **"I'm positive, sir":** Farago, *Patton*, Dell, New York, 1963, p. 282.

30 **Aboard a blacked-out ship:** Morison, *Sicily-Salerno-Anzio*, p. 64.

30 **An inch of vomit:** Buechner, *Sparks*, p. 65.

30 **The convoy nearing Sicily:** James Tobin, *Ernie Pyle's War*, p. 105.

32 **"After all, the original":** Lieutenant N. L. A Jewell, *Secret Mission Submarine* (Ziff-Davis Publishing, London 1944), pp. 114–15.

32 **"So many brave young":** Gilbert, *Churchill*, pp. 748–49.

33 **"I'm sure," recalled Pamela:** Ibid.

33 **The question that troubled:** D'Este, *Bitter Victory*, p. 313.

33 **"No matter what happens":** Whicker, *Whicker's War*, p. 89.

34 **According to one bystander:** Farago, *Patton*, p. 283.

35 **The commodore didn't say:** Felix Sparks, Colorado National Guard oral history.

35 **He belonged to:** Jack Hallowell, interview with author.

35 **It made one hell:** Hallowell et al., *Eager for Duty*, p. 21.

35 **Wisecarver promptly hit the:** Franklin, *Medic*, p. 6.

35 **Several were injured:** Hallowell et al., *Eager for Duty*, p. 21.

36 **"Go! Good luck!":** Franklin, *Medic*, p. 6.

36 **Although the wind:** Anse Speairs, interview with author.

36 **In bad weather:** Felix Sparks, Regis University interview.

36 **Once it had secured:** Ibid.

36 **the regiment's first objective:** After Action Report, National Archives.

CHAPTER FOUR—THE RACE FOR MESSINA

38 **Ramps dropped and the:** Franklin, *Medic*, p. 9.
39 **Twenty-seven men from:** 157th Infantry Regiment, After Action Narrative Report, June–August 1943, p. 2, National Archives.
39 **Cowboys in the regiment:** Franklin, *Medic*, pp. 5–11.
39 **"Hits on buildings near":** Morison, *Sicily-Salerno-Anzio*, p. 144.
39 **Five hundred Italian soldiers:** 157th Infantry Regiment, After Action Narrative Report, p. 2.
39 **"Those goddamn Italians came":** Felix Sparks, Colorado National Guard interview.
39 **He pressed on that:** Hallowell et al., *Eager for Duty*, p. 23.
39 **"Now we were men":** Edward Pepper, H Company, 157th Infantry Regiment, Colorado National Guard interview.
39 **By late on:** Hallowell et al., *Eager for Duty*, p. 23.
39 **Men would soon call:** Ibid.
40 **From now on:** Edward Pepper, Colorado National Guard interview.
40 **"Colonel," he told Ankcorn:** Felix Sparks, Colorado National Guard oral history.
40 **"I don't care how":** Buechner, *Sparks*, p. 66.
40 **He gathered them together:** Felix Sparks, Colorado National Guard oral history.
40 **Some had been stripped:** Felix Sparks, 157th Infantry Regiment Association newsletter, 2009.
40 **He also found the:** Ibid.
41 **Finally, they gathered wood:** Ibid.
41 **Caked in a dust:** Buechner, *Sparks*, p. 65.
41 **They have been in:** Felix Sparks, letter to his parents, August 4, 1943. Quoted courtesy of Blair Lee Sparks.
42 **Patton was being driven:** Cave Brown, *The Last Hero*, p. 352.
42 **"We've got a hard":** Felix Sparks, interview with author.
42 **Eighth Army's General Montgomery:** After Action Report, National Archives.
42 **"My God," US II Corps:** Bradley and Blair, *A General's Life*, p. 189.
42 **As far as Bradley:** Ibid., p. 188.
42 **"Tell Montgomery to stay":** Geoffrey Keyes, diary, July 13, 1943.
42 **It was a humiliating:** Ed Speairs, interview with author.
42 **as the Thunderbirds pulled:** Graham, *No Name on the Bullet*, p. 38.
43 **The ancient home:** *The World at War*, Thames Television.
43 **"We must take Messina":** Blumenson, *Patton*, p. 202.

43 **Facing the 45th was:** Fort Benning Report, "Infantry Combat Part Five: Sicily," 12-30-43, p. 5.
44 **So steep was the:** After Action Report, National Archives.
44 **A machine-gun squad:** Ibid.
44 **None would be alive:** Bernie Kaczorowski, Colorado National Guard interview, 2007.
44 **Fighting on Bloody Ridge:** Oliver R. Birkner, letter to editor, 45th Division News, February 1995.
44 **At the epicenter:** Vinnie Stigliani, interview with author.
44 **"Maybe that's why I'm":** Bernie Kaczorowski, Colorado National Guard interview, 2007.
45 **Men sat in the shade:** Guy Prestia, interview with author.
45 **"It's reassuring to know":** Felix Sparks, letter to his parents, August 4, 1943. Quoted courtesy of Blair Lee Sparks.
45 **"It's plenty hot over":** Ibid.
45 **Two days later:** After Action Report, National Archives.
45 **The same officer recommended:** Fort Benning Report, "Infantry Combat Part Five: Sicily," 12-30-43, p. 10.
45 **A davit failure caused:** Buechner, *Sparks,* p. 66.
45 **But these were:** After Action Report, National Archives.
46 **Men from Sparks's regiment:** Ibid.
46 **"Hello, you bloody bastards!":** Biddle, *Artist at War,* p. 113.
46 **Messina had endured earthquake:** Reynolds, *The Curtain Rises*, p. 345.
46 **He was the American:** Blumenson, *Patton*, p. 206.
46 **The Battle for Sicily:** The total regimental casualties for the 157th Infantry Regiment in the Sicilian campaign: killed in action, 58; wounded in action, 205; missing in action, 16. Source: Buechner, *Sparks,* p. 68.
46 **Crucially, Axis forces were:** Hallowell et al., *Eager for Duty,* p. 30.
46 **"It would have saved":** Anse Speairs, interview with author.
47 **He'd spent the whole:** Felix Sparks, Regis University interview.
48 **"We're going to go":** Felix Sparks, Colorado National Guard oral history.
48 **Through his "gentle persuasion":** Felix Sparks, 157th Infantry Association newsletter, June 30, 1993.
48 **"I don't think":** Felix Sparks, Colorado National Guard oral history.
48 **A reinvigorated E Company passed:** Ibid.
48 **Combat was what he:** Felix Sparks, Regis University interview.
48 **He loved being:** Ibid.
49 **With these men:** Ibid.

50 **"Do not go to":** Fisher, *Story of the 180th*, p. 55.

51 **"I know," replied:** Reynolds, *The Curtain Rises*, p. 227.

51 **Patton was forced to:** Whiting, *America's Forgotten Army*, pp. 40–42.

51 **A humiliated Patton sank:** Brighton, *Patton, Montgomery, Rommel*, p. 229.

51 **"I know I can":** Ibid.

51 **But would he ever:** D'Este, *Patton*, p. 536.

52 **A long column of:** Paul Cundiff, *45th Infantry CP*, p. 55.

CHAPTER FIVE—MOUNTAIN COUNTRY

54 **Known as Wayne:** Whicker, *Whicker's War*, pp. 86–87.

54 **"None":** Hickey and Smith, *Operation Avalanche*, pp. 52–53.

54 **The same could not:** Ibid.

55 **Montgomery also believed Clark's:** Buechner, *Sparks,* p. 70.

55 **The news of the:** Ibid., p. 71.

55 **In propaganda leaflets dropped:** Bishop et al., *The Fighting Forty-Fifth*, p. 41.

55 **Men vainly tried to:** Cundiff, *45th Infantry CP*, p. 60.

55 **More than two hundred men:** Bishop et al., *The Fighting Forty-Fifth*, p. 41.

55 **The Germans were lying:** Hickey and Smith, *Operation Avalanche*, p. 126.

56 **Kesselring sent a message to:** Cundiff, *45th Infantry CP*, p. 56.

56 **In the Temple of:** Hickey and Smith, *Operation Avalanche*, p. 34.

56 **The Allies were ashore:** Whicker, *Whicker's War*, p. 84.

56 **The Germans commanded all:** Cundiff, *45th Infantry CP*, p. 58.

56 **"The Germans actually needed":** Reynolds, *The Curtain Rises*, p. 319.

56 **What Churchill feared most:** Gilbert, *Churchill, A Life*, p. 753.

56 **It was all chillingly:** Ibid.

58 **"I have no reserves":** Clark, *Calculated Risk*, p. 165.

58 **"We are going to":** Buechner, *Sparks,* p. 72.

58 **Crucially, Allied artillery was:** Allen Beckett, interview with author.

58 **This "fire on time" coordination:** Mike Gonzales, interview with author.

58 **"We have made mistakes":** Clark, *Calculated Risk*, p. 171.

58 **Kesselring ordered his divisions:** After Action Report, National Archives.

59 **"It has just begun":** Reynolds, *The Curtain Rises*, pp. 342–43.

59 **"Just do it, get":** Sparks, *Déjà Vu*, p. 153.

59 **Before them lay the:** Morison, *Sicily-Salerno-Anzio*, p. 254.

60 **Evidence of fierce and:** After Action Report, National Archives.

60 **"Don't let that bother":** Felix Sparks, Colorado National Guard interview.

60 **Early on September 24:** After Action Report, National Archives.

60 **At first, it was:** Rex Raney, interview with author.

61 **Ankcorn's leg was so:** Hallowell et al., *Eager for Duty*, p. 42.

61 **His war was over:** Felix Sparks, 157th Infantry Regiment Association newsletter.

61 **Colonel John Church:** Ibid.

61 **On October 1, the Fifth:** After Action Report, National Archives.

61 **Its strongpoint was the:** Clayton D. Laurie, "Rapido River Disaster," www.military.com.

61 **Dead Germans lay by:** Franklin, *Medic*, p. 56.

62 **A cold mist clung:** After Action Report, National Archives.

62 **"Machine gun bullets passed":** Vinnie Stigliani, interview with author.

62 **He and his men:** Jack Hallowell, interview with author.

63 **Mortarman Jack Hallowell:** Ibid.

63 **He knew the next:** Ibid.

63 **Medics were busy tending:** Buechner, *Sparks,* p. 77.

63 **"You're going to be":** Jack Hallowell, interview with author.

63 **He was wearing an:** Vinnie Stigliani, Colorado National Guard interview.

64 **Among them was a:** After Action Report, National Archives.

64 **The medics had done:** Buechner, *Sparks,* p. 77.

64 **He had lost more than:** After Action Report, National Archives.

64 **Thankfully he had been:** Buechner, *Sparks,* p. 77.

64 **He had been able to think:** Felix Sparks, Regis University interview.

65 **But like all the:** Felix Sparks, Regis University lecture, "Stories from Wartime."

65 **The German had wanted:** Vinnie Stigliani, Colorado National Guard interview.

66 **Sparks set up his:** After Action Report, National Archives.

66 **He had reached the:** Grossman, *On Killing*, p. 44.

66 **Enemy planes came in:** Jack Hallowell, interview with author.

66 **So great was the:** After Action Report, National Archives.

67 **"It is essential for us":** Chandler, *Papers of Dwight Eisenhower*, vol. 3, p. 1529.

67 **Tying down German forces:** Gervasi, *The Violent Decade*, p. 518.

67 **"Ford a river—and":** Whicker, *Whicker's War*, p. 109.

67 **The Thunderbirds succeeded in:** Wallace, *The Italian Campaign*, p. 101.

67 **"The country was shockingly":** Pyle, *Brave Men*, p. 68.

67 **When they looked back:** Franklin, *Medic*, p. 69.

68 **It was destined to:** Buechner, *Sparks*, p. 78.

68 **The Germans had been:** Ibid.

68 **He had received the:** Warren Wall, Colorado National Guard interview.

69 **"Dry feet were something":** Hallowell et al., *Eager for Duty*, p. 49.

69 **"We've caught the torch":** Tregaskis, *Invasion Diary*, p. 193.

70 **Ankcorn had heard that:** Felix Sparks, Colorado National Guard interview.

70 **His mood improved further:** Buechner, *Sparks*, p. 77.

70 **One day that fall:** Mary Sparks, interview with author.

71 **So long as the:** Felix Sparks, interview with author.

71 **"You can't go back":** Felix Sparks, Colorado National Guard oral history.

71 **"Can I get on":** Ibid.

71 **"I've a war to":** Sparks, *Déjà Vu*, p. 158.

71 **Later that morning, Sparks:** Felix Sparks's Distinguished Service Cross recommendation file.

72 **To his amazement:** Mary Sparks, interview with author.

72 **Sparks told him to:** *Colorado Lawyer* 27, no. 10 (October 1998).

72 **"You're still here!":** Jack Hallowell, interview with author.

72 **Every one of his:** Felix Sparks, Colorado National Guard oral history.

73 **Orders had come from:** After Action Report, National Archives.

73 **He knew he could:** Bishop et al., *The Fighting Forty-Fifth*, p. 67.

73 **Later that morning, after:** After Action Report, National Archives.

73 **"I want to go":** Felix Sparks, Colorado National Guard interview.

73 **"No, Jack, you can't":** *Rocky Mountain News*, March 10, 2007.

73 **Under cover of darkness:** Felix Sparks, Colorado National Guard interview.

73 **They had even placed:** Ibid.

74 **"I'll take care of":** Felix Sparks, Colorado Army National Guard oral history.

74 **Instead of returning to:** Buechner, *Sparks*, p. 78.

74 **"That's a habit they'll":** Hallowell et al., *Eager for Duty*, p. 78.

75 **In some areas:** Lewis, *Naples 44*, p. 131.

PART THREE—ANZIO

77 **"The problem is staying":** Felix Sparks, Regis University lecture, "Stories of Wartime."

CHAPTER SIX—DANGER AHEAD

80 **The divisions at Anzio:** Buechner, *Sparks,* p. 80.
80 **"Either it was a":** Morison, *Sicily-Salerno-Anzio*, p. 336.
80 **Early on January 22, 1944:** Lucas also wrote in his diary before the landings: "Army has gone nuts again. The general idea seems to be that the Germans are licked and fleeing in disorder and nothing remains but the mop up. They will end up by putting me ashore with inadequate forces and get me into a serious jam. Then who will take the blame?" Source: Buechner, *Sparks,* p. 95.
80 **By midnight, more than thirty-six:** Morison, *Sicily-Salerno-Anzio*, p. 343.
80 **"This whole affair has":** Whicker, *Whicker's War*, p. 125.
81 **The sun shone brightly:** Hallowell et al., *Eager for Duty*, p. 51.
81 **Men scanned the shoreline:** Felix Sparks, Colorado National Guard oral history.
81 **Men had to step:** Franklin, *Medic*, p. 83.
81 **"Buck up, we got":** Hallowell et al., *Eager for Duty*, p. 51.
81 **He would soon be:** Felix Sparks, 157th Infantry Regiment Association newsletter, March 31, 1989.
81 **"Easy, boys, there's danger":** Cundiff, *45th Infantry CP*, p. 141.
82 **Once a man was:** Felix Sparks, Regis University lecture.
82 **Dead bodies lay strewn:** Felix Sparks, Regis University interview.
82 **Sparks began to suspect:** Buechner, *Sparks,* p. 83.
82 **Because the Allies had:** Hallowell et al., *Eager for Duty*, p. 53.
82 **They soon started to:** graffagnino.com/doctorslounge/anzio1944.htm.
83 **Here his regiment's Second:** Jack Hallowell, interview with author.
83 **The Germans were on:** graffagnino.com/doctorslounge/anzio1944.htm.
83 **"The Führer expects the":** Whicker, *Whicker's War*, p. 123.

CHAPTER SEVEN—HELL BROKE LOOSE

84 **All across the beachhead:** graffagnino.com/doctorslounge/anzio1944.htm.
85 **The horizon filled with:** Ellis, *The Sharp End*, pp. 70–71.
85 **Sparks had already seen:** Whitlock, *Rock of Anzio*, p. 196.
85 **After an hour:** graffagnino.com/doctorslounge/anzio1944.htm.
85 **"Then those are Krauts":** Whitlock, *Rock of Anzio*, p. 186.
86 **As far as the:** Morris, *Circles of Hell*, p. 288.
86 **They were confident of:** Felix Sparks, 157th Infantry Regiment Association newsletter, March 31, 1989.
86 **With their machine guns blinking:** Ibid.

86 **Sparks called to two:** Buechner, *Sparks,* p. 84.

86 **"Get them!":** Whitlock, *Rock of Anzio*, p. 186.

86 **"Hell, no—they're German":** Ibid.

86 **"Shoot them":** Felix Sparks, interview with Chris Miskimon, March 11, 2005. Quoted courtesy of interviewer.

87 **Two German tanks exploded:** Buechner, *Sparks,* p. 84.

87 **The third tank pulled:** Felix Sparks, 157th Infantry Association newsletter, March 31, 1989.

87 **An M10 moved thirty:** Whitlock, *Rock of Anzio,* p. 186

87 **Sparks saw dust fly:** Ibid.

88 **"Medics!" cried wounded men:** Bishop et al., *The Fighting Forty-Fifth*, p. 74.

88 **Heart rates soared and some men's:** Dave Grossman, *On Killing*, pp. 44–57.

88 **Finally, the German tanks:** Whitlock, *Rock of Anzio*, p. 187.

88 **Sparks and his company:** Hallowell et al., *Eager for Duty*, p. 58.

89 **"Would you agree to":** Buechner, *Sparks,* p. 85.

89 **"Yes, that would be":** Whitlock, *Rock of Anzio*, p. 196.

89 **The Germans now threatened:** Felix Sparks, 157th Infantry Association newsletter, February 1, 1985.

89 **It would have taken:** After Action Report, National Archives.

89 **"You can't do us":** Felix Sparks, interview with Chris Miskimon, quoted courtesy of interviewer.

89 **He radioed his Second:** After Action Report, National Archives.

90 **Seven enemy divisions were:** Allen, *Anzio*, p. 3.

90 **"My name is Müller":** Ibid., p. 1.

90 **"What's your name now":** Ibid.

90 **There were some five:** Jack Hallowell, "The Battle of the Caves", 45th Infantry Division Museum, p. 4.

91 **Sparks now had just:** D'Este, *Fatal Decision*, p. 246.

91 **"To hell with takin'":** Jack Hallowell, "The Battle of the Caves," 45th Infantry Division Museum, p. 4.

91 **McDermott ran off:** 157th Infantry Regiment, After Action Report, February 1944, National Archives.

91 **McDermott was never seen:** Hallowell et al., *Eager for Duty*, p. 66.

91 **"The enemy prevented":** Buechner, *Sparks,* p. 87.

92 **More German planes wreaked:** Hallowell et al., *Eager for Duty*, p. 65.

CHAPTER EIGHT—A BLOOD-DIMMED TIDE

93 **"If we ever get"**: Buechner, *Sparks,* pp. 99–100.
94 **Men shouldered their machine guns:** Hallowell et al., *Eager for Duty,* p. 60.
94 **"So they gave our"**: Whitlock, *Rock of Anzio*, p. 202.
94 **"It looks like a"**: Jack Hallowell, "The Battle of the Caves," 45th Infantry Division Museum, p. 4.
94 **Brown responded: "Withdraw and"**: Ibid.
95 **He was blubbering, mumbling:** D'Este, *Fatal Decision*, p. 234.
95 **Utterly exhausted, Sparks:** Hallowell et al., *Eager for Duty*, p. 65.
95 **Sparks knew every one:** Felix Sparks, Regis University interview.
97 **The Germans kept coming:** Sheehan, *Anzio*, p. 131.
97 **"Yeah," said the machine gunner:** Jack Hallowell, "The Battle of the Caves," 45th Infantry Division Museum, pp. 4–9.

CHAPTER NINE—THE BATTLE OF THE CAVES

98 **At noon on February 18:** Vaughan-Thomas, *Anzio*, p. 190.
99 **In some of the:** Fifth Army History, privately published, 1946, Part 4, Chapter 8, p. 138.
99 **Back in America:** Jack Hallowell, "The Battle of the Caves," 45th Infantry Division Museum, p. 7.
99 **An incredible six hundred:** Sheehan, *Anzio*, p. 146.
99 **Three men were killed:** Jack Hallowell, "The Battle of the Caves," 45th Infantry Division Museum, p. 6.
99 **He constantly swigged a lemonade:** Cundiff, *45th Infantry CP*, p. 46.
100 **One Thunderbird sniper finally:** Hallowell et al., *Eager for Duty*, p. 70.
100 **By the following morning:** Allen, *Anzio*, p. 5.
100 **In one sector, German:** Sheehan, *Anzio*, p. 138.
100 **"They [also] told of"**: Ibid., p. 139.
100 **"I've been lying under"**: D'Este, *Fatal Decision*, p. 237.
101 **And if his useless:** Clark, *Anzio, Italy and the Battle for Rome*, p. 195.
101 **At 2:55 A.M. on February 20:** 157th S-2 Journal, February 20, 1944, National Archives.
102 **Once the British arrived:** Whitlock, *Rock of Anzio*, p. 242.
102 **They made a hideous:** Franklin, *Medic*, p. 87.
102 **Dozens of men from:** Lloyd Wells, *Anzio* (University of Missouri Press, 2004), p. 69.
102 **By the time the:** Ibid.

103 **"His wounds were not life threatening":** Vincent P. Cookingham, "The Battle of the Caves, Results of Personal Research," pp. 3–4. Quoted with permission. Personal correspondence with the author.
103 **The next thing he:** Ibid.
104 **Men with terrible wounds:** Whitlock, *Rock of Anzio*, p. 211.
104 **The Germans opened fire:** Hallowell et al., *Eager for Duty*, p. 65.
104 **Though the water was:** Ibid.
104 **"They need me out":** Jack Hallowell, 'The Battle of the Caves," 45th Infantry Division Museum, p. 7.
105 **O'Neill and his Psalm-reciting:** Bill O'Neill, interview with author.
106 **Others made a thin:** graffagnino.com/doctorslounge/anzio1944.htm.

CHAPTER TEN—CROSSING THE LINE

107 **It was time to:** Whitlock, *Rock of Anzio*, p. 246.
108 **As Sparks prepared to:** Ibid.
108 **The position had been:** Ibid.
108 **Empty-handed and "spooked" by:** Ibid.
108 **Terrified Thunderbirds followed him:** graffagnino.com/doctorslounge/anzio1944.htm.
108 **Others lagged behind, slowed:** Vaughan-Thomas, *Anzio*, p. 188.
108 **He had not eaten:** Whitlock, *Rock of Anzio*, p. 246.
108 **He stuffed his mouth:** Jack Hallowell, interview with author.
109 **He did not return:** Jack Hallowell, "The Battle of the Caves," 45th Infantry Division Museum, p. 12.
110 **Every one of them:** Felix Sparks, Regis University interview.
110 **"We're Americans!" shouted Sparks:** Whitlock, *Rock of Anzio*, p. 247.
110 **He had gone without:** Jack Hallowell, interview with author.
110 **Sparks was barely able:** Ibid.
110 **Sparks was still carrying:** Ibid.
111 **It was, in Sparks's:** Felix Sparks, Regis University interview.
111 **Several could not walk:** Sheehan, *Anzio*, p. 148.
111 **The Thunderbirds had saved:** D'Este, *Fatal Decision*, p. 250.
112 **"First at Stalingrad, now":** Sheehan, *Anzio*, p. 139.
112 **"Our enemy was of":** Brooks, *With Utmost Spirit*, p. 378
112 **Sparks and his fellow:** graffagnino.com/doctorslounge/anzio1944.htm.
112 **"In the annals of":** John S. D. Eisenhower, *They Fought at Anzio*, p. 194.
112 **Their cries and groans:** Felix Sparks, 157th Infantry Association newsletter, March 31, 1989.

CHAPTER ELEVEN—THE BITCH-HEAD

113 **The streets of Naples:** DePastino, *Bill Mauldin*, p. 147.
114 **Even the hundreds of:** Lewis, *Naples 44*, p. 86.
114 **"Only five hundred":** Moorehead, *Eclipse*, p. 67.
114 **Naples was a vast:** Mauldin, *Up Front*, p. 117.
114 **"Beautiful signorina":** Moorehead, *Eclipse*, p. 67.
114 **For those with real:** By December 1944, more men were casualties of VD than of combat, according to some reports.
114 **No matter the rank:** John Piazza, interview with author.
115 **"A red rag was":** Franklin, *Medic*, p. 79.
115 **Of the tens of:** Atkinson, *Day of Battle*, p. 448.
115 **"We were taking more":** Moorehead, *Eclipse*, p. 70.
115 **Sparks would soon receive:** Felix Sparks, interview with author.
115 **The gorgeous San Carlo:** Atkinson, *Day of Battle*, p. 447.
115 **The cheap vermouth and:** Cundiff, *45th Infantry CP*, p. 154.
116 **He was said to:** Jack Hallowell, interview with author.
116 **Otherwise, every night before:** Mary Sparks, interview with author.
116 **The photographs of her:** Felix Sparks, letter to parents, April 29, 1944, quoted courtesy of Blair Lee Sparks.
117 **"Instead we have stranded":** Vaughan-Thomas, *Anzio*, p. 189.
117 **At Monte Cassino, where:** Allanbrook, *See Naples*, p. 175.
118 **The Soviets outnumbered the:** Keegan, *The Second World War*, p. 477.
118 **"If we old fools":** Westphal, *The German Army*, p. 160.
119 **One did not know:** Franklin, *Medic*, p. 101.
119 **"The one he used":** Guy Prestia, interview with author.
119 **But before they had:** Felix Sparks, Regis University Interview.
119 **Across the "Bitch-Head," what:** Hastings, *Winston's War*, pp. 33–35.
119 **Thunderbirds likened themselves to:** Hallowell et al., *Eager for Duty*, p. 73.
119 **The taller men like:** John Piazza, interview with author.
119 **Neither the propaganda leaflets:** Bill Lyford, interview with author.
120 **"A person would hold":** Pyle, *Brave Men*, p. 302.
120 **One day, Sparks received:** Felix Sparks, Regis University lecture.
120 **"Won't you please tell":** Buechner, *Sparks*, pp. 97–98.
120 **It ended with the:** Felix Sparks, Regis University lecture.
120 **It was not knowing:** Sparks, *Déjà Vu*, p. 165.

CHAPTER TWELVE—THE BREAKOUT

122 **Sparks wondered if he:** Felix Sparks, Regis University lecture.
122 **To confuse the enemy:** Hallowell et al., *Eager for Duty*, p. 81.
122 **Lyford at first enjoyed:** Bill Lyford, interview with author.
123 **He rolled back into:** Bill Lyford, Colorado National Guard interview.
123 **For two days, Sparks:** Winston Churchill, correspondence with George C. Marshall, April 16, 1944.
123 **Losing a limb might:** Hallowell et al., *Eager for Duty*, p. 82.
123 **Just like their forefathers:** Ibid., p. 83.
123 **Would inexperienced squad and:** Felix Sparks, Regis University lecture.
124 **Dawn cracked on the:** After Action Report, National Archives.
124 **Squads filed into gullies:** Hallowell et al., *Eager for Duty*, p. 83.
124 **"And after that I":** Ibid., p. 84.
124 **At 5:45 A.M., the horizon:** Felix Sparks, Regis University interview.
124 **"A wall of fire":** Truscott, *Command Decisions*, p. 371.
124 **To Sparks, it sounded:** Whitlock, *Rock of Anzio*, p. 288.
124 **Men climbed out of:** Felix Sparks, Regis University lecture.
124 **They were soon passing:** Bill Lyford, interview with author.
126 **Sparks ordered tank destroyers:** Whitlock, *Rock of Anzio*, p. 294.
126 **"I was yelling at":** Ibid., p. 297.
126 **Thanks to several tank:** After Action Report, National Archives, G-3 report.
127 **I Company took the hill:** Franklin, *Medic*, p. 113.
127 **A rampaging Barfoot:** Captain Van T. Barfoot, *The Operation of 3rd Platoon, Company L, 157th Infantry, 22–24 May*, Fort Benning Infantry Officers Course monograph, 1948.
128 **"Boy, you've made it":** Clark, *Anzio, Italy and the Battle of Rome*, p. 295.
128 **It had taken four:** Felix Sparks, Regis University lecture.
128 **Among the fatalities was:** Ibid.
129 **"Men looked down on":** Hallowell et al., *Eager for Duty*, p. 94.

CHAPTER THIRTEEN—ROME

131 **"He wore a somewhat":** Truscott, *Command Missions*, p. 548.
131 **Frederick would receive eight:** Clark, *Anzio, Italy and the Battle*, p. 316.
131 **Lithe and fit as:** Atkinson, *Day of Battle*, p. 282.
131 **At Anzio, his men:** Kemp, *Commemorative History*, p. 31.
131 **"What's holding you up":** Sevareid, *Not So Wild a Dream*, p. 411.
132 **In opting for a Roman:** Whicker, *Whicker's War*, p. 179.

132 **Clark's yearning to be:** Molony, *The Mediterranean and Middle East*, vol. VI, p. 234.

132 **"We Americans had slogged":** D'Este, *Fatal Decision*, pp. 370–71.

132 **"I'm holding off the":** Sheehan, *Anzio*, p. 210.

132 **"We can't be held":** Ibid.

132 **Flashbulbs popped as Clark:** Sevareid, *Not So Wild a Dream*, p. 411.

133 **"That's what's holding up":** Hicks, *The Last Fighting General*, p. 140.

133 **"I don't have time":** Ibid, p. 141.

134 **Ecstatic locals showered him:** Buechner, *Sparks*, p. 101.

135 **"On this historic occasion":** Sevareid, *Not So Wild a Dream*, p. 414.

135 **It was a great victory:** Atkinson, *Day of Battle*, p. 574.

135 **The Italian campaign:** Langworth, *Churchill by Himself*, p. 43.

136 **"How grateful they should":** Buechner, *Sparks*, p. 95.

136 **"As for the nectarines":** Ibid.

136 **"They didn't even let":** Walters, *Silent Missions*, p. 97.

136 **According to the journalist:** Whicker, *Whicker's War*, p. 182.

136 **As the Allies stormed:** Hallowell et al., *Eager for Duty*, p. 95.

137 **"We are all completely":** Felix Sparks, letter to parents, June 12, 1944, quoted courtesy of Blair Lee Sparks.

137 **"With that beachhead in":** Hallowell et al., *Eager for Duty*, p. 96.

137 **On June 19, the:** After Action Report, National Archives, June 1944.

138 **"Everyone fell in love":** Hallowell et al., *Eager for Duty*, p. 97.

138 **None other than Mark:** Rex Raney, interview with author.

138 **"I'm not crazy about":** Felix Sparks, letter to parents, June 12, 1944, quoted courtesy of Blair Lee Sparks.

139 **"And I've heard a":** Hallowell et al., *Eager for Duty*, p. 97.

139 **"Given their choices, they":** Ibid.

139 **On terraces along the:** Cundiff, *45th Infantry CP*, pp. 182–83.

139 **"They had been more":** Ibid., p. 184.

139 **"We speak about half":** "Report of William Russell Criss," 45th Infantry Division Museum.

139 **A nearby beach resembled:** Clarence Schmitt, interview with author.

139 **They had paid not:** Cundiff, *45th Infantry CP*, p. 223.

140 **In early August, the:** After Action Report, National Archives.

140 **Aged just twenty-six:** Felix Sparks, interview with Chris Miskimon.

PART FOUR—FRANCE

141 **"There were several times":** Felix Sparks, interview with author.

CHAPTER FOURTEEN—DAY 401

144 **He crept behind:** Adleman and Walton, *The Champagne Campaign*, pp. 107–8.
144 **"Jesus Christ!" blurted:** Hicks, *The Last Fighting General*, p. 155.
144 **"Your helmet in this":** Whiting, *America's Forgotten Army*, p. 58.
145 **Sparks and his men:** Munsell, *Story of a Regiment*, p. 71.
145 *Will I be alive*: Bill Lyford, letter to author, November 5, 2011.
145 **"How do you like":** Hallowell et al., *Eager for Duty*, p. 100.
145 **"Hell," said one grizzled:** Stars and Stripes, *The Story of the 45th Infantry Division*, Kessinger Publishing, LaVergne, Tennessee, 2007, p. 24.
145 **He had fiercely opposed:** Churchill had threatened to resign. Clark was also vehemently opposed: "Stalin . . . was one of the strongest boosters of the invasion of southern France. He knew exactly what he wanted and one of the things he wanted most was to keep us out of the Balkans, which Stalin had staked out for the Red Army." Source: Whiting, *America's Forgotten Army*, p. 59.
145 **"The best invasion":** Graham, *No Name on the Bullet*, p. 67.
146 **"We been waiting years":** Hallowell et al., *Eager for Duty*, pp. 100–2.
146 **On they marched beneath:** Adam Przychocki, Colorado National Guard interview.
146 **Perfumed with mimosa and:** Hallowell et al., *Eager for Duty*, pp. 100–3.
146 **Sparks's command post that:** Felix Sparks, Regis University interview.
146 **The casualty rate had:** Buechner, *Sparks*, p. 102.
148 **No wonder Hitler called:** Kershaw, *Hitler 1936–1945*, New York, p. 721.

CHAPTER FIFTEEN—THE CHAMPAGNE CAMPAIGN

149 **They pushed farther inland:** Adam Przychocki, Colorado National Guard interview.
150 **"And damn toot sweet!":** Hallowell et al., *Eager for Duty*, p. 105.
151 **Before the startled Germans:** Kirk Sparks, interview with author.
151 **Sparks joked that he:** Ibid.
151 **It wasn't long before:** *Denver Post*, April 30, 1995.
151 **In one village:** Kirk Sparks, interview with author.
151 **Sparks set a photograph:** Blair Lee Sparks, interview with author.
151 **There were battered Dodge:** Cundiff, *45th Infantry CP*, p. 197.
152 **The Coloradans in the:** Ibid., p. 199.
152 **There were fears it:** Whiting, *America's Forgotten Army*, p. 73.
152 **Survive its thirty days:** After Action Report, National Archives.

152 "The thrust of the": Whitlock, *Rock of Anzio*, p. 322.

153 It was a macabre: After Action Report, National Archives, September 1944.

153 Sparks moved from the: Felix Sparks, army personnel file.

153 As the battle to: Felix Sparks, interview with author.

155 Generals like George Patton: Buechner, *Sparks,* p. 102.

155 One of the greatest problems: Felix Sparks, interview with author.

155 After five years of: Had planners correctly predicted the far greater numbers of men that were actually required in the infantry, the war in Europe would probably already have ended, and fewer of Sparks's dogfaces would have died. Instead, they had placed their faith in airpower, and now the shortfall was showing.

156 The answer was sobering: Hastings, *Armageddon*, p. 380.

CHAPTER SIXTEEN—THE VOSGES

158 But they suffered heavy: After Action Report, National Archives.

158 One company lost: A. H. Speairs, *An Anzio Experience*, monograph, 45th Infantry Division Museum.

158 A signpost was placed: Stars and Stripes, *The Story of the 45th Infantry Division*, p. 27.

158 "You soon realized your": George Courlas, interview with author.

158 "It was sometimes a relief": Hallowell et al., *Eager for Duty*, p. 117.

158 Others became so tightly: Ibid.

159 "We took more small": Felix Sparks, Regis University interview.

159 One day, a patrol: After Action Report, National Archives.

159 Shell fragments and jagged: Franklin, *Medic*, p. 128.

160 "My men are going": Clarence Schmitt, interview with author.

160 "The strongest personality, subjected": Bruce C. Clarke, *Study of AGF Casualties*, September 1946, National Archives.

161 Well over a hundred thousand men: Hastings, *Armageddon*, p. 184.

161 Officially, eighteen thousand American deserters: Hastings, *Armageddon*, p. 185.

161 That way, they got: Guy Prestia, interview with author.

161 "He's not to come": Felix Sparks, Regis University lecture.

161 "You get pounded enough": Adam Przychocki, interview with author.

161 until he too was: Adam Przychocki, Colorado National Guard interview.

161 How long would his: Felix Sparks, Regis University lecture.

162 Few believed they would: Rex Raney, interview with author.

162 Only the letters and: Felix Sparks, Regis University lecture.

162 **Many communities had both:** Hallowell et al., *Eager for Duty*, p. 119.
163 **When he looked up:** Kirk Sparks, interview with author.
163 **A small French flag:** Buechner, *Sparks,* pp. 103–4.
163 **He pointed out where:** Ibid.
163 **"Apparently, they had no":** Felix Sparks, 157th Infantry Association newsletter, December 31, 1989.
164 **It had taken them:** After Action Report, National Archives.
164 **They had been in:** Hallowell et al., *Eager for Duty*, pp. 105–10.
164 **It felt as if:** Ellis, *The Sharp End*, pp. 101–2.
164 **That October 25:** "157th Combat Casualties" list, courtesy of Dave Kerr.
164 **Then came the crack:** After Action Report, National Archives.
164 **By dusk, Sparks's I Company:** Buechner, *Sparks,* p. 104.
164 **The Thunderbirds had now:** Cundiff, *45th Infantry CP*, p. 205.
165 **At Anzio, he had:** Sheehan, *Anzio*, p. 106.
165 **It was uncanny that:** Felix Sparks, 157th Infantry Association newsletter, September 1, 1989.
165 **According to Otis:** *Denver Post*, August 21, 2001.
166 **"Who the hell do":** Hallowell et al., *Eager for Duty*, p. 120.
168 **Sparks and his fellow:** Kirk Sparks, interview with author.

PART FIVE—GERMANY

169 **"It was a glorious bloodbath":** 101 U.S. Airborne Division, G-2 Report, January 1945, National Archives.

CHAPTER SEVENTEEN—BLACK DECEMBER

172 **The Germans had also:** Cundiff, *45th Infantry CP*, p. 228.
172 **"It will take these":** Hicks, *The Last Fighting General*, p. 168.
172 **"He's the greatest fighting":** Adleman and Walton, *The Champagne Campaign*, p. 32.
173 **"What are you waiting":** After Action Report, National Archives. See also Whiting, *America's Forgotten Army*, p. 98.
173 **The tired soldier waited:** Stars and Stripes, *The Story of 45th Infantry Division*, p. 3.
174 **The *Stars and Stripes* trumpeted:** Ibid., p. 130.
175 **"The meeting was crowded":** Whiting, *America's Forgotten Army*, p. 103.
175 **"There will be only":** Stephen Ambrose, *Citizen Soldiers*, p. 208.
176 **"Then we'll really cut":** D'Este, *Patton*, p. 679.
176 **To pull off his:** Whiting, *America's Forgotten Army*, p. 105.

176 **"But through the room":** Ibid.

176 **"You will start on":** Eisenhower, *The Bitter Woods*, p. 368.

177 **"And this time":** Whiting, *America's Forgotten Army*, p. 106.

177 **"And every time you":** D'Este, *Patton*, p. 681.

177 **Indeed, the Seventh would:** Whiting, *America's Forgotten Army*, p. 109.

179 **Until they appeared:** Antelme, *The Human Race*, pp. 102–4.

179 **"We exchanged Christmas greetings":** Buechner, *Sparks*, p. 106.

179 **"Maybe my luck will":** Sergeant John W. Kendall Jr., private correspondence, January 14, 1945.

180 **"I don't owe my":** Cundiff, *45th Infantry CP*, p. x.

180 **Sparks himself would fire:** Karl Mann, unpublished memoir of World War II, provided to the author.

181 **The German First and Nineteenth:** Whiting, *America's Forgotten Army*, pp. 112–13.

181 **"We will yet be":** Warlimont, *Inside Hitler's Headquarters*, p. 493.

182 **"I remember us singing":** "I remember that we fired a few machine-gun bursts of tracer ammo in the air—a breach of discipline, no doubt, and a bit childish." Source: Johann Voss, letter to author, December 4, 2011.

182 **"We switched off the":** Voss, *Black Edelweiss*, p. 179.

182 **Voss was one of:** "We weren't liberated by the Allies, not by the Russians, nor by the British or by the Americans," added Voss. "This is my view not only as a former soldier of the German Army but is also based on a lifelong reading of history. Nor was there an intent to 'liberate' us. Consider General Eisenhower's non-fraternization order: 'We come as victors, not as liberators, and I want you to behave as such towards the German people, who are defeated once and for all.' Not to speak of what the Russians did to the Germans when they entered Germany. Or were the Eastern Germans liberated by the Soviet politruk Ulbricht? But it is true of the persecuted; they were no doubt liberated by the Allied Powers. It was only later on that German politicians who were not persecuted by the Nazis, but were more or less involved in the dark schemes of the National Socialist leadership, felt it would be a good idea to say the German people as a whole was liberated by the Western Powers. This caught on in politics as well as in historiography, and is now a common view in Germany." Source: Johann Voss, letter to author, December 4, 2011.

182 **He and his comrades:** Johann Voss, letter to author, December 4, 2011.

182 **All were supplied with:** Voss recalled: "We got the MG42 during our short stay in Denmark, along with new rifles, uniforms and boots. Prior to that we were equipped with the MG34. The main feature of the new weapon was its simplicity and its stunning fire rate. Hugh can tell you

much more about it than I could ever do." Source: Johann Voss, letter to author, December 4, 2011.

182 **But that did not:** Voss, *Black Edelweiss*, p. ix. "Hitler's leadership was still undisputed in my environment," recalled Voss. "I remember wondering why Joseph Goebbels spoke on New Year's Eve instead of Hitler, who always had inspired the nation with his vision of victory. Goebbels was no substitute. I think I had a faint idea that Hitler himself didn't believe in victory any more." Source: Johann Voss, letter to author, December 4, 2011.

182 **In fact 62 percent:** Frederick Taylor, "The Road to Ruin," *Financial Times*, August 20/21, 2011.

183 **"I immediately thought of":** *Guardian*, April 16, 2011.

183 **BRITISH LAND IN GREECE:** May, *Witness to War*, p. 72.

183 **As it did so:** Evans, *The Third Reich at War*, p. 690.

184 **Twenty-one-year-old Jack Goldman was:** Ibid., p. 691.

184 **His father had in:** Jack Hallowell, The President's Column, 157th Infantry Association newsletter, 2009.

184 **Then they were ordered:** Rothchild, *Voices from the Holocaust*, pp. 163–64.

184 **Fifteen thousand of his:** Evans, *The Third Reich at War*, p. 691.

184 **Soon after, Goldman fell:** Jack Goldman, interview with author.

184 **One day, the SS:** Ibid.

184 **"Do what you want":** *Rocky Mountain News*, April 29, 2003.

184 **Those who couldn't were:** Rothchild, *Voices from the Holocaust*, p. 164.

185 **"The women who are":** Leonid Rabichev, "*Voina vse spishet*," *Znamya* 2 (2005): 163.

185 **"Fire for fire, blood":** Merridale, *Ivan's War*, p. 311. See also Bundesarchiv-Militärarchiv, RH2-2688, 13.

185 **No wonder that at:** Evans, *The Third Reich at War*, p. 711.

185 **He and his fellow:** "I was *Sturmmann* and NCO candidate as you'd say," recalled Voss. "Up front I was leader of a heavy machine-gun squad." Source: Johann Voss, letter to author, December 4, 2011.

186 **The last of Hitler's:** Voss, *Black Edelweiss*, p. ix.

CHAPTER EIGHTEEN—THE BREAKING POINT

187 **"Every man has a":** Felix Sparks, Regis University lecture.

187 **The sun pierced the:** After Action Report, National Archives.

188 **Having to turn their:** Hallowell et al., *Eager for Duty*, p. 129.

188 **"Ike or the Krauts":** Hicks, *The Last Fighting General*, p. 176.

188 **In Sparks's regiment:** After Action Report, National Archives.

189 **Medina had since tended:** Joe Medina, interview with Nate Matlock, Regis University.

189 **The rate of fire:** After Action Report, National Archives.

189 **He knew that without:** Felix Sparks, report to Inspector General 45th Division, January 27, 1945. Before the day was out, sixty-one men in the regiment would be wounded, mostly by flying hot splinters from artillery shells and mortars in hills near the Alsace village of Reipertswiller. Source: After Action Report, National Archives.

189 **He was with three:** The jeep's windshield had been either removed or folded down and covered with canvas, not only to avoid flying glass, but also to prevent glint from the sun giving away its presence, and so Sparks was able to spread out maps on the hood should they lose their way among the winding lanes and muddy tracks of the most rugged and least populated area of the Vosges.

189 **Sparks and Turk were:** Karl Mann, interview with author.

190 **Mann had first seen:** Ibid.

190 **With the often curt:** Ibid.

190 **The jeep sped down:** Ibid.

190 **All of a sudden:** Karl Mann, unpublished memoir of World War II, provided to the author.

190 **He lay sprawled in:** Felix Sparks's Distinguished Service Cross recommendation file.

190 **He climbed out of:** Karl Mann, interview with author.

190 **One of the jeep's:** Karl Mann, unpublished memoir of World War II, provided to the author.

191 **It was vital that:** Ray Merriam, *Waffen SS* (Bennington, Vermont: Merriam Press, 1999), p. 29.

191 **Soon I Company also arrived:** Louis Cody Wims, oral history, www.45thdivision.org/Veterans/Wims.

191 **"We were sitting up":** Felix Sparks, Regis University interview.

192 **Meanwhile other German units:** Ibid.

194 **At his forward command:** Ibid.

194 **The G-3 then conferred:** After Action Report, National Archives.

194 **Frederick's orders were to:** Bishop et al., *Fighting Forty-Fifth*, 1946, p. 142.

194 **The response to O'Brien's:** Felix Sparks, Regis University interview.

194 **When Sparks learned of:** Ibid.

194 **From crackling radio messages:** *Rocky Mountain News*, March 10, 2007.

196 **The conversation ended abruptly:** Hugh Foster, *Something Has to Be Done Quick*, manuscript on the Battle of Reipertswiller, October 1995, Chapter 10, pp. 1–2.

196 **The trees that had:** Buechner, *Sparks*, p. 114.

196 **The surrounding ridges controlled:** Hugh Foster, interview with author.

196 **Casualties had mounted through:** After Action Report, National Archives.

196 **Whenever a Thunderbird showed:** Bishop et al., *Fighting Forty-Fifth*, pp. 140–42.

196 **To his relief, around:** Hugh Foster, *Something Has to Be Done Quick*, manuscript on the Battle of Reipertswiller, October 1995, Chapter 10, pp. 1–2.

197 **The SS were, remembered:** Hallowell et al., *Eager for Duty*, p. 255.

197 **Their primary target was:** Hugh Foster, *Something Has to Be Done Quick*, manuscript on the Battle of Reipertswiller, October 1995, Chapter 10, pp. 1–2.

197 **Dawn was breaking as:** Ibid., p. 7.

197 **Soon the white-helmeted SS:** MacDonald, *Battle of the Huertgen Forest*, p. 20.

197 **Flares soared and cruelly:** Hugh Foster, *Something Has to Be Done Quick*, manuscript on the Battle of Reipertswiller, October 1995, Chapter 10, p. 8.

198 **It was still working:** "We had lost our regimental commander when the Finns succeeded in attacking our regimental HQ," recalled Johann Voss. "Raithel took over the 11th Rgt. in Pirmasens, the German town right at the border to Alsace, in January 1945. At that time we heard he was an old Lapland hand, and had come from the German *Heer.* That was OK with us. In the fighting at Reipertswiller we learned that he could lead. There, he changed the situation from reluctant defense to vigorous attack, which won him our complete respect. I saw him only once, and I remember him as very good looking with his sporty bearing and his faded mountain cap. I got to know him much better after the war, when he had returned from South Africa, where he was a plantation manager, and was studying history at the Munich University. Before the war, he was officer in a Mountain Division in southern Germany, and had won championships in skiing and mountain guiding. Two of his brothers were also colonels of German Mountain Regiments. Even when he was around seventy, he practiced mountaineering in the US and South America. He died when he crashed into a road barrier one night on his way from Bad Reichenhall to his home in Icking, south of Munich. His eyesight was impaired by the loss of his right eye during the last battle of the 'Nord.' After he was taken prisoner, severely wounded, he was interrogated, of which a record must exist. Raithel was very much interested in digging up that record." Source: Johann Voss, letter to author, December 4, 2011.

198 **The SS now knew:** Hugh Foster, *Something Has to Be Done Quick*,

manuscript on the Battle of Reipertswiller, October 1995, Chapter 10, p. 9.

198 **"G Company is captured!":** Ibid.

198 **More shells landed in:** After Action Report, National Archives.

198 **"When hit, men sank":** Hallowell et al., *Eager for Duty*, p. 133.

198 **An astonishing three:** Ibid., pp. 134–35.

199 **Waiting in ambush up:** Voss, *Black Edelweiss*, p. 186.

199 **Several men fell in:** Felix Sparks's Distinguished Service Cross recommendation file.

199 **Sergeant Bernard Fleming looked:** The armored car platoon leader, Lt. Baze, had been shot in the head and later died.

200 **"Give me a lot of":** Bernard Fleming, written account of January 18, 1945, rescue by Sparks, Felix Sparks's Distinguished Service Cross recommendation file.

200 **"They're going to watch":** Ibid.

200 **"I'm going to get":** Ibid.

200 **Now there were more:** Sparks, *Déjà Vu*, p. 170.

201 **"Help on the way":** Felix Sparks, Regis University interview.

201 **Soon, one was landing:** After Action Report, National Archives.

201 **One SS machine gunner:** Voss, *Black Edelweiss*, p. 187.

201 **Around 9 A.M., two Sherman:** Foster, *Something Has to Be Done Quick*, manuscript on the Battle of Reipertswiller, October 1995, Chapter 10, p. 13.

201 **They were nicknamed "Ronson":** Ellis, *The Sharp End*, p. 154.

201 **The tank crews went:** Felix Sparks's Distinguished Service Cross recommendation file.

202 **"Help is fighting to":** Foster, *Something Has to Be Done Quick*, manuscript on the Battle of Reipertswiller, October 1995, Chapter 10, p. 15.

202 **The Sherman tanks trundled:** 158th Artillery report for January 18, 1945, Felix Sparks's Distinguished Service Cross recommendation file.

203 **Several men from Bernard:** Eisenhower Presidential Library, Box 1392, Folder #1, pp. 5–6.

203 **It was ever more:** Ibid.

203 **Just as often:** Ellis, *The Sharp End*, p. 154.

203 **Some fifty yards away:** "When we clashed with the American Army it had already stormed through France and reached the borders of the Reich within seven months," recalled Voss. "So, we had no doubt that we faced a serious and tough adversary. I don't remember that we were told any disparaging or agitating things about the American soldiers in the field. We knew their resources were unlimited while ours were

sparse. While in Denmark, after our endless march through the Arctic winter, our thoughts were focused on an extended leave. But that didn't happen. Instead we found ourselves face to face with the Americans immediately upon our return to Germany. We had to learn from our own experience with them. From the beginning, we endured seemingly unlimited artillery fire that cost us unusually heavy casualties. Then, at Reipertswiller, the American soldiers won our respect." Source: Johann Voss, letter to author, December 4, 2011.

203 **He watched as Sparks:** Voss, *Black Edelweiss*, p. 188.

203 **"If [he] could pass":** Ibid.

203 **The tank slid sideways:** Voss, *Black Edelweiss*, p. 188.

204 **Several Thunderbirds lay bleeding:** Felix Sparks, Regis University interview.

204 **"Make a break for":** *Rocky Mountain News*, March 10, 2007.

204 **He looked around at:** Eisenhower Presidential Library, Box 1392, Folder #1, pp. 5–6.

204 **He had lost his:** Sparks, *Déjà Vu*, p. 170.

204 **Sparks climbed out of:** Ibid.

204 **There was no honor:** Voss, *Black Edelweiss*, p. 188.

204 **Killing him would be:** Johann Voss, letter to author, December 4, 2011.

204 **Incredibly, the SS still:** Felix Sparks, Regis University interview.

204 **Voss could still see:** Voss, *Black Edelweiss*, p. 188.

204 **Never had he witnessed:** Voss, letter to author, December 4, 2011.

205 **There was no way:** *Rocky Mountain News*, March 10, 2007.

205 **He watched as Sparks:** Buechner, *Sparks*, p. 118. See Joseph Crowley statement.

205 **The tanks' treads were:** Felix Sparks, Regis University interview.

205 **One had a broken:** Ibid.

205 **There was a hollow:** Bull, *World War II Infantry Tactics*, p. 21.

205 **Then the SS opened:** Felix Sparks, Distinguished Service Cross recommendation file.

205 **Bullets pinged and ricocheted:** Buechner, *Sparks*, p. 117.

205 **But neither tank was:** Ibid., p. 118. Crowley added: "Enclosed is a letter Sparks sent on my behalf dated 5 July, 1985, recommending me for the Bronze Star Medal (for the second time). In the citation it is to be noted that he deliberately left himself out of this action. Since Sparks was the major player in this effort, the only conclusion that I can draw from this is that he wanted to lend more credence to the actions of the tank crews. . . . There must have been a lot of animosity existing between the Division Commanders and Sparks. This was undoubtedly one of the reasons why he was cheated and possibly why his recommendations

were not honored. If anyone deserves this award, Sparks does. He was a courageous man if ever I saw one." According to Crowley: "It was Col. Felix Sparks who initiated the breakthrough attempt. He was the first to get out of the tank not knowing if anyone would follow. I think that he deserved more than he got (a higher award). All this leads to another question. To my knowledge Hanson, who did the same thing as Zeek, got no award and other recommendations were shelved. Quite arbitrary I would say."

205 **The front of his:** Certificate, 45th Cav Rcn TRP Mec Z 45th Inf Div, AFO 45, US ARMY, February 1, 1945, pp. 1–2, Carl O Winters, National Archives.

205 **"Our commander had proved":** Felix Sparks DSC Recommendation file.

206 *Why didn't they shoot*: *Rocky Mountain News*, March 10, 2007.

CHAPTER NINETEEN—DEFEAT

207 **Two companies from the:** Certificate, 45th Cav Rcn TRP Mec Z 45th Inf Div, AFO 45, US ARMY, February 1, 1945, pp. 1–2, Carl O Winters, National Archives.

208 **"We had no medical":** After Action Report, National Archives.

208 **The SS noose closed:** Merriam, *Waffen SS*, p. 29.

208 **It was announced in:** Ibid.

208 **"Impossible to get there":** National Archives, radio reports 18 January, 45th Div. 157th CP, p. 12.

208 **"We are being attacked":** Unit Journal, 158th Artillery Battalion, January 19, 1945, After Action Report, National Archives.

209 **German tanks were moving:** Richard Baron, Major Abe Baum, and Richard Goldhurst, *Raid!* (New York: Dell, 1981), p. 67.

209 **The SS promised Curtis:** Louis Cody Wims, oral history, 45th Infantry Division, www.45thdivision.org/Veterans/Wims.

209 **They were shivering, drenched:** 158th Artillery Battalion, After Action Report, National Archives.

209 **Two senior German officers:** According to Voss: "Degen was a paragon of the young *Waffen-SS* officer. By 'young' I mean that they differed to a great extent from the older officers who came from the *Allgemeine-SS* and took their civilian ranks with them, without having passed through the tough training in the officer candidate school of the *Waffen-SS*. He had a strong leadership style and demonstrated great personal bravery in several serious combat situations. There was unanimous agreement about his authority among the troops. One can say that we admired him and were proud to have such a leader among us, especially after he rescued the 11th Regiment from Russian encirclement at Tuchkalla,

near Kuusamo, when we were on our march toward the Finnish border. He was killed in the last battle of the Regiment at Pfaffenheck, where he was laid to rest in the military cemetery, together with ninety of his comrades." Source: Johann Voss, letter to author, December 4, 2011.

210 **The snow provided cover:** Hallowell et al., *Eager for Duty*, p. 135.

210 **At 1:30 P.M., Colonel O'Brien:** After Action Report, National Archives.

210 **"We are following thru":** 158th Unit Journal, January 20, 1945, AAR 158th Field Artilley Battalion, National Archives.

210 **Now poor visibility and:** Baron et al., *Raid!*, p. 67.

210 **Forward artillery observers were:** Merriam, *Waffen SS*, p. 29.

210 **I Company's Private Benjamin Melton:** After Action Report, National Archives.

210 **"I fortunately got back":** Joe Early, interview with Jeffrey Hilton, 157th Regiment's reunion, Colorado Springs, 2007.

211 **Finally, as dusk fell:** *Fighting Forty-Fifth*, p. 146

211 **Some attached white handkerchiefs:** After Action Report, National Archives.

211 **"You can imagine how":** Hallowell et al., *Eager for Duty*, p. 136.

211 **Everyone else, as far:** Ibid., p. 135.

212 **Twenty-five officers were taken:** "All I heard at that time was that the officers were honorably received by Raithel personally," recalled Voss, "and that their soldiers received the precious *Scho-Ka-Kola*, a piece of chocolate in a round tin box—the ration we used to be issued in the North before departure on some important mission. There was some grumbling among us that WE didn't receive them, too." Source: Johann Voss, letter to author, December 4, 2011.

212 **"Rumor had it that":** Voss, *Black Edelweiss*, p. 190.

212 **The SS were duly:** Johann Voss, letter to author, December 4, 2011.

212 **Franz stood in his:** Baron et al., *Raid!*, pp. 67–68. And Louis Cody Wims, oral history, 45th Infantry Division, www.45thdivision.org/Veterans/Wims.

212 **There was a bucket:** Joe Early, Colorado National Guard interview.

212 **All that mattered was:** Buechner, *Sparks*, p. 109.

212 **According to SS records:** Whiting, *The Other Battle of the Bulge*, p. 127.

213 **Even though he held:** Johann Voss, letter to author, December 4, 2011.

213 **First at Anzio:** Buechner, *Sparks*, p. 115.

213 **"It is still difficult":** Ibid.

213 **It was as if:** Johann Voss, letter to author, December 4, 2011. Voss also recalled: "Bodies still lying about in the devastated woodland, most of them separately, some already laid in rows by their comrades; they made

peculiar bundles, easily recognized even under the snow." Source: Voss, *Black Edelweiss*, p. 190.

213 **Roads were soon strips:** Hallowell et al., *Eager for Duty*, p. 137.

213 **They were moving back:** Ibid.

214 **Over three days, more:** National Archives, Box 1392, folder 1, 157th Inf. Regiment Narrative History, After Action Report.

214 **They were full of questions:** Hallowell et al., *Eager for Duty*, p. 137.

214 **He was "hurt badly":** Shoah Foundation, interview with Felix Sparks.

214 **It was quickly evident:** Buechner, *Sparks,* p. 115.

214 **"If I had it":** Cundiff, *45th Infantry CP*, p. 239.

214 **Harsh words were exchanged:** Kirk Sparks, interview with author.

214 **After a few minutes:** Felix Sparks's Distinguished Service Cross recommendation file.

214 **Generals didn't appreciate being:** *Rocky Mountain News*, March 10, 2007.

214 **As far as Sparks:** Felix Sparks, interview with author.

215 **Sparks also had a:** Buechner, *Sparks,* p. 116.

215 **In late January he:** Felix Sparks's Distinguished Service Cross recommendation file.

215 **Having finally passed the:** Kirk Sparks, interview with author.

215 **There was no excuse:** Ibid.

215 **"Frederick didn't see the":** Anse Speairs, interview with author. "I deserted my men," added Speairs in 2010 when asked how he felt about returning to the States on leave.

215 **Frederick must have deeply:** Cundiff, *45th Infantry CP*, p. 232.

215 **"The actions for which":** National Archives, HQ records 45th Infantry Division, January 29, 1945, letter from Robert T. Frederick.

CHAPTER TWENTY—THE RIVER

217 **"I do not suppose":** Gilbert, *Churchill*, p. 1182.

218 **Now they went on:** Earl Sparks, interview with author.

218 **In the American Officers':** Wilson, *If You Survive*, p. 229.

218 **"Any American city has":** Felix Sparks, letter to parents, February 12, 1945. Quoted courtesy of Blair Lee Sparks.

218 **He had not been:** Hugh Foster, e-mail to author, November 23, 2011. The commendation was never made.

219 **Green officers came in:** Felix Sparks, Regis University, "Stories from Wartime."

219 **Because men with at:** Dan Dougherty, Colorado National Guard interview.

219 **Private Dan Dougherty was:** Dan Dougherty, interview with author.

219 **There was a jeep:** Dan Dougherty, Colorado National Guard interview.

220 **In Berlin, Hitler was:** Musmanno, *Ten Days to Die*, p. 94. The *Gauleiters* were regional leaders. "They occupied party appointed positions and were responsible for government of one of 43 Party Regions with theoretical direct access to Hitler." Source: Major Quentin W. Schillare, *The Battle of Aschaffenburg: An Example of Late World War II Urban Combat in Europe*, (Fort Leavenworth, Kansas, 1989), p. 170.

220 **"That would be the":** Musmanno, *Ten Days to Die*, p. 94.

220 **"In any case only":** Speer, *Inside The Third Reich*, p. 440.

222 **"Get going, you guys":** Hechler, *The Bridge at Remagen*, pp. 115–21.

222 **"Hold on to it, Brad":** Hastings, *Armageddon*, p. 366.

223 **The Allied demand for:** Winston Churchill, *The Second World War*, vol. 4: *The Hinge of Fate* (London, 1951), pp. 616–18.

223 **"There are enough of":** Fritz, *Endkampf*, p. 203.

223 **Some ten thousand Germans would:** Ibid., p. 686.

224 **"That's why the Germans":** Rex Raney, interview with author.

224 **"Not the ordinary soldier":** Bundesarchiv, diary of Lieutenant Julius Dufner, April 7, 1945.

224 **Fear of the truly:** Tony Judt, *Postwar*, p. 20.

224 **But not even terror:** Ibid.

CHAPTER TWENTY-ONE—THE SIEGFRIED LINE

225 **They illuminated the dragon's:** Hallowell et al., *Eager for Duty*, p. 141.

225 **Heading back into combat:** Based on analysis of Hugh Foster's *Combat Days of the 157th Infantry Regiment in World War II.*

226 **Now he would have:** MacDonald, *Battle of the Huertgen Forest*, p. 16.

226 **In briefings, he had:** Hallowell et al., *Eager for Duty*, p. 144.

226 **Flushed from their concrete:** Charles Whiting, *West Wall* (Staplehurst, UK: Spellmount, 1999), p. 130.

226 **Two platoon leaders out:** After Action Report, National Archives.

226 **It was the only:** Witness affidavit, Cranston R. Rogers, April 25, 2006.

227 **Three hundred surrendered to:** After Action Report, National Archives.

227 **It had taken the:** Ibid.

227 **Unlike in France, where:** Ibid.

227 **"Every time you killed":** Anse Speairs, interview with author.

228 **"Straggling Germans, still wearing":** After Action Report, National Archives.

228 **In some homes that:** Ryan, *The Last Battle*, p. 17.

228 **"For an extra bar of chocolate":** Whiting, *America's Forgotten Army*, p. 177.
228 **"This is the scorched":** Ibid.
229 **He turned toward his:** Toland, *The Last 100 Days*, p. 285.
229 **"Thus, William the Conqueror!":** D'Este, *Patton*, p. 712.
229 **Men were greeted by:** MacDonald, *The Last Offensive*, p. 287.
229 **But there was now:** Whiting, *America's Forgotten Army*, p. 183.
229 **Sparks's Third Battalion crossed:** Rawson, *In Pursuit of Hitler*, p. 26.
230 **"Nonetheless it":** Vincent Presutti, Colorado National Guard interview.
230 **"Call that thing a river?":** Hallowell et al., *Eager for Duty*, p. 147.
230 **The worst was surely:** Ibid.
230 **Nazi flags were popular:** Cundiff, *45th Infantry CP*, p. 242.
230 **One day, he found:** Blair Lee Sparks, interview with author.
230 **On March 27, as:** AAR Narrative Form, March 1945, p. 8, L -1029, After Action Report, National Archives.
230 **He was to take:** Felix Sparks, 157th Infantry Association newsletter, July 22, 1982.
230 **It would be a simple:** Buechner, *Sparks,* p. 124.
230 **They had become indifferent:** History—Narrative Form, 157th Infantry Regiment, March 1945, p. 9, National Archives, L-1029.
231 **Soldiers, Men of the** ***Wehrmacht*****:** Felix Sparks, "The Aschaffenburg Battle," 157th Infantry Association newsletter, July 22, 1982.
231 **It instructed him and:** Quentin W. Schillare, *The Battle of Aschaffenburg*, master's thesis, Fort Leavenworth, Kansas, 1989, p. 99.
231 **He had fought in:** Cranston Rogers, interview with author.
231 **Concrete bunkers and pillboxes:** Michael Gonzales, *Brief History of the 45th*.
231 **But it had been:** Quentin W. Schillare, *The Battle of Aschaffenburg*, master's thesis, Fort Leavenworth, Kansas, 1989, p. 99.
232 **To ensure loyalty and:** Jack Hallowell, 157th Infantry Association newsletter, 2008.
232 **He was quickly tried:** Ibid.
232 **DEATH TO ALL TRAITORS:** Quentin W. Schillare, *The Battle of Aschaffenburg*, master's thesis, Fort Leavenworth, Kansas, 1989, p. 105.

CHAPTER TWENTY-TWO—CASSINO ON THE MAIN

233 **Icy-eyed GI's darted through:** Oleck, ed., *Eye Witness*, p. 137.
234 **Through his field glasses:** Quentin W. Schillare, *The Battle of Aschaffenburg*, master's thesis, Fort Leavenworth, Kansas, 1989, p. 17.
234 ***If the Third Army*****:** Felix Sparks, Regis University interview.

234 **Again the area was:** Ibid.

234 **Then Sparks heard the:** Harry Eisner, letter to Michael E. Gonzales, containing memoir "Poor Child," May 10, 1989. 45th Division Museum archives.

234 **His men scattered, looking:** Buechner, *Sparks*, p. 125.

234 ***What the goddamn hell?*****:** Felix Sparks, Regis University interview.

235 **They were dug in:** Ibid.

235 **"Colonel," said the captain:** Felix Sparks, interview with Chris Miskimon.

235 **Indeed, they had assumed:** Felix Sparks, Regis University interview.

235 **"There's no way I":** Ibid.

235 **Yet again, they had:** Quentin W. Schillare, *The Battle of Aschaffenburg*, master's thesis, Fort Leavenworth, Kansas, 1989, p. 92.

236 **It would certainly have:** Abe Baum, interview with author.

236 **There was, however, some:** Jack Hallowell, interview with author.

236 **Captain Anse Speairs:** Felix Sparks, interview with author.

236 **"Let's get rid of":** Anse Speairs, interview with author.

236 **One battalion issued twenty-six:** After Action Report, National Archives.

237 **It would be several:** Ibid.

237 **If it was Dutch:** Ainse Speairs, interview with author.

237 **The uneasy silence was:** Hallowell et al., *Eager for Duty*, p. 151.

237 **Some Thunderbirds got blind:** Ibid.

237 **According to his company:** Cranston Rogers, Colorado National Guard interview.

237 **After a sleepless night:** Ibid.

238 **Having come so far:** Cranston Rogers, interview with author.

238 **That morning, under a:** After Action Report, National Archives.

238 **By lunchtime, the advance:** Felix Sparks, interview with author.

238 **Not since Anzio had:** Quentin W. Schillare, *The Battle of Aschaffenburg*, master's thesis, Fort Leavenworth, Kansas, 1989, p. 103.

238 **He ordered his men:** Felix Sparks, "The Aschaffenburg Battle," 157th Infantry Association newsletter, July 22, 1982.

238 **That evening, unsettling rumors:** After Action Report, National Archives

238 **According to one report:** *45th Infantry Division News*, April 1945.

238 **"Whoever remains in the":** Quentin W. Schillare, *The Battle of Aschaffenburg*, master's thesis, Fort Leavenworth, Kansas, 1989, p. 97.

238 **"Now the people stand":** Ibid., p. 66.

239 **In some rooms, they:** After Action Report, National Archives.

239 **They did so, but:** Felix Sparks, "The Aschaffenburg Battle," 157th Infantry Association newsletter, July 22, 1982.

239 **joining fifty-nine other men:** After Action Report, National Archives.

239 **Later that afternoon, Sparks:** He would be cut down by men of Chan Rogers's platoon of G company. "A US newspaper photographer arrived after Heymann had been cut down, and expressed extreme anger that the GIs had ruined a great photograph!" Source: Chris Miskimon.

239 **In their absence:** Karl Mann, interview with author.

239 **Mann wondered what might:** Ibid.

239 **"There was a good":** A. H. "Ed" Speairs, "Two Ultimatums at Aschaffenburg," Second Platoon Newsletter, C Company, 157th Regiment, no. 10 (April 1999), courtesy of Dan Dougherty.

240 **Mortars opened up and:** Christopher Miskimon, "A City Destroyed," pp. 16–17.

240 **By daylight, the entire:** Felix Sparks, "The Aschaffenburg Battle," 157th Infantry Association newsletter, July 22, 1982.

240 **Yet casualties continued to:** After Action Report, National Archives.

240 **Every mobile piece available:** Felix Sparks, "The Aschaffenburg Battle," 157th Infantry Association newsletter, July 22, 1982.

240 **Then Thunderbirds stormed the:** Quentin W. Schillare, *The Battle of Aschaffenburg*, master's thesis, Fort Leavenworth, Kansas, 1989, p. 104.

240 **The Germans answered round:** Hallowell et al., *Eager for Duty*, p. 152.

241 **Speairs finally managed to:** Ed Speairs, interview with author.

241 **Speairs opened a window:** A. H. "Ed" Speairs, "Two Ultimatums at Aschaffenburg," Second Platoon Newsletter, C Company, 157th Regiment, no. 10 (April 1999), courtesy of Dan Dougherty.

241 **"Should you refuse to":** Hallowell et al., *Eager for Duty*, p. 154.

241 **Lamberth ignored the offer:** Felix Sparks, "The Aschaffenburg Battle," 157th Infantry Association newsletter, July 22, 1982.

241 **Snipers would crawl through:** After Action Report, National Archives.

241 **If nobody answered:** Whiting, *America's Forgotten Army*, p. 191.

242 **In some streets:** Cranston Rogers, interview with author.

242 **he had to fight:** Felix Sparks, "The Aschaffenburg Battle," 157th Infantry Association newsletter, July 22, 1982.

242 **It was the utter:** Cranston Rogers, interview with author.

242 **Ordered by his company:** Ibid.

242 **They were both cut:** Cranston Rogers, Colorado National Guard interview.

242 **In the Bois-Brule Barracks:** Miskimon, "A City Destroyed," p. 18.

242 **Unprecedented quantities of white:** After Action Report, National Archives.

242 **Nothing was sacred:** Oleck, ed., *Eye Witness*, p. 137.

243 **But the strafing runs:** After Action Report, National Archives.

243 **The napalm, essentially jellied:** Ibid.

243 **The air strikes seemed:** Ibid.

243 **So stubborn in fact:** Whiting, *America's Forgotten Army*, p. 191.

243 **Aschaffenburg was indeed what:** Felix Sparks, "The Aschaffenburg Battle," 157th Infantry Association newsletter, July 22, 1982.

243 **"Revenge is our battle":** Lucas, *Experiences of War*, pp. 168–69.

244 **Lamberth and his men:** Speer, *Spandau*, p. 39.

244 **Finally, that evening, facing:** After Action Report, National Archives.

244 **That March of 1945:** Evans, *The Third Reich at War*, p. 682.

244 **Two German soldiers, executed:** Felix Sparks, Regis University interview.

244 **As the Thunderbirds closed:** Quentin W. Schillare, *The Battle of Aschaffenburg*, master's thesis, Fort Leavenworth, Kansas, 1989, p. 105.

245 **She kept looking at:** Harry Eisner, letter to Michael E. Gonzales, containing memoir "Poor Child," May 10, 1989. 45th Division Museum archives. Eisner would later write that he saw the same child on a ferry in New York Harbor. He did not say anything to the girl.

246 **Colonel O'Brien was:** After Action Report, National Archives.

246 **There would be unconditional:** Whiting, *America's Forgotten Army*, pp. 192–93.

246 **Sparks was the most:** Felix Sparks, "The Aschaffenburg Battle," 157th Infantry Association newsletter, July 22, 1982.

246 **Sparks, his interpreter Karl:** Karl Mann, interview with author.

246 **Then he ordered all:** Felix Sparks, "The Aschaffenburg Battle," 157th Infantry Association newsletter, July 22, 1982.

246 **Soon, they had all:** Felix Sparks, Regis University interview. Sparks would keep the gun and later give it to his son.

246 **To the end of:** Blair Lee Sparks, interview with author.

246 **"Tell the major he's":** Karl Mann, interview with author.

246 **Lamberth rode on the:** Israel, *The Day the Thunderbird Cried*, p. 88.

246 **He had executed honorable:** Felix Sparks, "The Aschaffenburg Battle," 157th Infantry Association newsletter, July 22, 1982.

246 **When the last Germans:** Ibid.

247 **The German looked humiliated:** Franklin, *Medic*, p. 138.

247 **"Had I known it":** Ibid.

247 **It was a heavy:** Rüdiger Overmans, *Deutsche militärische Verluste* (Munich, 1999), pp. 238–39.

247 **The regiment had lost:** After Action Report, National Archives.

247 Such behavior meant he: Whiting, *America's Forgotten Army*, p. 193.

248 Thankfully, the counterattack: Cundiff, *45th Infantry CP*, p. 272.

248 "Sixty minutes to build": Whiting, *America's Forgotten Army*, p. 206.

248 "I left the old": Rex Raney, interview with author. "I can with luck smell something for a few seconds each month," said Raney in 2011. "I can be around some pretty ripe odors and I don't know it." Source: Rex Raney, interview with author.

249 So Sparks and others: Felix Sparks, interview with author.

CHAPTER TWENTY-THREE—DOWNFALL

251 "Yeah," replied one veteran: Hallowell et al., *Eager for Duty*, p. 158.

251 "Roosevelt died!": Hicks, *The Last Fighting General*, p. 185.

251 An editorial in the: "Person of the Century Runner-Up: Franklin Delano Roosevelt," *Time*, March 1, 2000.

252 "It is a miracle": Toland, *The Last 100 Days*, p. 377.

252 "Here, read it!" exclaimed: Speer, *Inside the Third Reich*, p. 463.

252 The Germans tried to: After Action Report, National Archives.

252 Sparks could stand in: Ibid.

253 The raid had in: www.raf.mod.uk/bombercommand/diary/jan45.html.

253 The airborne destruction, which: Johnson, *Churchill*, pp. 137–38.

253 Hidden in the skeletons: Hallowell et al., *Eager for Duty*, p. 159.

253 Himmler, although desperately trying: Bundesarchiv Berlin, NS19/3118, fo.3. Himmler's order was on January 21, 1945. Hitler's had been on November 25, 1944 (fo.2), a couple of weeks before the start of the Ardennes campaign.

253 They were told to: Felix Sparks, Regis University interview.

253 The Seventh Army, to: After Action Report, National Archives.

254 Sparks was able: Hallowell et al., *Eager for Duty*, p. 159.

254 Sparks consulted his map: Felix Sparks, Regis University interview.

254 That morning, Sparks's Third: After Action Report, National Archives.

254 Sparks had deployed two: Karl Mann, interview with author.

254 Yet again, he wanted: Cranston R. Rogers, affidavit, April 25, 2006, Felix Sparks DSC Recommendation file.

254 "Uh, oh. I think": Felix Sparks, Regis University interview.

254 Turk pulled up: Karl Mann, interview with author.

254 Sparks realized that he: Felix Sparks, Regis University interview.

256 The burst had gone: Ibid.

256 "Goddamn it": Ibid.

256 Now his only mementos: Mary Sparks, interview with author.

256 "The ruined city was": Buechner, *Sparks,* p. 135.
256 The regiment had lost: After Action Report, National Archives.
256 Many men treated themselves: Cranston Rogers, Colorado National Guard interview.
256 It had not been: Speer, *Inside the Third Reich*, p. 473.
257 Speer himself had been: Ibid., p. 472.
257 "Probably he sensed that": Ibid., p. 474.
257 The Slavic hordes Hitler: Duffy, *Red Storm*, p. 297.
257 A Soviet force of: Bessel, *Germany 1945*, p. 104.
257 Selected men from the: Whiting, *America's Forgotten Army*, pp. 196–97.
257 For newsreel cameras: *Die Letzen Tage von Nurnberg* (Nuremberg: 8 Uhr Blatt, 1952).
257 Fittingly, the men given: Allen Bennett, interview with author.
258 Sparks thought the whole: Felix Sparks, interview with author.
258 The sniper died not: Buechner, *Sparks,* p. 135.
258 "Clouds of lilac perfume": Anonymous, *A Woman in Berlin*, pp. 1–5.
260 Among the most morally: Bessel, *Germany 1945*, pp. 108–9.
260 "I'm staying here," said: Ryan, *The Last Battle*, pp. 434–36.
261 As the war progressed: Hugh Foster, e-mail to author, November 23, 2011.
261 He was to seize: Felix Sparks, interview with author.
261 The race was on: Ibid.
261 "Move as rapidly": Shoah Foundation, interview with Felix Sparks.
261 Finally, he was on the last straight: Hallowell et al., *Eager for Duty*, p. 162.
261 No one wanted to: Cranston Rogers, Colorado National Guard interview.
261 Occasionally, what remained of: After Action Report, National Archives.
261 "Men or parts of men": Cundiff, *45th Infantry CP*, pp. 242–43.
262 Sparks was within striking: Hallowell et al., *Eager for Duty*, p. 162.
262 But his task force: Felix Sparks, Regis University interview.
262 After refueling, Sparks ordered: After Action Report, National Archives.
262 The following day, April 27: Buechner, *Sparks,* p. 136.
262 There followed a short: Felix Sparks, interview with author.
262 In disgust, Sparks moved: Buechner, *Sparks,* p. 136.
263 If he managed to: Felix Sparks, Colorado National Guard interview.

PART SIX—THE HEART OF DARKNESS

265 **"Above all I charge":** Bullock, *Hitler*, p. 795.

CHAPTER TWENTY-FOUR—THE DAY OF THE AMERICANS

267 **"S-3 to all battalions":** Felix Sparks, interview with author.
268 **If either group ran:** Shoah Foundation, interview with Felix Sparks.
268 **Sparks set out:** Antelme, *The Human Race*, p. 286.
268 **Did they know something:** Ibid.
268 *Everything is ripe*: Ibid.
269 **Determined to get the first report:** *Denver Post*, August 26, 2001.
269 **Since its opening as Nazi Germany's:** Felix Sparks, 157th Infantry Regiment newsletter, June 15, 1989.
269 **More than thirteen thousand in:** *Denver Post*, August 26, 2001.
269 **Soon after, twenty-five-year-old Walsh:** *Boston Globe*, July 2, 2001.
269 **"I don't know what":** Felix Sparks, Regis University interview.
269 **On the outskirts of the town:** After Action Report, National Archives.
270 **There were fresh beds:** Smith, *The Harrowing of Hell*, p. 79.
270 **His interpreter, Karl Mann:** Karl Mann, interview with author.
270 **Several shots were fired:** Karl Mann, unpublished memoir of World War II, provided to the author, p. 16.
270 **Sparks then caught sight:** Karl Mann, interview with author.
270 **It resembled some kind:** Felix Sparks, Regis University interview.
270 **He did not know:** Felix Sparks, 157th Infantry Regiment Association newsletter, June 15, 1989.
270 **Sparks could see a:** www.scrapbookpages.com, "Who entered Dachau first on April 29 1945." This is the most authoritative Internet source on all aspects of Dachau.
270 **If the SS were:** Felix Sparks, interview with author.
272 **"We got all kinds":** *The Liberation of KZ Dachau*, a documentary by James Kent Strong, 1990.
272 **"Okay," said Walsh:** Felix Sparks, Regis University interview.
272 **Walsh and his men:** *The Liberation of KZ Dachau*, documentary by James Kent Strong, 1990.
272 **"What's a freight train":** Israel, *The Day the Thunderbird Cried*, p. 133.
272 **Degro was in fact:** *Cleveland Plain Dealer*, February 6, 2005.
272 **He had been in:** *The Liberation of KZ Dachau*, documentary by James Kent Strong, 1990.
272 **Human excrement was all:** Israel, *The Day the Thunderbird Cried*, p. 259.

272 **Corpses riddled with bullets:** John Lee, "Action at the Coal Yard Wall," Second Platoon newsletter, April 2001, issue 20.

273 **It was as if:** Ibid.

273 **The stump was covered:** Dachau and the Nazi Terror, 1933–1945 (Comite International de Dachau, Brussels, 2002), p.142

273 **The train had left:** Dan Dougherty, interview with Jeffrey Hilton, 157th Infantry Regiment reunion, Colorado Springs, 2007.

273 **It had first stopped:** Pierre C. T. Verheye, *The Train Ride into Hell*, unpublished manuscript.

273 **On April 21, when:** IfZ-Archiv, Nurnberger Dokumente, NO 2192, testimony Hans Mehrbach, "The Death Train from Buchenwald."

273 **Six days later:** Eye Witness Report of Johann Bergmann, Buchenwald, in Mahnung und Verpflichtung, *Dokumente und Berichte* (Berlin: Forth, 1983), pp. 503–5.

273 ***What the hell is*:** *The Liberation of KZ Dachau*, documentary by James Kent Strong, 1990.

273 **Sparks was next on:** Felix Sparks, interview with the author.

273 **His only weapon now was:** Blair Lee Sparks, interview with author.

273 **The sights and smells:** *The Liberation of KZ Dachau*, documentary by James Kent Strong, 1990.

273 **Then Sparks saw a:** *Rocky Mountain News*, April 29, 2003.

273 **He would never forget:** Ibid.

273 **"Why?":** Israel, *The Day the Thunderbird Cried*, p. 133. According to Israel, another GI "who came across the little girl would see her face in his mind every night for the next 60 years until he was mercifully able to fall asleep. Even as an old man he was unable to answer her innocent question."

273 **They had been killed:** Felix Sparks, interview with author.

273 **All he could do:** Ibid.

274 **How could human beings:** *Denver Post*, April 30, 1995.

274 **Disbelief and shock turned:** *Cleveland Plain Dealer*, February 6, 2005.

274 **"Let's kill every one":** I.G. Report.

274 **"Don't take any SS":** Ibid.

274 **"Okay, move!" Sparks ordered:** *Colorado Lawyer* 27, no. 10, p. 51.

274 **I Company scout Private:** John Lee, "Action at the Coal Yard Wall," Second Platoon newsletter, April 2001, Issue 20.

274 **"Let's get these Nazi dogs":** Shoah Foundation, interview with Felix Sparks.

274 **Lieutenant Walsh set the:** *Boston Globe*, July 2, 2001.

274 **He and others had been:** Felix Sparks, interview with author.

274 **It had not prepared:** *Times Picayune*, May 27, 2001.

274 **"Every man in the":** IG Report.

275 **Sparks snapped commands:** Felix Sparks, Regis University lecture.

275 **"We're going in the":** Felix Sparks, Regis University interview.

275 **He struggled for a:** Felix Sparks, Regis University lecture.

275 **KZ Dachau had been guarded:** For an excellent and exhaustive description of the American actions at Dachau on April 29, 1945, see Klaus-Dietmar Henke's *Die amerikanische Besetzung Deutschlands, München*, 1995, pp. 862–931.

275 **Before he could be brought:** Barbara Distel, *Die Befreiung des KZ Dachau* [The Liberation of the Concentration Camp Dachau], in *Dachauer Hefte 1,* 1985, p. 7.

275 **Then he changed his:** *Boston Globe*, July 2, 2001.

276 **"I never like to":** Ibid.

CHAPTER TWENTY-FIVE—THE HOUNDS OF HELL

277 **"The effect of it":** *Boston Globe*, July 2, 2001.

277 **He and his men:** Whitlock, *Rock of Anzio*, p. 362.

278 **Poplar trees in spring:** Ibid.

278 **"You sons of bitches":** *Rocky Mountain News*, April 29, 2003.

278 **Walsh began to beat:** Felix Sparks, interview with the author.

278 **"Bastards. Bastards. Bastards":** Felix Sparks, Regis University interview.

278 **So Sparks pulled out:** Felix Sparks, Colorado National Guard interview.

278 **Stunning him and knocking:** *Rocky Mountain News*, April 29, 2003.

278 **Walsh lay there, crying:** Felix Sparks, interview with author.

278 **"I'm taking over command":** Ibid.

278 **"He really lost it":** Sidney Horn, interview with Flint Whitlock, 1996.

278 **Walsh had gone "crazy":** Felix Sparks, Regis University interview.

278 **"This was the culmination":** William Walsh, interview with James Kent Strong, in *The Liberation of KZ Dachau*, documentary, 1990.

278 **His barrack:** Felix Sparks, Regis University lecture, "Stories of Wartime."

279 **"They're here!" someone cried:** Antelme, *The Human Race*, p. 286.

279 **"We're free!":** Ibid.

280 **"We kicked all the":** Israel, *The Day the Thunderbird Cried*, p. 259. Degro would never forget the scenes that greeted him that morning. "Those scenes at Dachau are impressed on my mind," he would say more than sixty years later. "Sometimes I get up at night and try to erase them, but I can't forget." Source: Ibid.

280 **One of the men:** T. Pauli, *Berkenkruis*, newsletter for volunteers of

Flemish SS, October 1988. The account in the magazine is based on Linberger's alleged testimony to the German Red Cross.

280 **The men rounded up:** *Dachau and Nazi Terror, 1933–1945, Studies and Reports* (Comité International de Dachau, Brussels), 2002, p. 34.

280 **They had massacred defenseless:** At a later trial for those accused of the Malmédy massacre, all mention of the killing of SS POWs by Americans was ordered stricken from the record.

281 **He and the platoon:** Shoah Foundation, interview with Felix Sparks.

281 **Then he discovered the:** *Dachau and Nazi Terror, 1933–1945, Studies and Reports* (Comité International de Dachau, Brussels, 2002), pp. 142–44.

281 **Other than Alsatians:** Israel, *The Day the Thunderbird Cried*, p. 116. "On special amusement days, Zill would have a table of food placed in front of starving prisoners who stood at attention. Should a prisoner relax his body, the dogs would react automatically." Source: Ibid. Zill, according to Israel, would die in 1974 in Dachau, having had a life sentence reduced to fifteen years. He in fact died within "walking distance" of the "horror camp" he had once commanded. Source: Ibid.

281 **The SS had made:** *Dachau and Nazi Terror, 1933–1945, Studies and Reports* (Comité International de Dachau, Brussels), 2002, p. 34.

281 **When the victims had been:** *Stars and Stripes*, May 3, 1945.

281 **The dogs died quickly:** In the cages, a single survivor was later found. Source: "A Survivor of Dachau Named Tell," personal communication from a soldier of the 72nd Signal Company, with Howard Buechner, June 6, 1986. "Lt. Lorin E. Fickle found a wounded dog at Dachau, the only known survivor of the 'Hounds of Hell.' The animal was a magnificent, black shepherd. Lt. Fickle nursed the dog back to health and named him 'Tell.' Somehow, permission was obtained to ship 'Tell' to the United States where he was a splendid pet for many years." Source: Ibid.

281 **A soldier apparently used:** Buechner, *Dachau*, pp. 149–50.

281 **Just one of the:** According to Gun, *The Day of the Americans*, p. 64: "A week later a GI pilfering in one of the abandoned SS barracks, heard a growling coming from behind some cases in a dark corner. He approached cautiously and was startled to see a German Shepherd dog—his head was bloody from a bullet wound. The animal had apparently been hiding there without food and water for several days, licking his wound. The GI ran away and no one knows what happened to the wretched animal."

281 **So blue- and green-tinged:** Buechner, *Sparks*, p. 142.

281 **Hundreds had died in:** Felix Sparks, "Dachau and Its Liberation," 157th Infantry Association newsletter, March 20, 1984.

282 **"One hears yelling and":** *Dachau and Nazi Terror, 1933–1945, Studies and Reports II* (Comité International de Dachau, Brussels), 2002, p. 152.

282 Inmates began to shout: Buechner, *Sparks*, p. 142.

282 A spine-chilling roar: Felix Sparks, interview with author.

282 "It was truly our": Whitaker, I.G. Report, Walenty Lenarczyk testimony, p. 51, National Archives.

283 It was as if: After Action Report, National Archives.

283 The German, it was: *New Orleans Times-Picayune*, May 27, 2001.

283 In another incident, Russian: *45th Infantry Division News*, May 13, 1945.

283 It is assumed that: www.scrapbookpages.com, Dr. Juergen Zarusky, "Dachauer Hefte Nr. 13."

284 The first to reach: *New York Herald Tribune*, May 1, 1945.

284 "My God! My God!": May, *Witness to War*, p. 90.

CHAPTER TWENTY-SIX—THE COAL YARD

285 Sparks did not know: Felix Sparks, "Dachau and Its Liberation," 157th Infantry Association, March 20, 1984.

286 Lieutenant Bill Walsh was: Felix Sparks, private correspondence, February 2, 1982.

286 To Sparks, the situation: *Boston Globe*, July 2, 2001

286 "Colonel, you should see": Felix Sparks, interview with Flint Whitlock, 1996.

286 Once Sparks had departed: IG Report, National Archives. See also Buechner, *Dachau*, pp. 78–79.

286 Lieutenant Walsh ordered a: Ibid.

286 Others muttered in German: John Lee, "Action at the Coal Yard Wall," Second Platoon newsletter, April 2001, no. 20.

286 "Keep your goddamn hands": Ibid.

286 Lieutenant Walsh then lined: Whitaker IG report, National Archives.

286 Curtin fired three bursts: Ibid.

287 Most of the SS did: Karl Mann, interview with author.

287 Thunderbird wouldn't let go: Whitlock, *Rock of Anzio*, p. 365.

287 Lieutenant Busheyhead also opened: Whitaker I.G. Report, National Archives.

287 The Thunderbirds fired from left: *Boston Globe*, July 2, 2001

287 "Stay calm, we die": Kern, *Verbrechen am deutschen Volk*, pp. 314–16.

287 It took him perhaps: Karl Mann, interview with author. Also see Karl Mann, unpublished memoir of World War II, provided to the author.

287 A film cameraman, Henry Gerzen: Felix Sparks, interview with author.

287 The firing got: Karl Mann, unpublished memoir of World War II, provided to the author.

287 **"There will be no":** Felix Sparks, interview with author.

287 **Curtin began to cry:** *Boston Globe*, July 2, 2001.

288 **"Colonel," he blurted:** Felix Sparks, "Dachau and Its Liberation," 157th Infantry Association newsletter, March 20, 1984.

288 **There were a few:** *New Orleans Times-Picayune*, May 27, 2001.

288 **"Lieutenant," said Sparks:** Whitlock, *Rock of Anzio*, p. 365.

288 **At least seventeen had:** Felix Sparks, interview with author.

288 **As many as seventy-five:** Whitaker IG Report, National Archives.

288 **A private standing in:** Ibid.

288 **Twenty-two-year-old Mills had not:** *The Liberation of KZ Dachau*, documentary by James Kent Strong, 1990.

288 ***We came over here*:** Ibid.

288 **It was not the:** IG Report, National Archives.

288 **Sparks ordered his men:** IG Report, National Archives.

288 **They included medic Peter:** Whitlock, *Rock of Anzio*, p. 365.

288 **Colonel Howard Buechner:** IG Report, National Archives.

288 **Among the SS:** Kern, *Verbrechen am deutschen Volk*, pp. 314–16.

288 **Then a Thunderbird medic:** IG Report, National Archives. See also the excellent account of the shooting: "That Is Not the American Way of Fighting,"in Wolfgang Benz and Barbara Distel, eds., *Dachau and Nazi Terror II* (Comité International de Dachau, Brussels, 2002), pp. 132–60.

289 **Jager took a blade:** Kern, *Verbrechen am deutschen Volk*, pp. 314–16.

289 **Beyond it, thousands of:** Karl Mann, unpublished memoir of World War II, provided to author. Also Karl Mann, interview with author.

289 **In a nearby barrack:** Jack Goldman, interview with author. Goldman's Auschwitz camp number was 69970—he would never forget it because it was tattooed on his arm. More than four hundred thousand numbers were assigned at Auschwitz. The tattoos were introduced so that the authorities could identify the corpses of registered prisoners who had died.

289 **He saw a young:** Rothchild, *Voices from the Holocaust*, p. 164.

289 **That felt a lot:** Ibid.

289 **Sparks's men asked him:** Jack Goldman, interview with author.

289 **He was a human:** *Rocky Mountain News*, April 29, 2003.

290 **"Okay, I'll go in":** Bill Walsh, interview with James Kent Strong, in *The Liberation of KZ Dachau*, documentary, 1990.

291 **"That's his everything":** Ibid.

291 **A few were utterly dazed:** Smith, *The Harrowing of Hell*, p. 285.

291 **Bodies flew through the:** Felix Sparks, "Dachau and Its Liberation," 157th Infantry Association newsletter, March 20, 1984.

291 "They're killing the informers": *Colorado Lawyer* 27, no. 10 (October 1998).

291 "We're bringing food, water": Felix Sparks, Regis University lecture, "Stories of Wartime."

292 "Don't throw them": Shoah Foundation, interview with Felix Sparks.

292 There were more than: Hallowell et al., *Eager for Duty*, p. 167.

292 Hundreds of their fellow: Wolfgang Benz and Barbara Distel, eds., *Dachau and Nazi Terror II* (Comité International de Dachau, Brussels), 2002, p. 31.

292 Some of these corpses: Felix Sparks, Regis University lecture.

292 They all claimed they: Ibid.

292 Young children cycled past: *Chicago Tribune*, April 30, 1945.

CHAPTER TWENTY-SEVEN—THE LINDEN INCIDENT

293 message on a sign: Brome, *The Way Back*, p. 226.

294 In the second was: Ibid., p. 240.

294 Her blond hair was: May, *Witness to War*, p. 90.

294 "It was the first": Ibid., p. 91.

294 To avoid embarrassment: Felix Sparks, Regis University interview.

294 He walked over to: Karl Mann, interview with author.

294 "She can't open that": Felix Sparks, interview with author.

294 "You're not in your area": Shoah Foundation, interview with Felix Sparks.

294 She named the Lutheran: Niemöller was a controversial figure. He had served on a U-Boat in World War I and initially supported the Nazis, making what some have claimed were anti-Semitic remarks before his arrest by the Gestapo in 1937 for opposing Hitler's attempt to Nazify Protestant churches.

294 She had a list: Whitlock, *Rock of Anzio*, p. 379. They had in fact been taken out of the camp days earlier.

294 "Lady, I don't give": Felix Sparks, interview with author.

295 Sparks was dead tired: Felix Sparks, Regis University interview.

295 "You can't go in": Felix Sparks, interview with author.

295 He began to argue: Buechner, *Dachau*, p. 75.

295 To Sparks, it seemed: Felix Sparks, interview with author.

295 He had never lost: Karl Mann, interview with author.

295 Linden and Sparks started: Whitlock, *Rock of Anzio*, p. 380

295 "There was a brigadier": San Marcos, California, *Today's Local News*, November 10, 2008.

296 **"Shoot over their heads!":** Felix Sparks, interview with author.
296 **"Charge the gate and":** Felix Sparks, Regis University interview.
296 **"No, you're not":** Felix Sparks, interview with Chris Miskimon.
296 **"I'm in my territory":** Felix Sparks, interview with author.
296 **"Escort the general":** Ibid.
296 **The blow was more:** Ibid.
296 **"I'll kill you right":** Whitlock, *Rock of Anzio*, p. 380.
296 **Sparks aimed at Linden's:** Karl Mann, interview with author.
296 **"I'm going to blow":** Whitlock, *Rock of Anzio*, p. 380.
296 **"I'll leave, but I'll":** Felix Sparks, Regis University interview.
296 **"Go ahead":** Felix Sparks, interview with author.
296 **Linden left with Higgins:** Karl Mann, interview with author.
297 **Fellenz backed off, returned:** Felix Sparks, interview with author.
297 **Then he walked with:** Karl Mann, unpublished memoir of World War II, provided to the author.
297 **"We need food and medicine":** Felix Sparks, Regis University interview.
297 **At 4:35 P.M., Sparks also:** 157th S-3 Journal, April 29, 1945, Box 11072, National Archives.
297 **"I don't have time":** Felix Sparks, Regis University interview.
298 **A Polish inmate explained:** After Action Report, National Archives.
298 **"Their blood drained into":** Ibid.
298 **Some of the victims:** Felix Sparks, interview with author.
298 **They had been dispatched:** Felix Sparks, "Dachau and Its Liberation," 157th Infantry Association newsletter, March 20, 1984.
298 **"I'll take care of":** Felix Sparks, Regis University interview.

CHAPTER TWENTY-EIGHT—THE LONG DAY CLOSES

299 **Michael DiPaulo, French consulate:** *Cape Cod Times*, September 7, 2001.
300 **That was all that:** Hicks, *The Last Fighting General*, p. 188.
300 **"We knew we had":** Dan Dougherty, interview with Jeffrey Hilton, 157th reunion 2007, Colorado Springs.
300 **One of the sergeants:** *Jewish Weekly News of Northern California*, April 2001.
300 **"He wanted an SS":** Dan Dougherty, interview with Jeffrey Hilton, 157th reunion 2007, Colorado Springs.
300 **"I don't think there":** John Lee, interviewed by James Kent Strong, *The Liberation of KZ Dachau*, documentary, 1990.
300 **THIS IS WHY WE:** *45th Infantry Division News*, May 1945.
301 **"I'd gladly go through":** After Action Report, National Archives.

301 **"Combat-hardened soldiers, Gentile":** Wolfgang Benz and Barbara Distel, eds., *Dachau and Nazi Terror II* (Comité International de Dachau, Brussels), 2002, p. 53.

301 **"Turned out they were":** Felix Sparks, interview with author.

302 **It was just as:** Hallowell et al., *Eager for Duty*, p. 169.

302 **"The chief is dead!":** Hugh Trevor Roper, *The Last Days of Hitler* (New York: Macmillan, 1965), p. 261.

302 **Sparks commandeered an apartment:** Whitlock, *Rock of Anzio*, p. 388. Also see "Liberating Dachau," *World War II*, March 2000.

302 **Soon, a three-inch blanket:** Joseph R. Bosa, Monograph 15, June 1990, *The 171st Field Artillery Battalion, 1942–1945*, 45th Infantry Division Museum, Oklahoma City.

302 **With an eye to:** Jack Hallowell, interview with author.

303 **the "Beer Hall Putsch":** Anse Speairs, interview with author.

303 **A white sign was:** Felix Sparks, 157th Infantry Regiment Association newsletter.

PART SEVEN—LAST BATTLES
CHAPTER TWENTY-NINE—THE LAST DAYS

307 **"Trying to keep warm":** Smith, *The Harrowing of Hell*, p. 101

308 **"A love letter. . . . Goodbye":** Adler, *Marguerite Duras*, p. 142.

308 **Mitterrand told Duras that:** Ibid., p. 141.

309 **Other Thunderbirds, by contrast:** Hicks, *The Last Fighting General*, p. 189.

309 **"Then someone said there":** Hallowell et al., *Eager for Duty*, p. 171. There were remarkably few cases of rape among the occupiers. The Soviets, by contrast, raped more than fifty thousand German women in Berlin alone in one week that May. Source: Judt, *Postwar*, p. 20.

309 **"Things are heating up":** Shoah Foundation, interview with Felix Sparks.

309 **Two Signal Corps men:** Colonel John H. Linden, letter to Historian of 45th Infantry Division Association, Oklahoma City, April 10, 1996, 45th Infantry Division Museum archives.

310 **"I'm going to send":** Felix Sparks, Regis University interview.

310 **"[Sparks] feels badly":** 3rd Battalion, 157th Journal, May 1, 1945, Box 11075, National Archives.

310 **Three men left Munich:** Felix Sparks, Regis University interview.

310 **By two o'clock:** 3rd Battalion, 157th Journal, May 1, 1945, Box 11075, National Archives.

311 **"As we passed the SS huts":** Adler, *Marguerite Duras*, pp. 141–44.

311 **A call was put:** Ibid.

311 **It would be many:** Ibid.

311 **Now he weighed just:** Edgar Morin, "Homage to Robert Antelme," *Le Monde*, November 2, 1990.

312 **Duras dared not tell:** Duras, *The War*, pp. 56–59

312 **He ordered Mann and:** Karl Mann, unpublished memoir of World War II, p. 19.

312 **"We went by Paris":** Felix Sparks, Regis University interview.

312 **"I have orders to":** Felix Sparks, "Dachau and Its Liberation," 157th Infantry Association newsletter, March 20, 1984.

312 **"I'll call my commander":** Felix Sparks, interview with author.

313 **"Sorry, Colonel":** Ibid.

313 **"Okay":** Felix Sparks, Regis University interview.

313 **In Bavaria, a Lieutenant Colonel:** Israel, *The Day the Thunderbird Cried*, p. 175.

314 **"Rumor had it that":** *Boston Globe*, July 2, 2001.

315 **Whitaker also went to:** This happened on May 8, 1945.

315 **"I was scared to":** *Boston Globe*, July 2, 2001.

315 **"I didn't see any":** Ibid.

316 **"At about the same":** Whitaker IG Report, National Archives.

316 **Under further questioning:** *Boston Globe*, July 2, 2001.

316 **He concluded that seventeen:** Whitaker IG Report, National Archives.

317 **After navigating the appalling:** Whiting, *'44*, p. 107.

317 **"Well, Colonel":** This disappearance of the Seventh was a shame. It was later described as America's "forgotten army"—one that never received any great recognition yet had done perhaps more than any other given its time in combat, to secure victory.

317 **Sparks set off once:** Felix Sparks, interview with author.

317 **He was tired after:** Blumeson, *The Patton Papers*, p. 706.

318 **He was hopeful, however:** Blumeson, *The Patton Papers*, p. 718.

318 **He reported to the:** Felix Sparks, 157th Infantry Association newsletter, March 20, 1984.

318 **He told Sparks that:** Felix Sparks, private correspondence, February 2, 1982.

318 **The charges were so:** Felix Sparks, interview with author.

318 **"General Patton's out now":** Felix Sparks, Regis University interview.

318 **"Colonel, sit here":** Six million copies of *Mein Kampf* had sold by 1940 in Germany, making Hitler a wealthy man.

318 **Behind the desk sat:** Felix Sparks, interview with author.

318 **"I have some serious":** Felix Sparks, "Dachau and Its Liberation," 157th Infantry Association newsletter, March 20, 1984.

318 Sparks looked over at: Felix Sparks, interview with author.

318 "Didn't you serve under": Felix Sparks, Regis University interview.

319 "I would like to": Felix Sparks, interview with author.

319 "I'm going to tear": Felix Sparks, "Dachau and Its Liberation," 157th Infantry Association newsletter, March 20, 1984.

319 Sparks would later remember: Felix Sparks, private correspondence, February 2, 1982.

319 "Now go home": Ibid. and Felix Sparks, "Dachau and Its Liberation," 157th Infantry Association newsletter, March 20, 1984.

319 Sparks saluted and left: Felix Sparks, Regis University interview.

319 George Patton was happy: Atkinson, *The Day of Battle*, p. 116.

319 "Unless their crimes were": D'Este, *Patton*, p. 742.

319 Besides, no one wanted: Johann Voss, letter to author, December 4, 2011.

320 "He was just kind": Whitlock, *Rock of Anzio*, p. 390.

320 "But in the light": *Boston Globe*, July 2, 2001.

320 A proud Thunderbird to: Ibid.

321 "I think they all": William Walsh, interview with James Kent Strong, in *The Liberation of KZ Dachau*, documentary, 1990.

CHAPTER THIRTY—VICTORY IN EUROPE

322 "In the United States": David Eichhorn, "Sabbath Service in a Dachau Concentration Camp," *Dachau and Nazi Terror 1*, Testimonies, p. 62.

324 He had sworn that: Carlo D'Este, *Eisenhower, A Soldier's Life* (New York: Henry Holt, 2002), p. 702.

324 "THE MISSION OF THIS": Ibid., p. 704.

324 The men of evil: Hastings, *Armageddon*, p. 487.

324 "It is the victory": Toland, *The Last 100 Days*, pp. 572–86.

325 "There is V-E Day": Murphy, *To Hell and Back*, p. 272.

325 "It takes a while": Guy Prestia, interview with author.

325 "There was great relief": Buechner, *Sparks*, p. 153.

325 Finally, after the death: D'Este, *Patton*, p. 730.

325 "I was just skin": Felix Sparks, Regis University interview.

325 So many of his: Soldiers of the regiment had received 4 Medals of Honor, 20 Distinguished Service Crosses, 376 Silver Stars, 1,054 Bronze Stars, and 1,694 Purple Hearts. Source: Hugh Foster, "Overview of 157th Infantry Regiment in WWII."

325 A total of 1,449: National Archives, Box #11063, "Personnel Reports Not Dated." Courtesy of Dave Kerr.

326 "Red and blue flares": Marguerite Higgins, "Finale in the West," *Mademoiselle,* July 1945.

326 **There were tears in:** May, *Witness to War,* p. 92. When the Korean War broke out, Higgins, as fearless and ruthlessly competitive as ever, was bureau chief in Tokyo for the *Herald Tribune*; she was among the first reporters to cover the ground war. Frank Gibney of *Time* had tried to warn her off, saying: "It was no place for a woman." To which another male reporter quipped: "But it's all right for Maggie Higgins." She was told there were inadequate lavatories and was ordered out of the field by the American Eighth Army commander, Lieutenant General Walton W. Walker: "This is not the type of war where women ought to be running around the front lines." She went over his head to MacArthur and returned to the battlefield, where her reports earned her the Pulitzer Prize; she was the first woman to win it for foreign reporting. Source: *Guardian*, April 16, 2011.

326 **The first woman to:** *Guardian*, April 16, 2011.

326 **That was the question:** Johann Voss, letter to author, December 4, 2011.

326 **The silver runes he:** Voss, *Black Edelweiss*, p. 202.

327 **Voss's unit, for example:** Hugh Foster, interview with author.

327 **His comrades in the:** In 2011, when asked how he looked back on his days with the SS, Johann Voss wrote: "With deep affection for my comrades, especially the ones who did not come back, their selflessness, their resilience and their morale, their sense of duty when there was no more hope. . . . Especially if seen against the background of today's selfishness and greed and the loss of values like the simple German saying *Gemeinnutz geht vor Eigennutz.* And I look back with gratitude to my tightly-knit unit as I always felt sure they would never let one of us down." Source: Johan Voss, letter to author, December 4, 2011.

327 **Like their fellow Germans:** SS veteran Johann Voss had changed his views on Hitler. "After all the revelations about the mass killings in the extermination camps, which after a period of disbelief I couldn't doubt anymore, his reputation was completely ruined. . . . I think he suffered from megalomania like so many dictators before him. His nature was extremely complex; he had a high intelligence mixed with a brutal will to further his vision combined with a strong tendency to gamble. His anti-Semitism was an aberration, in the clinical sense of the word. His magnetism overwhelmed not only the masses but even sober German Generals when they came to see him face to face. Of his visions at least one was right: that it was Germany's European mission to contain the expansion of the communist world revolution as declared by the Komintern in the twenties and thirties. Germany had always been the main goal of the Komintern. To this day I believe that Germany under the weak and feeble democratic system of the Weimar Republic would have shared the fate of other Soviet satellites sooner or later, as we witnessed in Finland and the Baltic States before the war and Eastern

Europe and the Balkans after the war." Source: Johann Voss, letter to author, December 4, 2011.

327 **"It can only be":** Johann Voss, letter to author, December 4, 2011.

327 **"Unconditional surrender was not":** Voss, *Black Edelweiss*, p. 201.

328 **Never had so many:** Judt, *Europe*, p. 18

328 **"He asked if one":** Adler, *Marguerite Duras*, p. 149.

328 **"But Antelme showed us":** Edgar Morin, "Homage to Robert Antelme," *Le Monde*, November 2, 1990.

329 **Then General Robert Frederick:** Bishop et al., *The Fighting Forty-Fifth*, p. 188.

329 **General Alexander Patch, Seventh:** Nelson, *Thunderbird*, p. 191.

329 **High praise also came:** Buechner, *Sparks*, p. 192.

329 **Even senior Pentagon officials:** D'Este, *Patton*, p. 89.

330 **"We were busy killing":** *Saturday Evening Post*, November 30, 1946.

330 **"Oh God, how I":** Hicks, *The Last Fighting General*, p. 188.

CHAPTER THIRTY-ONE—PEACE BREAKS OUT

331 **"A pretty girl is":** Fritz, *Endkampf*, p. 201.

332 **"Thunderbird Paul Cundiff dated":** Cundiff, *45th Infantry CP*, p. 279.

332 **"However, noncompliance was widespread":** Buechner, *Sparks*, p. 154.

333 **"How do you know":** Hicks, *The Last Fighting General*, p. 190.

334 **"It took three weeks":** Felix Sparks, Regis University interview.

334 **Sparks's fellow Thunderbirds also:** "Thunderbird Afloat," 1, no. 5 (September 7, 1945).

334 **"On board," remembered one:** Hallowell et al., *Eager for Duty*, p. 178.

334 **After 827 days overseas:** Hugh Foster, "Summary of Combat Activities, 157th Infantry Regiment in WW11."

334 **The division's artillery had:** Buechner, *Sparks*, p. 203.

334 **The Thunderbirds approached New York:** "Thunderbird Afloat," 1, no. 5 (September 7, 1945).

334 **"It's the most beautiful":** Cundiff, *45th Infantry CP*, p. 286.

335 **To his right, across:** Felix Sparks, interview with author.

335 **"Come to El Paso":** Mary Sparks, interview with author.

335 **She booked into a hotel:** Ibid.

337 **An estimated ten million:** Clodfelter, *Warfare and Armed Conflicts*, pp. 584–91.

337 **That night of V-J:** Mary Sparks, interview with author.

337 **It was the happiest:** Ibid.

337 **The thought of being:** Felix Sparks, interview with author.

338 **"Well, as soon as":** Felix Sparks, Regis University interview.
338 **Kirk recognized his father:** Mary Sparks, interview with author.
338 **"He didn't take to":** Felix Sparks, interview with author.
339 **Other than diving to:** Ibid.
339 **He would never forget:** *Rocky Mountain News*, March 10, 2007.
340 **Their first home as:** *Colorado Lawyer,* 27, no. 10 (October 1998).
340 **"There were still a":** *University of Denver Water Law Review* (Fall 1999).
340 **Sparks took two months' leave:** Felix Sparks, Colorado National Guard interview.
341 **Sparks told Turner's parents:** *Rocky Mountain News*, March 10, 2007.
341 **In the rich farmland:** Felix Sparks, Colorado National Guard interview.
341 **"'This man knows Daddy'":** *Rocky Mountain News*, March 10, 2007.
341 **He then passed his:** "Law school was always easy for me," he later said. Source: *University of Denver Water Law Review* (Fall 1999).
342 **In 1948, Sparks "campaigned":** Kirk Sparks, interview with author.
342 **In Johnson's jaundiced eyes:** www.colorado.gov./dpa/doit/archives
342 **Sparks added that while:** Undated press clipping, Felix Sparks scrapbook, courtesy of Blair Lee Sparks.
343 **"They're Democratic . . . you'll need":** *Colorado Lawyer,* 27, no. 10 (October 1998).
343 **Far too blunt and:** Kirk Sparks, interview with author.
343 **He served just two:** *Denver Post,* September 28, 2007.
343 **Sparks's colleagues savored:** *Rocky Mountain News*, September 26, 2007.
343 **He always fought:** Blair Lee Sparks, interview with author.
343 **"Colorado can never repay":** *Denver Post,* September 28, 2007.
344 **Now Sparks was no:** Vincent Stigliani, interview with author.
344 **Sparks would boom out:** Jack Hallowell, personal notes on Sparks, provided to the author.
344 **"I don't know what":** Buechner, *Sparks,* p. xxxvi.
344 **"He didn't hesitate to":** Ainse Speairs, interview with author.
344 **Speairs had gone on:** Ibid.
344 **Among those who attended:** Joe Medina, interview with Nate Matlock, Regis University.
344 **Medina had retreated into:** Ibid.
345 **"No, I don't remember":** Ibid.
345 **"She had a little":** Rex Raney, interview with author.
345 **"It's Vinnie!" cried Sparks:** Vincent Stigliani, interview with author.
346 **No action had been:** Hugh Foster, e-mail to author, November 23, 2011.
346 **At a reunion in:** *Boston Globe,* July 2, 2001.
346 **Brazenly false accounts of:** Kirk Sparks, interview with author.

347 **At a reunion shortly:** Theresa Lynn Ast, "Confronting the Holocaust: American Soldiers Who Liberated the Concentration Camps," Ph.D. thesis, Emory University Library, E11.5.A87 2000. Also Mike Gonzales, interview with author.

347 **The number was:** Howard Buechner I.G. Report, National Archives. The report stated that Buechner "violated his duty both as a physician and a soldier by ignoring the possibility of saving the wounded, but still living prisoners who had been shot." Source: Summary of IG Report, p. 7.

347 **A former good friend:** Buechner, *Dachau*, p. 99.

347 **The report concluded that:** Whitaker IG Report, National Archives.

348 **"It didn't look good":** Shoah Foundation, interview with Felix Sparks.

348 **In early 1994, Israel:** Robert Goebel to David Israel, February 8, 1994.

348 **"Look, if I recover":** David Israel, interview with author.

348 **Israel knew from others:** Henry Gerzen to David Israel, March 14, 1994.

349 **The four clearly showed:** Israel, *The Day the Thunderbird Cried*, p. 177.

349 **According to Israel, Sparks:** David Israel, interview with author.

CHAPTER THIRTY-TWO—THE LAST BATTLE

350 **"The content of your":** Grossman, *On Killing*, p. 364.

351 **The fifteen-year-old pulled out:** *Denver Post*, January 12, 1994.

351 **Indeed, Lee Pumroy's killing:** Blair Lee Sparks, interview with author.

351 **He was particularly close to:** Kirk Sparks, interview with author.

351 **Sparks had once scolded:** Ibid.

351 **Days later, at his:** Sparks, *Déjà Vu*, p. 178.

352 **"They were like: 'Who's' ":** Blair Lee Sparks, interview with author.

352 **"It will be my":** Felix Sparks to Jack Hallowell, from Jack Hallowell's private correspondence. Quoted courtesy of Jack Hallowell.

352 **At the ensuing trial:** *Denver Post*, January 12, 1994.

352 **"I'm not the type":** Ibid.

352 **"I'll put in $50,000":** *Chicago Sun-Times*, December 12, 2003.

352 **I told him he:** *Rocky Mountain News*, September 14, 1993.

353 **"I don't have a low":** Ibid.

353 **Among his backers were:** *Chicago Sun Times*, December 12, 1993.

353 **"Just within the past few":** Felix Sparks, 157th Infantry Association newsletter, June 30, 1993.

353 **Also he tried to:** Felix Sparks, Regis University interview.

353 **After reestablishing the Colorado:** *Colorado Lawyer* 27, no. 10 (October 1998).

353 **Eventually, the governor of:** Felix Sparks, Regis University interview.

353 **Sparks believed that:** Shoah Foundation, interview with Felix Sparks.
353 **He had not seen:** Felix Sparks, interview with author.
354 **Among those who attended:** *Chicago Sun-Times*, December 12, 1993.
354 **The "goddamn NRA":** Ibid.
354 **But Sparks's proposed law:** Ibid.
354 **"They didn't know what":** Felix Sparks, Regis University interview.
354 **"Just call me Felix":** *Rocky Mountain News*, September 14, 1993.
355 **"This business of letting":** Felix Sparks, Regis University interview.
355 **In the nineties, Sparks:** Blair Lee Sparks, interview with author.
356 **"Tell that to my":** Felix Sparks, Holocaust Museum Speech, May 8, 1995.
356 **"He has advanced America":** *Rocky Mountain News*, undated clipping, Jack Hallowell's personal files.
356 **A housing association deemed:** *Richmond Times-Dispatch*, December 2, 2009.
356 **"or a place I've":** Fox News, December 3, 2009, foxnews.com/us/2009/12/03/.
356 **"He just goes into":** *Rocky Mountain News*, undated clipping, Jack Hallowell's personal files.
356 **"If you're going to":** *Times-Call*, Longmont, Colorado, August 3, 2001.
357 **"I don't need any":** *Rocky Mountain News*, March 10, 2007.
357 **His most prized memento:** www.c-spanvideo.org, U.S. representative, Colorado, Edwin Perlmutter speech before Congress, October 17, 2007.
357 **"I love you":** Mary Sparks, interview with author.
358 **"He just cared about":** *Rocky Mountain News*, October 3, 2007.
358 **According to tradition:** Ibid.
358 **"[It] doesn't bring my":** Felix Sparks, Regis University interview.

SELECTED BIBLIOGRAPHY

Abzug, Robert. *Inside The Vicious Heart.* Oxford University Press, New York, 1985.

Adleman, Robert H., and George Walton. *The Devil's Brigade.* Chilton Books, New York, 1966

———. *The Champagne Campaign.* Little Brown, New York, 1969.

Adler, Laure. *Marguerite Duras, A Life.* University of Chicago Press, 2000.

Allanbrook, Douglas. *See Naples.* Houghton Mifflin, Boston, 1995.

Allen, William L. *Anzio, Edge of Disaster.* Dutton, New York, 1978.

Anonymous. *A Woman in Berlin*, trans. Philip Boehm. Metropolitan Books, New York, 2005.

Antelme, Robert. *The Human Race.* The Marlboro Press, Evanston, Illinois, 1998.

Arnold-Foster, Mark. *The World at War.* New York, Stein & Day, 1973.

Atkinson, Rick. *The Day of Battle.* Henry Holt, New York, 2007.

Beevor, Anthony, and Artemis Cooper. *Paris—After the Liberation.* Penguin, London, 2004.

Bessel, Richard. *Germany 1945.* Harper Collins, New York, 2009.

Biddle, George. *Artist at War.* Viking, New York, 1994.

Bishop, Leo V., George A. Fisher, and Frank J. Glasglow. *The Fighting Forty-Fifth: The Combat Report of an Infantry Division.* Army & Navy Publishing Co., Baton Rouge, Louisiana, 1946.

Blumenson, Martin. *Bloody River.* Houghton Mifflin, Boston, 1970.

———. *The Patton Papers.* Houghton Mifflin, New York, 1974.

———. *Patton.* William Morrow, New York, 1985.

Bonn, Keith E. *When the Odds Were Even: The Vosges Mountains Campaign, October 1944–January 1945*: Presidio Press, Novato, California, 1994.

Bowditch, John III, ed. *Anzio Beachhead*, vol. 14 in the *American Forces in Action* series. Department of the Army Historical Division, Washington, DC, 1947.

Bradley, Omar N. *A Soldier's Story*. Rand McNally, Chicago, 1951.

Bradley, Omar N., and Clay Blair. *A General's Life*. Simon & Schuster, New York, 1983.

Brighton, Terry. *Patton, Montgomery, Rommel*. Three Rivers Press, New York, 2008.

Brome, Vincent. *The Way Back*. W.W. Norton & Company, New York, 1957.

Brooks, Barbara. *With Utmost Spirit*. University of Kentucky Press, 2004.

Buechner, Emajean. *Sparks: The Combat Diary of a Battalion Commander*. Thunderbird Press, Metairie, Louisiana, 1991.

Buechner, Howard A. *Dachau—Hour of the Avenger*. Thunderbird Press, Metairie, Louisiana, 1986.

Bull, Stephen. *World War II Infantry Tactics, Company and Battalion*. Osprey, Oxford, UK, 2005.

Bullock, Alan. *Hitler*. Konecky and Konecky, New York, 1962.

Capa, Robert. *Slightly Out of Focus*. Henry Holt, New York, 1947.

Cave Brown, Anthony. *The Last Hero*. Times Books, New York, 1982.

Chandler, Alfred. *Papers of Dwight Eisenhower*, vol. 3. Johns Hopkins University Press, 1970.

Clark, Lloyd. *Anzio, Italy and the Battle for Rome*. Grove Press, New York, 2006.

Churchill, Winston S. *The Second World War: Closing the Ring*. Houghton Mifflin, Boston, 1951.

Clark, Mark W. *Calculated Risk*. Harper & Bros., New York, 1950.

Clodfelter, Michael. *Warfare and Armed Conflicts, A Statistical Reference to Casualty and Other Figures, 1500–2000*. McFarland and Company, Jefferson, North Carolina, 2002.

Cundiff, Paul A. *45th Infantry CP—A Personal Record from World War II*. Privately published, Tampa, Florida, 1987.

Dachau and Nazi Terror, 1933–1945, Studies and Reports II, Comité International de Dachau, Brussels, 2002.

Dann, Sam. *Dachau, 29 April 1945*. Texas Tech University Press, Lubbock, 1998.

Darby, William O., and William H. Baumer. *We Led the Way*. Presidio Press, San Rafael, California, 1980.

DePastino, Todd. *Bill Mauldin: A Life Up Front*. W. W. Norton & Company, New York, 2008.

D'Este, Carlo. *Bitter Victory: The Battle for Sicily, 1943*. Dutton, New York, 1988.

———. *Fatal Decision: Anzio and the Battle for Rome*. HarperCollins, New York, 1991.

———. *Patton: A Genius for War*. HarperCollins, New York, 1995.

Die Letzen Tage von Nurnberg. Edited 8 Uhr Blatt, Nuremberg, 1952.

Distel, Barbara. "The Liberation of the Concentration Camp Dachau." *Dachauer Hefte* 1, Verlag Dachauer Hefte, Dachau, 1985.

Dorrance, William H. *Fort Kamehameha.* White Mane Publishing, Shippensburg, Pennsylvania, 1993.

Duffy, Christopher. *Red Storm on the Reich.* Da Capo Press, New York, 1993.

Duras, Marguerite. *The War.* The New Press, New York, 1985.

Eisenhower, D. *Crusade in Europe.* Doubleday, New York, 1948.

———. *Letters to Mamie.* Doubleday, New York, 1978.

Eisenhower, John S. D. *The Bitter Woods.* Putnam's Sons, New York, 1969.

———. *They Fought at Anzio.* University of Missouri Press, Columbia, 2007.

Ellis, John. *The Sharp End: The Fighting Man in WWII.* Charles Scribner's Sons, New York, 1980.

Embry, John. *The 45th Infantry Division at Anzio* (Monograph no. 8). 45th Infantry Division Museum, Oklahoma City, 1986.

Evans, Richard J. *The Third Reich at War.* Penguin, New York, 2009.

Farago, Ladislas. *Patton.* Barker, London, 1966.

Fest, Joachim. *Speer: The Final Verdict.* Harcourt, New York, 2003.

Fisher, George A. *The Story of the 180th Infantry Regiment.* Newsfoto Publishing Co., San Angelo, Texas, 1947.

Franklin, Robert. *Medic.* University of Nebraska Press, Lincoln, 2006.

Fritz, Stephen. *Endkampf.* The University Press of Kentucky, Lexington, 2004.

Fussell, Paul. *Wartime.* Oxford University Press, New York, 1989.

Gavin, James. *On to Berlin.* Bantam, New York, 1978.

Gervasi, Frank. *The Violent Decade.* Norton, New York, 1989.

Gilbert, Martin. *The Second World War* (rev. ed.). Henry Holt, New York. 1989.

———. *Churchill, A Life.* Henry Holt, New York, 1991.

Graham, Don. *No Name on the Bullet.* Penguin, New York, 1989.

Grossman, Dave. *On Killing.* Back Bay Books, Little Brown, New York, 2009.

Gun, Nerin. *The Day of the Americans.* Fleet Publishing, New York, 1966.

Hallowell, Jack, et al. *Eager for Duty: History of the 157th Infantry Regiment (Rifle).* Army & Navy Publishing Company, Baton Rouge, Louisiana, 1946.

Hastings, Max. *Armageddon.* Knopf, New York, 2004.

———. *Winston's War.* Vintage, New York, 2011.

Hechler, Ken. *The Bridge at Remagen.* Pictorial Histories Publishing Company, Missoula, Montana, 1993.

Hickey, Des, and Gus Smith. *Operation Avalanche: The Salerno Landings, 1943.* McGraw-Hill, New York, 1984.

Hicks, Anne. *The Last Fighting General.* Schiffer Military History, Atglen, Pennsylvania, 2006.

Hitchcock, William I. *The Bitter Road to Freedom*. Free Press, New York, 2008.

Irving, David. *The War Between the Generals*. Allen Lane, London, 1980.

Israel, David. *The Day the Thunderbird Cried*. Emek Press, Medford, Oregon, 2005.

Johnson, Paul. *Churchill*. Penguin, New York, 2009.

Jones, James. *WWII*. Ballantine, New York, 1975.

Judt, Tony. *Europe*. Penguin, New York, 2005.

Keegan, John. *The Second World War*. Penguin, New York, 1989.

Kemp, Ted. *A Commemorative History: First Special Service Force*. Taylor Publishing, Dallas, 1995.

Kershaw, Ian. *Hitler, 1936–1945, Nemesis*. W.W. Norton, New York, 2000.

Kesselring, Albert. *The Memoirs of Field-Marshal Kesselring*. Presidio Press, Novato, California, 1989.

Langworth, Richard. *Churchill by Himself*. Public Affairs, New York, 2008.

Lewis, Norman. *Naples 44*. Carol and Graff, New York, 2005.

Lucas, James. *Experiences of War: The Third Reich*. Arms and Armour Press, London, 1990.

MacDonald, Charles. *The Last Offensive*. Office of the Chief of Military History, Washington, DC, 1973.

———. *The Battle of the Huertgen Forest*. University of Pennsylvania Press, 2003.

Marshall, S. L. A. *Men Against Fire*. University of Oklahoma Press, Norman, 2000.

Mauldin, Bill. *Up Front*. Norton, New York, 1991.

May, Antoinette. *Witness to War: A Biography of Marguerite Higgins*. Beaufort Books, New York and Toronto, 1983.

Merridale, Catherine. *Ivan's War*. Henry Holt, New York, 2006.

Middleton, Drew. "The Seventh Army." *Combat Forces Journal*, August 1952.

Molony, C. J. C. *The Mediterranean and Middle East*, vol. VI. Naval & Military Press, London, 2004.

Moorehead, Alan. *Eclipse*. Harper, New York, 1968.

Morison, Samuel E. *History of United States Naval Operations in World War II*, vol. 9: *Sicily-Salerno-Anzio*. Little, Brown, Boston, 1954.

Morris, Eric. *Salerno. A Military Fiasco*. Stein & Day, New York, 1983.

———. *Circles of Hell: The War In Italy, 1943–1945*. Crown, New York, 1993.

Munsell, Warren P., Jr. *The Story of a Regiment: A History of the 179th Regimental Combat Team*. Privately published, place unknown, 1946.

Murphy, Audie. *To Hell and Back*. Corgi, London, 1950.

Musmanno, Michael A. *Ten Days to Die*. MacFadden, New York, 1962.

Nelson, Guy. *Thunderbird: A History of the 45th Infantry Division*. 45th Infantry Division Association, Oklahoma City, 1970.

Nichols, David, ed. *Ernie's War: The Best of Ernie Pyle's World War II Dispatches.* Random House, New York, 1986.

Oleck, Major Howard. *Eye Witness World War II Battles.* Belmont Books, New York, 1963.

Orange, Vincent. *Tedder: Quietly in Command.* Frank Cass, London, 2004.

Overy, Richard. *Why the Allies Won.* W. W. Norton, New York, 1995.

Patch, Alexander. "The Seventh Army: From the Vosges to the Alps." *Army and Navy Journal*, December 1945.

Patton, George. *War As I Knew It.* Houghton Mifflin, Boston, 1947.

Perry, Michael W. *Dachau Liberated.* Inkling Books, Seattle, 2000.

Pyle, Ernie. *Brave Men.* Henry Holt, New York, 1944.

Rawson, Andrew. *In Pursuit of Hitler.* Pen and Sword, Barnsley, UK, 2008.

Reynolds, Quentin. *The Curtain Rises.* Random House, New York, 1944.

Robinson, Don. *News of the 45th.* Grosset & Dunlap, New York, 1944.

Rothchild, Sylvia. *Voices from the Holocaust.* New American Library, New York, 1981.

Ryan, Cornelius. *The Last Battle.* Simon & Schuster, New York, 1966.

Salerno: American Operations from the Beachhead to the Volturno. Military Intelligence Division, War Department, Washington, DC, 1944.

Salpeter, Norbert, ed. *Ready in Peace and War: A Brief History of the 180th Infantry Regiment.* F. Bruckmann KG, Munich, 1945.

Sevareid, Eric. *Not So Wild a Dream.* Knopf, New York, 1946.

Shapiro, L. S. B. *They Left the Back Door Open.* Ryerson, Toronto, 1944.

Sheehan, Fred. *Anzio: Epic of Bravery.* University of Oklahoma Press, Norman, 1964. Reprint 1994.

Silvestri, Ennio. *The Long Road to Rome.* Etic Grafica, Latina, Italy, 1994.

Smith, Marcus J. *The Harrowing of Hell. Dachau.* University of New Mexico Press, Albuquerque, 1972.

Sparks, Blair Lee. *Déjà Vu.* Author House, Bloomington, Indiana, 2008.

Speer, Albert. *Inside the Third Reich.* Macmillan, New York, 1970.

———. *Spandau, the Secret Diaries.* Macmillan, New York, 1976.

Stanton, Shelby L. *World War II Order of Battle.* Galahad Books, New York, 1984.

Starr, Chester G., ed. *From Salerno to the Alps—A History of the Fifth Army, 1943–45.* Infantry Journal Press, Washington, DC, 1948.

Terkel, Studs. *The Good War.* Hamish Hamilton, London, 1985.

Tobin, James. *Ernie Pyle's War.* Free Press, New York, 1997.

Toland, John. *The Last 100 Days.* Random House, New York, 1966.

Tregaskis, Richard. *Invasion Diary.* Random House, New York, 1944.

Trevelyan, Raleigh. *The Fortress: A Diary of Anzio and After.* Collins, London, 1956.

Trevor Roper, Hugh. *The Last Days of Hitler.* Macmillan, New York, 1965.

Truscott, Lucien K. *Command Decisions.* Dutton, New York, 1954.

Uys, Errol Lincoln. *Riding the Rails.* TV Books, New York, 1999.

Vaughan-Thomas, Wynford. *Anzio.* Longmans, Green, London, 1961.

Vega, Santos. *Around Miami.* Arcadia Publishing, Charleston, South Carolina, 2011.

Verney, Peter. *Anzio 1944: An Unexpected Fury.* B. T. Batsford, London, 1978.

Voss, Johann. *Black Edelweiss.* Aberjona Press, Bedford, Pennsylvania, 2002.

Wallace, Robert. *The Italian Campaign.* Time-Life Books, New York, 1981.

Walters, Vernon. *Silent Missions.* Doubleday, New York, 1978.

Warlimont, General Walter. *Inside Hitler's Headquarters.* Presidio Press, Novato, California, 1964.

Westphal, Siegfried. *The German Army in the West.* Cassel, London, 1951.

Whicker, Alan. *Whicker's War.* HarperCollins, London, 2006.

Whiting, Charles. *Siegfried: The Nazis' Last Stand.* Stein & Day, New York, 1982.

———. *America's Forgotten Army.* St. Martin's Press, New York, 2001.

Whitlock, Flint. *Rock of Anzio.* Basic Books, New York, 1998.

Whitman, Bill. *Scouts Out!* Authors Unlimited, Los Angeles, 1990.

Wilson, George. *If You Survive.* Ivy Books, New York, 1987.

Wilt, Alan F. *The French Riviera Campaign of August 1944.* Southern Illinois University Press, Carbondale, 1981.

Zoepf, Wolf T. *Seven Days in January.* Aberjona Press, Bedford, Pennsylvania, 2001.

INDEX

ABOUT THE AUTHOR

Alex Kershaw is the *New York Times* bestselling author of several books on World War II, including *The Bedford Boys* and *The Longest Winter.* He lives in Williamstown, Massachusetts.

www.AlexKershaw.com